Management of Transboundary Water Resources under Scarcity

A Multidisciplinary Approach

Management of Transboundary Water Resources under Scarcity

A Multidisciplinary Approach

Edited by

Ariel Dinar *(University of California, Riverside)*

Yacov Tsur *(The Hebrew University of Jerusalem, Israel)*

 World Scientific

NEW JERSEY · LONDON · SINGAPORE · BEIJING · SHANGHAI · HONG KONG · TAIPEI · CHENNAI · TOKYO

Published by

World Scientific Publishing Co. Pte. Ltd.

5 Toh Tuck Link, Singapore 596224

USA office: 27 Warren Street, Suite 401-402, Hackensack, NJ 07601

UK office: 57 Shelton Street, Covent Garden, London WC2H 9HE

Library of Congress Cataloging-in-Publication Data

Names: Dinar, Ariel, 1947–   editor. | Tsur, Yacov, editor.

Title: Management of transboundary water resources under scarcity :
    a multidisciplinary approach / edited by Ariel Dinar, Yacov Tsur.

Description: New Jersey : World Scientific, 2017. |
    Includes bibliographical references and index.

Identifiers: LCCN 2016049468 | ISBN 9789814740043 (hardcover : alk. paper)

Subjects: LCSH: Water-supply--Management.

Classification: LCC TD345 .M23 2017 | DDC 333.91--dc23

LC record available at https://lccn.loc.gov/2016049468

British Library Cataloguing-in-Publication Data

A catalogue record for this book is available from the British Library.

Copyright © 2017 by World Scientific Publishing Co. Pte. Ltd.

All rights reserved. This book, or parts thereof, may not be reproduced in any form or by any means, electronic or mechanical, including photocopying, recording or any information storage and retrieval system now known or to be invented, without written permission from the publisher.

For photocopying of material in this volume, please pay a copying fee through the Copyright Clearance Center, Inc., 222 Rosewood Drive, Danvers, MA 01923, USA. In this case permission to photocopy is not required from the publisher.

Desk Editor: Philly Lim

Typeset by Stallion Press
Email: enquiries@stallionpress.com

Printed in Singapore

CONTENTS

ACKNOWLEDGMENTS

We would like to acknowledge the financial and in-kind support from several organizations that helped us organize the conference (http://transboundaryconf.wix.com/transboundary-water) leading to this book: The Center for Agricultural Economic Research; The Hebrew University of Jerusalem R&D Fund; The Robert H. Smith Faculty of Agriculture, Food and Environment, The Hebrew University of Jerusalem; The Lady Davis Fellowship Trust; LIDM Software Systems; The School of Public Policy, University of California, Riverside; and Keren Kayemet Le'Israel (Jewish National Fund).

And last but not least, we are indebted to Omri Hason who supported the organization of the conference and the review process.

FOREWORD

At its most basic level, the problem of transboundary waters is deceptively simple. Figure 1 should help.

To the left is a map where the Jordan River basin exists as it does in nature: the only boundaries are those of the watershed itself, which represents the unit within which everything is connected — surface water, groundwater, quality, and quantity. There are no human interventions and no divisions save for those of nature herself — what stands out are the aspects of the space that unify.

To the right is a map of the same basin within the actual human landscape, a place crowded with political boundaries and all the sovereignty issues and national aspirations they represent; a place where a convoluted network of infrastructure brings water from its sources to where the people are, even out of basin; in short, a place where all the divisions of the region are only too apparent.

"All" one needs to do with transboundary waters is manage the resource as if the world looked the way it does on the left map, in a way that balances all the needs and divisions of the world on the right map.

And then we try.

First, to train ourselves, we need some understanding of basic atmospheric sciences, biology, engineering, environmental sciences, fluvial mechanics, geochemistry, hydrogeology, hydrology — that's only the first eight letters of the alphabet and only in the natural sciences! Now we need political science, economics, law, cross-cultural

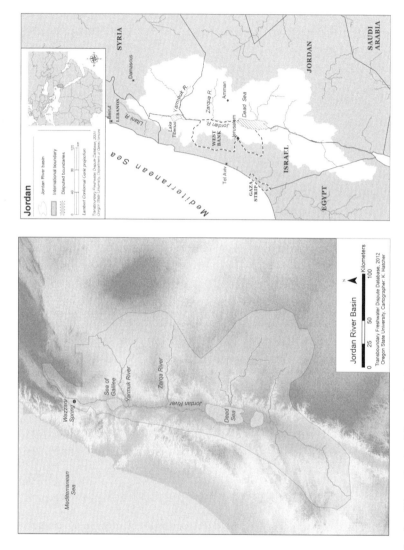

Figure 1: Jordan River Basin. Map to the left shows the watershed borders. Map to the right shows the political borders.

Notes: Product of the Transboundary Freshwater Dispute Database, College of Earth, Ocean, and Atmospheric Sciences, Oregon State University. Additional information about the TFDD can be found at: http://www.transboundarywaters. orst.edu.

communications, diplomacy, religious studies, and so much more. (Of course, in geography, we call all of this, "geography".)

This is the problematique that this book grappled with. So many disciplines, so many approaches, so many case studies, and so many ways this could have gone wrong. And it is strong testament to the editors — to their own vast interdisciplinary experience and commitment to water — that you have the tightly organized, informative, document that you are holding and, despite all odds, it tells a cohesive story.

The motivation is clear and compelling, as described in Chap. 1. Despite its apparent simplicity, the problem of transboundary waters is deeply complex, nowhere more so than in the arid and hostile Middle East. Yet for the very survival of the people and ecosystems that rely on this scarce, precious resource — not to mention all the economic, cultural, and spiritual activity that is equally dependent — we have to get it right.

As the editors state, populations and economies are growing, bringing ever increasing pressure on both quality and quantity, all the while that the amount of water that exists today is roughly the same as it has been throughout human history. Adding to the pressures is global climate change, bringing more variability and intensity to already fragile and stressed systems.

These are the problems.

Fortunately, this compilation makes an important contribution to the solutions.

What stands out starkly to an alert reader, then, is a profound disconnect between the problems of the transboundary water world, which care as little for disciplinary boundaries as they do for political ones, and the solutions, which, whether in universities or in water agencies, are deeply disciplinary. (In a state in the US Southeast, which should remain unnamed, water quality was in one agency, while quantity was in another. While the arrangement is not uncommon, the rationale is, as explained off the record by one of their directors: it was designed by the governor so that no agency would gain too much power.)

Within the academic world, while the concept and need for interdisciplinarity is well-recognized, its implementation is not. Not only are our jargons and tenure-tracks disjointed, so too are allocations of such "administrivia" as returned overhead and incentive structures.

The inertia required to overcome these barriers makes volumes such as this all the more rare and valuable. Take just one problem addressed within these covers — figuring out the benefits of cooperation. Why, for example, would any downstream country acquiesce to upstream development? It's a wonderful problem, rich for its apparent simplicity, yet practically intractable in its application, and at the heart of today's most vociferous hydropolitics, from the Nile to Central Asia to the Mekong.

Parts of the answer, we find in this volume, are found in a variety of disciplines, from economics to international relations to law. And should one wish to see these concepts implemented successfully, this volume offers a rich section of regional case studies from which to draw. The bottom line is that upstream and downstream riparians have been finding ways to accommodate each other's needs from time immemorial — this volume goes a longway to explaining how.

While much of my time is spent as an analyst of shared waters, much is also spent as a facilitator within the settings described here. And I, and any number of others can attest that stakeholders and country representatives generally care not a whit about which discipline has contributed to a solution; they care about whether it works. I have been in too many rooms where someone overly grounded in their particular framework has said something like, "I'm sorry, my model will not allow you to take that position." The case studies here confirm that the tools must support the process, not the other way around.

As I mentioned, to really grapple with the problem of transboundary waters, as well as to find helpful approaches to mitigate tomorrow's basins at risk, one needs both broad experience and deep commitment. To our fortune, our editors possess just such credentials, and the story they weave from the authors and their perspectives leave one better prepared to help in the struggle to craft more efficient, effective, and equitable management of our transboundary water resources.

Aaron Wolf
Oregon State University, USA

ABOUT THE EDITORS

Ariel Dinar is a Professor of Environmental Economics and Policy at the School of Public Policy, University of California, Riverside. He teaches courses in water and environmental economics and conducts research on various aspects of water and the environment, regional cooperation, international water, impact of and adaptation to climate change, and strategic behavior and the environment. He is the founder and the editor in chief of two journals and two book series, respectively: *Strategic Behavior and the Environment* (now Publishers), *Water Economics and Policy* (World Scientific), *Global Issues in Water Policy* (Springer), and *World Scientific Lecture Notes in Economics* (World Scientific).

Yacov Tsur is the Ruth Ochberg Professor of Agricultural and Resource Economics at the Department of Environmental Economics and Management, Faculty of Agriculture, Food and Environment, the Hebrew University of Jerusalem. He received a PhD in Agricultural and Resource Economics from the University of California, Berkeley in 1984. Before joining the Hebrew University (in 1994), he served on the faculty of the Department of Applied Economics at the University of Minnesota, and the Department of Economics at Ben-Gurion University of the Negev. His research includes natural resource management under uncertainty and catastrophic threats, with a particular focus on water resource management. He publishes widely in economic outlets and has been actively involved in advising Israel's Water Authority and the World Bank on various issues concerning water resource management and regulation.

ABOUT THE CONTRIBUTORS

Nir Becker is a Professor of Economics at Tel-Hai Academic College. He is currently the Dean of the Social Sciences and Humanities faculty. He specializes in environmental and resources economics. He has published more than 50 referred papers and 20 chapters. He also had written a book on the economics of marine protected areas and edited a book on water policy in Israel. In recent years, his interest is in the economics of nature and energy conservation. He is a consultant to the nature protection agency, the ministry of the environment and other environmental organizations on various issues related to the economics of nature conservation and environmental quality.

Maksud Beckhanov has a PhD in agricultural economics from the Center for Development Research, Germany. He is currently a Postdoctoral Researcher with the International Water Management Institute. His dissertation focused on the Aral Sea Basin (efficient water allocation and water conservation policy modeling in the Aral Sea Basin) and he has published multiple pieces of research on the key rivers in the Central Asia region. Most recently he has focused on extending a hydro-economic model to better reflect energy concerns in the Ganges river basin of South Asia.

Anik Bhaduri is the Executive Director of the Sustainable Water Future Programme (SWFP) and Associate Professor at Australian

River Institute, Griffith University. Previously, he served as an Executive Officer of Global Water System Project (GWSP). With a background in environment and natural resource economics, he has specialized in water resource management. He has worked on several topics and projects, ranging from transboundary water sharing to adaptive water management under climate change. He also serves as a senior fellow at Centre of Development Research, University of Bonn.

Christine Bismuth is a Scientific Coordinator at the Helmholtz Centre Potsdam-GFZ German Research Centre for Geosciences. At the Berlin-Brandenburg Academy of Sciences and Humanities, she was the responsible scientific coordinator for the Interdisciplinary Research Group Science Water Technology. Her major research fields are public participation in water management and international cooperation in integrated water resources management.

Sabine Blumstein is a Project Manager at Adelphi Consult in Berlin where she coordinates research and consulting projects in the fields of resource governance and water cooperation. Prior to that, she was a researcher at the Helmholtz-Centre for Environmental Research — UFZ as well as a lecturer at the Global and European Studies Institute in Leipzig. She is furthermore a fellow at the Earth System Governance Project. Her research focuses on transboundary water management institutions (in particular, International River Basin Organizations), environmental change and adaptation capacities, as well as international relations theories. Dr. Blumstein earned her PhD in political science at the University of Leipzig.

David B. Brooks was educated in geology and economics, and spent much of his professional career with the International Development Research Centre. His main research interests are split between water soft paths in Canada and water demand management in the Middle East. Among his books are *Watershed: The Role of Fresh Water in the Israeli-Palestinian Conflict* (1994, coauthor with Stephen C. Lonergan) and *Making the Most of the Water We Have: The Soft Path Approach to Water Management* (2009, coeditor with Oliver M. Brandes and Stephen Gurman). In 2012, Dr Brooks received an honorary doctorate of environmental studies from the University of Waterloo.

Bernd Hansjürgens, PhD, is a Professor of Environmental Economics at Martin Luther University Halle-Wittenberg and Head of the Department of Economics at the Helmholtz Centre for Environmental Research — UFZ. He is the study leader of TEEB Germany (Natural Capital Germany). His major research fields include environmental valuation, TEEB — The Economics of Ecosystems and Biodiversity, instrument choice in environmental policy, and sustainable water management.

David Katz is a Lecturer in the Department of Geography and Environmental Studies at the University of Haifa in Israel. He specializes in environmental economics and policy, with a focus on water resource management. Much of his work has addressed transboundary resource policy and management issues.

María Milanés-Murcia, an environmental attorney, earned her MA in economics from New Mexico State University in May 2007 and LLM in international water resources from the University of the Pacific in December 2008. She became the fifth person to also earn Pacific McGeorge's unique JSD in International Water Resources Law. Throughout the years, she has developed a great amount of experience as her profession has led her to work in various and diverse areas of the world. For example, North and South Sudan, where she developed specific research on water resources and collected information. She has also worked on the development of a national irrigation policy and strategy in Nigeria. In addition, she has been a member of the legal team representing Uruguay before the International Court of Justice (ICJ) in the Pulp Mill Case (Argentina v. Uruguay). Moreover, she has worked on the Nicaragua v. Costa Rica case representing Nicaragua before the ICJ. She is currently working as an International Legal Consultant for several institutions and organizations such as Food and Agriculture

Organization of the United Nations (FAO) and United Nations Organization for Education, Science and Culture (UNESCO).

Getachew Nigatu is an Economist in the Market and Trade Economics Division at Economic Research Service/USDA. His current activities include supporting the international baseline analysis and examining policy factors affecting near- and long-term prospects for domestic and global markets. In addition, he undertakes research works on the impacts of energy prices and policies on global commodity supply, demand, and trade; the effect of global macroeconomic developments on the US agricultural exports; and the changing role of the United States in the price determination of major agricultural commodities. Dr. Nigatu has also continued working on issues of water resource economics and policy, focusing on the Nile River and international treaties affecting basin resource allocation and management. He received a PhD in economics from the University of California, Riverside in 2012.

Kim Hang Pham Do is a Senior Lecturer at the School of Economics and Finance (Palmerston North), Massey University, New Zealand. She teaches courses in quantitative methods, applied economics, and environmental economics and resource management. Her interests includes analyzing the interactions between agroecosystem and social systems on economic growth and sustainable development. Her research includes theoretic and empirical frameworks to address the analytical issues related to cooperation in multilateral setups with externalities and the role of issue linkage for arriving efficient and equitable arrangements in transboundary resource management. She has published prestigious international journals, including *Mathematical Social Sciences*, *International Game Theory Review*, and *Environment and Development Economics*.

Susanne Schmeier is currently the Coordinator for Transboundary Water Management at the Deutsche Gesellschaft für Internationale Zusammenarbeit (GIZ). Prior to this, she has worked as an advisor to the Mekong River Commission (MRC), at the World Bank and with a number of other international and regional organizations and river basin organizations on water resources management. She is also a fellow at the Earth System Governance Project and contributes to a number of research projects. She has published extensively on water management topics, with a particular focus on the legal and institutional dimensions of transboundary water management. Dr. Schmeier holds a PhD in transboundary water management.

Julie Trottier is the Research Professor at France's Centre National de la Recherche Scientifique (CNRS). With formal studies in chemistry, politics, and Islamic studies, she has focused her research for the last 20 years on the politics of water in Israel/Palestine. She published *Hydropolitics in the West Bank and Gaza Strip* (1999); *Water Management, Past and Present* (2004, co-edited with Paul Slack); and *A Wall, Water and Power: The Israeli 'Separation Fence'* (2007).

INTRODUCTION AND CONCLUSION

ARIEL DINAR[*] and YACOV TSUR[†]

University of California, Riverside, USA
† The Hebrew University of Jerusalem, Israel

Water scarcity becomes a critical political and policy matter in many international basins, sometimes leading to conflicts and sometimes to cooperation among the riparian states. This book presents approaches originating from various disciplines, all aimed to address likely risk from water scarcity in the basin. Recent works on the subject of international water management under scarcity have focused mainly on a narrow disciplinary approach. Developments in recent years in several international basins indicate the importance of interdisciplinary approach to management of transboundary water resources under conditions of increased scarcity. The book presents an array of approaches, including economics, politics, legal, hydrology, and ecology. Basins featured in the book include: Jordan, Nile, Mekong, Aral Sea, Rio Bravo/Grande, and Tajos.

Motivation, Purpose, and Objectives of the Book

Due to climate change processes and population growth, water scarcity becomes a critical issue in many semiarid and arid regions. Water scarcity is exacerbated through increased water fluctuations and quality deterioration. While these phenomena are not new, they are especially critical in regions where water is shared by several riparian states — international water — and used for competing purposes (irrigation, domestic, industry, and hydropower). Historical and recent events suggest that increased water scarcity gives rise to new conflicts and intensifies existing conflicts among riparian states sharing water basins (Bernauer and Böhmelt, 2014). At the same time, with proper institutions in place (Dinar *et al.*, 2014; Dinar and Dinar, 2017), transboundary water sources create a basis for cooperation, which is a necessary condition for economic development, environmental sustainability, and poverty reduction. Agricultural production is one of the main concerns in the field of shared water, especially in international river basins that are shared by two or more developing countries.

Recent works on the subject of international water management under scarcity have focused mainly on a single disciplinary approach. Recent developments in several international basins around the world indicate the importance of a multidisciplinary approach to the management of transboundary water resources under conditions of increased scarcity. New phenomena associated with climate change, such as increased variability of water supply and extreme events of flooding and droughts necessitate the use of more comprehensive approaches. For example, a water treaty is necessary but far from sufficient condition to deal with scarcity in an international basin. Therefore, the legal approach needs to be amended by other considerations, such as economics, technology, political, and incentive-based mechanisms.

The purpose of this book is to assemble a set of works from various disciplines to deal with the impact of water scarcity and variability on the welfare of international basins and to learn from their experience in applying a multidisciplinary approach to address such problems in water basins around the globe. Addressing similar problems by different approaches enables exchange of information and collaboration necessary for the development of multidisciplinary approaches to dealing with the problem of agricultural production, energy generation, and environmental pollution needed for regional welfare and stability.

The book is organized in three parts, reflecting on the geographical coverage of the river basins analyzed and the various disciplines used. Part I includes chapters that employ modeling of economic, institutions, and technologies used to address water scarcity in the Jordan River Basin, the Amu-Darya subbasin of the Aral Sea, the Blue Nile, and the Mekong. Part II addresses treaties for managing surface and groundwater conjunctively as applied by the United States and Mexico in the Rio Bravo/Grande and by Israel and the Palestinian Authority on the Mountain Aquifer. Part III includes chapters that present approaches that support regulation, water allocation, and environmental rehabilitation decisions of shared water in the Nile, the Mekong, the Tagus, the Fergana Valley of the Aral Sea, and the Lower Jordan River.

The next section of the Introduction and Conclusion chapter places the book in the context of the existing works in the literature. It reviews relevant work from political and international relation disciplines, planning, legal and institutional, and game theory (GT) approaches. The chapter then provides a summary of the main analyses in each of the chapters and follows with a conclusion of lessons learned from the analyses presented and the (long) way ahead.

Literature Background

Management of water for various uses in international river basins is not new to the literature. In the following, we provide background on the work undertaken by various disciplines that will feature also in our book.

Political and International Relation Approaches

Studies in this discipline focused mainly on whether or not the existing agreements between the riparian states of the international water basins adequately address reduction and increased variability of water supplies resulting from climate change processes. Climate change and water variability are also expected to intensify security concerns within international river basins (Nordås and Gleditsch, 2007). A report entitled "National Security and the Threat of Climate Change" claims that one of the most destabilizing impacts from climate change will be in the form of reduced access to freshwater (CNA Corporation, 2007, pp. 13–16). Despite the often cited claim that "water is a source of cooperation, rather than violent conflict" (Wolf and Hamner, 2000), some observers have stressed that climate change and the projected increase in water variability may further complicate existing shared water management policies and will have significant economic, social, environmental, and political consequences (Adger *et al.*, 2005).

Given the links between climate change, water variability, and interstate tensions, the role of institutions in assuaging potential conflicts between states seems paramount (Salehyan, 2008, p. 317). In the realm of international water, treaties often constitute the main governing apparatus and have been shown to assuage conflict and promote cooperation (Brochmann, 2012). Yet, beyond the mere existence of a treaty, the design of the agreement is also important for understanding the treaty's ability to deal with water variability (Zentner, 2012). That is, different mechanisms codified in a given treaty should impact differently on treaty effectiveness in promoting cooperation and reducing conflict. Guided by recent research exploring treaty effectiveness in the area of international water (particularly, De Stefano *et al.*, 2012; Drieschova and Fishhendler, 2011; Drieschova *et al.*, 2008; Stinnett and Tir, 2009).

A number of studies have demonstrated that institutions help prevent or moderate disputes between countries. According to Chayes and Chayes (1993), treaties alter states' perception of each other, thereby affecting behavior and relationships that support cooperation. Specific to water, evidence suggests that the likelihood of political tensions is related to variability or rates of changes of water availability within a basin, and the absence of institutions (particularly treaties) to deal with such changes (Wolf *et al.*, 2003). Treaties that govern river basins constitute an important means for managing transboundary water resources by preventing or mitigating disputes (Tir and Stinnett, 2012). Moreover, water agreements can promote wider cooperation and enhance basin security more generally (Brochmann, 2012; Conca and Dabelko, 2002).

Despite the role of water agreements in assuaging conflicts (Brochmann, 2012), some scholars have suggested that the mere presence of an international water regime does not provide any guarantee that it will ultimately promote sustained cooperation (Dombrowsky, 2007, 2009, 2010). In regions already governed by a water treaty, climate change and water supply variability could affect the ability of basin states to meet their water agreement commitments and effectively manage transboundary waters (Ansink and Ruijs, 2008; Drieschova *et al.*, 2008). This is particularly salient in agreements that are not appropriately designed to deal with environmental changes and similar forms of uncertainty. Increased variability may thus raise serious questions about the adequacy of many existing transboundary arrangements even in areas that have exemplified cooperation in the past (Cooley *et al.*, 2009, p. 28). As such, administrative instruments for transboundary basins, and specifically the mechanisms codified in treaties should be assessed for their ability to address potential impacts of climate change (Alavian *et al.*, 2009, p. 24). Treaty design and treaty capacity are, therefore, directly related to the ability of the treaty to lessen tension. As the existing qualitative literature points out, the presence of particular allocation and institutional mechanisms can identify the type of treaties that are more effective under conditions of water variability and climatic change (Odom and Wolf, 2008). Various mechanisms can potentially mitigate grievances and enhance cooperation over water thus contributing to the effectiveness of the treaty over time (Cooley *et al.*, 2009). This study seeks to contribute to existing empirical research on international water treaty design (De Stefano *et al.*, 2012; Tir and Stinnett, 2012) by examining an array of water allocation and institutional mechanisms.

We discuss these treaty instruments below in the context of the extant literature. In the case of water allocation mechanisms, in particular, it is noteworthy that no systematic empirical work has been conducted to scrutinize their effectiveness in a comparative fashion.

Planning Approaches

Many planning models in the literature focus on the allocation of the available water among competing users in the basin. Such allocation of water to users in a river basin is based on a set of imposed or agreed upon priorities assigned to water users. Often, the criterion used to calculate the allocation of water to users in a river basin model is to minimize deficits of water delivery to all users in each time period, which is critical for agricultural production. This method is used in the Water Evaluation and Analysis Program (WEAP) software discussed in a later chapter. There are different methods that can be used to endogenously or exogenously estimate the demands for water in the basin (primarily agricultural and municipal); however, an exogenous determination is the most common. In the priority allocation method, for each time step a network flow solver attempts to satisfy the demands of the water users with the highest priority first. Then the lower priority users are satisfied in decreasing order of priority. This is a typical method of solution for several well-known river basin models, including WEAP (Stockholm Environment Institute [SEI], 2004) and ModSim (Labadie, 2004).

As an alternative to priority-based allocation, economic optimization can be used to allocate water based on economic criteria, such as priority to those uses that return the highest net benefits in the basin. Agricultural water demand can be determined endogenously within such a model using crop production functions (yield vs. water, irrigation technology, salinity, etc.) and a municipal and industrial (M&I) water demand function based on a market inverse demand function. Water supply can be determined through a hydrologic water balance in the river basin with extension to the irrigated areas. Water demand and water supply are integrated into an endogenous system and balanced based on the economic objective of maximizing net benefits from water use, including irrigation, hydropower, and M&I benefits (Rosegrant *et al.*, 2000). The net benefit (profit) from agricultural water use at a particular site can be expressed as crop revenue minus fixed crop cost, irrigation technology improvement cost, and water supply cost. A river basin model based on this development will also include institutional rules, including minimum required water supply for users, minimum and maximum crop production, and environmental flow requirements. In such a case, the objective is to maximize net benefits in the basin from the supply of water to agriculture and M&I water uses, and hydroelectric power generation, subject to institutional, physical, and other constraints. An application to the Jordan River Basin of such planning approach can be found in Tsur (2015) and Malkawi and Tsur (2016).

Because water resources problems are inherently multifaceted with conflicting uses of water where trade-offs must be made between stakeholders with differing goals. An objective function with three components representing the net benefits from allocating water to agricultural use, municipal and industrial use, and hydropower generation is typical. When the components are equally weighted, then each component is being given equal priority in the solution process according to its contribution to net benefits. That is, a dollar of agricultural benefit is equivalent to a dollar of hydropower benefit. However, these components or objectives can often be in conflict with one another, such as when agricultural water demand peaks in the summer growing season and hydropower demand peaks in the winter heating season. Modeling methods that are used to determine the trade-offs between various conflicting objectives in water resources problems are used in multiobjective analyses. Multiobjective modeling methods have been used for several decades to determine the trade-offs between various objectives in water resources problems. Examples of multiobjective modeling in water resources planning include Bogardi and Duckstein (1992), who presented an interactive multiobjective analysis method to embed the decision-maker's implicit preference function; Ridgley and Rijsberman (1992), who employed multicriteria decision aid for policy analysis of the Rhine estuary; and Theissen and Loucks (1992), who presented an interactive water resources negotiation support system. In these last two examples, multicriteria evaluation to support group decision making was emphasized. Other work has focused on integrating technologies to support multiobjective analysis.

The Syr Darya basin was modeled by McKinney (2004) to allow management of upstream reservoir so that it operates in an irrigation mode with minimal winter season releases. A multiobjective optimization model was developed to promote understanding of, and aid in the development of, efficient and sustainable water allocation options for the republics (Cai *et al.*, 2003). The multiple objectives combined in the model included minimizing upstream winter power deficits and maximizing downstream irrigation water supply. By integrating these objectives with the system's physical, political, and operational constraints in an optimization model, the trade-offs between the conflicting objectives of satisfying agricultural water demand, and generating hydroelectric power were elaborated and used to develop a number of water allocation scenarios to aid decision making. Further analysis of the economic consequences of the proposed options was prepared using hydroelectric and agricultural input and output costs and prices (Keith and McKinney, 1997). The model has also been used as a basis for analyzing proposed changes to the basin agreement through the application of GT techniques (Teasley and McKinney, 2011).

The development of the scenarios informed the process of assembling the data to populate the planning model. In constructing the management scenarios, a 30–50 year planning horizon was used so that the issue of climate variability and climate change could be considered (Sandoval-Solis *et al.*, 2011).

Legal and Institutional Approaches

Work on legal and institutional aspects of water management in international river basins is probably the most long-standing ones. Several examples presented below indicate the wide spectrum of legal arrangements to address water flow variability by riparian states.

In their analysis of selected treaties, Kliot *et al.* (2001) identify institutions for management of droughts in the Rio Grande (Bravo) shared by Mexico and the United States. The October 1995 Rio Grande treaty update provides for a standby water loan by the United States to Mexico in order to provide for unforeseen water needs of Mexican border communities along the river path. This agreement led to some long-term water debt conflict that was finally solved in 2012 as we discuss in more details below. Dinar (2005) Selects several treaties that can help with the resolution of the Syr Darya and Amu Darya water dispute.

Drieschova *et al.* (2008) reviews several mechanisms to address flow variability on international rivers and uses several examples to demonstrate the awareness of riparian states to flow variability issues and how they were addressed. The Meuse treaty of 1863 between Belgium and the Netherlands already identified the flow variability problem and allocated water among the riparian states conditioned on actual annual flow. The 1995 Danube agreement calls for the 17 parties/countries along the river to provide mutual support to allow all parties that face flow variability to sustain extreme situations.

Fischhendler (2008) identifies some ambiguities in the Jordan-Israel 1994 water treaty over the Jordan River. The treaty includes institutions that can mitigate physical variability in water flow and provides Jordan with a water package of three components to close a fixed gap in the supply, shall the variability in water flow lead to scarcity that triggers the need for one of these components. This treaty will also be further discussed in the following section.

In a recent comparative study, Salman (2006) surveys several international water disputes that indicate a new brand of disputes and the way they have been addressed from a legal point of view of these disputes. They include water quantity and quality issues, the lines across boundary rivers where the borders between states fall and water rights and prior appropriation of such rights across borders. They also include claims for compensation by both individuals and legal entities against foreign governments, as well as navigational rights over border creating rivers. The parties are no longer one state against another state. Such parties now include individuals, legal entities and nongovernmental organizations (NGOs), as well as multinational corporations of one state against another state. The settlement institutions have also changed and include both international as well as national courts and third and fourth parties.

GT Approaches

Applications of GT approaches to issues of water allocation among international water sharing riparian states have seen a major rise in the past decade. Most applications deal with the cooperative nature of sharing water and how cooperation is likely to provide stability to the basins under conflict. Several works apply noncooperative GT frameworks and demonstrate how under such behavior solutions to water conflicts are also possible.

Early work by Rogers (1969) develops a cooperative GT framework and applies it to the conflict in the Ganges river basin at that time. The author identifies issues which are of mutual interest to India and Bangladesh, such as navigation, flood control, and irrigated agriculture, and builds an optimization mathematical programming model linked with cooperative GT solution concepts that allow us to realize the cooperation potential between the two riparian nations which will result in significant benefits to each. The model in Rogers (1969) was refined and expanded in Rogers (1994) to include both unidirectional externalities (mainly floods and pollution originating in India and affecting Bangladesh) and allocation schemes such as the nucleolus and the Shapley value.

In a series of works Becker and Easter (1999, and their earlier works that they cite) model Great Lakes Basin management issues among Canada and various states in the United States. In their early work they consider alternative diversion restrictions and their impact on the basin and players' (states in the United States and provinces in Canada) benefits. Later they compare the results of two game structures: two players (United States and Canada) and eight players (six states in the United States and two Canada provinces) to the social planner solution. The results suggest that states do not divert water necessarily because they stand to gain but because they may lose more if they do not. The application in one of their work considers the economically desirable diversions and how the gains from such diversions should be distributed among the players. The work shows that in most cases, new institutional arrangements will be needed before agreements can be reached. A similar approach is used in the 1999 work, but here the approach addresses different configurations of the lakes that are being regulated (starting from one lake and ending up with all lakes.)

A series of works develop and apply the concept of interlinked games to international water. This concept is very useful in the case that deals with conflicting issues that lead to gridlock. The existence of issues that have asymmetric interest on the part of the parties involved may lead to an acceptable set of solutions. Bennett *et al.* (1998) apply the idea of interconnected/linked games to the problem of international water quantity and quality externalities. The authors argue that in the presence of unidirectional externalities the traditional GT approach produces unsatisfactory solutions leaving the victim to pay and unable to transfer payments to incentivize the upstream country to change its practices. Instead, the authors suggest that nations in weak negotiating positions try to improve their leverage by linking issues. If the linked issues are selected carefully, it can generate outcomes that cannot be obtained when games over issues are modeled separately. The authors demonstrate the interlinked game model for the case of the Aral Sea in Central Asia and in the cases of the Euphrates and Orontes River Basins in the Middle East.

A similar approach has been implemented by Pham Do *et al.* (2012) to the case of the Mekong River Basin. They analyze whether issue linkages can be used as a form of negotiation on sharing benefits and mitigating conflicts in the presence of unidirectional externalities, such as in the case of the Mekong (navigation, irrigation water quality). In particular, if the linked games are convex, the grand coalition is the only optimal level of social welfare. An extension of their work to include multilevel linked issues is provided in Pham Do and Dinar (2014).

Another application of the interconnected game concept can be found in Just and Netanyahu (2004) where they consider modeling bilateral agreements for sharing common pool resources (such as groundwater aquifer) under conditions of unequal access. Their work shows how game structure and benefits suggested by interconnected games are modified when the victim pays strategies are removed from the feasibility set.

The peace agreement between Jordan and Israel, and Egypt and Israel, and the establishment of the Palestinian Authority led to several attempts at addressing the water conflict between Israel and its Arab neighbors, which at that time were very promising.

Several works use the relative advantage of the players in a game of water creation and/or exchange and water use efficiency in irrigation. Dinar and Wolf (1994a, 1994b, 1997) develop the concept of "water for irrigation technology" in the lower Nile Basin. They demonstrate the economic rationale for exchange of irrigation technology and knowhow for the water saved by using that technology. If allocations (water or income) are assumed among countries with some level of hostility, political considerations which are usually not incorporated in economic analysis can hinder or even block the most efficient arrangement. Dinar and Wolf (1994a, 1994b, 1997) demonstrate, using several cooperative GT concepts that are amended by political models (PRINCE Political Accounting System; and the Generalized Shapley Value with political probabilities), how incorporating political considerations in the analysis may provide a more acceptable regional solution compared to the economic-related allocations.

A different focus on possible cooperation via exchange is discussed in Brill *et al.* (1999). The authors depart from the situation of water scarcity in the Gaza Strip and technological capacity for wastewater treatment in Israel. They suggest the following scheme that does make a lot of economic sense: wastewater from Gaza will be sent to Israel for treatment and fresh water (either treated or desalinated), in exchange will be sent from Israel to Gaza. The cooperative Nash bargaining solution and the noncooperative Nash-Cournot solution are compared. The results suggest that as scarcity level increases the gap between cooperative and noncooperative solutions increases. More examples on the application of GT to water conflicts in this part of the world can be found in Becker *et al.* (2001). An example of application of GT to the sharing of the Mountain Aquifer between Israel and the Palestinian Authority is analyzed in Netanyahu *et al.* (1998) using both cooperative and noncooperative bargaining GT and other solutions and suggesting that GT approaches are robust with regards to demand elasticity, user costs, and pumping costs.

Interest has grown in the first part of the 21st century as more work was published on aspects related to international water treaties — treaties on management of joint international waterways. Kilgour and Dinar (2001) address variation in water supply and its impact on the stability of international agreement (see also work cited in the section "Political and International Relation Approaches"). Kilgour and Dinar (2001) claim that most water allocation agreements refer to the long-term mean flow and as such treaties are unable to accommodate variations in conditions. They develop a flexible mechanism that produces a Pareto-efficient allocation for every possible flow volume in a river, which is also able to be extended to accommodate other kinds of variation, such as changes in water demand. They apply the mechanism to historical water flow data for the Ganges, using stylized water demand relationships for India and Bangladesh. They derive equilibrium negotiation solutions and conclude that variable allocation substantially outperforms fixed allocation, improving regional welfare by at least 10%.

A series of studies focused on achieving stable agreements in stylized river basin structures followed the seminal work by Ambec and Sprumont (2002). These authors refer to a group of agents arranged sequentially along a river, and are characterized by a given set of preferences for water and money. The aim is to find an allocation that will be efficient, stable (in the sense of the core), and fair. They show that a cooperative game of this problem is convex, thus implying a large core that would guarantee the three requirements: efficiency, stability, and fairness. They prove that only one welfare vector in the core can satisfy the three requirements — the allocation based on the marginal contribution vector that corresponds to the order of the agents along the river.

The work by Ambec and Sprumont (2002) was extended by Ambec and Ehlers (2008) to include two extensions — a satiation point in the benefit function of the players along the river, and unidirectional externalities. The authors observe that the cooperative core might be empty; instead, they suggest a unique allocation of the water — the downstream incremental distribution — is the unique distribution which is both fair-according to the "aspiration welfare" principle and satisfies the noncooperative core lower bounds. In addition, it satisfies all core lower bounds for all connected coalitions if and only if each agent's individual rationality constraint is independent of the behavior of the other agents.

The ideas of Ambec and Ehlers were further extended by Ambec *et al.* (2013) to include fluctuations in the water flow of the river due to droughts. Their river geography is again a sequential river where the players along the river agree (or not) to release an amount of river water in exchange for a negotiated compensation. The work addresses the vulnerability of such agreements to reduced water flows. Among all types of agreement, they find one, which is self-enforced under the most severe drought scenarios, the upstream incremental allocation assigns to each country its marginal contribution to its followers in the river. Its mirror image, the downstream incremental allocation that featured in previous works, is not sustainable to reduced flow at the source. They demonstrate the usefulness of the model in the case of the Aral Sea basin.

Ansink and Ruijs (2008) address the sharing problem by assessing the effect of climate change and the choice of a sharing rule on stability of the agreement using a game theoretic model. The results of their work suggest that a decrease in mean river flow decreases the stability of an agreement, while an increased variance can have a positive or a negative effect on stability, depending on the institutions in place. An agreement where the downstream country is allocated a fixed amount of water has the lowest stability compared to other sharing rules.

Another work that addresses the impact on stochastic river flow in stability of treaties is Ansink (2009). The author tries to find water allocation agreements that can be self-enforcing under stochastic situations. An agreement is an outcome of a bargaining game which is the result of a repeated extensive-form game in which countries decide whether or not to comply with the agreement. The work suggests that, for sufficiently low discounting rates, every efficient agreement can be sustained in subgame perfect equilibrium. The solution induced by this particular agreement implements the downstream incremental allocation (see also Ambec *et al.*, 2013), an axiomatic solution to water allocation that assigns all gains from cooperation to downstream countries.

Van den Brink *et al.* (2010) expands the results of downstream incremental allocation in Ambec and Sprumont (2002) by adding a class of weighted hierarchical solutions that satisfy the "Territorial Integration of all Basin States" principle for sharing water of international rivers (in the International Water Law). They find that when all players have increasing benefit functions, every weighted hierarchical solution is core-stable. In case of satiation points, every weighted hierarchical solution is independent of the externalities.

Other works that is worth mentioning include van der Laan and Moes (2012) who model international river pollution problems. The unique feature of the model is that each player along the river benefits from activities that cause pollution downstream, and, at the same time, players (except the first one) are also harmed by pollution that originates upstream. Using principles from International Water Law, the authors determine that cooperation is the best strategy and suggest "fair" ways of solving the pollution problem, based on property rights' doctrines from International Water Law, such as Absolute Territorial Sovereignty, Unlimited Territorial Integrity, and Territorial Integration of all Basin States.

The Main Messages

The various chapters in the book provide a range of important messages that are synthesized below. Tsur's chapter addresses water management in the Jordan River Basin, comprising Israel, Jordan, and the Palestinian Authority. The main message that comes out of this chapter is the need for a comprehensive, long-term approach in managing transboundary water resources. As is usually the case, water diversions come at the expense of damage to environmental amenities. In the case of the Jordan River Basin, such diversions have led to the destruction of the lower Jordan River, with its reach and unique ecosystem, and to a rapid decline of the Dead Sea level, with far reaching environmental consequences (see also Becker and Katz). The chapter offers policies for satisfying the domestic, irrigation, and environmental water needs of a growing population pattern alternatives. The main policy tools suggested are demand management, in the form of appropriate water pricing-quota system, and supply management, in the form of recycling and desalination.

Bhaduri and Bekchanov analyze the scope for cooperation in the Amu-Darya River subbasin with and without the controversial Rogun Dam that is being constructed. With the strict cross-border geography of the river they find out that the interaction between food production and energy production poses a sensitive trade-off, which is dependent on the subjective value assigned to each use by each of the upstream and downstream users. The authors suggest that in light of the unstable cooperative solution they obtained, it is probably useful to introduce the issue linkage principle to expand the zone of agreement between the players in the Amu-Darya game. The authors do not perform issue linkage analysis, and leave it to future extension of their model.

Similar to Bhaduri and Bekchanov analysis of the role of a controversial dam in regional cooperation, Nigatu and Dinar apply a basin-level mathematical model to the Blue Nile region in order to address the phenomena that the basin states engage in unilateral building of irrigation projects and hydropower big dams. In order to evaluate the performance of these big dams, they compare model results for unilateral and social planner regional outcomes for three big dams in each of the respective riparian countries: Grand Ethiopian Renaissance Dam (GERD) in Ethiopia, Merowe Dam in Sudan, and Aswan High Dam in Egypt. Since the results of the unilateral scenario, which is the actual state of business in the basin, are suboptimal, the authors introduce the concept of "allocate-and-trade," which suggests first that a regional institution such as Nile Basin Initiative will assign water rights to the three riparian countries, monitor and evaluate the performance of each riparian country, and then facilitate an intrabasin water trade among riparian countries so that water could be used for projects within the basin. The institution of water rights arrangement (WRA) and intrabasin water trade happen to be very efficient also in the case of soil degradation (erosion) abatement. The proposed WRA with trade are therefore an attractive alternative to optimize the utilization of the Nile River water in a situation where subbasin or basin-wide agreements are infeasible in a foreseeable future (as is the case now). Beyond creating a desired solution to the ENRB, long-standing water allocation challenges the intrabasin trade in water rights could also lead to enhancing the Nile dialogue that is stalled right now.

Pham Do and Dinar do address the important role of issue linkage when otherwise the players in the basin game are pushed to the unfavorable prisoner dilemma solution. They demonstrate the possible role of issue linkage in moving a gridlock negotiation process in the Mekong River Basin into a cooperative agreement. They apply concepts from GT to the conflict between Lower Mekong Basin countries and China and demonstrate how GT concepts are useful in pulling the basin from a prisoner dilemma's situation when water issues and trade issues (as an example) are handled separately in the basin to a situation where both water and trade issues are linked into one negotiation set. The example demonstrates how the zone of agreement expands and allows much more flexibility when the issues are linked. While the example addresses only two issues (water and trade), the chapter argues that the linkage can be extended to more than only two issues, if necessary.

Minales-Murcia develops and demonstrates the implementation issues of a model treaty to the Mexico–US region of the Rio Bravo/Grande. The delimitation of the US–Mexico border region proposed in this agreement goes beyond the political border, and it is established according to existing International Water Law principles. The proposed treaty covers the entire border region using the basin approach, taking into account the social, physical, and environmental conditions in each region and leading to conservation and environmental protection. A unique feature in the treaty is the Water Bank institution, which provides a basis for cooperation as well as reasonable and equitable utilization, and avoids harm between the United States and Mexico. In addition, the proposed treaty provides the integration of water resources management with the goal of maximizing benefits along the border region at the basin level. To achieve such goal, the treaty includes a new water use right as a mechanism to achieve a unique system of water allocation based on uses, and treating groundwater and surface water as one source in the Water Bank allocation system.

Brooks and Trottier present a model treaty to manage the water shared by the Palestinians and Israelis and the unilateral pollution of unregulated wastewater. The authors argue that with the new technological and institutional realities in the region, a systematic focus of both parties on secured water stock maintains the gridlock in their negotiations on water issues. Instead, the model treaty suggests that both parties face the fact that the quantities in conflict reflect water that flows through several users' hands, both Israeli and Palestinian. The authors argue that with its new desalination capacity, Israel created excess water resources, which makes it ideal to introduce considerations of water flows. The proposed treaty takes into consideration that the Palestinians are upstream on the aquifers and the Israelis are upstream on the desalination capacity. The authors argue that reformulating the negotiating stock/quantities to flow is now feasible and benefit both parties more by allowing the opposite party to use the same flow of water they both interact with.

Blumstein and Schmeier show the importance of functioning river basin organizations (RBOs) is addressing conflicts. They address the questions whether or not RBOs are relevant for dispute resolution, and whether or not the dispute resolution mechanism they employ is effective in solving these disputes. The chapter provides a very relevant review of dispute resolution mechanisms in the existing RBOs around the world and then a two case studies in the Mekong and the Nile River Basins to assess the performance of the dispute-resolution effectiveness of existing mechanisms. The chapter reveals that more than 50% of the identified 121 RBOs do not have dispute resolution mechanisms, which allows the authors to refer to the natural experiment and test whether or not dispute resolution mechanisms are relevant in addressing conflict. One of the useful findings is that the distribution of dispute resolution mechanisms is a reflection of regional history of cooperation. This by itself suggests that conflicts have interpretations that vary across geographies. The two case examples suggest that dispute resolution mechanisms have to be amended by other supporting mechanisms such as information sharing and transparency, so that they may be effective.

Milanes-Murcia demonstrates how the international treaty between Portugal and Spain can support domestic development of one of the parties by an interbasin transfer, using the Tagus-Segura transfer in Spain as an example. The chapter shows how customary law at the local level can be used as an instrument to maintain uses already established and recognized among the parties. The chapter demonstrates how regional allocation mechanisms such as aqueducts and other instruments could be a component of strategies that promote resilience to climate change and mitigate the impacts of drought conditions. The author argues that European Union (EU) Solidarity Funds should be used to build infrastructure needed for promoting cooperation among different regions and improving the economic and social life of Spanish citizens. An infrastructure able to transfer water surplus from one region to another will be one of the solutions to the current hydrologic disequilibrium between northern and southern Spain. Furthermore, the chapter uses various international treaties to argue that it is the objective of the international treaties to enhance solidarity/cooperation in order to prevent drought impacts between countries and domestically. The chapter provides legal support, using European legislation and the principles of International Water Law, to the argument that the Aqueduct Tagus-Segura fulfills the concept of sustainable development as it protects the environment for present and future generations while promoting the development of the region.

Bismuth and Hansjürgens analyze the appropriateness of existing institutions and legal means in regions facing economic, social, and political instability and where water is a scarce resource both present and future scenarios. Using the International Water Law as a model for the analysis of their hypotheses, and two case studies — the Lower Jordan River Basin in the Middle East and the Fergana Valley in Central Asia, the chapter demonstrates the shortfall of existing agreements based on International Water Law in the two cases to produce adaptive and participative water basin management. The authors suggest several modifications to the International Water

Law that include: (i) Linking water allocation to the availability of renewable water resources; (ii) Linking water quality objectives to the ecological status of a river course; (iii) Strengthening monitoring and data collection and sharing among the riparians; (iv) Introducing instruments for mitigation and conflict resolution and a RBO (see Blumstein and Schmeier); and (v) Providing economic incentives. The chapter concludes that as long as there is no internalization of benefits from cooperation for each riparian, the legal system in the basis of the agreement will not function.

Becker and Katz demonstrate the use of economic benefit estimation from rehabilitation of a shared river. The authors apply various nonmarket valuation methods to the lower Jordan River Basin that is shared by Jordanians, Israelis, and Palestinians to estimate the attributed benefits to each group from different levels of rehabilitation of the environmentally deteriorated region. Using the travel cost method, the contingent valuation method, and the choice modeling, the authors provide a range of benefit values that by themselves suggest a basis for a joint interest in the rehabilitation project and future benefits from a rehabilitated, well-functioning river ecosystem.

Conclusions and Future Research Needs

The book chapters provide a comprehensive coverage of river basin conflict and cooperation issues and approaches designed and applied to address them. One important conclusion is that policy intervention to address water scarcity at a basin level would fair better if it is based on several intervention mechanisms and addresses several sectors. This was the conclusion in Chap. 1 (Tsur) and in Chap. 10 (Becker and Katz) for the Jordan River Basin. Tsur suggests addressing both the demand for and supply of water in order to allow both the irrigation and domestic sectors to grow, while dealing with environmental calamities that devastate the basin. Becker and Katz demonstrate how the value of the environment in the basin can be estimated and used in the process of public decision making. It is clear that environmental amenities can make a difference in the decision to allocate water and funding for rehabilitation projects, which will improve the basin ecosystem and increase the benefits to the basin population.

Two chapters (Pham Do and Dinar, and Bhaduri and Bekchanov) address the role of issue linkage in designing a cooperative solution to water conflict at the basin level. Both chapters identify economic benefits associated with cooperation. While Bhaduri and Bekchanov realize that the allocation solution they suggest for the case of the Amu-Darya is not stable and could benefit from issue-linkage approach (although they do not develop this approach in the chapter), Pham Do and Dinar demonstrate for the Mekong how linkage between water issues and regional trade issue could expand and stabilize the suggested regional arrangements. An important conclusion from these two chapters is that the more relevant issues are linked, the higher is the likelihood for stronger and more stable cooperative arrangement.

Bhaduri and Bekchanov and Nigatu and Dinar address the role of mega dams in reaching sustainability of the economies in the basin. While Bhaduri and Bekchanov find relatively small incremental benefits from the cooperative arrangement resulting from the dam on the Amu-Darya, Nigatu and Dinar demonstrate that with appropriate institutions, the benefits from a dam on the Blue Nile could be significant and attractive for all countries involved in the analysis, by providing economic incentives to promote cooperation. Hence, combining institutional framework for enhancement of the allocated benefits with the infrastructure investment turns to be important.

The chapters by Milanes-Murcia and by Brooks and Trottier highlight the role of international treaties as a useful framework to manage resources under scarcity and quality constraints. Both chapters analyze the role of institutional arrangements on the likely performance of the treaty. Milanes-Murcia develops the concept of conjunctive use of groundwater and river water. She introduces the concept of water trading (banking) and Brooks and Trottier frame the treaty in terms of all water resources, surface water and groundwater, freshwater and recycled and produced water. Milanes-Murcia also suggests institutions to manage these multilateral and multifaceted resources. The conclusion from these two chapters is that a framework agreement among riparian states has to look at the whole set of water resources and be supported by working institutions.

One of the institutions that features in many transboundary river basins is RBO. The Blumstein and Schmeier analyze the population of transboundary basins for their performance as affected by the RBO and then focus on two case studies — the Nile and the Mekong. Their important conclusion is that one feature that matters most is the existence of a dispute resolution mechanism in the RBO and whether or not it is adaptable to the existing institutional, social, and political situations of the basin riparian states. As in previous chapters, the effectiveness of a dispute resolution mechanism depends on other existing supporting mechanism that will enhance the effectiveness of the dispute resolution mechanism.

Dealing with another transboundary basin Milanes Murcia shows for the Tagus the importance of adequate infrastructure to allow the functioning of the Albufera treaty. Similarly to Bhaduri and Bekchanov, and Tsur, the conclusion is that appropriate infrastructure is necessary to carry out important development project in the basin. Investment in the downstream may be a good inhibitor for cooperation even if it is benefiting directly only part of the riparians in the basin.

Very similar conclusions are apparent from the chapter by Bismuth and Hansjürgens. The conclusion from the analysis of existing institutions of international treaties in their chapter calls for modification of the existing International Water Law by introducing opportunities for linkage between suggested mechanisms to the situation in the basin, strengthening the conflict resolution mechanisms, and introducing more transparent economic incentives (See Nigatu and Dinar, Pham Do and Dinar, Bhaduri and Bekchanov, and Becker and Katz).

The interdisciplinary set of chapters in this book suggest that while there are different options to approach a water conflict in a basin under scarcity, literally all approaches recognize the importance of comprehensive framework that allows a multifaceted mechanisms and policies to work in concert and support each other. This is the overall conclusion that underlies the book chapters.

While the book chapters demonstrate the usefulness of a multi-disciplinary approach, yet they also admit that much more work is needed. One aspect that could promote the analysis of transboundary water is a better communication between the different disciplines, including also joint projects that will allow input and feedback links between legal, political, economic, and engineering scholars. Another aspect that needs to be addressed in the future for quantitative work on transboundary river basins is the harmonization of datasets that exist now without any possible comparison with each other. Related to the above is the need to expand the data collection so that more relevant variables that were identified in past research could be part of the available information at the global level.

References

Adger, N, T Hughes, C Folke, S Carpenter, and J Rockstrom (2005). Social ecological resilience to coastal disasters. *Science*, 309(5737), 1036–1039.

Alavian, V, H Qaddumi, E Dickson, S Diez, A Danilenko, R Hirji, G Puz, C Pizarro, M Jacobsen, and B Blankespoor (2009). *Water and Climate Change: Understanding the Risks and Making Climate-Smart Investment Decisions.* Washington: World Bank.

Ambec, S and L Ehlers (2008). Sharing a River Among Satiable Agents. *Games and Economic Behavior*, 64(1), 35–50.

Ambec, S and Y Sprumont (2002). Sharing a river. *Journal of Economic Theory*, 107(2), 453–462.

Ambec, S, A Dinar, and D McKinney (2013). Water sharing agreements sustainable to reduced flows. *Journal of Environmental Economics and Management*, 66(3), 639–655.

Ansink, E (2009). *Game-Theoretic Models of Water Allocation in Transboundary River Basins.* The Netherlands: Wageningen Universiteit (Wageningen University).

Ansink, E and A Ruijs (2008). Climate change and the stability of water allocation agreements. *Environmental and Resource Economics*, 41, 133–287.

Becker, N and KW Easter (1999). Conflict and cooperation in managing international water resources such as the Great Lakes. *Land Economics*, 75, 233–245.

Becker, N, N Zeitouni, and D Zilberman (2001). *Issues in the Economics of Water Resource.* Cheltenham: Edward Elgar Publishing.

Bennett, LL, ER Shannon, and Y Peter (1998). Facilitating international agreements through an interconnected game approach: The case of river basins. In *Conflict and Cooperation on Transboundary Water Resources*, J Richard and N Sinaia (eds.). Boston: Kluwer.

Bernauer, T and T Böhmelt (2014). Basins at risk: Predicting International River Basin Conflict and Cooperation. *Global Environmental Politics*, 14(4), 116–138.

Bogardi, J and L Duckstein (1992). Interactive multiobjective analysis embedding the decision maker's implicit preference function. *Water Resources Bulletin*, 28(1), 75–78.

Brill, E, U Chakravorty, and E Hochman (1999). Transboundary water allocation between Israel and Gaza Strip. In *New Economic Developments and Their Impact on Arab Economies*, A Al-Kawaz (ed.), pp. 599–626. Amsterdam, New York, and Oxford: Elsevier Science, North-Holland.

Brochmann, M (2012). Signing river treaties: Does it improve cooperation? *International Interactions*, 38, 141e163.

Cai, X, DC McKinney, and LS Lasdon (2003). An integrated hydrologic-agronomic-economic model for river basin management. *Journal of Water Resources Planning and Management*, 129(1), 4–17.

Chayes, A and A Chayes (1993). On compliance. *International Organization*, 47, 175–205.

CNA Corporation (2007). *National Security and the Threat of Climate Change.* Alexandria: CNA Corporation.

Conca, K and G Dabelko (eds.) (2002). *Environmental Peacemaking.* Baltimore: Johns Hopkins University Press.

Cooley, H, J Christian-Smith, P Gleick, L Allen, and M Cohen (2009). *Understanding and Reducing the Risks of Climate Change for Transboundary Waters.* Oakland: Pacific Institute.

De Stefano, L, J Duncan, S Dinar, K Stahl, K Strezepek, and A Wolf (2012). Climate change and the institutional resilience of international river basins. *Journal of Peace Research*, 49(1), 193–209.

Dinar, S (2005). Treaty principles and patterns: Selected international water agreement as lessons for the resolution of the Syr Darya and Amu Darya water dispute. In *Transboundary Water Resources: Strategies for Regional Scarcity and Ecological Stability*, H Hogtmann and N Dobretsov (eds.), pp. 147–168. Dordrecht: Springer.

Dinar, A and A Wolf (1994a). Economic-potential and political considerations of regional water trade — The western Middle-East example. *Resource and Energy Economics*, 16, 335–356.

Dinar, A and A Wolf (1994b). International markets for water and the potential for regional cooperation — Economic and political perspectives in the western Middle East. *Economic Development and Cultural Change*, 43, 43–66.

Dinar, A and A Wolf (1997). Economic and political considerations in regional cooperation models. *Agricultural and Resource Economics Review*, 26, 7–22.

Dinar, S, D Katz, L De Stefano, and B Blankespoor (2014). Climate change, conflict, and cooperation: Global analysis of the effectiveness of international river treaties in addressing water variability. *Political Geography*, 45, 55–66.

Dinar, S and A Dinar (2017). *International Water Scarcity and Variability: Managing Resource Use Across Political Boundaries*. Berkeley, California: University of California Press.

Dombrowsky, I (2007). *Conflict, Cooperation, and Institutions in International Water Management*. Cheltenham: Edward Elgar.

Dombrowsky, I (2009). Revisiting the potential for benefit sharing in the management of Transboundary Rivers. *Water Policy*, 11, 125–140.

Dombrowsky, I (2010). The role of intra-water sector issue linkage in the resolution of transboundary water conflicts. *Water International*, 35(2), 132–149.

Drieschova, A and I Fischhendler (2011). *Toolkit: Mechanisms to Reduce Uncertainty in International Water Treaties. CLICO Report.* Hebrew University of Jerusalem.

Drieschova, A, M Giordano, and I Fischhendler (2008). Governance mechanisms to address flow variability in water treaties. *Global Environmental Change*, 18(2), 285–295.

Fischhendler, I (2008). When ambiguity in treaty design becomes destructive: A study of transboundary water. *Global Environmental Politics*, 8(1), 115–140.

Just, RE and S Netanyahu (2004). Implications of "victim pays" infeasibilities for interconnected games with an illustration for aquifer sharing under unequal access costs. *Water Resources Research*, 40, 1–11.

Keith, J and DC McKinney (1997). Options analysis of the operation of the Toktogul reservoir, Issue Paper No. 7, United States Agency for International Development (USAID) Environmental Policy and Technology (EPT), Almaty, Kazakhstan, August.

Kilgour, MD and A Dinar (2001). Flexible water sharing within an international river basin. *Environmental and Resource Economics*, 18(1), 43–60.

Kliot, N, D Shmueli, and U Shamir (2001). Institutions for management if transboundary water resources: Their nature, characteristics, and shortcoming. *Water Policy*, 3, 229–255.

Labadie, J (2004). ModSim: Decision support system for river basin management, Documentation and User Manual-2000. http://modsim. engr.colostate.edu/ (Accessed on 29 December 2014).

Malkawi, AIH and Y Tsur (2016). Reclaiming the Dead Sea: Alternatives for action. In *Society–Water–Technology: A Critical Appraisal of Major Water Engineering Projects*, RF Hüttl, O Bens, C Bismuth, and S Hoechstetter (eds.). London: Springer (Open).

McKinney, DC (2004). Cooperative management of transboundary water resources in Central Asia. In *In the Tracks of Tamerlane-Central Asia's Path into the 21st Century*, D Burghart and T Sabonis-Helf (eds.). Washington, DC: National Defense University Press.

Netanyahu, S, EJ Richard, and KH John (1998). Bargaining over shared aquifers: The case of Israel and the Palestinians. In C*onflict and Cooperation on Transboundary Water Resources*, Richard J and Sinaia N (eds.). Boston: Kluwer.

Nordås, R and NP Gleditsch (2007). Climate change and conflict. *Political Geography*, 26, 627–638.

Odom, O and A Wolf (2008). Defining and redefining needs in international water law. In *Defining Water Needs in Areas of Fully Exploited Resources*. Palais des Nations, Geneva: International Workshop.

Pham Do, KH and A Dinar (2014). The role of issue linkage in managing non-cooperating basins: The case of the Mekong. *Natural Resource Modeling* (Accepted for publication 27 October 2014).

Pham Do, KH, A Dinar, and D McKinney (2012). Transboundary water management: Can issue linkage help mitigate externalities? *International Game Theory Review*, 14(1), 39–59.

Ridgley, M and F Rijsberman (1992). Multicriteria evaluation in a policy analysis of a Rhine estuary. *Water Resources Bulletin*, 28(6), 1095–1110.

Rogers, P (1969). A game theory approach to the problems of international river basins. *Water Resources Research*, 5, 749–760.

Rogers, P (1994). *A Model to Generate Pareto-Admissible Outcomes for International River Basin Negotiations*. Milan, Italy: Nota di Lavoro Fondazione Enrico Mattei.

Rosegrant, MW, C Ringler, DC McKinney, X Cai, A Keller, and G Donoso (2000). Integrated economic-hydrologic water modeling at the basic scale: The Maipo River basin. *Agricultural Economics*, 24(1), 33–46.

Salehyan, I (2008). From climate change to conflict? No consensus yet. *Journal of Peace Research*, 45(3), 315e326.

Salman, MA (2006). International water disputes: A new breed of claims, claimants, and settlement institutions. *Water International*, 31(1), 2–11.

Sandoval-Solis, S, DC McKinney, RL Teaseley, and C Patino-Gomez (2011). Ground-water banking in the Rio Grande Basin. *Journal of Water Resources Planning and Management*, 137(1), 62–71.

Stinnett, D and J Tir (2009). The institutionalization of river treaties. *International Negotiation*, 14, 229–251.

Stockholm Environment Institute (SEI) — Boston (2001). Tellus Institute, WEAP water evaluation and planning system, user guide for WEAP 21, Boston, MA. http://www.weap21.org/downloads/weapuserguide.pdf (Accessed on 29 December 2014).

Teasley, RL and DC McKinney (2011). Calculating the benefits of transboundary river basin cooperation: Syr Darya Basin. *Journal of Water Resources Planning and Management-ASCE*, 137, 481–490.

Theissen, EM and DP Loucks (1992). Computer assisted negotiation of multiobjective water resources conflicts. *Water Resources Bulletin*, 28(1), 163–177.

Tir, J and D Stinnett (2012). Weathering climate change: Can institutions mitigate international water conflict? *Journal of Peace Research*, 49(1), 211–225.

Tsur, Y (2015). Closing the (widening) gap between water resources and water needs in the Jordan Basin region: A long term perspective. *Water Policy*, 17(3), 538–557.

Van den Brink, R, G Van der Laan, and N Moes (2010). *Fair Agreements for Sharing International Rivers with Multiple Springs and Externalities.* Tinbergen Institute, Tinbergen Institute Discussion Papers: 10-096/1: VU University Amsterdam.

van der Laan, G and N Moes (2012). Transboundary Externalities and Property Rights: An International River Pollution Model. Social Science Research Network, http://papers.ssrn.com/sol3/papers.cfm?abstract_id=1988838.

Wolf, A and J Hamner (2000). Trends in transboundary water disputes and dispute resolution. In *Water for Peace in the Middle East and Southern Africa*. Geneva: Green Cross International.

Wolf, A, K Stahl, and M Macomber (2003). Conflict and cooperation within international river basins: The importance of institutional capacity. *Water Resources Update*, 125, 31–40.

Zentner, M (2012). *Design and Impact of Water Treaties: Managing Climate Change* (Springer theses). Heidelberg: Springer.

Part I

ECONOMIC, INSTITUTIONAL, AND TECHNOLOGICAL ASPECTS IN MANAGEMENT OF TRANSBOUNDARY WATER UNDER SCARCITY

CHAPTER 1

CLOSING THE (WIDENING) GAP BETWEEN NATURAL WATER RESOURCES AND WATER NEEDS IN THE JORDAN RIVER BASIN: A LONG-TERM PERSPECTIVE

YACOV TSUR

Department of Environmental Economics and Management, The Hebrew University of Jerusalem, Rehovot, Israel

The supply of renewable natural water available in a sustainable fashion in the Jordan River Basin (JRB), comprising Israel, Jordan, and the Palestinian Authority (PA), will soon drop below 100 cubic meters (m^3) per person per year. Drawing on recent technological progress and policy innovations, a comprehensive policy to address the region's water problems in the long run is offered. The policy has a dual goal: to satisfy the needs of a growing population (domestic, irrigation, and industry) and to preserve important environmental amenities, including restoration of the lower Jordan River (LJR) and stabilization of the Dead Sea. The gap between natural water supplies and the basic needs of the growing population will be closed by conservation and desalination; at the same time, all domestic water will be recycled and will be available for reuse in irrigation and environmental restoration. Over time, the supply of recycled water that *should* be allocated for environmental restoration (accounting for the compensation of irrigators) will suffice to partially restore the LJR and contribute to the stabilization of the Dead Sea. The analysis is relevant in a wide range of real-world situations, where satisfying the basic needs of a growing population and preserving environmental amenities become critical.

Reprinted from *Water Policy* vol. 17, issue 3, pp. 538–557 (2015) with permission from the copyright holders, IWA Publishing.

Keywords: Dead Sea; Desalination; Environmental amenities; Lower Jordan River; Recycling; Water scarcity

1.1. Introduction

The average supply of natural water available in a sustainable fashion (without systematically drawing down water stocks) in the JRB, comprising Israel, Jordan, and the PA, will soon drop below 100 m^3 per person per year. As a result, extensive diversions from natural sources have led to the deterioration, if not complete demolition, of natural stream flows and ecosystems. Two prominent environmental "victims," shared by the three parties, are the LJR and the Dead Sea: the LJR's flow has been reduced to a trickle of mostly brackish water and partially treated sewage and its historically rich ecosystem no longer exists (Gafny *et al.*, 2010); the Dead Sea level has been declining at a rate exceeding 1 m per year with far reaching detrimental consequences to its surrounding environment (Becker and Katz, 2009; Tahal and Geological Survey of Israel, 2011; Rawashdeh *et al.*, 2013). In this chapter, we propose a comprehensive policy to address the water problems of the JRB in the long run. The policy has a dual goal: first and foremost, to satisfy the essentials of the growing population in subsistence (drinking, hygiene) as well as agricultural (irrigation) and industrial production; and second, to maintain an acceptable level of environmental amenities, including partial restoration of the LJR and stabilization of the Dead Sea level. The proposed policy draws on recent technological progress and policy innovations. The analysis is relevant in a wide range of real-world situations, where the limited water resources make the dual goal of satisfying the needs of a growing population and preserving environmental amenities — a critical problem.

Water scarcity is a fuzzy and complex concept because of the "liquid" nature of the resource, which often exhibits large temporal and spatial variability, variation in quality, and dependence on idiosyncratic climate conditions (e.g., evapotranspiration). At the root level, water scarcity has to do with the availability of water needed to satisfy human livelihoods, including drinking, washing, and food production as well as environmental preservation. The ability to satisfy these needs depends both on the available quantity of renewable, natural water as well as on how this water is managed. A region can experience abundance of water some of the time (e.g., in the winter or monsoon periods) and a severe shortage in other times (e.g., in the summer or dry periods) and water shortage depends also on demand management and on the ability to transfer water across time and across space (from water-abundant periods/locations to water-scarce periods/locations), requiring, inter alia, storage and conveyance facilities. It is thus understandable that multiple indices of water scarcity exist with no consensus regarding which one to use in any given circumstance (discussions of the different water scarcity indicators can be found in Rijsberman [2006], Gleick [2002], and references they cite).

These qualifications notwithstanding, a rough and widely used index of water scarcity is the supply of renewable (i.e., available in a sustainable fashion) natural water suitable for human use, measured in units of cubic meters per person per year. Widely accepted measures of water scarcity defined by this index are due to Falkenmark *et al.* (1989). Based on estimates of water requirements for households, agricultural, industrial, and environmental needs, Falkenmark *et al.* (1989) proposed the following thresholds: regions whose renewable water supplies fall below 1700, 1000, or $500 \, \text{m}^3$ per person per year are said to experience *water stress*, *water scarcity*, or *absolute scarcity*, respectively. The threshold of $100 \, \text{m}^3$ per person per year is often mentioned as the water supply needed to satisfy basic human needs (Gleick, 1996) and we call this threshold *subsistence scarcity*. Water scarcity measures based on annual supplies of natural renewable water available per person are popular because their calculation requires data that are often available. Notice that these indices change over time due to population growth.

We begin in the next section with a description of the water scarcity situation in the JRB and its projected time evolution. We shall see that the region as a whole will soon suffer from subsistence scarcity, and parts of it have already entered this phase. In Section 1.3, we discuss recent technological progress in desalination and policy innovations that have been used to deal with water scarcity in Israel and show in Section 1.4 how these policies underline the basic principles of a comprehensive solution to the water shortage problem in the region. Section 1.5 discusses how the environmental goals of partially restoring the LJR (the stretch of the river between Lake Tiberias-Kinneret and the Dead Sea) and stabilizing the Dead Sea level can be incorporated within this comprehensive water policy. Section 1.6 concludes.

1.2. Water Scarcity in the JRB

We consider the part of the JRB that comprises Israel, Jordan, and the PA (see Fig. 1.1).[1] The situation of the three parties is not symmetric: while Israel and Jordan are free to set their water policies, the PA is limited as it does not yet possess the same state status. While this political obstacle has consequences regarding feasible water policies in the short run, one hopes that it will be resolved and once this happens, these (short term) restrictions will no longer be effective. As this work takes a long-term perspective (as the title suggests), current political restrictions and mutual mistrusts among the parties are ignored and the emphasis is on what *could* be done under collaborative political conditions.

1.2.1. *Water Resources*

We discuss first the water resources of Israel and the PA jointly, followed by the water resources of Jordan.

1.2.1.1. *Water resources in Israel and the PA*

Table 1.1 presents average recharge into the main water sources west of the Jordan River for the periods 1976–1992 and 1993–2009. It also gives the quantities of brackish water recharge, where brackish water refers to water with chloride concentration above

---

[1]The JRB contains also parts of southern Lebanon and southwest Syria. Due to lack of data on these regions, they will not be included in this study.

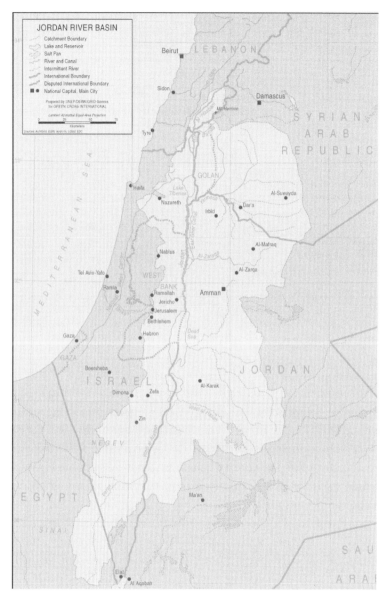

Figure 1.1: The JRB. The upper Jordan River extends between its headwater (at the confluence of the Dan, Banias, and Hatzbani) and Lake Tiberias-Kinneret. The LJR is the southern stretch of the river between Lake Kinneret and the Dead Sea.

Source: United Nations Environment Programme (http://www.grid.unep.ch/products/4_Maps/jordanb.gif).

Table 1.1: Average annual recharge (MCM/y) of main water sources
west of the Jordan River and the share of brackish water (with chloride
concentration above 400 mg/L).

| Basin | 1976–1992 | | 1993–2009 | |
	Average Recharge	Brackish	Average Recharge	Brackish
Kinneret	623	18	540	14
Coastal	252	124	232	116
Western Mountain	369	0	333	0
Eastern Mountain	211	0	174	0
NortheastMountain	151	0	134	0
Lower Galilee	30	6	26	6
Western Galilee	139	30	132	30
Carmel	42	15	40	15
Negev andArava	32	28	32	28
Gaza	44	31	40	23
Total	1893	252	1683	232

Source: Weinberger *et al.* (2012).

400 mg/L. To obtain quantities of fresh water recharge (with chloride
concentration below 400 mg/L) one needs to subtract the brackish
from the average, for example, the total average recharge of fresh
water during 1993–2009 was $1683 - 232 = 1451$ million cubic meters
per year (MCM/y).[2] Figure 1.2 provides a map view of Table 1.1.
These are the quantities of natural water available to Israel and the
PA on a sustainable fashion. Brackish water is unsuitable for drinking
and when used for irrigation often requires mixing with good quality
water to reduce salinity.

Figure 1.3 shows the actual realizations of natural recharge for
the period 1976–2009. It illuminates two features of renewable water
resources in the JRB: high (temporal) fluctuations and a declining
trend. Part of the declining trend (of 8.92 MCM/y) could be the
result of climate change processes.

---

[2]The breakdown into subperiods in Table 1.1 shows temporal changes of water
recharge, which could be the result of climate trends.

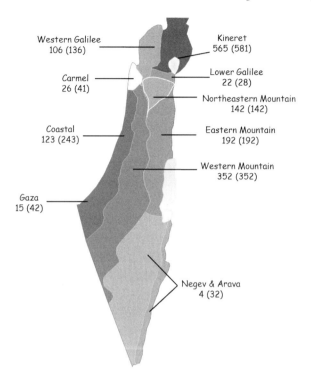

Figure 1.2: Average renewable (natural) supplies (with chloride concentration <400 mg/L), based on the 1993–2009 data of Table 1.1 (numbers in parenthesis give brackish water — with chloride concentration >400 mg/L).

Source: Weinberger *et al.* (2012).

1.2.1.2. *Water resources in Jordan*

Table 1.2 presents Jordan's renewable water resources. The total average supply of renewable natural water in Jordan is 745 MCM/y on average.[3]

---

[3]The total of 745 MCM/y in Table 1.2 also includes brackish water (with chloride concentration above 400 mg/L). As the share of brackish water is not clearly indicated, it will not be subtracted from the total supplies, as was done for Israel and the PA earlier. It is thus likely that the total supply of 745 MCM/y overestimates the natural supplies of fresh water in Jordan.

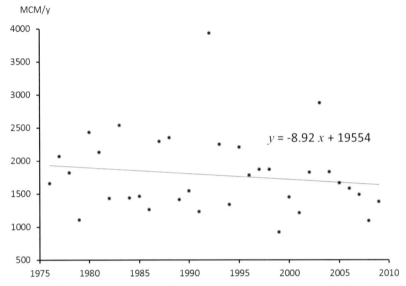

Figure 1.3: Actual observations of total natural water recharge of all major water sources (including brackish water) west of the Jordan River during the period 1976–2009.

Source: Weinberger *et al.* (2012).

Table 1.2: Jordan's renewable water resources.

Source	MCM/y
Groundwater (safe yield)	275
Surface water (by 2022)	365
Artificial recharge (in 2007)	55
1994's peace treaty (from Lake Kinneret)	50
Total	**745**

Source: Hashemite Kingdom of Jordan's Ministry of Water and Irrigation (2010, Executive Summary, p. 7).

1.2.1.3. *Water resources in the JRB*

The average supply of renewable natural water in the JRB (available to Jordan, Israel, and the PA in a sustainable fashion, i.e., without drawing down stocks) is therefore 2428 (1683 + 745) MCM/y, of which (at least) 232 MCM/y is of brackish quality (with chloride concentration exceeding 400 mg/L, unsuitable for drinking and for irrigation of many crops without mixing). The annual supply of renewable, fresh natural water (with chloride concentration below 400 mg/L) available in the JRB is therefore 2196 ($=1683-232+745$) MCM/y on average.

1.2.2.   *Population and Per Capita Water Supplies*

Figure 1.4 presents actual (up to 2011) and projected populations of Israel, Jordan, and the PA from 1950 to 2050.

Dividing the annual natural water supplies of 2196 MCM/y by the population gives the per capita annual water supplies, presented in Table 1.3.[4]

As Table 1.3 reveals, the region as a whole is already far below the absolute scarcity mark of 500 m^3 per person per year and within two decades will cross the subsistence scarcity mark of 100 m^3 per

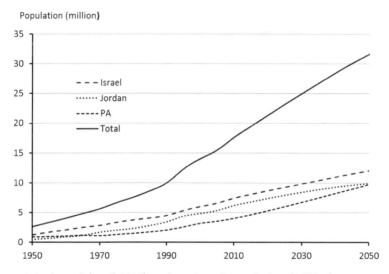

Figure 1.4: Actual (until 2011) and projected population (million).
Source: United Nations (2011).

___

[4]The average per capita water supplies presented in Table 1.3 mask a considerable spatial variability among the three parties, with Jordan suffering the most acute water shortage.

Table 1.3: Population and per capita supplies of natural water in the JRB. The latter is obtained by dividing natural water supply (2196 MCM/y) by the population.

Year	Population (million)	m^3/person/year
2013	18.8	117
2030	25.0	88
2050	31.6	69

person per year. At such an acute scarcity, the problem of allocating natural, potable water becomes also a human right issue, implying that any water allocation policy in the region should give priority to the supply of domestic (potable) water. Increasing the allocation of domestic water can be achieved by reallocating water from irrigation or by introducing new water supplies or a combination of these. In the next section, we describe recent experience of Israel's water policy, which can serve as a guide for water policy in the regions as a whole.

1.3. Dealing with Water Scarcity: Israel's Experience

Water scarcity in Israel has been addressed by demand management aimed at improved conservation and efficiency of water use, and by supply management through augmenting water supplies in the form of desalinated and recycled water. We discuss demand and supply measures in turn.

1.3.1. *Demand Management*

Policy measures aimed at affecting water demand must rely in one way or another on a combination of water pricing and water quotas and these tools have always been the foundations of Israel's water policy (see Tsur [2009] for a discussion of water pricing in general, and Kislev [2011] for a detailed account of water pricing in Israel). The efficacy of strict volumetric pricing of domestic water is demonstrated in Fig. 1.5, which presents domestic water consumption during the period 1996–2011. As the figure shows, domestic water consumption increased more or less in proportion with the population growth until 2007, reaching a peak of 767 MCM

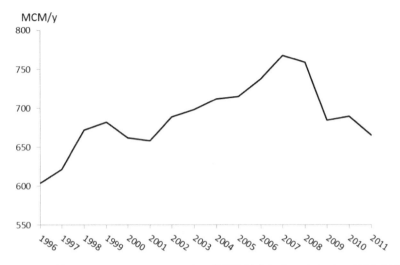

Figure 1.5: Domestic water consumption (MCM/y) in Israel during 1996–2011.
Source: Israel Water Authority (2011). Water consumption by sectors: 1996–2011 (in Hebrew). Available at: http://www.water.gov.il/Hebrew/ProfessionalInfoAnd Data/Allocation-Consumption-and-production/20112/1996-2011.pdf.

in that year. Thereafter, it decreased to 665 MCM in 2011 — a decline of more than 10% or 100 MCM/y (the equivalent of a large-scale desalination plant). As population continues along its secular growth trend, water consumption per person has decreased even more drastically. What happened in 2007 that led to such a shift in domestic water consumption?

A number of measures are responsible for this shift. First, Israel's Water Authority was formed in 2007 as an independent, statutory regulatory body with authority to set extraction permits and water prices in all sectors.[5] Second, municipal water management shifted from the municipalities (city, regional, and local councils) to Water Corporations. Third, 2007 was the third winter in a sequence of five of

---

[5]Prior to 2007, water policies were spread over a number of agencies and committees: the Water Commission (the agency that preceded the Water Authority) was responsible for protecting the natural water resources, thus providing extraction permits; a Knesset (Parliament) committee was responsible for setting prices in various sectors; and a number of governmental committees for allocating quotas (see Kislev, 2011).

below average precipitation (see Fig. 1.2). These three events have led to a number of interventions. First, domestic water prices increased sharply to reflect the cost of water supply (including scarcity cost).[6] Second, the transfer of the management of municipal water to Water Corporations has reduced water loss (due to leakage or theft) and improved collection of water fees from users. Third, the prolonged period of below-average rainfall has increased the public awareness for the need to reform the water sector and was conducive to the implementation of drastic measures to conserve water and improve management.

These three processes combined have acted to reverse the domestic water consumption trend, as seen in Fig. 1.5. This episode illuminates the importance of demand management tools: an effective implementation of a number of demand measures (strict volumetric pricing, effective management practices, reduced leakage, and unaccounted water) resulted in water-saving equivalent to the quantity produced by a large-scale desalination plant.

Similar processes took place in Israel's agriculture, albeit more gradually. Figure 1.6 shows trajectories of two price indices during the period 1952–2011 (adjusted for consumer price index): the price index of natural, fresh (nonbrackish) water in agriculture; and a price index of agricultural output (crop prices). The crop price declined moderately until the late 1990s and has been stable since then. The water price index, on the other hand, has increased fivefold during this period, with a sharp increase following the early 1990s. This price trend has led to a decline in the demand for irrigation water from fresh, natural sources and accelerated the transition of Israel's agriculture to recycled water (see Fig. 1.7).[7]

---

[6]A description of municipal water tariffs during 1975–2008 can be found in Kislev (2011, pp. 62–72). Current rates can be found in the Water Authority's tariffs book (in Hebrew) at http://www.water.gov.il/Hebrew/Rates/DocLib1/prices-books-1.1.14.pdf.

[7]The actual water prices are based on historical (1986–1987) quotas, where actual quotas are adjusted each year according to precipitation, with a base rate that applies up to a certain percentage of the quota and add on fees for deviations (details can be found in the above-cited water tariffs book).

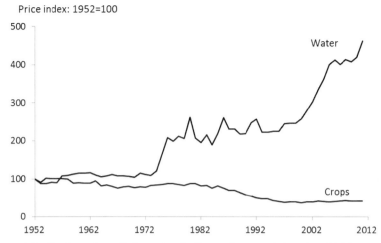

Figure 1.6: Trajectories of the price indices of natural (nonbrackish) water in agriculture and of crop prices during 1952–2011 (1952 = 100, adjusted for consumer price index).

Source: Kislev and Tzaban (2013).

1.3.2. *Supply Management*

In addition to the above-mentioned demand management measures, the supply of water has been increased by the development of recycling and desalination. We discuss each in turn.

1.3.2.1. *Recycling*

Figure 1.7 shows the water allocation in Israel's agriculture sector during the period 1996–2011. As the figure reveals, the allocation of natural water to agriculture has reduced from 892.3 MCM in 1996 to 413.7 MCM in 2011 — a decline of 54%. At the same time, the supply of recycled water increased from 270 MCM in 1996 to 414.8 MCM in 2011. Israel's growers now use more recycled water than natural water and this trend (of replacing natural water by recycled and brackish water) is ongoing.

The direct effect of reallocating natural water from agriculture to households is to increase the supply of (potable quality) domestic water. However, each cubic meter reallocated to households provides 0.6–$0.65\,\mathrm{m}^3$ of recycled water that in turn is allocated

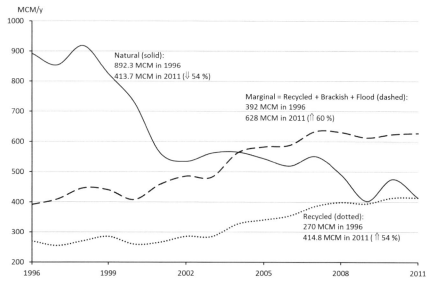

Figure 1.7: Water allocation in Israel's agriculture during 1996–2011 (brackish refers to water with chloride concentration above 400 mg/L).

Source: Israel Water Authority (2011). Water consumption by sectors: 1996–2011 (in Hebrew). http://www.water.gov.il/Hebrew/ProfessionalInfoAndData/Allocation-Consumption-and-production/20112/1996-2011.pdf.

to irrigation.[8] Thus, the overall effect of reallocating $1\,\text{m}^3$ from agriculture to households is to increase domestic supply by $1\,\text{m}^3$ and reduce agricultural supply by only 0.3–$0.4\,\text{m}^3$. Almost all domestic and industrial water supplies in Israel are now recycled and made available to irrigation (pending conveyance facilities). Moreover, all recycling facilities are expected (required by law) to be upgraded to tertiary level by 2015, reducing the limitation on the use of recycled water for most crops.

1.3.2.2. *Desalination*

The cost of desalination has declined substantially during the last decade mainly due to learning by doing associated with the

---

[8]The conversion rates in Israel's water economy master plan range from 0.592 in 2010 to 0.64 in 2030 (Israel Water Authority, 2012, p. 14).

increased scale of installed desalination capacity. Figure 1.8 presents the desalination costs ($/m^3 at the plant's gate) of the major desalination plants in descending order. Also shown, for each plant, are the year operation began (all plants are in operation except for Ashdod, which is expected to begin operation soon) and the plant's production capacity (MCM/y). At the completion of Ashdod plant, Israel's desalination capacity will exceed 600 MCM/y, which is about 90% of the total household consumption in 2011. The desalination capacity will reduce reliance on natural water sources and allow a more sustainable management of the natural water sources, by reducing average extractions in order to increase stock levels, thereby eliminating risks such as seawater intrusion into the coastal aquifer or potentially detrimental algal bloom in Lake Kinneret. In addition, more water will be allocated for environmental purposes such as river restoration.[9]

To sum up, the recent Israeli experience emphasizes the potential of demand management measures in dealing with water scarcity. The pricing and management practices that were implemented in 2007 reduced domestic water use by more than 10% or 100 MCM/y. Regarding supply management, recycling is an immediate and relatively cheap way to increase water supply. It is cheap because of the rapid technological progress in recycling and because the alternative environmental cost of not recycling is high. A cubic meter allocated to household or industrial use can generate 0.6–0.65 m^3 of recycled water suitable for irrigation and environmental restoration. Technological progress due to research and development (R&D) and learning by doing associated with increased desalination activities have led to a substantial decrease in the cost of desalination. These trends, together with the fact that the bulk of Israel's population is concentrated along the coast, imply that desalination is an economically viable source of water supply for households.

---

[9]See the planned fivefold increase in freshwater allocated to nature and landscape in Israel's long-term master plan of the water sector (Israel Water Authority, 2012, p. 14).

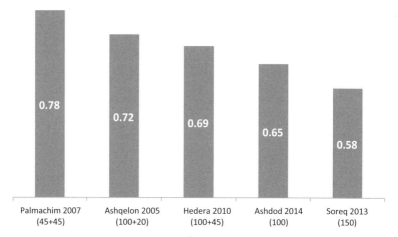

Figure 1.8: Cost of desalination ($/m^3 at the plant's gate calculated under the exchange rate: \$1 = 3.6 NIS). The numbers in parentheses give the capacity in MCM/y ($x + z$ means that the original capacity of x MCM/y has been or will soon be expanded by z MCM/y to give a total capacity of $x + z$ MCM/y).

Source: Israel Water Authority (2012).[10]

1.4. Managing Water Scarcity in the JRB

Is the Israeli experience relevant to Jordan and the PA? Regarding recycling, the answer is clearly in the affirmative, as recycling can be applied in Jordan and the PA in much the same way as in Israel.[11] This means that most of the fresh (potable) natural water should be allocated to domestic use, collected, treated, and reused in agriculture and environmental (rivers, ecosystems) restoration. The household demand over and above the natural water supplies (which increases over time due to population growth) can come from desalination plants. Regarding desalination, the case of Jordan differs

---

[10]The desalination prices are based on the original prices at the time the contracts were signed. Over time, these prices have been adjusted for inflation and changed with the capacity expansions. The prices listed in the figure, thus, should be taken as estimates.

[11]Indeed, water reuse captures an important role in Jordan's plans for future water policy reforms (Jordan's Ministry of Water and Irrigation, 2010, Chap. 6). Regarding the PA, construction of sewage treatment plants has been delayed mainly due to political obstacles (associated with reluctance to share plants with Israeli settlements). One hopes that these obstacles will be resolved soon.

from that of Israel and the PA. I, therefore, discuss Jordan and the PA separately.

1.4.1. *Jordan*

The bulk of Jordan's population resides in the Amman area at about 1000 m above sea level and more than 300 km away from Jordan's only sea access (the Gulf of Aqaba). Desalination in Aqaba and conveyance to Amman is an expensive operation: the cost in Amman of $1\,m^3$ desalinated in Aqaba (before distribution to households and sewage treatment) is estimated above $\$2/m^3$ — about four times the cost of supplying desalinated water to Israel's densely populated areas (see Fig. 1.8). Moreover, discharging large quantities of brine ($1\,m^3$ of desalinated water generates about $1.22\,m^3$ of brine) in the Gulf of Aqaba could have detrimental effects on the sensitive coral reef ecology and is objected to by the other Gulf of Aqaba's riparian states (Egypt, Saudi Arabia, and Israel). For these two reasons, desalination in Aqaba (with brine discharge in the Red Sea) and conveyance to Amman is nonviable as a comprehensive solution to Jordan's water scarcity problems in the long run.

These demographical and topographical features of Jordan imply that reallocating fresh (natural) water from irrigation to urban use requires considerable pumping. However, the cost associated with such reallocation is still lower than the cost of desalinating in Aqaba and conveyance to Amman due to the shorter distances (see World Bank, 2012). At the same time, these features are conducive to using recycled water in irrigation. This is so because conveyance of the recycled water from treatment plants near higher urban centers to lower agricultural areas (e.g., in the Jordan Valley) can be based more on gravitation and less on energy, and hence entails a lower cost.[12]

---

[12]The alternative cost of fresh (natural) water allocated for irrigation in Jordan is the cost urban dwellers are willing to pay for fresh water, which is very high (due to the acute shortage of potable water) and cannot be afforded by Jordanian farmers (although this is the price they *should* pay for irrigating with fresh water). On the other hand, the price of recycled water in irrigation is very low, since it consists only of the cost of conveying this water from treatment plants located

1.4.1.1. *Water management: pricing, conservation, and reduction of water loss*

Water losses from Jordan's municipal supply networks were estimated at 43%, which amounts to 137 MCM/y of total municipal allocation of 320 MCM/y (Yorke, 2013, p. 100). A reduction of water loss, through improved management and pricing practices, to internationally conventional levels would increase the supply of potable water by more than 100 MCM/y. Water tariffs for irrigation do not cover the operational costs of conveyance, let alone the fix cost of the infrastructure (Yorke, 2013, p. 46). In the Jordan Valley, for example, farmers pay an average tariff of JD $0.012/m^3$ ($\$0.017/m^3$), while domestic and industrial tariffs are much higher, ranging between JD $0.250/m^3$, or $\$0.35/m^3$, and JD $1.800/m^3$, or $\$2.55/m^3$ (Yorke, 2013).

The existing water allocation (Jordan's Water Strategy, 2008–2022) could be changed by reallocating at least 300 MCM/y of good quality natural water from irrigation to domestic use, while fully compensating farmers with recycled water. This reallocation will increase the supply of potable water (by 300 MCM/y) and will add about 200 MCM/y of recycled water (60%–65% of the 300 MCM/y) to total water supplies that were not available before the reallocation. Overall, improved management and allocation practices could increase the supply of potable water by more than 400 MCM/y.

1.4.1.2. *Water swap*

On Monday, 9 December 2013, a memorandum of understanding was signed between Israel, Jordan, and the PA, at the World Bank's Washington headquarters, with the following basic principles: Jordan will desalinate about 80–100 MCM/y near Aqaba and discharge

---

near urban centers (which are mostly in higher plains) to the agricultural areas located mostly in lower plains (notice that the cost of conveying the fresh natural water to the urban centers as well as the cost of recycling should be paid by urban dwellers). Thus, reallocating fresh water to urban, recycling and reusing in irrigation are the correct way to keep the cost of irrigation water low.

the brine in the Dead Sea (to be conveyed via a pipeline).[13] Israel will buy about 50 MCM/y from the Aqaba plant to be used in Eilat (for drinking) and the Arava valley (for irrigation) and will sell Jordan 50 MCM/y from Lake Kinneret (to be conveyed to Amman via existing conveyance facilities). The agreement also involves additional water allocation to the PA, but its main feature is a water swap between Jordan and Israel, where Israel obtains water from Aqaba's desalination and provides the same quantity from Lake Kinneret in the north. The cost of Lake Kinneret water in Amman is about \$1–\$1.2 per m^3,[14] which is about half the cost of the Aqaba-Amman default alternative. The potential scale of such a water swap is, however, limited by the annual flow of water into Lake Kinneret (see Weinberger *et al.* [2012], for a description of Lake Kinneret's water balance). At most it could support an additional 50 MCM/y, bringing the total amount of Lake Kinneret water allocated to Jordan to 150 MCM/y (including the 50 MCM/y supplied to Jordan following the 1994 peace treaty).

1.4.1.3. *Red Sea–Dead Sea conveyance projects*

A recurrent idea that has recently been studied in detail entails conveyance of water from the Red Sea (or the Mediterranean) to the Dead Sea, desalination near the Dead Sea, discharge of the brine reject in the Dead Sea, using the elevation difference (of about 350–400 m) to generate electricity, and conveyance of the desalinated water mostly to Amman (see Vardi [1990], for a survey of studies prior to 1990). The recent incarnation of this idea is the Red Sea–Dead Sea (RSDS) Conveyance Project, investigated by a suit of feasibility studies conducted under the World Bank's auspices (see Markel *et al.*, 2013, for an overview; the detailed studies can be found

---

[13]As was already mentioned, discharging brine in the Gulf of Aqaba could have detrimental effects on the sensitive coral reef ecosystem and discharging the brine in the Dead Sea overcomes this obstacle. In addition, it will provide information on possible effects of mixing seawater or brine in the Dead Sea, relevant for the implementation of the RSDS project (see discussed in the following).

[14]This cost consists of \$0.3–\$0.4 per m^3 purchasing price plus \$0.7–\$0.8 per m^3 treatment and conveyance (see World Bank, 2012).

in www.worldbank.org/rds). The RSDS project is planned to be constructed in phases over three to four decades. Upon completion, a full-scale RSDS project will convey 2000 MCM/y from the Red Sea to the Dead Sea, desalinate 850 MCM/y (near the Dead Sea), to be conveyed mostly to Amman (but also to the PA and Israel), discharge the 1150 MCM/y brine in the Dead Sea and generate electricity. A number of environmental (e.g., effects on the Dead Sea due to mixing with large quantities of brine and/or sea water, potential hazards associated with earthquake threats) and economic (ability to finance a large and expensive project) issues render the realization of a full-scale project questionable.

The Study of Alternatives (World Bank, 2012) considered a small-scale RSDS project, under which only 200 MCM/y will be desalinated and conveyed mostly to Amman. This requires conveyance of 440 MCM/y from the Red Sea to the Dead Sea and will generate 240 MCM/y of brine, to be discharged in the Dead Sea. No reliable estimates of the cost of potable water in Amman associated with this small-scale RSDS project exist, but it is expected to be lower than the cost in Amman of water desalinated in Aqaba (see World Bank, 2012).

1.4.1.4.   *Water from the Mediterranean*

The Study of Alternatives (World Bank, 2012) examined also the cost in Amman of water derived from the Mediterranean Sea. One of the options considered (the northern alignment) entails desalination along the Mediterranean coast (between Haifa and Atlit) and conveyance to Amman via Naharayim-Bakura (at the confluence of the Jordan and Yarmouk Rivers). The cost in Amman (desalination and conveyance) was calculated to be in the range of $1/m^3–$1.2/m^3 (World Bank, 2012), which is substantially lower than the $2/m^3 cost in Amman of water desalinated in Aqaba. The cost advantage is due to the shorter conveyance distance. The scale of this operation can reach 200 MCM/y.[15]

---

[15]As noted by a reviewer, the Jordanians have been explicit about not wanting to be dependent on Israel (or the PA) for all of their water supply, but may

1.4.1.5.   *Actions combined*

The above four actions combined will augment Jordan's supply of potable water by about 900 MCM/y (about 400 MCM/y from improved management and allocation practices, 100 MCM/y from Lake Kinneret by water swaps, 200 MCM/y from the Mediterranean via Naharayim-Bakura, and 200 MCM/y from a mini RSDS project). These additional supplies will satisfy Jordan's potable water needs in the long run.

1.4.2.   *Palestinian Authority*

The many issues on which the Palestinians and Israelis disagree include ownership of the mountain aquifer (see Fig. 1.2). I have nothing to contribute to this particular dispute. I note, however, that water rights over natural sources are of lesser importance once water scarcity reaches a point where existing natural supplies can at most satisfy basic human needs and water allocation policies are driven by human right considerations. The Israelis and Palestinians will reach this point very soon, as Table 1.4 reveals. The implications are that, independent of ownership rights, the mountain aquifer's water should be allocated to satisfy basic human needs in the most economical way.

The renewable supply of drinking quality water available from the water basins west of the Jordan River is currently 1451 MCM/y on average (see Table 1.1). The population of Israel and the PA

Table 1.4: Annual per capita supplies of natural (potable) water available for Israel and the PA.

Year	Population (million)	m^3/person/year
2011	11.5	127
2030	16.6	88
2050	21.8	67

Source: Data from Weinberger *et al.* (2012) and United Nations (2011), as per Table 1.1 and Fig. 1.4.

---

not object to a fraction of the total water supply (say 100–200 MCM/y) at a substantial lower cost than that of water desalinated in Aqaba.

combined is expected to reach 16.6 million in 2030 and 21.8 million in 2050 (see Fig. 1.4). The corresponding expected annual supplies per person from natural sources are similar to those given in Table 1.3 (will reach 88 or 67 m³/person/year in 2030 or 2050, respectively).

As far as recycling and desalination are concerned, the PA's situation is similar to that of Israel, in that it has an easy access to the Mediterranean (Gaza strip) and a large share of its population resides near the sea. The actions needed to deal with the water scarcity can therefore be similar to those taken by Israel.

1.5. Water for the Environment

The water policy discussed so far focused on direct human needs (domestic, irrigation, and industry). Satisfying these needs entails extractions and diversions from natural sources, which inevitably come at the expense of environmental needs (see Beyth [2006] for a historical account of diversions by Israel and Jordan). In this respect, two environmental assets, shared by Israel, Jordan, and the PA, stand out: the LJR and the Dead Sea (see map in Fig. 1.1). Diversions from Lake Kinneret and the upper Jordan River, mostly by Israel, have virtually eliminated the water flow from the lake to the LJR. Diversions from the Yarmouk basin (mostly by Syria) have diminished its flow into the LJR. Further diversions downstream (by Jordan, Israel, and the PA) have deprived the LJR of an additional 200–300 MCM/y. The historic flow of 1300 MCM/y on average has been diminished to a trickle of mostly brackish water and sewage (Gafny *et al.*, 2010). The most pronounced environmental consequences have been the destruction of the LJR's ecosystem and declining Dead Sea levels.[16] I discuss here how partial restorations of the LJR and stabilization of the Dead Sea level can be incorporated within the water policy discussed earlier. The approach taken here is

---

[16]Additional diversions (e.g., from the Mujib at the Dead Sea's eastern escarpment) as well as the Dead Sea potash industries (of Israel and Jordan) also contribute to the decline of the Dead Sea level.

similar to the alternative called "Combined Alternative 1" in World Bank (2012).

1.5.1. *Partial Restoration of the LJR*

Gafny *et al.* (2010) conclude that the LJR requires an annual flow of 400–600 MCM/y in order to restore its ecosystem. We explain how such a flow can be implemented over a period of three to four decades. Water for LJR restoration can come from three possible sources: Lake Kinneret, desalination plants, and recycled water; the cost of each is determined by its alternative cost. The alternative cost of potable water (from Lake Kinneret or from desalination plants) is the cost of providing Amman with the same quantity of potable water (either from Lake Kinneret or by desalination along the Mediterranean and conveyance via Naharayim-Bakura). As was discussed previously, this cost exceeds $1/m^3. The alternative cost of recycled water is the cost farmers are willing to pay for this water.[17] This cost can be estimated by the cost of recycled water to Israeli growers, which currently is in the range of $0.2–$0.4/m^3 (see Kislev, 2011).

The associated benefit is the willingness to pay (WTP) for restoring the LJR. Because the LJR, in addition to the environmental services it provides to the local population, has historical, religious, and cultural values, the WTP for its restoration has local and international components. Estimates of regional (Israel, Jordan, and the PA) WTPs for LJR restoration were recently calculated by Becker *et al.* (2014) for different annual flows (220 and 400 MCM/y) and water quality levels. Their WTP values for restoration involving annual flow of 400 MCM of water of different quality range between $0.23/m^3 and $0.87/m^3.[18] These values fall below the alternative costs of potable water but are compatible with costs of recycled water. We conclude, given the WTP estimates of Becker *et al.*

---

[17]The technical cost of recycling is borne by the domestic sector (i.e., households), since, for environmental reasons, the water must be treated disregarding how it is used afterward.

[18]These estimates are obtained by dividing the total WTP corresponding to scenarios S3 and S4 by the restoration flow of 400 MCM/y (see Becker *et al.*, 2014, Tables 2–3).

(2014), that the use of potable water (either from Lake Kinneret or from desalination plants) for LJR restoration cannot be justified on economic grounds.[19] In the remainder of this subsection we consider LJR restoration by recycled water.

According to Israel's master plan of the national water sector (Israel Water Authority, 2012, p. 14), the allocation of water to agriculture in 2050 is planned to reach 1450 MCM/y, of which 900 MCM/y will come from recycling plants,[20] 100 MCM/y will be brackish (saline) water, and 450 MCM/y will come from fresh natural sources. An allocation of 80 MCM/y is planned for environmental purposes. The value in agricultural production of the 1000 MCM/y of recycled and brackish water allocated to irrigation depends on how and where it is used (crops in different locations). The value of *some* of this allocation will fall below the value that would be generated had this water been reallocated to LJR restoration (which, as noted earlier, generates benefit in the range of $0.23/m^3$–$0.87/m^3$). The quantity of reallocated water that will satisfy this criterion (i.e., will generate higher benefit in LJR restoration than in irrigation) is expected to exceed 20% of the total recycled and brackish water allocation, that is, around 200 MCM/y by 2050. Thus, in three to four decades, about 200 MCM/y of recycled water planned for agriculture use in Israel would generate a higher value in LJR restoration, and hence *should* be reallocated for that purpose.[21]

By the same calculation applied to Jordan and the PA (recalling from Fig. 1.4 that their population will be similar to that of Israel), it is expected that by 2050, each will be able to supply

---

[19]This conclusion could be changed if international WTP were high enough. Unfortunately, such estimates are not available and will not be considered here.

[20]Recent legislation requires all recycling plants in Israel to be upgraded to tertiary level by 2015.

[21]The demand for irrigation water is expected to increase over time as food prices rise with the increased demand from a growing population. However, the WTP for environmental amenities will also increase with economic growth and wealthier population, and there is no reason to assume that the former process will outpace the latter. While the evaluation based on current irrigation water demand and WIP for environmental amenities should be updated as new data come along it is unlikely to change in any substantial way.

at least 100 MCM/y for LJR restoration. We conclude that by 2050, the allocation of recycled water for LJR restoration from the three parties combined *should* (according to a cost–benefit criterion) exceed 400 MCM/y, which is the flow necessary for LJR restoration (Gafny *et al.*, 2010). This process, however, will be gradual and will evolve over time. It is a direct outcome of the water policy discussed earlier, namely, of providing enough potable water to satisfy the needs of the growing population, while recycling all domestic and industrial water use.

Using recycled water for LJR restoration requires conveyance (of the recycled water) from where it is produced (treatment plants) to the upper end of the LJR (near Naharayim-Bakura) and the associated cost will increase the cost of the restoration water. Mekonen (2013) calculated the cost of conveying 100 MCM/y of recycled water from the Jerusalem-Ramallah area to Naharayim-Bakura, while using the elevation difference (of about 1000 m) to generate electricity. Mekonen (2013, Table 6) calculated the conveyance cost at $0.19/m^3 (equivalent to 0.68 NIS/m^3)[22] and the hydroelectricity profit at $0.12/m^3. The compensation to farmers was estimated at $0.26/m^3. The net cost of using this water for LJR restoration (conveyance minus hydroelectricity profit plus compensation to irrigators) is therefore $0.33/m^3, which falls at the lower part of the benefit range (WTP) from LJR restoration, estimated by Becker *et al.* (2014) between $0.23/m^3 and $0.87/m^3.

1.5.1.1. *Stabilizing the Dead Sea*

The second most notable effect of the extensive upstream diversions discussed earlier is the declining Dead Sea levels (Klein, 1982; Salameh and El-Naser, 1999, 2000; Tahal and Geological Survey of Israel, 2011). The Dead Sea level, which has recently been declining at an annual rate above 1 m, is measured now at about 428 meters below sea level (mbsl) — about 35 m below its historical level of 390–400 mbsl (Fig. 1.9). Most proposals for reclaiming the Dead Sea,

---

[22]At the time of writing, the exchange rate is $1 = 3.63 NIS.

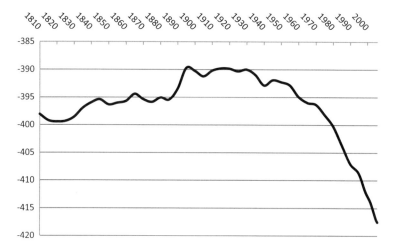

Figure 1.9: Dead Sea levels: 1810–2006.
Source: Rawashdeh *et al.* (2013).

by either stopping its decline or restoring its level to the pre-
diversions state, involve conveyance of large quantities of sea water to
the Dead Sea either from the Mediterranean or from the Red Sea (see
Vardi [1990] and Beyth [2007] for overviews of past proposals, and
the studies in www.worldbank.org/rds of the recent "Red Sea–Dead
Sea Conveyance Study Program," compiled under the World Bank
auspices). The approach taken here is based on the actions needed
for solving the water shortage problem considered above and avoids
a major sea-to-sea water conveyance project.

Stabilizing the Dead Sea at its current level requires increasing
the water inflow by 700–800 MCM/y (Tahal and Geological Survey of
Israel, 2011). Over time, due to the LJR restoration discussed earlier,
the flow of the LJR into the Dead Sea will increase by 400 MCM/y
or more. In addition, 360 MCM/y of brine will be discharged into the
Dead Sea at its southern end: 240 MCM/y from the desalination near
the Dead Sea associated with the small-scale RSDS project discussed
earlier and 120 MCM/y of brine from the desalination in Aqaba
(associated with the water swap action). The total flow into the Dead
Sea will thus increase by about 760 MCM/y — about the flow needed
to stabilize the Dead Sea at the current level.

The cost of discharging seawater or brine from the Red Sea into the Dead Sea is estimated between $0.1/m^3 and $0.27/m^3, depending on assumptions made regarding the interest rate and cost of electricity (see World Bank, 2012, p. 156). The risks associated with mixing the Dead Sea with sea water or brine (stratification, gypsum precipitation, and biological bloom) are low for a discharge flow below 400 MCM/y (Tahal and Geological Survey of Israel, 2011, p. 6). The 360 MCM/y of brine discharge, therefore, is unlikely to inflict detrimental effects on the Dead Sea and can be considered safe.

Regarding the cost of the recycled water, it was discussed previously that the residual cost after paying for the LJR restoration is negligible. However, the inflow of recycled water is filled with nutrients and, without further treatment, could give rise to severe biological bloom. Avoiding this risk will therefore require further treatment before the water enters the Dead Sea. No estimates are available regarding the cost of such further treatment.

The total cost of Dead Sea stabilization should be compared to the benefit associated with stabilizing the Dead Sea at about its current level. This benefit includes the cost avoided as a result of stopping the decline of the Dead Sea level. Becker and Katz (2009) estimated this cost to be in the range of 73–227 million dollars a year. Like in the case of LJR restoration, the unique characteristics of the Dead Sea imply that the benefit of its preservation extends beyond the region and includes the international community as a whole. The total benefit of preventing the decline of the Dead Sea is therefore likely to be much larger.

1.6.   Concluding Comments

The JRB, comprising Israel, Jordan, and the PA, suffers from acute water scarcity: the average supplies of natural water available in a sustainable fashion (without drawing down stocks) in this region will soon drop below $100\,m^3 per person per year. This is far below the supplies needed for human activities and the ensuing diversions have deprived many environmental sites of the minimal water supplies required to sustain living ecosystems. The three parties share some of the water sources, and thus must coordinate their water policies.

A water policy consists of demand management and supply management measures. The purpose of a demand management policy is to increase the efficiency of water use, that is, to do more with the same quantity of water. It includes measures such as water pricing and water quotas as well as institutional arrangements such as the delegation of municipal water to special corporations designed for that purpose, which (in the case of Israel) improved collection of water fees and reduced water leakage and theft. The purpose of supply management policies is to increase the available supply of water mainly from recycling and desalination plants. Drawing on recent Israeli experience, we offer a comprehensive, long-run policy to address the region's water shortage problems based on demand and supply management measures.

Special attention is given to environmental water and in particular to the restoration of two environmental assets shared by the three parties: the LJR and the Dead Sea. We show how a partial restoration of the LJR and a stabilization of the Dead Sea level can be achieved within the water policy that addresses human needs. A key element of this policy is that each cubic meter allocated to households and industrial use should be collected, treated, and be available for reuse in irrigation and environmental restoration. Over time, the supply of this water grows (with the population) to the extent that it can support comprehensive environmental policies. This approach is gradual and depends on the rate of population growth. In the case under study, it was found that within three to four decades the supply of (high quality) recycled water will suffice to partially restore the LJR and stabilize the Dead Sea level while fully compensating farmers for reallocating the recycled water from irrigation to environmental restoration.

Far from being anecdotal, the case of the JRB involves elements common in many water basins, where population growth and rising living standards have increased water scarcity and intensified the tradeoffs associated with the multidimensional role of water. These elements include transboundary management of water resources shared by multiple parties, the need to balance environmental and human water consumptions, and the combination of demand and supply management policies in an erratically fluctuating environment. The main lessons drawn from this study are therefore relevant in many real-world situations.

References

Becker, N and DL Katz (2009). An economic assessment of Dead Sea preservation and restoration. In *The Jordan River and Dead Sea: Cooperation Amid Conflict*, C Lipchin, D Sandler, and E Cushman (eds.), pp. 275–296. Dordrecht, the Netherlands: Springer.

Becker, N, J Helgeson, and D Katz (2014). Once there was a river: A benefit-cost analysis of rehabilitation of the Jordan River. *Regional Environmental Change*, 14, 1303–1314.

Beyth, M (2006). Water crisis in Israel. In *Water Histories, Culture and Ecologies*, M Leybourne, and A Gynor (eds.), pp. 117–181. Perth: University of Western Australia Press.

Beyth, M (2007). The Red Sea and the Mediterranean–Dead Sea canal project. *Desalination*, 214, 364–370.

Falkenmark, M, J Lundquist, and C Widstrand (1989). Macro-scale water scarcity requires micro-scale approaches: Aspects of vulnerability in semi-arid development. *Natural Resources Forum*, 13, 258–267.

Gafny, S, S Talozi, B Al Sheikh, and E Ya'ari (2010). *Towards a Living Jordan River: An Environmental Flows Report on the Rehabilitation of the Lower Jordan River*. EcoPeace/Friends of the Earth Middle East, Amman, Bethlehem, Tel Aviv.

Gleick, PH (1996). Basic water requirements for human activities: Meeting basic needs. *Water International*, 21, 83–92.

Gleick, PH (2002). *The World's Water: The Biennial Report on Freshwater Resources 2002–2003*. Washington: Island Press.

Israel Water Authority (2011). Water consumption by sectors: 1996–2011 (in Hebrew). http://www.water.gov.il/Hebrew/ProfessionalInfoAnd Data/Allocation-Consumption-and-production/20112/1996-2011.pdf

Israel Water Authority (2012). Long-term master plan for the National Water Sector. http://www.water.gov.il/Hebrew/Planning-and-Develop ment/Planning/MasterPlan/DocLib4/MasterPlan-en-v.4.pdf

Jordan's Ministry of Water and Irrigation (2010). Jordan's water strategy, water for life, 2008–2022, Executive Summary, pp. 1–7. Ministry of Water and Irrigation, Amman. http://www.joriew.eu/uploads/private/ joriew_org_jordan_national_water_strategy.pdf

Kislev, Y (2011). The water economy of Israel. *Taub Center for Social Policy Studies in Israel*. (Policy Paper No. 2011.15). http://depart ments.agri.huji.ac.il/economics/teachers/kislev_yoav/water_English%20 edition.pdf

Kislev, Y and S Tzaban (2013). Statistical atlas of Israel's agriculture (in Hebrew). http://departments.agri.huji.ac.il/economics/teachers/kislev_ yoav/atlas2013.pdf

Klein, C (1982). Morphological evidence of lake level changes: Western shore of the Dead Sea. *Israel Journal of Earth Sciences*, 31, 67–94.

Markel, D, J Alster, and M Beyth (2013). The Red Sea–Dead Sea feasibility study, 2008–2012. In *Water Policy in Israel*, N Becker (ed.). London: Springer.

Mekonen, S (2013). Economic alternatives for rehabilitation of the lower Jordan River. MSc Thesis, Department of Agricultural Economics and Management, the Hebrew University of Jerusalem, Rehovot, Israel (in Hebrew).

Rawashdeh, S, R Ruzouq, A Al-Fugara, B Pradhan, S Ziad, and A Ghayda (2013). Monitoring of Dead Sea water surface variation using multi-temporal satellite data and GIS. *Arabian Journal of Geosciences*, 6, 3241–3248.

Rijsberman, FR (2006). Water scarcity: Fact or fiction? *Agricultural Water Management*, 80, 5–22.

Salameh, E and H El-Naser (1999). Does the actual drop in the Dead Sea level reflect the development of water sources within its drainage basin? *Acta Hydrochimica Hydrobiologica*, 27, 5–11.

Salameh, E and H El-Naser (2000). Changes in the Dead Sea level and their impacts on the surrounding groundwater bodies. *Acta Hydrochimica Hydrobiologica*, 28, 24–33.

Tahal and Geological Survey of Israel (2011). Red Sea–Dead Sea water conveyance study program: Dead Sea study (final report). http://sitere sources.worldbank.org/INTREDSEADEADSEA/Resources/Tahal_Init ial_Final_Report_August_2011.pdf

Tsur, Y (2009). On the economics of water allocation and pricing. *Annual Review of Resource Economics*, 1(1), 513–536.

United Nations (2011). Department of Economic and Social Affairs, Population Division: World Population Prospects DEMOBASE extract. https:// docs.google.com/a/mail.huji.ac.il/spreadsheet/ccc?key=0Aon YZs4MzlZbcGhOdG0zTG1EWkVOb3FVbVRpa0Y5REE#gid=10

Vardi, J (1990). *Mediterranean-Dead Sea Project–A historical Review*. The Geological Survey of Israel, Report GSI/9/90.

Weinberger, G, Y Livshitz, A Givati, M Zilberbrand, A Tal, M Weiss, and A Zurieli (2012). The natural water resources between the Mediterranean Sea and the Jordan River. *Israel Hydrological Service, Israel's Authority for Water and Sewage.* http://www.water.gov.il/Hebrew/about-reshut-hamaim/The-Authority/FilesWatermanagement/water-report-MEDITERRANEAN-SEA-AND-THE-JORDAN.pdf

World Bank (2012). *Red Sea–Dead Sea Water Conveyance Study Program: Study of Alternatives* (Preliminary Draft Report). http://siteresources.worldbank.org/INTREDSEADEADSEA/Resources/Study_of_Alternatives_Report_EN.pdf

Yorke, V (2013). *Politics matter: Jordan's path to water security lies through political reforms and regional cooperation.* NCCR Trade Working Paper No 2013/19.

CHAPTER 2

EXPLORING BENEFITS AND SCOPE OF COOPERATION IN TRANSBOUNDARY WATER SHARING IN THE AMU DARYA BASIN

ANIK BHADURI* and MAKSUD BEKCHANOV†

*Griffith University, Brisbane Australia
†International Water Management Institute (IWMI)

This chapter assesses ex-ante the Rogun Dam project in Tajikistan and examines different possibilities of water allocation between the riparian countries and trade-offs across competing uses for water resources. A hydro-economic optimization model is used in the chapter to quantify the impacts of dam operations on energy production and irrigation water availability. The chapter finds that the economic impacts of the dam depend on its operation. Under the case of sustained cooperation, loss of the downstream countries, Uzbekistan and Turkmenistan, could be insignificant from the construction of Rogun Dam by the upstream country, Tajikistan. However, any unilateral diversion of water in the upstream for increased hydropower benefits may lead to a larger loss for downstream countries. This justifies for a strong need for trust and cooperation among the riparian countries over managing water infrastructural resources and for achieving sustainable growth.

Keywords: Transboundary; Central Asia; Water-Energy-Food Nexus; Cooperation

2.1. Introduction

One of the key challenges for riparian countries in many river basins is to attain water, food, and energy security altogether. The interdependence among food, water, and energy sectors is evident today due to a higher degree of correlation between energy and food prices and stronger dependence of food production on water availability (Beckchanov *et al.*, 2015; Bhaduri *et al.*, 2015; Ringler *et al.*, 2013). These cross-sectoral interdependences complicate identification of relevant policies for improved security, for instance, through hydraulic developments such as hydropower development, especially in transboundary river basins. Today, the increased attention to developing dams in transboundary river settings in developing countries escalates the debates over the relevance of water–energy–food nexus approaches. Many of such dams are mainly for multipurpose schemes, serving energy production, irrigation, domestic supply, and flood control needs. In a transboundary context, the sharing of rivers by different sectors and across political boundaries has led to direct competition between water use for energy and for food production.

The case of the Aral Sea basin (ASB) is worth mentioning in this context because it illustrates how water–energy–food nexus has created trade-offs, dilemmas, and conflicts in the region which are deeply rooted in historical circumstances. Under the centralized governance during the Soviet era, an institutional setting was created among the subregions over the sharing of water and energy resources in the ASB to achieve an efficient out (in Soviet terms) regarding resource allocation between regions capitalizing on the water abundance in the upstream and wealth of fossil fuel in the downstream. The Central Asia Power System (CAPS) was developed under the Soviet Union, comprising of the national grids of Uzbekistan, Tajikistan, Southern Kazakhstan, Kyrgyzstan, and Turkmenistan. CAPS allowed the exchange of power across countries dependent on their excess demand. In the winter, Tajikistan and the Kyrgyzstan Republic would depend on energy imports from the other countries, and in the summer, the upstream countries would supply excess hydropower to the downstream states.

With the disintegration of Union of Soviet Socialist Republics (USSR) and liberalization of energy markets, the mutual beneficial institutional setting of water–energy exchange turns out to futile and a conflict arose between the regions over the sharing of water after

Turkmenistan, Uzbekistan, and Kazakhstan withdrew themselves from the CAPS. As a result, regional energy trade dropped significantly contributing to severe winter energy shortages in the upstream countries. The upstream country, Kyrgyzstan then operates the Toktogul reservoir which generates hydropower demanded mainly in winter for heating while the downstream countries — Uzbekistan and Kazakhstan need irrigation water in summer primarily to grow cotton and wheat (Abbink *et al.*, 2005). Although water usage is nonconsumptive for hydropower generation, the conflict stemmed from the time of release and the seasonal differences in water demand for irrigation and energy production.

Recently, the revitalization of the Rogun hydropower dam project in Tajikistan has led to another water–energy dispute between Tajikistan and Uzbekistan. The proposed Rogun Dam is designed to increase upstream energy generation in the Amu Darya Basin but creates similar potential trade-offs with existing downstream irrigation needs due to the intertemporal differences in energy and irrigation water demands (Beckchanov *et al.*, 2015).

Rogun is a planned hydropower power project on the Vakhsh River, one of the main tributaries of the Amu Darya River in Tajikistan. As envisioned, the dam will be one of the tallest dams in the world with a power generating capacity of 13.3 TWh annually. Tajikistan not only aims at increasing its industrial income by investing in the aluminum sector but also has the ambition to export surplus power to neighboring countries like Afghanistan and Pakistan, which will help the country's economy.

The dam construction started in 1976, but its progress slowed down due to several reasons such as flooding, political upheaval, and civil unrests. It finally got suspended in 1991 during the collapse of the Soviet Union. In 2014, the World Bank submitted a detailed analysis report on the feasibility of the Rogun Dam that addressed the technical, economic, environmental, and social aspects of the project. The study showed that the current design of the dam subject to certain modifications meets most of the international safety norms. The study also found that the dam has the longest project life due to the planned height of the dam, and could guarantee low-cost energy production for a long period. However, the report does not specify in details the effects of the dam on the downstream countries Uzbekistan and Turkmenistan (World Bank, 2014). The report does not specify also in details about the effects of the dam on the downstream countries Uzbekistan and Turkmenistan.

This chapter assesses the Rogun Dam project and examines different possibilities of water allocation and trade-offs across competing uses for water resources; it computes benefits of the Rogun Dam to Tajikistan, and benefits forgone to the downstream countries, Uzbekistan and Turkmenistan under the scenarios of cooperation and unilateral benefit maximization. Differing from the earlier work (Bekchanov *et al.*, 2015) that looked at sectoral benefits or costs due to dam development, here we consider possible benefits or costs for the countries in the basin due to dam construction. The chapter applies a hydro-economic optimization model to quantify the impacts of dam operations on energy production and irrigation water availability and explores how cooperation between countries can reduce the risks to downstream users while ensuring benefits to all users. Cooperation here indicates that all riparian countries agree for allocating water to achieve the highest basin-wide benefits and consequently sharing these benefits fairly. Meantime, unilateral maximization of water corresponds with prioritization of either irrigation or hydropower production in water allocation decisions. All the above three cases are simultaneously assessed considering the cases with and without the Rogun Dam. The chapter finds that there will be a loss of 0.5 billion USD per year to all the three countries if there is a unilateral diversion of water in the upstream with prioritization of hydropower development (without Rogun) compared to a case of cooperation (with Rogun). The results also indicate that there will be a substantial decrease in agricultural benefits to all countries, particularly Uzbekistan. The agricultural benefits forgone by Uzbekistan and Turkmenistan will be more than 40% higher than the benefits that will be enjoyed by Tajikistan under the case of unilateral diversion of water for hydropower generation. However, under the cooperation scenario, the losses to the countries

are marginal, and there is scope for gain for all countries from the
Rogun Dam.

2.2. Brief Description of the Amu Darya Basin

The Amu Darya, part of the larger ASB, is one of the largest rivers
in Central Asia with a catchment area of above 300,000 km^2 and an
average annual flow of 73 km^3 (Bekchanov, 2014). The river known
in ancient times as Oxus is formed by the junction of the Vakhsh
(Tajikistan) and Pandj (Tajikistan and Afghanistan) rivers, which
rise in the Pamir Mountains of Central Asia. The river flows 2574 km
northwest from the headwaters of the Pyanj River on the Afghan-
Tajik border to the Aral Sea (Dukhovny and de Schutter, 2011), and
its water is shared among four countries — Tajikistan, Uzbekistan,
Turkmenistan, and Afghanistan (McKinney, 2004). The basin is
characterized by a diversity of natural landscapes and has a distinctly
continental climate (UNEP, 2005). The precipitation in the basin
occurs mainly during the winter in the form of snow which provides
the majority of river flows discharge through snow melt as well as
melting of the glacier.

Over centuries, a large proportion of the downstream population
is dependent on the irrigated agriculture along the banks of the Amu
Darya (Tolstov, 2005). During the Soviet period, large investments
were made to ensure irrigation water availability in the downstream
for cotton production. Such extensive withdrawal of water leads to
gradual desiccation of the Aral Sea, which has already reduced to
one tenth of its original size. It is considered to be the world's one of
worst ecological disasters, with economic and social impacts on the
local populations. Most of the eastern part of the basin is completely
dried up as recent as two years back. Today, agriculture continues to
play a major role in the regional economy through its contribution
to incomes and employment (Bekchanov and Bhaduri, 2013). There
are views that the downstream agriculture could get affected by
increasing development of the river's hydropower potential upstream
(Wegerich *et al.*, 2007; Weinthal, 2001). Since the dissolution of the
Soviet rule in Central Asia, rivers in Central Asia become the subject

of competing interests and demands by the independent states. The countries followed unilateral development paths in ensuring food and energy security and affirmed their individual rights to control land, water, and other natural resources within their territories. On one side, countries like Tajikistan suffered severe winter energy shortages that caused serious deprivation to its population (World Bank, 2014). While the downstream countries suffer water deficiency to meet the demands of downstream irrigators, indicating that further upstream developments to generate hydropower may affect the availability of irrigation water (Micklin, 2007; O'Hara, 2000).

2.3. Model

The chapter develops a node-link based optimization model to analyze the potential trade-offs between water users across different sectors and for determining the socially optimal patterns of water releases from the Rogun dam. The model considers distinct features of the Amu Darya basin such as the prevailing land and water allocation. The model is static and does not capture the interannual effects. Given the seasonal differences for peak water demand by irrigation and hydropower generation, a monthly time step has been considered to capture intra-annual variability. The model is coded in GAMS and solved using the CONOPT 3 solver. The basic schematic model considers 13 major tributaries, water diversions from five river nodes to 14 irrigated areas across three countries — Tajikistan, Uzbekistan, and Turkmenistan. The nodes are described in Table A1. As more than 90% of water available in the Amu Darya basin is used for irrigation and energy, and there is a potential trade-off between agriculture and hydropower, the model considers these two sectors only and analyzes the agricultural and hydropower production impacts of the Rogun Dam.

The trade-offs between irrigation and hydropower are captured under three institutional scenarios with and without the existence of the Rogun Dam. Three institutional scenarios include basin-wide cooperation, prioritization of downstream irrigation water use, and unilateral use of upstream reservoirs for hydropower generation. Basin-wide cooperation aims at maximizing the benefits from irrigation and hydropower production basin wide and sharing benefits among the parties fairly. The scenario with irrigation prioritization scenario emphasizes irrigation benefits from reservoir operation while considering hydropower production as by-product. Hydropower prioritization scenario represents the case when reservoir operations are mainly meant to maximize hydropower generation benefits and only allowing the remaining water to be available for irrigation purposes. This situation reflects the case during the post-Soviet period when upstream countries influence the reservoir water release regimes to increase hydropower generation during winter without considering downstream irrigation effect. These above three institutional scenarios can be modeled respectively through basin-wide optimization (cooperation scenario), the sequential optimization of irrigation and energy water uses (irrigation prioritization scenario), or optimizing energy first and then irrigation (hydropower prioritization scenario). Alternative modeling approach may consider different weights for sectoral benefits in a single objective function. Especially when irrigation and hydropower production and benefits are linearly dependent on water uses as in our case this weighting approach is relevant since the optimization model automatically considers much higher water use to the sector with higher weight. Thus, these three institutional scenarios are assessed in the model through changing weights in the objective function of the model, for example, considering equal weights for both irrigation and hydropower production benefits under cooperation scenario, higher weighting factor (10 times higher than the weight for hydropower production) for irrigation benefit under irrigation prioritization scenario (w^{irr}), and higher weights (10 times higher weights than irrigation) for hydropower production benefit (w^{hp}) under unilateral use of reservoirs for energy generation purposes. The value of weighting factor can be different than the value of the weight currently assumed here (i.e., 10) however, the outcome of the model in terms of marginal changes will not vary much with other values of relative weights.

2.3.1.   *Model Objective Function*

The model maximizes the sum of irrigation and hydropower production benefits (π)[1]:

$$\pi = \varepsilon^{\text{IRR}} \sum_d B_d^{\text{IRR}} + \varepsilon^{\text{HP}} \sum_n B_n^{\text{HP}} \tag{2.1}$$

where:

The terms, ε^{IRR} and ε^{HP}, are weights that determine either irrigation or hydropower is prioritized;

n is the set that defines the river nodes (here the nodes with reservoir and hydropower stations);

d is the set that defines irrigation sites;

B_d^{IRR} and B_n^{HP} are benefits from irrigation and hydropower production, respectively.

Irrigation benefits (in million \$) are calculated as the difference between total crop production revenues and the costs. The costs included the costs of crop production, water supply, pumping drainage water, and groundwater:

$$
\begin{aligned}
B_d^{\text{IRR}} = \sum_c 10^{-6} \cdot \left(A_{d,c} \left(P_{d,c}^{\text{CROP}} Y_{d,c} - c_{d,c}^{\text{A\_PROD}} \right) \right) \\
- c_d^{\text{SWS}} \sum_t W_t^{\text{SWS}} - c_d^{\text{RUS}} \sum_c \sum_t W_{d,c,t}^{\text{DRN}} \\
- c_d^{\text{GWP}} \sum_g \sum_c \sum_t W_{g,d,c,t}^{\text{GWP}}
\end{aligned}
\tag{2.2}
$$

where:

c and g are sets to define crop type and groundwater aquifer;

$A_{d,c}$ is the cropland area (in hectares);

$P_{d,c}^{\text{CROP}}$ is price of crop c (in \$/metric ton);

---

[1]Endogenous variables are written using upper case letters while exogenous factors (model parameters) and identifiers (sets) are written with lower case letters in this section.

$Y_{d,c}$ is yield of crop c in irrigation site d (in metric ton/hectare);
$c_{d,c}^{A\_PROD}$ is the cost of cultivation that does not consider water use related costs (in \$/hectare);
c_d^{SWS} is the cost of supplying a unit of surface water for irrigation (in \$/m^3);
W_t^{SWS} is the monthly water supply to irrigation site in each month (in million m^3/month);
c_d^{RUS} is the cost of pumping drainage for irrigation (in \$/m^3);
$W_{d,c,t}^{DRN}$ is the amount of drainage water reused (in million m^3/month);
c_d^{GWP} is the cost of pumping groundwater (in \$/m^3);
$W_{g,d,c,t}^{GWP}$ is the volume of water pumped from groundwater aquifer (g) (in million m^3/month).

Crop yields are determined as dependent on monthly and overall water scarcity as modeled using FAO method (Doorenbos and Kassam, 1979; see also Ringler *et al.*, 2004; Cai *et al.*, 2006):

$$1 - \frac{Y_{d,c}}{y_{d,c}^{MAX}} = \max_t \left\{ k_{c,t} \left(1 - \frac{ET_{d,c,t}^{ACT}}{10^{-5} \times A_{d,c} et_{d,c,t}^{POT}} \right) \right\} ; \qquad (2.3)$$

where:

$y_{d,c}^{MAX}$ is maximum attainable yields;
$k_{c,t}$ is crop coefficient;
$ET_{d,c,t}^{ACT}$ is total amount of actual crop evapotranspiration by month (in million m^3);
$et_{d,c,t}^{POT}$ is crop reference evapotranspiration (in mm).

Hydropower generation benefits (in million \$) are calculated as:

$$B_n^{HP} = 10^{-3} \times \sum_t l_{n,t}^{HP} Q_{n,t}^{HP} ; \qquad (2.4)$$

where:

$l_{n,t}^{HP}$ is the net benefit per unit of electricity (in \$/kW-hr in month t);
$Q_{n,t}^{HP}$ is the amount of hydropower generated (in MW-hr in month t).

Hydropower production $(Q_{n,t}^{HP})$ is calculated as a multiplicative function of production efficiency, water elevation at reservoir, and reservoir water release:

$$Q_{n,t}^{HP} = \rho \times e_{n,t}^{HP} \left(0.5 H_{n,t}^{HP} + 0.5 H_{n,t-1}^{HP} - h_n^{TAIL} \right)$$
$$\times \sum_{nl \in NNLINK} W_{n,nl,t}^{FLOW} \qquad (2.5)$$

where:

$W_{n,nl,t}^{FLOW}$ is river flow (in million m^3/month) from node with reservoir (n) to downstream node (nl) if a link between these exists $(NNLINK)$;

$H_{n,t}^{HP}$ the head (in m) of the reservoir at node n;

h_n^{TAIL} is the tail-water level of the reservoir (in m);

$e_{n,t}^{HP}$ is production efficiency of the reservoir;

ρ is a coefficient for conversion to power units.

2.3.2. *Model Constraints*

The model considers a range of water balance constraints for each river node:

$$\sum_{nu \in NNLINK} W_{nu,n,t}^{FLOW} + w_{n,t}^{SRC}$$
$$+ \sum_{d \in DNLINK} W_{d,n,t}^{RETF} + \sum_{g \in GNLINK} W_{g,n,t}^{SEEP}$$
$$= \sigma_n^{RES} \left[(V_{n,t} - V_{n,t-1}) + 10^{-3} \theta_{n,t} (0.5 S_{n,t-1} + 0.5 S_{n,t}) \right]$$
$$+ \sum_{nl \in NNLINK} W_{n,nl,t}^{FLOW} + \sum_{d \in NDLINK} \left(W_{n,d,t}^{SWS} + w_{n,d,t}^{INM} \right)$$
$$(2.6)$$

where:

$W_{nu,n,t}^{FLOW}$ is the river flow (in million m^3) from the upper node (nu) to node n;

$w_{n,t}^{SRC}$ is the source flow (in million m^3);

$W_{d,n,t}^{RETF}$ is return flow to the river from upstream irrigation site (in million m^3);

$W_{g,n,t}^{SEEP}$ is water seepage (in million m^3) to the river node from the connected groundwater aquifer g (*GNLINK*);

$W_{n,d,t}^{SWS}$ and $w_{n,d,t}^{INM}$ are water diversions (in million m^3) from river to irrigation and industrial-municipal sites (assumed fixed in this model given the prioritization of the residential sector in water allocation decisions);

σ_n^{RES} is a binary parameter indicating if the node is reservoir or not;

$V_{rev,t}$ is water storage in the reservoir;

$\theta_{n,t}$ evaporation form the surface of the water reservoir (in mm);

$S_{n,t}$ is the surface area (in million m^2) of the water reservoir.

The surface area of the reservoir depends on its water storage volume:

$$S_{n,t} = b0 + b1V_{n,t} + b2V_{n,t}^2 + b3V_{n,t}^3 \qquad (2.7)$$

where $b0$, $b1$, $b2$, and $b3$ are the parameters of the cubic function that relates water storage volume with the surface area of the reservoir.

The water level in the reservoir ($H_{n,t}$) also related to the reservoir storage volume:

$$H_{n,t} - h_n^{TAIL} = a0 + a1V_{n,t} + a2V_{n,t}^2 \qquad (2.8)$$

where $a0$, $a1$, and $a2$ are the parameters of the corresponded quadratic function.

The model also considers other constraints related to the reservoir storage limit, hydropower production capacity, and irrigated area availability. Furthermore, the levels of all reservoirs at the beginning and the end of the planning period are modeled to be equal to each other.

2.3.3. *Data Source of the Model*

The model database uses various primary and secondary sources. Most of the water-related data such as source flows, irrigation, and industrial-municipal withdrawals were from CAREWIB database (SIC-ICWC, 2011). The same data source also provides data on crop production areas, patterns, and yields. Data on reference crop evapotranspiration and the amounts of effective rainfall were derived from IFPRI's IMPACT model database (2013). Reports from local water management organizations (MAWR, 2007; SIC-ICWC, 2008) and surveys (ZEF/UNESCO Uzbekistan Project) provide data on crop production costs and prices, costs of conveyance, costs of pumping groundwater across the Amu Darya basin. Data on hydropower production capacity, prices for electricity, capacity of water reservoirs, and the parameters for the relationships between the reservoir water volume, elevation and surface area parameters are based on previous modeling studies such as Cai (1999), EC IFAS (2013), and SIC-ICWC (2003).

2.4. Results

In this section, we present different results related to optimal water allocation; corresponding irrigated land use change, and hydropower benefits to Tajikistan, Uzbekistan, and Turkmenistan. The institutional scenarios include the case of basin-wide cooperation, unilateral use of upstream reservoirs for hydropower generation as well as prioritization of downstream irrigation water use. All these scenarios are tested without and with Rogun which resulted in total of six cases. Table 2.1 presents the irrigated land and water use under the above these tests. Uzbekistan uses more than 50% of the total water usage and accounts for more than 55% of the irrigated area in all the scenarios. The results indicate that overall water usage will increase marginally if there is prioritization in downstream irrigation as explained earlier. There will be a decrease in the water usage for all countries under the case where water is unilaterally diverted for hydropower production, and the decrease will be significant with the construction of Rogun Dam. The decrease in water usage (16%) is also noteworthy in Tajikistan with Rogun Dam if the latter country continues to prioritize energy rather than resorting to cooperation.

Table 2.1: Comparison of optimal irrigated land and irrigation water use with and without Rogun Dam.

	Irrigated Area (1000 ha)			Water Use (km³)		
	Cooperation	Irrigation Prioritized	Hydropower Prioritized	Cooperation	Irrigation Prioritized	Hydropower Prioritized
Without Rogun						
Tajikistan	416.95	416.95	416.95	4.13	4.13	4.77
Uzbekistan	2312.46	2355.76	2253.11	44.21	45.42	43.79
Turkmenistan	1451.44	1464.77	1300.23	27.76	28.27	22.50
Total	4180.84	4237.47	3970.29	76.10	77.82	71.06
With Rogun						
Tajikistan	416.95	416.95	416.95	4.13	4.13	3.99
Uzbekistan	2347.44	2410.61	2358.88	43.05	45.48	41.79
Turkmenistan	1451.27	1451.56	1344.93	27.59	29.43	22.24
Total	4215.66	4279.12	4120.76	74.77	79.04	68.03

Other than in Tajikistan, however, there will be an increase in irrigated area in Uzbekistan and Turkmenistan after the construction of Rogun Dam. The positive effects of hydropower dam on water availability and the expansion of irrigated areas when irrigation is prioritized makes logical sense while slight increase in irrigation land use when upstream dam is unilaterally used for hydropower generation is puzzling.

Table 2.2 presents agricultural and hydropower benefits of the countries under different scenarios of cooperation with and without Rogun Dam. The results suggest that the decrease in agriculture benefits in Uzbekistan will be substantial even from a moderate 4% decrease in water usage if there is no cooperation. Overall, there will be a decrease in agricultural benefits of 352 million USD per year for all the countries in the case Tajikistan unilaterally diverts water, and most of the decrease in irrigation benefits will be in Uzbekistan. Such decrease in agriculture benefits will be less for all the countries when they cooperate. Results under the scenario of downstream agriculture prioritization show that there is the little scope of gains for Uzbekistan while Turkmenistan can gain only by 4%. Under hydropower prioritization scenario, large water releases upstream for hydropower generation may increase downstream water availability during winter and thus increased releases from downstream reservoirs for additional hydropower generation may slightly increase hydropower benefits from the Tuyamuyun hydropower station of Uzbekistan.

Tajikistan will enjoy substantial hydropower benefits of around 200 million dollars from Rogun Dam if upstream hydropower production benefits are unilaterally maximized. However, in this scenario, the agricultural benefits forgone will be much higher compared to the hydropower generation benefits incurred (Table 2.3).

Summing the results, the analysis in the chapter finds that overall combining the agricultural and hydropower benefits, Tajikistan will gain under the cooperation scenario compared to other scenario which maximizes either downstream irrigation benefits or hydropower benefits from upstream reservoir operations. If Rogun

Table 2.2: Comparison of agricultural and hydropower benefits to upstream and downstream countries with and without Rogun Dam.

	Agricultural Benefits (Million USD)			Hydropower Benefits (Million USD)		
	Cooperation	Irrigation Prioritized	Hydropower Prioritized	Cooperation	Irrigation Prioritized	Hydropower Prioritized
Without Rogun						
Tajikistan	270.83	270.84	272.99	166.94	144.74	195.78
Uzbekistan	892.93	901.59	872.33	6.82	6.72	7.80
Turkmenistan	595.66	601.95	413.32	0.00	0.00	0.00
Total	1759.42	1774.39	1558.64	173.76	151.46	203.58
With Rogun						
Tajikistan	270.83	270.84	214.92	328.95	276.49	366.83
Uzbekistan	879.93	899.08	600.34	7.11	6.79	8.77
Turkmenistan	593.35	616.67	391.16	0.00	0.00	0.00
Total	1744.11	1786.60	1206.42	336.05	283.29	375.60

Table 2.3: Share and total (agricultural plus hydropower) benefits to upstream and downstream countries with and without Rogun Dam.

	Percentage of Total Benefits (%)		
	Cooperation	Priority to Irrigation	Priority to Energy
	Without Rogun		
Tajikistan	22.65	21.58	26.60
Uzbekistan	46.54	47.16	49.94
Turkmenistan	30.81	31.26	23.45
Total Benefits (million USD)	1933.19	1925.85	1762.22
	With Rogun		
Tajikistan	28.83	26.44	36.77
Uzbekistan	42.64	43.76	38.50
Turkmenistan	28.52	29.79	24.73
Total Benefits (million USD)	2080.16	2069.88	1582.02

dam is operational, then cooperation will allow the countries to gain 0.5 million USD per year. Overall, Uzbekistan loss will be insignificant from Rogun Dam under cooperative case, but a noncooperation situation can lead to significant loss in benefits of around 250 million USD compared to the case without Rogun Dam. Downstream Turkmenistan may also lose similarly in such case.

2.5. Discussion and Conclusion

Rogun Dam is the now the flash point of another water conflict in Central Asia. It is conceived that the Dam will generate substantial benefits to Tajikistan and the latter country believes that the Dam will be beneficial for all countries of the basin. There are opposite views that the Dam would significantly reduce summer water availability, which will affect cotton, wheat, fruits, vegetables, and rice production downstream. Yet, as the modeling results showed new dam obviously increases hydropower benefits and may have negligible losses downstream even under cooperation scenario.

However, unilateral maximization of upstream hydropower benefits may further increase hydropower benefits but at the expense of much larger downstream irrigation losses. Considering that the scenario under hydropower prioritization without Rogun Dam approximate the current situation, the results of the model show that Rogun Dam can be beneficial for all countries, Tajikistan, Uzbekistan, and Turkmenistan, only under the cases without any attempt by Tajikistan to divert water unilaterally for more hydropower benefits.[2] Thus, in the case where Tajikistan constructs Rogun Dam, cooperation is a necessary condition for all countries to gain. Current scenarios show that Tajikistan loss from deviating from cooperation is much lower compared to the losses of Uzbekistan and Turkmenistan combined. Experience from Toktogul Dam suggests that Tajikistan may resort to the unilateral diversion of water to serve various political interests (Bank Information Center, 2013). Moreover, there are effects of extreme events stemming from climate change which may narrow down the difference in benefits from cooperation. Thus, establishing mutual trust and cooperation over the use and regulation of the existent dams are prerequisite for new infrastructural developments. The relevant question arises: What kind of cooperation model can sustain the benefits of countries and mitigate the conflicts. Side payments are often viewed to overcome difficulties in attaining international treaties. However, side payments do not necessarily facilitate cooperation (Bennett *et al.*, 1998), as it can result in the classic victim pays outcome, as the downstream countries are essentially bribing the upstream countries to share more water. In a more recent paper, Pham Do *et al.* (2014) test the concept of issue linkage to resolve unidirectional externalities in the Mekong River Basin. The paper shows that the downstream countries in the basin can consider the use of linkage as a form of side payment in achieving a basin-wide agreement.

---

[2]The results emerge if we compare the total benefits under the cases of unilateral diversion of water in the upstream with prioritization of hydropower development (without Rogun) with that of the case with cooperation (with Rogun).

Under such conditions, issue linkage has often been regarded as a potential strategy to mitigate conflicts and sustain cooperation (Bennett *et al.*, 1998; Daoudy, 2007; Dinar, 2006; Dombrowsky, 2010; Just and Netanyahu, 2004; LeMarquand, 1977; Mostert, 2003; Priscoli, 1990; Wolf, 1997). Issue linkage brings in a better chance of sustained cooperation as it broadens strategy set to prevent noncooperative behavior and contributes to avoiding unreasonable outcomes while balancing uneven "power" potentials (Eleftheriadou and Mylopoulos, 2008). Wolf *et al.* (1999) already found that such issue linkages are common and out of more than 100 treaties analyzed, 40% are an issue linked. Just and Netanyahu (2004) showed that linking negotiations to issues with reciprocal benefits can yield international cooperation without resorting to a less satisfactory "victim pays" outcome. Pham Do *et al.* (2011) discussed the role of linkage between water and nonwater issues and examined how linkage between issues could be used to promote stable agreements.

Bennett *et al.* (1998) demonstrated the possibility of attaining bilateral or even multilateral agreement in international river basin management by linking water allocation negotiations to outcomes in non-water issues of mutual interest to the parties. The chapter has linked the water allocation issue between Uzbekistan and Tajikistan with air pollution abatement and found that issue linkage can lead to enhanced bargaining sets where the players have the opportunity to cooperate and gain.

Water is a multifunctional resource, there may, in principle, also be opportunities for issue linkage within the water sector (Bernauer, 1997; Dombrowsky, 2007, 2010). Dombrowsky (2009, 2010) demonstrates in a simple bilateral context how riparian countries may increase their shared benefits from intro water-sector issue. In the context of the water and energy nexus in Central Asia, Teasley and McKinney (2011) studied hydropower export in exchange for imported water, and analyzed a newly developed Draft Agreement on the allocation of water and energy resources among the four riparian countries of the Syr Darya basin, considering transboundary cooperation and benefits sharing. Bhaduri and

Liebe (2012) evaluates issue linkage in cooperative transboundary water sharing, which concerns the discounted trade of hydroelectric power as compensation for greater transboundary water flow to the hydropower generating plant. The study shows how such issue linkage of water and energy can enhance the scope of cooperation between the upstream-downstream countries.

Pham *et al.* (2012) find that if there is a scope of issue linkage, the countries indeed find it mutually beneficial to cooperate. The policy question arises here in the context of the Amu Darya basin: can we design such a cooperative framework of issue linkage which will allow all the countries to gain from the upstream dams (Nurek and Rogun). Or in other words, is it possible to create a cooperate arrangement of benefit-sharing of 0.5 billion USD to facilitate transboundary cooperation which can be sustained in the long run. Here in this chapter, we understand that cooperation is a prerequisite to gain a Pareto efficient outcome with all countries gaining from existent and new dams, however, further studies should look into the feasibility and transaction costs of such a cooperative model in the basin and explore the case of sustained cooperation. These transaction costs may consider the costs of the measures to prevent the unilateral diversion of water for hydropower. New infrastructural developments which can cause serious downstream losses when unilaterally managed for hydropower generation can occur only with agreement of all riparian countries in the basin. Otherwise, these developments may escalate the conflicts in the basin and may result in unexpected and unwanted outcomes. Further consideration of energy and agricultural markets within and across the countries as well as price and demand relationships in the improved versions of the model would provide additional insight on potential gains from introducing the issue linkage across the sectors.

References

Abbink, K, LC Moller, and S O'Hara (2005). The Syr Darya River conflict: an experimental case study. Centre for Decision Research and Experimental Economics Discussion Papers, No. 2005–14.

Bank Information Center (BIC) (2013). *Tajikistan's Rogun Hydro: Social and environmental aspects.* Available at http://www.bicusa.org/wp-content/uploads/2013/02/Rogun+Hydro+Brief.pdf [Last accessed on 28 November 2014].

Bekchanov, M, C Ringler, A Bhaduri, and M Jeuland (2015). How would the Rogun Dam affect water and energy scarcity in Central Asia? *Water International*, 40(5–6), 856–876.

Bekchanov, M and A Bhaduri (2013). National tendencies and regional differences in small business development in Uzbekistan. Chapter presented at IAMO Forum, pp. 19–21 June 2013, Halle, Germany.

Bekchanov, M (2014). Efficient water allocation and water conservation modeling. PhD Thesis, Bonn University, Bonn. Available at http://hss.ulb.uni-bonn.de/2014/3609/3609.pdf.

Bennet, LL, SE Ragland and P Yolles (1998). Facilitating international agreements through an interconnected game approach: The case of the river basin. In *Conflict and Cooperation in Transboundary Water Resources*, R Just and S Netanyahu (eds.). Norwell: Kluwer Academic Publishing.

Bernauer, T (1997). Managing international rivers. In *Global Governance: Drawing Insights from the Environmental Experience*, OR Young (ed.), pp. 155–195. Cambridge: MIT Press.

Bhaduri, A, C Ringler, I Dombrowski, R Mohtar, and W Scheumann (2015). Sustainability in the water–energy–food nexus. *Water International*, 40(5–6), 723–732.

Cai, X (1999). A modeling framework for sustainable water resources management. Unpublished PhD dissertation, the University of Texas at Austin.

Cai, X, C Ringler, and MW Rosegrant (2006). *Modeling water resources management at the basin level: Methodology and application to the Maipo River Basin.* IFPRI Research Report 146. Washington: IFPRI.

Daoudy, M (2007). Benefit-sharing as a tool of conflict transformation: Applying the inter-SEDE model to the Euphrates and Tigris river basins. *Economics of Peace and Security Journal*, 2(2), 26–32.

Dinar, S (2006). Assessing side-payments and cost-sharing patterns in international water agreements: The geographic and economic connection. *Political Geography*, 25(4), 412–437.

Dombrowsky, I (2007). *Conflict, cooperation and institutions in international water management.* Cheltenham: Edward Elgar.

Dombrowsky, I (2009). Revisiting the potential for benefit-sharing the management of transboundary rivers. *Water Policy*, 11(2), 125–140.

Dombrowsky, I (2010). The role of intra-water sector issue linkage in the resolution of transboundary water conflicts. *Water International*, 35(2), 132–149.

Doorenbos, J and AH Kassam (1979). *Yield response to water*. FAO Irrigation and Drainage Chapter No. 33. Rome: FAO.

Dukhovny VA and JLG de Schutter (2011). *Water in Central Asia: Past, present, future*. London, UK: Taylor and Francis.

EC IFAS (Executive Committee of International Fund for Saving the Aral Sea) (2013). *The Aral Sea basin economic allocation model BEAM. Report*. Available at www.ec-ifas.org [Accessed on 20 August 2013].

Eleftheriadou, E and Y Mylopoulos (2008). Game theoretical approach to conflict resolution in transboundary water resources management. *Journal of Water Resources Planning and Management*, 134, 466.

Just, RE and S Netanyahu (2004). Implications of "victim pays" infeasibilities for interconnected games with an illustration for aquifer sharing under unequal access costs. *Water Resources Research*, 40, W05S02, doi:10.1029/2003WR002528.

LeMarquand, DG (1977). *International rivers. The politics of cooperation*. Vancouver: Westwater Research Center, University of British Columbia.

Ministry of Agriculture and Water Resources of Uzbekistan (MAWR) (2007). Conveyance costs of delivering one cubic m of water to the irrigation regions in 2006. Unpublished report. Tashkent, Uzbekistan.

McKinney, DC (2004). Cooperative management of transboundary water resources in Central Asia. In *In the Tracks of Tamerlane: Central Asia's Path to the 21st Century*, D Burghart and T Sabonis-Helf (eds.), pp. 187–220. Washington: National Defense University.

Micklin, P (2007). The Aral Sea disaster. *Annual Review of Earth and Planetary Sciences*, 35, 47–72. http://www.annualreviews.org/doi/pdf/10.1146/annurev.earth.35.031306.140120 [Accessed on 28 July 2011]

Mostert, E (2003). Conflict and co-operation in international freshwater management: A global review. *International Journal of River Basin Management*, 1(3), 1–3.

O'Hara, S (2000). Central Asia's water resources: Contemporary and future management issues. *Water Resource Development*, 16(3), 423–441.

Pham Do, KH, A Dinar, and D McKinney (2011). Can issue linkage help mitigate externalities and enhance cooperation? *International Game Theory Review*, 14(1), pp. 39–59.

Pham Do, KH, A Dinar, and D McKinney (2012). Transboundary water management: Can issue linkage help mitigate externalities? *International Game Theory Review*, 14(1), 1250002.

Pham Do, KH and A Dinar (2014). The role of issue linkage in managing noncooperating basins: The case of the Mekong. *Natural Resource Modeling*, 27(4), 492–518.

Priscoli, J. (1990). Does water integrate or separate us? *Water International*, 236–239.

Ringler, C, J von Braun, and MW Rosegrant (2004). Water policy analysis for the Mekong River Basin. *Water International*, 29(1), 30–42.

Ringler, C, A Bhaduri, and R Lawford (2013). The nexus across water, energy, land and food (WELF): Potential for improved resource use efficiency? *Current Opinion in Environmental Sustainability*, 5(6), 617–624.

SIC-ICWC (Scientific-Information Center of Interstate Commission of Water Coordination in the Aral Sea Basin) (2003). The database of the Aral Sea basin optimization model (ASCOM). Excel file. Tashkent, Uzbekistan.

SIC-ICWC (2008). Crop production costs and revenues across the regions of Uzbekistan in 2006. Unpublished database. Tashkent, Uzbekistan.

SIC-ICWC (2011). CAREWIB (Central Asian Regional Water Information Base). www.cawater-info.net [Accessed on 27 January 2012].

Teasley, RL and DC Mckinney (2011). Calculating the benefits of transboundary river basin cooperation: The Syr Darya Basin. *Journal of Water Resources Planning and Management*, 137, 481–490.

Tolstov, SP (2005). *Following the Tracks of Ancient Khorezmian Civilization*. First published in the Russian language in 1948 by the publishing house of the Academy of Sciences of the USSR, Moscow-Leningrad. Tashkent, Uzbekistan: UNESCO.

UNEP (2005). Severskiy, I, I Chervanyov, Y Ponomarenko, NM Novikova, SV Miagkov, E Rautalahti, and D Daler. The Aral Sea, GIWA Regional assessment 24. The University of Kalmar, Kalmar, Sweden.

UNEP and ENVSEC (2011). Environment and security in the Amu Darya basin. UNEP, Bresson, France.

Wegerich, K, O Olsson, and J Froebrich (2007). Reliving the past in a changed environment: Hydropower ambitions, opportunities and constraints in Tajikistan. *Energy Policy*, 35(7), 3815–3825.

Weinthal, E (2001). Sins of omission: Constructing negotiating sets in the Aral Sea Basin. *Journal of Environmental Development*, 10(1), 50–79.

Wolf, A (1997). International water conflict resolution: Lessons from comparative analysis. *International Journal of Water Resources Development*, 13(3), 333–365.

Wolf, A, J Matharius, J Danielson, B Ward, and J Pender (1999). International river basins of the world. *International Journal of Water*, 15(4), 387–427.

World Bank (2014). *Assessment studies for proposed Rogun hydropower project in Tajikistan*. Washington: World Bank. http://www.world bank.org/en/region/eca/brief/rogun-assessment-studies.

Appendix A

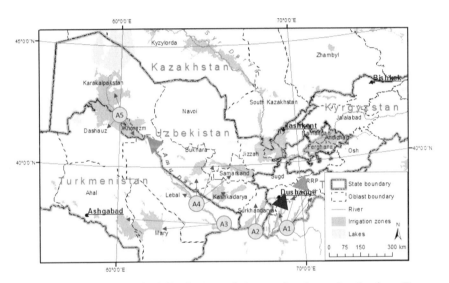

Figure A.1: Map of the Aral Sea basin and river node scheme for the Amu Darya basin as considered in the model. Notes: five river nodes are depicted with circles, reservoirs with triangulars (blue for Rogun, dark blue for Nurek, and orange for Tuyamuyun), water diversion for irrigation sites with arrows.

Source: The map is prepared at GIS center of KRASS at Urgench State University based on MODIS database. The second author holds right to the map.

Table A1: Water supply at source nodes (in million m^3).

Country	Tributary	Jan	Feb	Mar	Apr	May	Jun	Jul	Aug	Sep	Oct	Nov	Dec
Tajikistan	Vakhsh	1713	1386	1157	1012	1940	1886	2748	2988	1557	942	837	917
Tajikistan	Pyandj	1153	1090	1466	2357	3675	5464	6734	5653	2911	1879	1439	1323
Tajikistan	Kafirnigan	273	287	635	1481	2259	2139	1576	814	419	321	304	297
Tajikistan	Yavansu	46	39	49	49	78	83	94	192	92	78	77	45
Afghanistan	Kunduz	122	127	149	272	350	638	616	513	290	193	140	125
Uzbekistan	Sherabad	15	14	17	26	37	24	9	1	3	8	13	8
Uzbekistan	Surhandarya	143	128	156	245	349	223	84	7	31	76	125	80
Turkmenistan	Atrek	26	27	30	21	0	10	9	0	0	14	31	17
Turkmenistan	Murgab	92	109	194	233	196	108	72	54	61	82	88	89
Turkmenistan	Tedjen	60	86	198	341	327	66	5	0	0	1	4	21
Uzbekistan	Kashkadarya	83	87	149	172	86	88	63	21	33	37	74	75
Uzbekistan	Guzardarya	8	10	12	25	9	8	5	4	4	6	10	11
Uzbekistan	Zarafshan	200	176	178	180	371	814	103	876	492	254	208	201

Source: SIC-ICWC (2011).

Table A2: Maximum crop yield (ton per ha).

Country	Irrigation Sites (Provinces)	Cotton	Fodder	Fruit	Wheat	Maize	Cords	Potato	Rice	Beet	Vegetables	Grapes
Tajikistan	GBAO	2.1	7.4	2.8	2.4	3.4	22.1	15.1	3.3	23.9	27.0	7.5
Tajikistan	Khatlon	3.2	34.3	9.1	11.3	5.7	14.8	19.5	5.1	110.5	28.7	4.6
Tajikistan	RRP	3.1	26.2	12.5	4.0	10.7	17.6	14.5	7.0	50.0	21.6	7.0
Uzbekistan	Surkhandarya	2.3	6.7	1.4	2.4	6.6	18.5	16.9	3.1	23.9	17.4	10.0
Turkmenistan	Mary	3.1	23.8	7.4	6.8	4.2	22.6	16.3	5.6	48.0	21.6	5.7
Turkmenistan	Ahal	2.4	3.3	11.8	1.6	4.7	11.6	16.3	3.3	23.9	26.4	5.9
Turkmenistan	Lebap	2.7	5.6	4.7	1.3	3.5	9.0	11.7	3.3	23.9	13.9	8.2
Uzbekistan	Kashkadarya	3.3	3.9	8.5	10.2	4.3	21.6	13.8	3.7	96.7	28.4	8.3
Uzbekistan	Samarkand	2.5	9.6	2.1	13.6	6.6	7.0	6.1	3.3	23.9	6.3	3.1
Uzbekistan	Navoi	2.4	2.6	3.2	1.5	3.7	11.3	9.5	1.0	27.0	18.2	2.8
Uzbekistan	Bukhara	2.1	0.8	3.1	3.2	2.0	7.5	18.4	1.9	27.0	21.2	12.9
Uzbekistan	Khorezm	2.4	2.2	4.8	1.7	2.6	10.1	11.6	3.0	13.9	15.8	4.2
Uzbekistan	Karakalpakstan	2.4	13.8	4.9	3.6	2.6	14.6	6.7	4.4	5.5	12.6	1.9
Turkmenistan	Dashauz	2.8	13.6	2.3	2.6	4.2	14.0	6.8	2.5	23.9	22.9	9.6

Source: SIC-ICWC (2011).

Table A3: Crop prices (US$ per ton).

Country	Irrigation Sites (Provinces)	Cotton	Fodder	Fruit	Wheat	Maize	Cords	Potato	Rice	Beet	Vegetables	Grapes
Tajikistan	GBAO	494	49	151	98	98	202	226	478	49	201	224
Tajikistan	Khatlon	453	45	136	90	90	169	210	478	45	158	424
Tajikistan	RRP	494	49	151	98	98	202	226	478	49	201	224
Uzbekistan	Surkhandarya	439	65	240	130	130	193	244	478	65	155	319
Turkmenistan	Mary	425	52	237	103	103	307	168	478	52	203	203
Turkmenistan	Ahal	479	55	146	109	109	212	161	478	55	208	242
Turkmenistan	Lebap	479	55	146	109	109	212	161	478	55	208	242
Uzbekistan	Kashkadarya	439	65	240	130	130	193	244	478	65	155	319
Uzbekistan	Samarkand	425	52	237	103	103	307	168	478	52	203	203
Uzbekistan	Navoi	454	46	228	92	92	220	253	478	46	212	408
Uzbekistan	Bukhara	439	65	240	130	130	193	244	478	65	155	319
Uzbekistan	Khorezm	462	49	339	98	98	297	212	478	49	169	424
Uzbekistan	Karakalpakstan	439	65	240	130	130	193	244	478	65	155	319
Turkmenistan	Dashauz	494	49	151	98	98	202	226	478	49	201	224

Source: CIS-ICWC (2008).

Table A4: Crop production costs (US$ per ha).

Country	Irrigation Sites (Provinces)	Cotton	Fodder	Fruit	Wheat	Maize	Cords	Potato	Rice	Beet	Vegetables	Grapes
Tajikistan	GBAO	371	169	192	148	121	1341	1387	796	478	2975	887
Tajikistan	Khatlon	797	894	519	478	380	1631	2473	1400	1819	3130	1242
Tajikistan	RRP	691	738	593	203	351	2152	1346	1047	828	2904	743
Uzbekistan	Surkhandarya	534	284	213	205	470	1576	1531	658	647	1702	1155
Turkmenistan	Mary	688	715	303	326	266	3795	1479	1226	1536	2533	455
Turkmenistan	Ahal	495	123	631	122	330	1231	1717	796	624	3262	772
Turkmenistan	Lebap	406	224	416	112	306	1326	1201	994	624	1600	1190
Uzbekistan	Kashkadarya	725	156	1525	497	362	2425	2216	1240	1591	2305	1644
Uzbekistan	Samarkand	550	285	283	915	497	1329	690	1052	485	800	318
Uzbekistan	Navoi	445	92	444	83	163	1895	1714	204	385	2532	544
Uzbekistan	Bukhara	427	33	525	132	124	796	2730	505	821	2182	2443
Uzbekistan	Khorezm	443	70	628	107	163	1926	1489	633	234	2058	885
Uzbekistan	Karakalpakstan	523	450	607	203	214	1608	1114	1245	142	742	363
Turkmenistan	Dashauz	586	336	188	168	232	1627	777	665	478	2441	761

Source: CIS-ICWC (2008).

Table A5: Water supply costs (US$ per m^3).

Country	Irrigation Sites (Provinces)	Conveyance Cost	Groundwater Use Cost	Water Reuse Costs
Tajikistan	GBAO	0.003	0.006	0.049
Tajikistan	Khatlon	0.013	0.006	0.049
Tajikistan	RRP	0.003	0.006	0.049
Uzbekistan	Surkhandarya	0.009	0.005	0.079
Turkmenistan	Mary	0.002	0.009	0.080
Turkmenistan	Ahal	0.012	0.009	0.080
Turkmenistan	Lebap	0.002	0.009	0.080
Uzbekistan	Kashkadarya	0.013	0.009	0.080
Uzbekistan	Samarkand	0.003	0.005	0.069
Uzbekistan	Navoi	0.005	0.009	0.080
Uzbekistan	Bukhara	0.012	0.009	0.080
Uzbekistan	Khorezm	0.002	0.007	0.074
Uzbekistan	Karakalpakstan	0.001	0.007	0.074
Turkmenistan	Dashauz	0.002	0.007	0.074

Source: MAWR (2007).

Table A6: Parameters related to hydropower generation.

Reservoir	Parameters of Functional Relationship Between Reservoir Elevation and Volume			Parameters of Functional Relationship Between Reservoir Surface Area and Volume				Reservoir Level at the Tail (m)	Power Station Efficiency	Electricity Price in Summer (US$ per kWh)	Electricity Price in Winter (US$ per kWh)
	a0	a1	a2	b0	b1	b2	b3				
Rogun	85.719	0.020	0.000	1.314	0.021	0.000	0.000	935	0.9	0.3–0.5	0.5–0.7
Nurek	10.314	0.056	0.000	14.498	0.021	0.000	0.000	620	0.8	0.3–0.6	0.5–0.8
Tuyamuyun	1.538	0.002	0.000	0.000	0.100	0.000	0.000	85	0.8	0.3–0.7	0.5–0.9

Source: EC IFAS (2013).

CHAPTER 3

DISTRIBUTIONAL IMPACTS OF WELFARE
ALLOCATIONS FROM DAMMING
THE NILE RIVER

GETACHEW NIGATU* and ARIEL DINAR†

*Economist, ERS/USDA, Washington, DC, USA
†Professor, University of California, Riverside, CA, USA

Using a partial equilibrium optimization model, we evaluate the performance of existing and future dams in the eastern Nile River basin (ENRB) for countries consisting of Ethiopia, Sudan, and Egypt. On top of unilateral allocation, we also propose three alternative water rights arrangements (WRAs) with and without intraregional water rights trade and internalizing the resource degradation externality. We found that the social planner would assign the Nile River water for economic sectors and basin countries that could generate more than $10 billion, the highest economic benefit to the region regardless of initial WRA. Unilateral use of Nile water would benefit Ethiopia and Sudan, but it would reduce the economic benefit for Egypt, a country that has relatively efficient irrigated agriculture. In addition, the proposed WRAs and trade could lead to efficiency, recovering up to 99% of the social planner's outcomes. Allocate-and trade could also be cost-effective alternative to raise around $680 million for short- to medium-term abatement investment that can be used for reducing or eliminating resource degradation problem.

Keywords: Eastern Nile Basin; Efficient allocation; Water rights arrangements; Externalitiest

The views expressed are those of the authors and do not necessarily reflect the views of the Economic Research Service or the U.S. Department of Agriculture.

3.1.   Introduction

Egypt, Sudan, and Ethiopia are located within the ENRB system. They use the Nile River water for a number of purposes, but the predominant uses are for irrigated agriculture and hydropower generation. These countries are, however, unable to satisfy their overall demand for food and electricity. Food imports and power outages are common challenges facing these countries. The region is forced to import millions tons of food commodities and crude petroleum for generating electricity. Other challenges for the region come from climate change that may alter mean annual river flow by up to 70% (Kilgour and Dinar, 1995) and resource degradation that reduces the resource base (Nigatu, 2012).

Agricultural production in Sudan and Egypt depends exclusively on irrigation since rainfall in these countries is insufficient to sustain food production. Both countries use water from dams constructed at various districts along the Nile River. The Aswan High Dam (AHD) in Egypt and the Merowe dam in Sudan are the prominent existing dams along the Nile River. In 2011, Ethiopia announced the construction of the Grand Ethiopian Renaissance Dam (GERD) along the Blue Nile River, a subbasin within the Nile River basin system. GERD will have the potential to change the hydrological position in controlling the Nile River flow and the economic benefit that riparian countries can derive from the Nile River (Gebreluel, 2014; Jeuland and Whittington, 2014; Nigatu and Dinar, 2016).

As many international river basins, such as the Mekong, the Nile basin faces a complex management challenge that has not yielded subbasin or basin-wide cooperation in allocating and managing the resource. The GERD introduces a new challenge for loosing up the existing and future hydro-political relationship among the riparian countries in the basin. With lack of water allocation agreement and management of the Nile River, the current situation with regards to unilateral dam construction could complicate relations among the riparian states and slow or derail the cooperative process that has started under the umbrella of the Nile Basin Initiative (NBI) two decades ago (NBI, 2015).

Furthermore, the prevalent resource degradation problem of about 525 million cubic meters of topsoil erosion in Ethiopia significantly threatens the basin's capacity to sustain fresh water supply, food production, hydropower generation, and ecological life (Arsano and Tamrat, 2005; Elhance, 1999). Hence, managing ENRB without dealing with resource degradation problem may worsen the existing water scarcity challenges facing these nations and the food security of their vulnerable citizens.

Since the riparian countries are increasingly interested in unilaterally developing the Nile River along their national borders, a long-sought basin-wide agreement may not be a viable strategy acceptable for Nile River water allocation (Cascão, 2009; McCartney and Menker-Girma, 2012). It is widely recognized that, basin-wide agreement on Nile River water allocation and management is rather a difficult objective (Dinar, 2004; Waterbury, 2002). This is because, among other factors, riparian countries differ in their economic strengths, political powers, and hydrologic and climatic situations (Just and Netanyahu, 1998; Martens, 2011).

Using a partial equilibrium economic optimization model originally developed by Nigatu and Dinar (2011), we model the effect of existing and future irrigation and hydropower production in the ENRB in light of the planned GERD and the other two existing dam projects: AHD in Egypt and Merowe dam in Sudan. In addition, we propose three alternative WRAs with and without intraregional water rights trade and internalizing the resource degradation externality. In this chapter we evaluate the performance of each of the WRAs, and the three big dams by estimating the efficient allocation using social planner settings. We assess the distribution of welfare among the three riparians under each set of WRAs and assumptions regarding the physical parameters.

3.2. Modeling Nile River and Introducing Water Trade

Most Nile River basin models have been designed to study the impact of cooperation on the relationship among Nile riparian countries (Whittington *et al.*, 1995), water allocation in a game theory setting without GERD (Dinar and Nigatu, 2013; Wu, 2000; Wu and Whittington, 2006), the hydrological impacts of four dams in the Ethiopian highland (Block and Strzepek, 2010; McCartney and Menker-Girma, 2012), the physical water use (Kirby *et al.*, 2010), or water resources planning under climate change (Jeuland and Whittington, 2014). Recently, Kahsay *et al.* (2015) developed a static computable general equilibrium (CGE) model to analyze the impacts of GERD on the three riparian countries by distinguishing impounding and operational stages of the dam. Nigatu and Dinar (2016) quantified the economic and hydrological impact of GERD on the region and assessed damming impact on efficient allocation.

Studies show that the problem of burgeoning water scarcity and deteriorating water quality could be addressed if water is properly treated as an economic good (Sunding, 2000). In a regional setting, water markets are used to promote economic development and political stability (Whittington *et al.*, 1995), increase income and crop yield (Meinzen-Dick, 1998), improve income distribution and produce the highest economic return (Saliba and Bush, 1987), and encourage economic agents to undertake conservation and protection efforts and accommodate changing patterns in society's demand (Easter *et al.*, 1998).

In practice, formal and informal water markets exist in a number of countries (Easter *et al.*, 1998). Analytically, water markets are designed to address a wide variety of economic and ecological issues (Aytemiz, 2001; Becker, 1996; Bhaduri and Barbier, 2008; Dinar and Wolf, 1994). For the Nile River in particular, the potential benefits of establishing regional water markets have been considered in the literature in the past (The Economist, 1992; Whittington *et al.*, 1995; Wu, 2000). For the first time, Nigatu and Dinar (2011) developed, and then Nigatu (2012) updated and refined the Nile economic and environmental optimization model (NEEOM) that explicitly included water rights trade in an ENRB context.

3.2.1. *NEEOM*

The model specified both the theoretical and practical impacts of water trade in an "allocate-and-trade" settings and internalizing resource degradation. The model has been used in a number of published papers, for instance, Dinar and Nigatu (2013) applied it in game theory settings, and Nigatu and Dinar (2016) used it to assess the economic and hydrological impact of GERD.

NEEOM is a nonlinear partial equilibrium model where irrigation and hydropower are the two economic sectors on the demand side of the model. The economic value of the volume of water used for irrigation (D_{dt}^{IR} in cubic meter [cm]/month) is defined by a nonlinear inverse demand equation for each individual riparian country at each demand district, d and month, t. It is the integral of the inverse demand function that maximizes welfare based on economic surplus, similar to the specification used in Fisher and Huber-Lee (2005). For hydropower, the economic surplus can be captured using the net benefit of producing hydropower calculated by the product of the amount of electricity produced (in kilowatt hour, kWh_{dt}) and its unit net price (P_d^{HP} in \$/kWh). This formulation is also widely used in several basin-based hydropower research works (Aytemiz, 2001; Fisher and Huber-Lee, 2005; Wu, 2000).

Under the water rights trading scenario, riparian countries trade excess demand, ED_{dt}, using a price, P^w, that can be identified through the marginal product of the relatively water abundant country (seller) and the shadow value of the water scarce country (buyer) obtained from the optimization model. In addition, in order to deal with the resource degradation problem, we included average cost (c), for the ENRB, estimated at US\$0.009/cm of Nile water by Nigatu (2012). The generalized objective function can be specified as

$$\text{Max}G = \frac{\sum_d \sum_t \beta (D_{dt}^{\text{IR}})^{(\alpha+1)}}{(\alpha+1)} + \sum_d \sum_t P_d^{\text{HP}}(\text{kWh}_{dt})$$

$$+ P^w \sum_d \sum_t \text{ED}_{dt} - c \sum_d \sum_t [D_{dt}^{\text{IR}} + D_{dt}^{\text{HP}}]. \quad (3.1)$$

where β is a coefficient of the inverse demand function; α is an exponent of the inverse demand function standing for demand elasticity, and $\alpha \langle 0; \beta \rangle 0$. Based on literature reviews, we use -0.2 for the price elasticity of irrigation water demand in all countries (Fisher and Huber-Lee, 2005). The objective function is subject to the following major constraints: irrigation water demand, hydropower water demand, the water mass balance, and the allocation constraints.[1]

Using the initial WRAs, $\bar{W}^i$, the excess demand and the related constraint can be further specified as

$$\sum_d \sum_t |_i \mathrm{ED}_{dt} = \sum_d \sum_t |_i (D_{dt}^{\mathrm{IR}} + D_{dt}^{\mathrm{HP}} + \mathrm{Ev}_{dt}) - \sum_i \bar{W}^i, \quad (3.2)$$

where Ev_{dt} is evaporation losses at the various dams (cm/month); and country $i = $ Et, Su, and Eg, standing, respectively, for Ethiopia, Sudan, and Egypt. With the following additional condition for supply constraint:

$$\sum_i \bar{W}^i \leq \sum_k \sum_t S_{kt}, \quad (3.3)$$

where $\sum_k \sum_t S_{kt}$ is total volume of water supplied to riparians from Nile River tributaries, k, namely Atbara, Blue Nile, Sobat, and White Nile (cm/month).

3.2.2. *Damming the Nile River*

Egyptian civilization was established on a long narrow strip of the Nile River. Along the Nile River, there are several traditional and modern dams, among them the one that stood up the most is the AHD. This dam was built in the 1970s on the border between Sudan and Egypt and it has ever changed the Nile River allocation. The reservoir created by this dam extends over a surface area of 6276 square kilometers (sq.km), and stores up to 164 billion cubic meters (bcm). It has a capacity to produce around 8 billion kilowatt

---

[1] A more detailed specification, and data and parameter used, and the limitation of the model can be found in Nigatu (2012) and Nigatu and Dinar (2016).

hours (bkWh) of electricity and provide irrigation water for millions hectares of land in Egypt (Fahim, 2013).

Another big project along the Nile River that changed the existing allocation is the Merowe Dam in Sudan that was built at the end of 2009. This dam covers a surface area of around 800 sq.km with a capacity to store around 12.4 bcm. Merowe dam is intended to produce around 5.6 bkWh of electricity and to irrigate hundred thousands of hectares of land (Bosshard, 2007).

The dialogue surrounding the Nile River, however, has taken an extraordinary new course when Ethiopia started the construction of the GERD in 2011. This dam will have a storage capacity of 60–70 bcm of water that will be primarily intended to produce 15 bkWh of electricity from hydropower, and, to a lesser extent, to irrigate agricultural land (Chen and Swain, 2014). With the estimated cost of more than $4 billion, for the first time in its history, Ethiopia will finance the construction of this mega dam from its own resources (GOE, 2014; Salini Impregilo, 2014). This is the first big project that has ever been attempted by the upstream Nile River riparian states.

3.2.3.   *Policy Scenario Runs*

We present results for various scenarios that we run with the model. We start with the efficient or usually called social planner's allocation. We then compare it with a unilateral allocation where each riparian acts on its own. We follow by producing results for the case where several big dams are introduced with their planned flow regime. We also present the comparison among the three WRAs, with and without an intrabasin trade in water rights and resource degradation abatement.

3.2.4.   *Results from the Model*

The setup of the NEEOM is similar to the approach used in McKinney and Savitsky (2006), and the model is written and solved using General Algebraic Modeling System (GAMS) software NLP (nonlinear programming) solver. The mean annual runoff of

98.5 bcm, calculated using the last 50 years of Nile River flow, is used as the main input for estimation of the various allocation scenarios and their economic benefits (GRDC, 2010). The main choice variables are irrigation water released, land irrigated, hydropower water released, electricity generated, and volume of water traded. The model performs an annual dynamics only because interannual dynamics will not change the results as there is no inter-temporal parameter in the model that affects the objective function.

3.2.4.1. *Efficient allocation*

One of the basic economic implications for the social planner's allocation is that Nile water that generates the maximum economic benefit is allocated optimally for economic activities regardless of where riparians are located. The economic theory further indicates that other allocations could lead to a welfare value that is inferior to the social planner's outcome. Consequently, efficiency from the social planner's outcome can be used as a benchmark by which the performance of other allocation schemes can be assessed.

Based on their respective efficiency conditions in producing agricultural commodities and generating hydropower, and maximizing the region's welfare, the social planner would allocate around 21.1, 14.7, and 62.7 bcm of Nile water to Ethiopia, Sudan, and Egypt, respectively. This allocation is similar to the proposed allocation by the experts working in the region (Whittington *et al.*, 1995). In addition, the efficient allocation would produce more than $10 billion in economic benefit to the countries involved, as shown in Table 3.1.[2]

The ENRB countries would have different economic dynamics in utilizing and producing economic benefits from the Nile River water, as shown in Table 3.1. Ethiopia would use the least amount of water to irrigate agricultural land, 5189 cm/hectare and to generate hydropower, 0.62 cm/kWh, implying that it could attain technical efficiency in both activities. Sudan could produce the highest economic benefit of $0.18/cm of water in irrigation projects, while,

---

[2]Prices and values are expressed in 2010 US$ price level.

Table 3.1: Model results for efficient allocation.

Sectors	Description	Units	Riparian Countries			
			Ethiopia	Sudan	Egypt	ENRB
Irrigation						
	Total water use	bcm	8.8	13.3	38.3	60.4
	Land irrigated	1000 hectare	1696	1999	3299	6994
	Economic benefit	billion US$	1.42	2.42	4.64	8.48
	Average water use	cm/hectare	5189	6653	11610	8636
	Average economic benefit generated from land	US$/hectare	837	1211	1406	1212
	Average economic benefit generated from water	US$/cm	0.16	0.18	0.12	0.14
Hydropower						
	Total water use	bcm	9.8	0	5.1	15.0
	Hydropower produced	bkWh	15.8	0	7.8	24
	Economic benefit	billion US$	0.95	0	0.62	1.57
	Average water use	cm/kWh	0.62	—	0.65	0.64
	Average economic benefit generated from kWh	US$/kWh	0.06	—	0.08	0.07
	Average economic benefit generated from water	US$/cm	0.10	—	0.12	0.10
	Evaporation loss	bcm	2.4	1.4	19.3	23.1
	Total water allocation	bcm	21.1	14.7	62.7	98.5
	Share of water allocation	per cent	21	15	64	100
	Total economic benefit	billion US$	2.4	2.4	5.3	10.1
	Share of economic benefit	per cent	24	24	52	100
Data						
	Land irrigated[a]	1000 hectare	88	1831	3402	5321
	Hydropower produced[b]	bkWh	4.9	6.2	13	24.1

Notes: Total and average values can be affected by rounding off.
[a]Hilhorst (2011).
[b]IEA (2014).

on efficiency ground, there is no economic benefit of producing hydropower in Sudan. Egypt could produce around $1406/hectare from irrigation and $0.08/kWh from producing hydropower, the highest among the three countries. This is because Egypt could use Nile water more efficiently than other riparian countries.

One of the inherent economic theory implications for the main cause of efficiency in Egypt is economies of scale, through accumulated experience and technological advancement compared with other riparians. The optimization result confirms the efficiency condition of using water in a place where it could generate the highest welfare benefits for the basin although Ethiopia and Sudan get water ahead of Egypt due to their geographic location.

When evaluating the results of the efficient allocation and the economic benefit with the current situation based on the data, we can see a stark difference in some of the findings. The one that attracts immediate attention is the difference between the model's results and the data for Ethiopia for both hectares of irrigated land and hydropower produced. Ethiopia could produce more than 1.7 million hectare of irrigated land, and 16 bkWh of electric power if Nile water were allocated based on efficiency conditions. But the reality is that Ethiopia is currently irrigating around 5% and generating around 31% of hydropower compared with the social planner allocation. On the other hand, Egypt and Sudan have already used more than 90% of their irrigation and hydropower potentials.

Even though efficiency condition does not explicitly address the issue of welfare or benefit distribution among the riparian countries, the notion of comparative advantage could help countries engage in the production of goods where resources could be used relatively efficient. The findings from the social planner also indicate the relative efficiency in producing agricultural products and hydropower in the region. Ethiopia, the relatively water abundant country could use the Nile water for more nonconsumptive water used in generating hydropower, whereas Sudan and Egypt, the relatively water scarce countries, could use Nile water for consumptive water use in producing agricultural products. This is in line with the factor-proportion theory in producing different goods based on the proportion in which factors of productions are available (Krugman *et al.*, 2012). Doing so could help distribute 24%, 24%, and 52% of the basin's economic benefit to Ethiopia, Sudan, and Egypt, respectively. Whether this share of the basin's benefit would be feasible in the current hydro-political situation remains to be addressed and is beyond the scope of this chapter.

3.2.4.2. *Unilateral allocation*

Unlike the social planner solution, which would not take into account geographical location of the countries in the ENRB, the unilateral allocation scenario could enable us understand if countries decide to use the Nile water unilaterally along their national boarder without considering their immediate or distant neighbors. This scenario follows current hydro-political situation in the ENRB where riparian countries are increasingly interested in unilaterally developing the Nile River (Cascão, 2009; McCartney and Menker Girma, 2012). Moreover, unilateral allocation is more prevalent because of the lack of a subbasin or basin-wide water allocation treaty (Wu and Whittington, 2006). This allocation is often supported by Ethiopia, the upstream riparian country, which advocates for an "absolute territorial sovereignty" in water rights for managing its transboundary rivers (Dinar and Wolf, 1994).

As shown in Table 3.2, the welfare value for the ENRB from unilateral allocation could reach $9.6 billion, which is about 5% less than the efficient allocation. Unilateral use of Nile water among the three riparian countries would reduce the economic benefit for Egypt as compared to the social planner's allocation scenario. On the other hand, Ethiopia and Sudan, which are upstream to Egypt, would benefit the most from the unilateral allocation scenario. More specifically, Sudan, which would not produce hydropower if water were allocated based on relative efficiency, would produce around 5 bkWh hydropower in unilateral allocation. In addition, Ethiopia and Sudan would bring about 20% and 40%, respectively, more land under irrigation compared with the social planner allocation. As a result, Ethiopia and Sudan could use around 24 and 29 bcm of Nile River water, respectively.

Table 3.2: Model results for unilateral use arrangement.

Sectors	Description	Units	Ethiopia	Sudan	Egypt	ENRB
Irrigation						
	Total water use	bcm	10.8	18.4	22	51.2
	Land irrigated	1000 hectare	1987	2765	1900	6652
	Economic benefit	billion US$	1.52	2.65	3.53	7.7
	Average water use	cm/hectare	5435	6655	11579	7697
	Average economic benefit generated from land	US$/hectare	765	958	1858	1158
	Average economic benefit generated from water	US$/cm	0.14	0.14	0.16	0.15
Hydropower						
	Total water use	bcm	11.1	7.7	5.1	23.9
	Hydropower produced	bkWh	16.4	4.9	7.8	29.1
	Economic benefit	billion US$	0.99	0.27	0.62	1.88
	Average water use	cm/kWh	0.68	1.57	0.65	0.82
	Average economic benefit generated from kWh	US$/kWh	0.06	0.06	0.08	0.06
	Average economic benefit generated from water	US$/cm	0.09	0.04	0.12	0.08
	Evaporation loss	bcm	2.4	2.5	18.4	23.3
	Total water allocation	bcm	24.2	28.7	45.6	98.5
	Share of water allocation	per cent	25	29	46	100
	Total economic benefit	billion US$	2.51	2.92	4.15	9.58
	Share of economic benefit	per cent	26	30	43	100

In this chapter we assume intrabasin water use, which means that diverting water out of the designated basin or natural river flow stream is not expected. We use Frenken and Faurès (1997) data for irrigation potential that countries could cultivate within the Nile basin. If, on the other hand, irrigated land were not constrained in this way, Ethiopia and Sudan could irrigate several million additional hectares of land, and the economic benefit from using more water would be more than $2.5 and $2.9 billion, respectively.

The relatively efficient irrigation practice in Egypt, which could produce around $0.16/cm of water and $1858/hectare of land, would be affected the most if Sudan and Ethiopia would continue to implement irrigation and hydropower projects along the Nile River without regard to Egypt. After, first Ethiopia, then Sudan uses the Nile water, what is left in the system would go to Egypt, the most downstream riparian country along the Nile River basin. As a result of scarcity of water, Egypt would not irrigate more than 40% of its agricultural land. This condition would further complicate the availability of food in Egypt where food imports have drained much of the country's foreign reserve, and food availability is closely related to the country's stability (Cook, 2014).

3.3. Are Big Dams Efficient?

As unilateral allocation becomes the predominant strategy, ENRB countries have engaged in building irrigation projects and hydropower dams. One of a typical features of these dams is that they have become bigger and bigger over time. In order to evaluate the performance of these big dams, we compare the unilateral and social planner outcomes for the three big dams in each of the respective riparian countries: GERD in Ethiopia, Merowe dam in Sudan, and AHD in Egypt as shown in Table 3.3. This approach helps us evaluate whether big dams are necessary efficient, and identify their comparative advantage in utilizing the Nile River water.

GERD would irrigate more than twice the land, and produce around 90% of hydropower in unilateral allocation than the social

Table 3.3: Model results for unilateral and efficient use of Nile River water for big dams.

		GERD		Merowe		AHD	
		Unilateral	Social Planner	Unilateral	Social Planner	Unilateral	Social Planner
Irrigation							
Total water use	bcm	4.2	1.8	9.1	6.3	19.0	32.9
Land irrigated	1000 hectare	500	211	1000	692	1713	2971
Economic benefit	billion US$	0.31	0.20	0.75	0.62	3.05	4.02
Average water use	cm/hectare	8352	8332	9135	9132	11069	11074
Average economic benefit generated from land	US$/hectare	614	944	746	896	1783	1353
Average economic benefit generated from water	US$/cm	0.07	0.11	0.08	0.10	0.16	0.12
Hydropower							
Total water use	bcm	8.4	9.3	4.9	0	5.1	5.1
Hydropower produced	bkWh	13.2	14.6	3.6	0	7.8	7.8
Economic benefit	billion US$	0.79	0.88	0.20	0	0.62	0.62
Average water use	cm/kWh	0.68	0.63	1.37	—	0.66	0.66
Average economic benefit generated from kWh	US$/kWh	0.06	0.06	0.06	—	0.08	0.08
Average economic benefit generated from water	US$/cm	0.09	0.09	0.04	—	0.12	0.12
Evaporation loss	bcm	1.0	1.0	1.3	0.3	16.5	17.3
Total water allocation	bcm	13.5	12.0	15.4	6.6	40.6	55.3
Share of water allocation	per cent	14	12	16	7	41	56
Total economic benefit	billion US$	1.10	1.08	0.94	0.62	3.68	4.65
Share of economic benefit	per cent	11	11	10	6	38	46

planner one. Hence, GERD would be relatively efficient in producing hydropower in the region. In efficiency terms, it would produce around 15 bkWh of electricity, which is around its maximum physical potential. In both cases, the dam would produce around $1.1 billion in economic benefits, using different irrigation and hydropower production mix for the social planner and unilateral allocation solutions.

Merowe dam in Sudan could irrigate 1 million hectares of land in the unilateral allocation scenario, which is around 45% more than under the efficient allocation. On the other hand, the dam could produce around 5 bkWh of electricity if Sudan would decide to use Nile water unilaterally. On efficiency ground, this dam, and any other dams in Sudan, would produce no hydropower. Hence, Sudan's comparative advantage is to use the Nile River water only for irrigation.

The other big dam, considered to be one of the wonder of the world, is the AHD in Egypt (Fahim, 2013). The adverse effect of being the downstream to the system of the Nile River basin could be seen from the performance of this dam if Ethiopia first and then Sudan decide to use the Nile water unilaterally. In unilateral allocation, this dam could irrigate about 40% less land than under the efficient allocation. It, however, could produce about 7.8 bkWh, or 98% of its installed potential, in both allocation scenarios. This is because, hydropower generation is considered as a nonconsumptive water use: around 80% of water that hits a turbine would return to the basin stream and can be used for irrigation or other purposes (Hutson, 2004). Results are presented in Table 3.3.

Since water scarcity in Egypt would be more intense under unilateral allocation scenario than under the efficient allocation, the average economic benefit generated from water under the unilateral allocation in Egypt, $0.16/cm, is higher than under the social planner scenario, $0.12/cm. This is due to one of the intricate features of the model, which optimally allocates water for the various economic sectors, based on marginal productivity and water availability.

3.4.   A New Institution for Water Allocation

In a river basin, such as the Nile, where unilateral use has become more prevalent at present than ever before, and a subbasin or basin-wide cooperation has become less feasible, attaining efficient allocation requires some institutional mechanisms. One of the many institutions that support efficiency and that have been tested both in economic theory and in practice is trade in water rights among riparian countries, which we call here "allocate-and-trade."

The basic concept of "allocate-and-trade" is that, first, a regional institution such as NBI will assign water rights to the three riparian countries, monitor, and evaluate the performance of each riparian country, and then facilitate an intrabasin water trade among riparian countries so that water could be used for projects within the basin. The ENRB countries are not required to divert water out of the basin, or to transfer water to other riparian countries that are not included in the agreement, or to sell water to other countries outside of the Nile basin. The design of the intended water trade is framed in an analogy to the emission market (Olmstead and Stavins, 2008). The preliminary condition for such trade institution is WRAs which we will identify in the next section.

3.5.   Water Rights Arrangements

In the case of common-pool resource such as river water, clearly defined property rights play a vital role in addressing a number of issues, including sharing benefits (equity) and internalizing the externality (Schlager and Ostrom, 1992). Here, we propose three WRAs (Table 3.4) to initiate water trade, based on suggestions from Nile River experts, historical facts, and past and present hydro-politics in the basin.

For WRA I, a Nile basin institution will assign 12.2% of Nile water to the upstream country, Ethiopia, and 87.8% to downstream riparian countries, Sudan and Egypt (Whittington *et al.*, 1995). For WRA II, we base our assumption on the United Nations Convention's *Article 5 "equitable and reasonable utilization and participation"* (United Nations, 1997), and on a per capita water use using the

Table 3.4: Proposed WRA among ENBR countries.

	WRA					
	I	II	III	I	II	III
ENRB Riparian	per cent share			(bcm)		
Ethiopia	12.2	38.4	50	12.0	37.8	49.2
Sudan	22	14.1	12.5	21.7	13.9	12.3
Egypt	65.8	47.5	37.5	64.8	46.8	37.0
Total	100	100	100	98.5	98.5	98.5

2015 population in the basin. This will enable us to account for current population in the three countries. WRA III is based on principles described in Beaumont (2000) that would allocate 50% of Nile water to Ethiopia because it is the source of the Nile River, and the remaining 50% to downstream riparian countries based on their historic status. Sudan and Egypt will share 25% and 75%, respectively, of the combined downstream portion according to the 1959 water sharing agreement for WRA I and WRA III.

3.6. Model Results for Intrabasin Trade

As shown in the generalized model in Eq. (1), an intrabasin water rights trade mechanism (henceforth "trade") attaches a positive price to each unit of water traded among riparian countries, by applying the equimarginal principle. It helps us identify the condition under which water is transferred to a riparian country with a higher marginal benefit. At the same time, a buyer riparian country is willing to compensate (not necessarily in the form of monetary terms, but could be in the form of providing other goods or services) a seller riparian country that has a lower shadow value of water.

As seen in Table 3.5, every trade scenario could increase the basin's economic benefits up to $10 billion compared with the without trade scenario. The results indicate that the region's economic benefit will be increased by up to $500 million depending on the WRA. This is supported by the economic theory of managing common-pool resources.

Table 3.5: Trade and WRA scenario results.

Trade Scenario	Country/ Dam	WRA I	WRA II	WRA III	WRA I	WRA II	WRA III
		(bcm)			(Billion $US)		
Without trade							
	Ethiopia	12.0	24.2	24.2	1.5	2.5	2.5
	Sudan	21.7	28.7	28.7	2.7	2.9	2.9
	Egypt	64.8	45.6	45.6	5.5	4.2	4.2
	Basin	98.5	98.5	98.5	9.8	9.6	9.6
Big dams	GERD	5.0	13.5	13.5	0.4	1.1	1.1
	Merowe	12.8	15.4	15.4	0.8	0.9	0.9
	AHD	56.7	40.6	40.6	4.2	3.7	3.7
With trade							
	Ethiopia	20.7	20.8	21.2	1.7	3.0	3.1
	Sudan	12.9	17.1	19.2	2.9	2.6	2.4
	Egypt	64.8	60.5	58.0	5.3	4.4	4.5
	Basin	98.5	98.5	98.5	10.0	9.9	10.0
Big dams	GERD	11.7	11.6	12.3	1.1	1.0	1.1
	Merowe	5.3	8.6	10.3	0.5	0.7	0.7
	AHD	57.3	53.6	51.3	4.7	4.4	4.5

Except for the inefficient Merowe dam in Sudan, the other two dams would perform better in terms of generating economic returns in trade scenario. Egypt (under WRA II and WRA III) and Ethiopia (under WRA I) would buy more water if they were allocated lower volume of water under the WRA. Sudan would be involved in water rights trade in limited number of cases. For the without trade case, Ethiopia and Sudan could use the level of water similar to the unilateral allocation if they were allocated more water than they could possibly use in their respective Nile Basin.

3.7. Trade and Efficiency

In the case of without trade scenario, the region's economic benefits could reach up to $9.8 billion, and this scenario could recover 95% to 97% of the social planner's economic benefits (Table 3.6). On the other hand, trade could recover up to 99% of the social planner's

Table 3.6: Proportion of social planner's benefit recovered under trade.

Scenario	Trade Scenario	
	Without Trade (%)	With Trade (%)
WRA I	97	99
WRA II	95	98
WRA III	95	99

outcomes. Hence, it can be inferred that allocation of water under water rights trading also leads to a Pareto efficient outcome, with the restrictive assumptions of limited number of buyers and no transaction costs, reaching up to 99% of total benefits guaranteed by the social planner.

Even though the underlying economic theory suggests that trade could attain the optimal efficiency level, our model indicates that the time needed to transfer water from one district to another and evaporation losses in the reservoirs prevent the model from attaining 100% of the social planner's economic benefit. One possible strategy to increase the region's economic benefits can be reducing evaporation losses in the various dams along the Nile River. In some cases, evaporation losses could reach as much as 25% of the total volume of Nile water.

3.8. Trade and Resource Degradation

The generalized objective function shown in Eq. (1) also enables us to estimate the amount of abatement investment that each country could make for reducing or eliminating resource degradation. As shown in Fig. 3.1 the social planner's solution could raise around $685 million in protecting the resource base, among one of the highest amount compared to other allocation schemes. Except WRA I, trade could provide more abatement dollars than without trade. Riparian countries could decide to share the level of abatement investment in different proportion, based on their use. In all of the cases, riparian countries that could use the Nile water most efficiently, Egypt, would

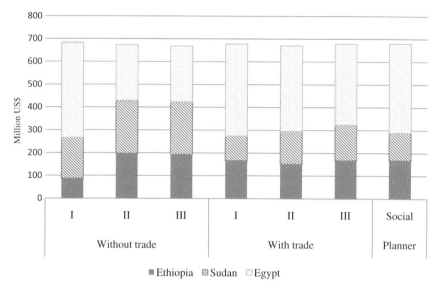

Figure 3.1: The amount of abatement investment in various allocation scenarios.

be responsible for the lion's share of the total abatement needed to restore the resource.

This result is consistent with the merit of trade in resource management where trade provides sufficient abatement based on incentive and marginal returns from resource use (Hanley et al., 1997). This abatement could solve the leading causes of soil erosion in Ethiopia and siltation in Sudan and Egypt that arise as the result of unsustainable agricultural practices and deforestation (Longin et al., 2005).

3.9. Conclusion

The results indicate that unilateral use arrangements, and the various big dams along the Nile River could result in suboptimal level of benefits compared to the social planner. The social planner would assign the Nile River water for an economic sector and agent that could generate the highest economic benefit to the region regardless of initial WRA. The welfare gain is the "first-best" economic solution, which is practically and politically challenging to implement in the real world, but the gains could help evaluate the performance of other allocations. In addition, the social planner's outcomes indicate that Egypt could use the Nile water more efficiently for irrigation and hydropower; Ethiopia could have a comparative advantage in generating hydropower; and Sudan could engage in using the Nile water for irrigation purpose.

The proposed WRA with trade could provide a plausible alternative to utilize the Nile River water in a situation where subbasin or basin-wide agreements are infeasible in a foreseeable future. But the issue that trade and the relevant institutions could provide the desired solution to the ENRB long-standing water allocation challenges depend on political will and further consideration of transaction costs. Water rights trade could lead to an important development in the Nile dialogue that is stalled by the fear that any intervention could affect the economic benefit of the downstream riparian countries.

If there is a regional or basin-wide consensus in the form of a treaty or formal negotiation among riparian countries, which adopts the prevailing realities of the basin, water rights trade will provide more cost-effective tool for resource protection than water rights alone. Such trade will compensate negatively affected countries and will promote sustainable resource management practices.

Our results highlight the possibility to address food shortage and energy outages while maintaining the natural resource base through investment. A relatively water abundant country, Ethiopia, could engage in the generation of hydropower, a nonconsumptive water use, that could sale excess power to Sudan and, in some extent to Egypt. Otherwise, these riparians could use the Nile water for the sector they do not have relative efficiency. In the meantime, water scarce countries, mostly Egypt, could use water for relatively efficient sector, irrigation. Hence, water-food-energy-environment nexus, as a package of considerations at the basin- or subbasin level, demonstrates the likelihood for cooperation and trade (including agricultural products, electricity) in the region.

References

Arsano, Y and I Tamrat (2005). Ethiopia and the Eastern Nile basin. *Aquatic Science*, 69, 15–27.

Aytemiz, L (2001). The optimal joint provision of water for irrigation and hydropower in the Euphrates River: The case of conflict between Turkey and Syria. Doctoral dissertation, Oklahoma State University, Stillwater.

Beaumont, P (2000). The 1997 UN Convention on the Law of Non-navigational uses of international watercourses: Its strengths and weaknesses from a water management perspective and the need for new workable guidelines. *Water Resources Development*, 16, 475–495.

Becker, N (1996). Reallocating water resources in the Middle East through market mechanisms. *International Journal of Water Resources Development*, 12(1), 17–32.

Bhaduri, A and EB Barbier (2008). International water transfer and sharing: The case of the Ganges River. *Environment and Development Economics*, 13(1), 29–51.

Block, P and K Strzepek (2010). Economic analysis of large-scale upstream river basin development on the Blue Nile in Ethiopia considering transient conditions, climate variability, and climate change. *Journal of Water Resources Planning and Management*, 136(2), 156–166.

Bosshard, P (2007). China's role in financing African infrastructure. *International Rivers Network*, 14.

Cascão, AE (2009). Changing power relations in the Nile River Basin: Unilateralism vs. cooperation? *Water Alternatives*, 2(2), 245–268.

Chen, H and A Swain (2014). The Grand Ethiopian Renaissance Dam: Evaluating its sustainability standard and geopolitical significance. *Energy Development Frontier*, 3(1), 11–19.

Cook, SA (2014). *Egypt's Solvency Crisis*. Council on Foreign Relation Contingency Planning Memorandum No. 20.

Dinar, A (2004). Cooperation in managing transboundary water resources: Evaluation approaches and experiences. Paper presented at the 4th Rosenberg International Forum on Water Policy, 3–9 September, Ankara, Turkey.

Dinar, A and G Nigatu (2013). Distributional considerations of international water resources under externality: The case of Ethiopia, Sudan and Egypt on the Blue Nile. *Water Resources and Economics*, 2(3), 1–16.

Dinar, A and A Wolf (1994). International markets for water and the potential for regional cooperation: Economic and political perspectives in the western Middle East. *Economic Development and Cultural Change*, 43, 43–66.

Easter, WK, MW Rosegrant, and A Dinar (1998). *Markets for Water: Potential and Performance*. Boston: Kluwer Academic Publisher.

Elhance, AP (1999). *Hydropolitics in the 3rd World: Conflict and Cooperation in International River Basins*. Washington: United States Institute of Peace Press.

Fahim, HM (2013). *Dams, People and Development: The Aswan High Dam Case*. New York: Pergamon Press.

Fisher, F and A Huber-Lee (2005). *Liquid Assets: An Economic Approach for Water Management and Conflict Resolution in the Middle East and Beyond*. Washington: RFF Press.

Frenken, K and JM Faurès (1997). *Irrigation Potential in Africa: A Basin Approach*, Vol. 4. Rome: Food and Agricultural Organization of the United Nations.

Gebreluel, G (2014). Ethiopia's Grand Renaissance Dam: Ending Africa's oldest geopolitical rivalry? *The Washington Quarterly*, 37(2), 25–37.

GOE (2014). The Government of Ethiopia. Retrieved from http://grand millenniumdam.net [6 May 2016].

GRDC (2010). Global Runoff Data Centre: The Nile River Runoff Data. Retrieved from http://www.bafg.de/GRDC/EN/ [6 May 2016].

Hanley, N, JF Shogren, and HB White (1997). *Environmental Economics: In Theory and Practice*. New York: Oxford University Press.

Hilhorst, B (2011). *Information Products for Nile Basin Water Resources Management*. Synthesis report. Rome: FAO.Retrieved from http://agris.fao.org/agris-search/search.do?recordID=XF2006450235 [6 May 2016].

Hutson, SS (2004). *Estimated Use of Water in the United States in 2000*. Washington: U.S. Department of the Interior/Geological Survey Circular No. 1268.

IEA (2014). International Energy Agency: Electricity and Heat 2010 data. Retrieved from http://www.iea.org/statistics/ [6 May 2016].

Jeuland, M and D Whittington (2014). Water resources planning under climate change: Assessing the robustness of real options for the Blue Nile. *Water Resources Research*, 50(3), 2086–2107.

Just, R and S Netanyahu, S (1998). *Conflict and Cooperation on Trans-Boundary Water Resources, Natural Resource Management and Policy*, Vol. 11. New York: Springer.

Kahsay, TN, O Kuik, R Brouwer, and P van der Zaag (2015). Estimation of the transboundary economic impacts of the Grand Ethiopian

Renaissance Dam: A computable general equilibrium analysis. *Water Resources and Economics*, 10, 14–30.

Kirby, M, J Eastham, and M Mainuddin (2010). *Water-Use Accounts in CPWF Basins: Simple Water-Use Accounting of the Nile Basin.* Colombo, Sri Lanka: The CGIAR Challenge Program on Water and Food.

Kilgour, DM and A Dinar (1995). *Are Stable Agreements for Sharing International River Waters Now Possible?* (No. 14774). Washington: The World Bank.

Krugman, P, M Obstfeld, and M Melitz (2012). *International Economics: Theory and Policy*, 9th Ed. Boston: Pearson.

Longin, N, S Sadd, A Eldaw, O Naggar, A Nindamutsa, B Chane, and H Faudul (2005). *Watershed Erosion and Sediment Transport.* UNESCO-IHE: Nile Basin Capacity Building Network (NBCBN): River Morphology Research Cluster, AX Delft.

Martens, AK (2011). *Impacts of Global Change on the Nile Basin: Options for Hydropolitical Reform in Egypt and Ethiopia* (No. 01052). Washington: International Food Policy Research Institute (IFPRI).

McCartney, MP and M Menker Girma (2012). Evaluating the downstream implications of planned water resource development in the Ethiopian portion of the Blue Nile River. *Water International*, 37(4), 362–379.

McKinney, DC and AG Savitsky (2006). *Basic Optimization Models for Water and Energy Management.* Austin: University of Texas.

Meinzen-Dick, R (1998). Groundwater markets in Pakistan: Institutional development and productivity impact. In *Markets for Water*, pp. 207–222. Boston: Springer.

NBI (2015). Nile Basin Initiative. Retrieved from http://www.nilebasin.org [6 May 2016].

Nigatu, G (2012). *Essays on resource allocation and management, price volatility and applied nonparametrics.* Doctoral dissertation, University of California Riverside, Riverside.

Nigatu, G and A Dinar (2011). Modeling efficiency, equity and externality in the Eastern Nile River Basin. Paper No. 02-0611. Riverside, CA: Water Science and Policy Center.

Nigatu, G and A Dinar (2016). Economic and hydrological impacts of the Grand Ethiopian Renaissance Dam on the Eastern Nile River Basin. *Environment and Development Economics*, 21(4), 532–555.

Olmstead, SM and RN Stavins (2008). Comparing price and non-price approaches to urban water conservation. *Water Resource Research*, 45(4).

Saliba, BC and DB Bush (1987). *Water Markets in Theory and Practice: Market Transfers, Water Values and Public Policy.* Boulder: Westview Publisher.

Salini Impregilo (2014). Grand Ethiopian Renaissance Dam Project. Retrieved from http://www.salini-impregilo.com/en/projects/in-progress/dams-hydroelectric-plants-hydraulic-works/grand-ethiopian-renaissance-dam-project.html [6 May 2016].

Schlager, E and E Ostrom (1992). Property-rights regimes and natural resources: A conceptual analysis. *Land Economics*, 68, 249–262.

Sunding, D (2000). The price of water: Market-based strategies are needed to cope with scarcity. *California Agriculture*, 54, 56–63.

The Economist (1992). The first commodity. *The Economist*, 11(12).

United Nations (1997). *The United Nations Convention on the Law of the Non-Navigational Uses of International Watercourses.* New York: United Nations Press.

Waterbury, J (2002). *The Nile Basin: National Determinants of Collective Action.* Yale: Yale University Press.

Whittington, D, J Waterbury, and E McClelland (1995). Toward a new Nile waters agreement. In *Water Quantity/Quality Management and Conflict Resolution*, pp. 167–178. Westport: Praeger.

Wu, X (2000). Game-theoretical approaches to water conflicts in international river basin: A case study of the Nile Basin. Doctoral dissertation, University of North Carolina, Chapel Hill.

Wu, X and D Whittington (2006). Incentive compatibility and conflict resolution in international river basins: A case study of the Nile Basin. *Water Resources Research*, 42, 1–15.

CHAPTER 4

ISSUE LINKAGE: A MECHANISM FOR MANAGING CONFLICT, APPLIED TO THE MEKONG BASIN

KIM HANG PHAM DO* and ARIEL DINAR[†]

*School of Economics and Finance, Massey University,
Palmerston North, New Zealand

[†]School of Public Policy, University of California,
Riverside, USA

Using the notion of externality games with issue linkage, this chapter demonstrates the advantages of issue linkage for the Mekong region in achieving a more efficient, more stable basin agreement. In a game that includes the Lower Mekong Basin (LMB) States and China, it is shown that the LMB states can benefit more from issue linkages. In particular, linking issues of water flow to the Lower Mekong with issues of regional trading will increase likelihood of regional cooperation.

Keywords: Issue linkage; transboundary water resource; Mekong region; sustainable development; externality games; conflict; cooperation.

4.1. Introduction

The Mekong is one of the world mighty rivers (in Tahi or Lao, Mekong means "mother of rivers"), shared by six countries: China, Myanmar, Thailand, Laos, Cambodia, and Vietnam (Fig. 4.1). The Mekong is managed under the 1995 Mekong Agreement (Dinar *et al.*, 2013) that includes Thailand, Laos, Cambodia, and Vietnam operating under

---

This chapter is based on the works by Pham Do *et al.* (2012) and Pham Do and Dinar (2014).

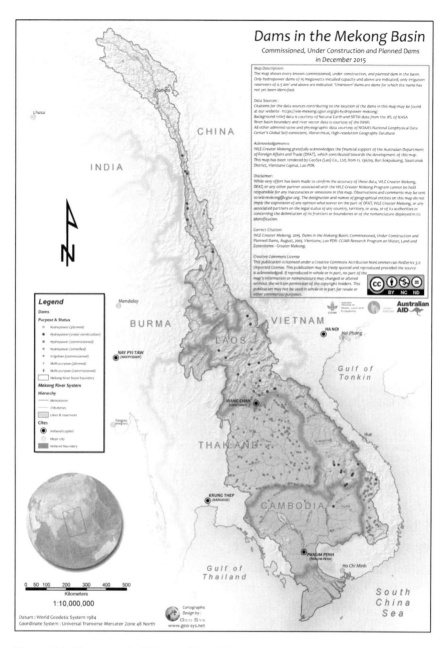

Figure 4.1: Dams in the Mekong River Basin.
Source: WLE (2015).

the Mekong River Commission (MRC). Having had a long history of frequent war and peace; and previously representing a division line between the capitalist and socialist worlds, the Mekong River and its Basin (MRB) are of global importance, whether in terms of population size, land use and resource base, regime, gross domestic product (GDP) size, GDP per capita, or comparative advantages (Table 4.1).

With the total catchment area of 795,000 km^2, the Mekong provides not only a source of energy through hydropower production but also many environmental, economic, and other benefits for the region, including fisheries, wetlands, ecosystem services, navigation, trade, water supply, and tourism (ABD, 2004; Mehtonen *et al.*, 2008; MRC, 2005). At present both economic and population, particularly in urban centers, have remarkable growth rates leading to increase in the demand for energy and natural resources. The rush to acquire sources of alternative energy and other benefits to meet rapid growth in demand has led to risk of existing infrastructure and resources within the Mekong Region.

Each of the six Mekong nations has its own ambitious hydropower plans. Six massive dams are already in operation or under construction in China on the upstream Mekong (known in China as the Lancang). Over 100 large dams are planned for the main stream of the Mekong River and its tributaries (Fig. 4.1). Dam construction has almost always created conflicts between energy supply and related economic interests, versus their social and environmental impacts (King *et al.*, 2007; MRC, 2010). Together with climate change adaptation and mitigation, the livelihoods of some 100 million rural people across the Mekong region are affected by degradation and depletion of natural resources. In particular, about 75 million people that depend on its resources for food production (Cronin and Hamlin, 2012; Osborne, 2004) are likely to face some monumental challenges in the years to come. In developing the Mekong, the world's fastest growing population region, this challenge is exacerbated by rapid and often chaotic social and economic change, environmental degradation, and limited understanding of the complex web of interaction between water-related uses in different sectors.

Table 4.1: Selected aggregate indicators for MR and China in the Great Mekong Subregion in 2014.

	Population (Million)	Population Growth (%)	Population Density (per/km^2)	Land Areas (10^{3}km^2)	Water (10^{3}km^2)	GDP Growth (%)	GNI per Capita (US$ 2014)[a]
Cambodia	15.18	1.50	84	181.04	4.5	7.0	1020
Laos	6.77	2.00	29	236.80	6.0	7.4	1650
Myanmar	51.42	1.17	76	676.59	23.1	7.7	1270
Thailand	67.09	0.40	131	513.12	2.2	0.7	5370
Vietnam	91.52	1.05	274	330.95	21.1	6.0	1890
China	1367.82	0.48	143	9569.96	27.1	7.4	7380

Source: ADB (2015).

[a]http://data.worldbank.org/country (Accessed 12 September 2015).

The aim of this chapter is to provide a comprehensive overview and contribute to the understanding of the existing knowledge gaps in managing the Mekong. The questions addressed by this chapter include: (i) Do existing MRB's institutions limiting opportunities and ability of nations to mitigate conflicts and enhance cooperation? (ii) What political regimes have facilitated (or limited) the expansion of MRC? (iii) How issue linkage can be considered as a mechanism for achieving sustainable development in the MRB? Based on the notions of games with externalities, and on the feasible solution concepts and linkage issues (Pham Do *et al.*, 2012), the chapter demonstrates that (i) the MRC is far from being a sufficient institution for achieving sustainable development and cooperation; (ii) though the future of hydropower seems to be shaped mainly by economic development under the Greater Mekong Subregion (GMS) initiative, the role of the MRC remains unclarified; (3) despite currently each riparian nation tries to capitalize on its domestic river location, regardless of the pending consequences for the health of the Mekong ecosystem, all Mekong countries are involved in the regional power trade triggered by the initiative.[1] If all members of MRC do not commit themselves to empowering their organization to plan and implement river basin management, the MRC (as weak governance) should expand its ability of current powerful trade interactions within Association of Southeast Asian Nations (ASEAN) Economic Community (AEC) and other external actors to influencing the role in sustaining and developing the basin.[2]

---

[1]In 1992, with ADB's assistant, Cambodia, Yunnan Province and Guangxi Zhuang Autonomous Region (China), Laos, Myanmar, Thailand, and Vietnam, entered into a program to enhance economic relations among the countries in transport, energy, telecommunications, environment, human resource development, tourism, trade, private sector investment, and agriculture (details, see ADB, 2015).

[2]According to Xuecui (2015), hydropower has run rampant in Yunnan province in south-west China, but up to half its capacity could be idle by 2015 (https://www.chinadialogue.net/reports/6811-The-uncertain-future-of-the-Mekong-River/en).

In this chapter, water and nonwater issues are considered as strategic interactions among players; under the assumption that the objective functions of players are linearly separable in the payoffs, and "linking" issues may either facilitate cooperation in payoff (i.e., substituted issues), or leave players' ability to cooperate unchanged (complemented issues). By constructing empirical-linked MRB game from separated externality games, based on the framework of the GMS and AEC developments,[3] the chapter shows that managing the MRB is not only countries that are the winners or losers from the hydropower development schemes, but rather parts of the Mekong nations' strategies in sustaining the basin/region-wide. Although linkage issue can be used as a mechanism for managing the MRB's conflicts, it is also supporting the integrated water resource management (IWRM) and water nexus solutions adopted by the MRC and the region-wide recently.[4]

The next section represents an overview of the Mekong Region status and its water resources. Section 4.3 provides a brief review of issue linkage approach for achieving cooperation and demonstrates a framework of linked games as a mechanism for conflicts management. Concluding remarks follow in the last section.

4.2. The Mekong and Its Water Resources

The Mekong River is the longest river in Southeast Asia and the world's largest inland fishery resource. Originating at over 4500 m elevation in the Tibet Qinghai plateau and flowing for more than 4800 km before entering the South China Sea, the MRB encompasses a vast range of geographic and climatic zones and is divided into the Upper Mekong Basin (UMB) constituting China and Myanmar

---

[3]The agreement of an AEC as a single market and production base signed on 22 November in Kuala Lumpur and entered into force on 31 December 2015. Thus, "the AEC will transform the Asean economy into a region with free movement of goods, services, investment, skilled labour and freer flow of capital" (AEC, 2015).
[4]China seems being more closely involved in cross-border cooperation on hydropower and water management after the six Mekong countries signed a landmark agreement (called the Lancang-Mekong Cooperation Mechanism) on 12 November 2015.

(24% of the total drainage area) and LMB constituting Cambodia, Laos, Thailand, and Vietnam (76% of the total drainage area). The basin is economically and politically diverse, consisting of three so-called least-developed economies (Cambodia, Laos, and Myanmar), and three diverse larger economies (Thailand, Vietnam, and Yunnan Province of China). As can be seen from Table 4.1, economic disparities exist, ranging from four lower income members (Cambodia, Laos, Myanmar, Vietnam) with a low gross national income (GNI) per capita (formerly GNP — gross national product — per capita) of $1020–$1890 (current US$) to two middle-income members (Thailand and China) with a high GNI per capita of $5370–$7380. Populations range from 6.7 million people in Laos to over 90 million in the combined Yunnan and Guanxi regions of China. Poverty is a critical issue across the basin, despite the significant economic growth of China. The MR's average growth of real GDP has continuously increased in recent years (ADB, 2015), regardless of Thailand's economy, which continued to struggle with declining growth and political instability. However, the proportion of the population living below the poverty line exceeds 30%, including over 100 different ethnic groups, in parts of Laos, Cambodia, and Vietnam (UNEP, 2008).

The MRB is home to nearly 75 million people with 90 distinct ethnic groups (Matthews and Geheb, 2015). It also possesses the region's largest potential water resources and related resources that support ongoing economic development and a basis for community livelihoods. A summary of the distribution of water and land resources in the MRB is presented in Table 4.2.

According to Goh (2004), although only 16% of the total discharge in the basin originates from the upper Mekong, China is the important part of the basin. During the critical dry season, China's discharge amounts to most of the Mekong mainstream flow in Laos and Thailand and contributes to almost 45% of the average flow in Cambodia. The Mekong riparian states have quite different long-term major use patterns of the river. However, the river's water resources are used mainly for hydropower production and irrigation (MRC, 2010).

Table 4.2: The water resource profile of the MRB.

	China	Myanmar	Laos	Thailand	Cambodia	Vietnam
Area (10^3 km^2)	165	24	202	184	155	65
Area as % of MRB	21	3	25	23	20	8
Flows as % of MRB	16	2	35	18	18	11
Average flow (m^3/sec)	2410	300	5270	2560	2860	1660

Source: MRC (2005).

4.2.1. *Overview of Development and Cooperation Obstacles in the Mekong*

As all countries in the MR are undergoing rapid economic growth and modernization, hydropower is seen as a key component in this transition. The six riparian states of the Mekong have grouped into different water institutions and programs for managing the Mekong since 1950. China views the upper Mekong primarily as a source of hydropower and as a trade route. Laos also considers the Mekong primarily as a source of hydropower. More than 90% of the electricity in Laos is produced from hydroelectric plants (Campbell, 2009). Thailand considers the Mekong as a water resource for irrigation. The main value of the Mekong for Cambodia is for fishery production, while Vietnam relies on the water to support the Mekong delta's agricultural production. There are clear potential conflicts between these demands for water, which will require trade-offs among water-using sectors. Can such diversity of interests allow reaching cooperation? Particular, hydropower development will be the core of water resources collaboration (Yu, 2015).

Since early 1990s, an increasing number of river-based cooperation institutions have emerged in mainland Southeast Asia. Among these are the MRC, the GMS, and the Mekong Basin Development (MBD) that take place under the overarching framework of the ASEAN. As the MRC is troubled by the diversity of expectations among the member countries, the ASEAN has played an important role in economic development of the Mekong region and has attracted international attention (for details, see Hensengerth, 2009; Weatherbee, 1997). These institutions will play a role in analyzing opportunities of issue linkage in reaching a basin-wide agreement.

Recent hydropower project developments in the MRB are largely unbridled because of the lack of legal hurdles and international coordination on such projects (Bearden, 2010; Osborne, 2010; Phillips *et al.*, 2006). The MRC's mission is to promote and coordinate sustainable management and development of water and related resources for the countries' mutual benefit and the people's well-being by implementing strategic programs and activities and providing scientific information and policy advice (MRC, 2005). The absence of China, however, is one of the MRC's main weaknesses. Governments in the LMB face critical decisions about the future of the mainstream MR, as will be discussed in the next section.

4.2.2. *Impacts of Hydropower Projects on the MRB*

With quite impressive economic growth (Table 4.1), electricity demand in the Mekong region has grown rapidly at annual rates ranging from 4.9% to 20.9% since 2000 (ECA, 2010). In particular, China's economy has been doubling since its reform period began in 1978, leading to surging energy demand. The fast export-led growth in Thailand, Laos, Cambodia, and Vietnam has also increased demand for electricity in the middle and lower Mekong regions. China has more than doubled its consumption between 1997 and 2007. Its electricity production capacity in 2012 is estimated at 4.94 trillion kWh of which nearly 22% are from hydropower (CIA, 2013). China's energy demand has been an important driving force for the development of hydropower projects along the MR mainstream.

Due to the regional diversity in economic development and population growth, increase in primary energy demand will differ by nations. Table 4.3 presents the primary energy demand for 2010 and the expected annual growth rates in the period 2010–2035 for all six Mekong countries with and without advanced technology. As a whole, primary energy demand is projected to increase at 2.1% per year over the outlook period (2010–2035) — faster than the projected

Table 4.3: Energy demand in two scenarios: BAU and alternative cases.

	Primary Energy Demand (Unit Mtoe)		Annual Growth Rate (%)	Primary Energy Demand per Capita (Unit toe)		Primary Energy Demand and Growth Rate with Advanced Technology	
	2010	2035		2010	2035	2035 (Mtoe)	Growth Rate (%)
Cambodia	5.0	8.9	2.3	0.36	0.5	7.4	1.7
Laos	2.8	7.9	4.3	0.45	0.99	7.7	4.0
Myanmar	14.0	30.3	3.1	0.29	0.55	29.2	3.0
Thailand	117.4	204.8	2.2	1.70	2.79	183.5	1.8
Vietnam	67.7	186.0	4.1	0.77	1.80	167.9	3.7
China	2471.1	4218.1	2.3	1.80	3.05	3418.7	1.4

Source: ADB (2013).

world average growth rate of 1.5% per year during the same period in the business-as-usual (BAU) case (ADB, 2013). With the deployment of advanced technologies, however, there will be a significant addition to the installed generating capacity of new and renewable energy, a reduction in the capacity of coal-fired power plants, and expanded nuclear power capacity in 2035 (ADB, 2013).

Currently, there are 392 individual dams[5] that exist in various stages. Of these, 258 are completed, 38 are under construction, 94 are in planning, and 2 were cancelled on the Mekong mainstream and its tributaries (WLE-CGIAR, 2015). According to Li (2012), the total monetary value of benefits from hydropower operations in the next 20 years in the region is estimated to be US$15–20 billion. Most of the recent interest in developing hydropower on the mainstream focused on locations in Laos, Laos-Thai border, and the Cambodia reaches of the Mekong mainstream. Hydropower projects in the Mekong region have generally been profitable for both host governments and private-sector sponsors. However, dam-building may have both

[5]Of which 198 are for hydropower dams of 15 MW installed capacity and above, 190 for irrigation, and 4 for multi-purposes (WLE-CGAIR, 2015).

positive and negative impacts that should also be taken into account in a regional analysis. Like any transboundary river, the hydropower resources of the Mekong are limited because too many dams may lead to the tragedy of the common (i.e., multiple parties acting independently in non-cooperative behavior will ultimately deplete a shared limited resource). Studies have already shown that upstream dams can lower water levels downstream. Lowering the water levels and flow, upstream dams will also lower downstream hydropower potential and its expected economic return (Biba, 2012; Kubiszewski *et al.*, 2012; Ziv *et al.*, 2012).

As can be seen in Table 4.3, China has the highest potential for energy saving than any other nation in the MR: its annual growth rate is reduced from 2.3% in the BAU case to 1.4% in the advanced technology case. Within the MR, it must be recognized that hydropower is only one of a number of purposes for which water is diverted or stored. At present the LMB's hydropower generation takes place in the tributaries and produces only 2% of the total economic value of the LMB (Table 4.4). This low value reflects the undeveloped hydropower potential, particular in Laos where 90% of the land area lies in the basin.

According to King *et al.* (2007), Cambodia has a hydropower potential of 10,000 MW but installed capacity of only 160 MW. Laos has the greatest potential for hydropower development (13,000 MW) within the MRB and could become a power hub for Thailand,

Table 4.4: Annual economic value (in billion US$) from different types of water uses in 2010.

	China	The LMB	The entire MRB
Households and industrial	0.408 (17)	1.956 (14)	2.364 (15)
Hydropower mainstream	0.758 (32)	0	0.758 (5)
Hydropower tributaries	0	0.206 (2)	0.206 (1)
Irrigation	0.961 (41)	8.619 (62)	9.580 (59)
Fisheries	0.237 (10)	3.000 (22)	3.237 (20)
Total	2.364 (100)	13.781 (100)	16.145 (100)

Source: Houba *et al.* (2013).

Note: In parentheses are rounded percentages of the types of water-use values.

Vietnam, and the ASEAN power grid. Although Thailand is an important importer of hydropower and a potential hub for the ASEAN power grid, Vietnam and Myanmar are important both as hydropower developers and potential importers. The MRC has proposed many plans for developing this potential through dam projects; there are 11 mainstream dam proposals and 30 planned tributary dams to be developed between 2015 and 2030 (Kubiszewski *et al.*, 2012). However, these dam projects are not going to be realized due to lack of legal and procedural elements in the 1995 LMB treaty. Currently, Yunnan installed 68% of its provincial power generation and is constructing a cascade of hydropower plants on the mainstream of the Mekong with 15,600 MW by 2025 (King *et al.*, 2007: xi). Construction of dams on the Mekong River may pose immediate and long-term threats to the food security and livelihoods of over 60 million people in the LMB (MRC, 2010).

As trade is an important issue driving economic growth, and infrastructure is necessity for trade, infrastructure development has a key role in economic development in the MRB. The GMS countries have grown rapidly since 1992. Openness, as measured by the ratio of the sum of exports and imports of goods and services to GDP, increased in all the GMS countries, except Myanmar, during the last two decades (Srivastava and Kumar 2012). Although there are some variations across the GMS, overall it remains a relatively poor region (Stone and Strutt, 2010). Srivastava and Kumar (2012) find that in the five lower Mekong countries (GMS5), the growth of trade has been rapid even without China. In terms of intraregional trade dependence (Table 4.5) and the degree to which China plays a role in that dependence, China has grown faster than the overall GMS5.

China is the world's factory, producing goods and serving export markets around the world. As such it needs inputs such as energy and raw materials (Eyler, 2014). On 1 January 2010, the China-ASEAN Free Trade Agreement (CAFTA) came into force. This established the third-largest free trade area (FTA) in the world, just behind the European Union (EU) and the North American Free Trade Area (NAFTA). However, China is now facing a great challenge in getting the agreement formally implemented because the trade structure

Table 4.5: Intra-GMS exports.

Export from/to (US$ mil)	Cambodia	Laos	Myanmar	Thailand	Vietnam	China
Cambodia		0.57	0.36	49.78	43.86	55.38
Laos	0.31		0.02	101.24	0.38	16.26
Myanmar	0.24	0.01		1089.4	0.44	206.04
Thailand	555.8	454.2	613.4		1978.0	12786.0
Vietnam	51.1	0.2	0.3	451.7		2516.1
China	624.3	86.1	969.8	7148.2	4863.4	

Source: Adjusted from Stone and Strutt (2010).

between China and ASEAN countries (AFTA) is competitive rather than complementary (Wang, 2011).

With all that background data on the potential embedded in the basin and the political and institutional barriers, one has to wonder what can be done to enhance cooperation in the basin. Various studies (e.g., Barrett, 1994; Dinar *et al.*, 2013; and references therein) show that allocation procedures and mechanisms are more problematic in transboundary water resources.[6] Recent research (see Pham Do *et al.*, 2012 and reference therein), however, has also shown that whenever opportunities for linkages exist, countries may indeed lean toward cooperation. If the benefits that result from the joint cooperation in the linked games exhibit growing incremental benefits by more participants joining the coalition (convexity principle), the grand coalition (that includes all riparian states) is the only optimal level maximizing social welfare. Within this context, static games may generate outcomes in which the dominant strategy for the upstream country (China) is not to cooperate, whereas the downstream country's (LMB nations) dominant strategy is to

---

[6]The two main characteristics of the problem are: countries' welfare is interdependent, through water quantity/quality externalities; and all solutions to the allocation problem must be consistent with the principle of national sovereignty — that is, a country's compliance with the agreement must be strictly voluntary and self-enforcing.

cooperate.[7] To achieve an efficient outcome, side payments have been suggested (Barrett, 1994; Porter, 1988) as means to internalize the externality by the upstream country. With such option for enhanced cooperation it is obvious that an evaluation of a possible issue linkage would necessitate the use of a normative model.

4.3. Issue Linkage as a Mechanism in Managing Conflicts

Game theory is essentially the mathematical study of decision making, of conflict, and strategy in social situations. Conflict or noncooperative strategy refers to the fact that a binding agreement cannot be achieved, whereas in cooperative strategy it is possible. Game theory incorporates key elements of both realist and liberal views of international politics (Stein, 1990). It provides a framework for studying the strategic actions of individual decision makers to develop more broadly acceptable solutions. In the following, we apply the notions of externality games[8] in approaching the Mekong situation and management of its water and resources.

We consider a negotiation process between upstream (China) and downstream (four LMB countries, represented by MRC) for achieving a basin-wide agreement as a two-stage game of two players with two strategies. China and LMB are assumed to have a unitary will, that is, each part of MRB acts as a single agent rather than some kind of a complex organization in the first stage. This means that countries (China and LMB)[9] can play noncooperative over independent policy[10] issues (strategies) such as energy (hydropower generation), trade, and the ecosystem (fishery and agricultural productions) to determine (evaluate) their policy (variables). Then in

---

[7]The resulting equilibrium is often not efficient.
[8]For further details, see Pham Do *et al.* (2012).
[9]Myanmar is excluded both due to its political separation policy and thus, lack of data, and its minute contribution of water to the Mekong runoff.
[10]We assume for simplicity that the LMB states act in one voice. While this is a simplifying assumption given the present ongoing disagreements between the LMB states, still we believe that they have a common threat and interest in the conflict with China.

the second stage, the final outcomes are calculated in a linked game structure for the negotiating countries. Note that, we assume that the outcomes can be ranked (meaning that the outcomes can reflect the players'/country preferences). The payoffs of the games are given in simple matrices, each cell of which has two elements (identified by the two players: *row* and *column*), the payoff for *row* followed by the payoff for *column*. The generic payoff matrix is shown following (Fig. 4.2).

Lower's strategy

		Cooperation	Noncooperation
	Cooperation	$\left(w_{Ui}^{cc}, w_{Li}^{cc}\right)$	$\left(w_{Ui}^{cd}, w_{Li}^{cd}\right)$
Upper's strategy			
	Noncooperation	$\left(w_{Ui}^{dc}, w_{Li}^{dc}\right)$	$\left(w_{Ui}^{dd}, w_{Li}^{dd}\right)$

Figure 4.2: The matrix game between Lower and Upper Mekong states.

For example, w_{Ui}^{cc} in the upper left cell in Fig. 4.2 is the payoff for Upper, if Upper chooses the strategy cooperation, and Lower chooses the strategy cooperation. Similarly, w_{Li}^{cc} is Lower's payoff from this pair of strategy choices. In the following, we use LMB for Lower and China for Upper.

4.3.1.   *First Stage: Independent Games*

Since the MRC has weak-policy institutions and seems politically biased in favor of hydropower generation (Grumbine *et al.*, 2012), on the water issue, the LMB riparian nations seem to face two strategies (regimes): weak governance (i.e., the four countries act individually) or strong governance (the four countries can act collectively, via MRC); whereas China has two strategies, either cooperate or not with the LMB on water uses. In addition to the water issues, on the trade issue, each player also has two strategies, open and restrict regional trade.

Currently, governments in the LMB face critical decisions that involve trade-off between (i) the economic benefits from hydropower generation and (ii) potentially irreversible negative impacts on the ecosystems that provide livelihoods and food security to the rural people. As a means of analyzing the potential of cooperation even though China has refused to be a member of the MRC, we assume that both the LMB and China (UMB) are faced with two strategies (i.e., cooperation and noncooperation) in each game.

4.3.1.1.   *A water issue game*

We adopt the physical hydrological basin model in Houba *et al.* (2013), with a unidirectional water flow from China to the LMB to construct the water issue game. The annual economic net values of water uses determined by aggregating four main activities in each region, UMB and LMB, and for each season (wet and dry), namely industry and households, hydropower generation, agricultural irrigation, and fishery. Table 4.6 represents the Mekong water game.

In this water game, under LMB's weak governance, if China cooperatives with LMB, the total welfare is 24.808 (billion US$) whereas it is 22.756 if China not. Hence, one can easily see that the total basin-level annual incremental welfare gains are 2.052 (billion US$) for moving from noncooperation to cooperation under weak governance. The same explanation suggests a 0.142 billion US$ gains from cooperation under strong governance. In addition, almost all of the maximal joint welfare gains can be realized by strengthening the LMB's governance (regardless of China's strategy) because LMB obtains almost the same payoff under both cooperation

Table 4.6: The Mekong water game.

		LMB	
		Strong Governance	**Weak Governance**
China	Cooperation	$(2.753, 22.055)^{a}$	$(3.755, 21.053)$
	Non-cooperation	$(2.729, 22.031)$	$(2.729, 20.027)$

[a]Nash equilibrium.
Source: Adapted from Table 7 in Pham Do and Dinar (2014).

(22.055) and noncooperation (22.031) with strong governance. From the perspective of China, the incentives are quite different because China can gain (3.755) more when it cooperates while LMB is weak in governance. This could help explain why China is interested in signing bilateral agreements rather than multilateral ones, namely enhance the weak governance status of the LMB states (Naohiro, 2012; Yongqi and Anfei, 2013).

4.3.1.2. *A trade issue game*

In January 2007, the 10 ASEAN countries agreed to implement the AEC by 2015, committing to provide a comprehensive framework for economic integration (Petri *et al.*, 2012). Taking AEC as a benchmark, the strategies of LMB as members of ASEAN are either to retain barriers with non-ASEAN partner economies (such as China); or to remove the barriers, that is create open trade with more partners of the world. UN COMTRADE (cited in Petri *et al.*, 2012, p. 97) reports that the region's share pattern is essentially symmetric: the shares of ASEAN, the United States and the EU, China and Japan, and the rest of the world each account for about one-quarter of the overall ASEAN trade.

Due to lack of data from Yunnan, we adapt the results from Table 4.6 in Petri *et al.* (2012) to address the welfare gains from regional cooperation and from external partnerships in deriving a trade game. The trade game (Table 4.7) is based only on trade results related to the four LMB nations and China. We consider China as

Table 4.7: The Mekong trade game.

		LMB	
		Open	**Restrict**
China	CAFTA	$(-7.8, 15.4)^a$	(0.4, 2.8)
	AFTA	$(-12.2, 52.9)$	$(-4.6, 12.0)$

[a]Nash equilibrium.

Source: Adapted from Pham Do and Dinar (2014).

Note: (CAFTA; Open), (CAFTA; Restrict), (AFTA; Open), and (AFTA; Restrict) values are taken from Column AEC, AFTA, AEC++, and AFTA+, respectively, in Petri *et al.* (2012, Table 4.6).

a partner of ASEAN but it can be involved with AEC only under two arrangements/conditions: (i) either increased bilateral free trade region with the four LMB states (under CAFTA), where LMB are members of AFTA and (ii) or enjoy bilateral FTA with AEC (under AFTA).

Note that the welfare gain of the LMB is defined as the aggregated gains obtained from all four LMB nations in ASEAN plans. One can realize that the LMB has "open" trade as the dominant strategy; while China's dominant strategy is CAFTA. In this game, the Nash equilibrium (CAFTA, Open) is not efficient as the total outcome is less than in (AFTA, Open).

Scrutiny of the Mekong water game and the Mekong trade game (Tables 4.6 and 4.7) suggests very clearly that playing each game separately will lead to a gridlock. Therefore, we turn to constructing a linked game as the sum of the two independent games in expectation that it would lead the regional players to cooperation. Since the water game and the trade game are expressed in 2010 monetary values, we can sum across the games in moving to the second stage game.

4.3.2. *Second Stage: Issue Linked Game*

As Cooperation is the dominant strategy in the water game above, while open is the dominant strategy in the trade game, we will take two outcomes of the water issue and two outcomes of the trade issue to construct a linked game[11] following (Table 4.8).

Table 4.8: The linked Mekong game.

		LMB	
		Liberalize (c)	Status quo (d)
China	Liberalize (c)	$(-5.047, 37.455)^{\text{a}}$	$(-4.045, 36.453)$
	Status quo (d)	$(-9.247, 74.955)$	$(-8.245, 73.955)$

[a]Nash equilibrium.

---

[11]From any two independent games, a two-issue-linked game can be constructed in which the payoff values are determined as the sum of the two values in the two independent games.

where:

$$(-5.047, 37.455) = (\mathit{2.753} - \mathbf{7.8}, \mathit{22.055} + \mathbf{15.4})$$
$$(-4.045, 36.453) = (\mathit{3.755} - \mathbf{7.8}, \mathit{21.053} + \mathbf{15.4})$$
$$(-9.247, 74.955) = (\mathit{2.753} - \mathbf{12.0}, \mathit{22.055} + \mathbf{52.9})$$
$$(-8.245, 73.953) = (\mathit{3.755} - \mathbf{12.0}, \mathit{21.053} + \mathbf{52.9})$$

The linked game indicates that the total social welfare will increase, when water is linked to trade considerations in the region. As a result, with a higher outcome, the LMB could make a side payment to China. The losses and gains are similar for both China and the LMB in the linked game. For example, see the last row of Table 4.8: for $(-9.247, 74.955)$ the total payoff is 65.708 ($74.955 - 9.247$); for $(-8.245, 73.953)$, the total payoff is 65.708. For the first row, the total outcome is 32.408 ($-5.047 + 37.455$) and 32.408 ($-4.045 + 36.453$). Thus, linking issues provides more opportunities for the countries in the negotiation process.

4.3.3. *A Mechanism*

The Mekong River has always been an important trade route between Western China and Southeast Asia flowing through six different countries. Recently China has become more engaged with all Mekong countries via the ASEAN. Therefore, the four LMB nations as members of ASEAN have advances on the trade issue (such as introducing the elements of the AEC as well as the AFTA) for negotiating with China. In particular, China is more closely involved in cross-border cooperation on hydropower and water management after the foreign ministers of the six Mekong countries announced the establishment of the Lancang-Mekong Cooperation (LMC) Mechanism on 12 November 2015 (CCTV, 2015). Guangsheng (2016) reports that since early 2000 "China has been seeking to upgrade sub-regional cooperation" for establishing and achieving the "Silk Road Economic Belt and 21st Century Maritime Silk Road Initiative in 2013." A joint declaration[12] (a so-called Sanya declaration) was

---

[12]Based on the Sanya Declaration, China and LM nations agree that "the LMC practical cooperation will be carried out through the three cooperation pillars":

issued after the first LMC Leaders' Meeting in Sanya, China on 23 March 2016 (Sanya, 2016).

In managing the Mekong water resources, decentralized decisions (noncoopeartive behavior) are generally less efficient than a centralized mechanism (strong cooperation) maximizing a regional utility function. Thus, countries can consider the option of issue linkage as alternative choice and opportunities in the negotiation process.

4.4. Concluding Remarks

Water is essential for promoting inclusive sustainable development, as it supports human communities, maintains the functions of ecosystems, and ensures economic development (WWAP, 2015). In the Mekong, the challenges at the interface of water and sustainable development vary from one region (upper and lower Mekong) to another. In particular, when decisions are decentralized with different issues, a dominant actor can get the maximal value of its strategy, while the other are maintained at their minimal acceptable satisfaction level. In spite of this unbalance/social optimum, however, such equilibrium may induce a global loss of efficiency and not correspond to global optimal conditions.

Using the notion of externality games with issue linkage, this chapter demonstrates the advantages of issue linkage for the Mekong region in achieving a wiser-basin agreement. Having provided issue linkages, each country or a sub-region of the Mekong can consider their own objectives for a shift of local equilibria toward regional optimal values and propose adjustment mechanisms for sustainable development.

Conflicts of interests and the distribution nature of the Mekong water resources may induce a global loss of efficiency. This chapter shows that the LMB can benefit more from issue linkages; particular trading will become more important issue for China when Trans-Pacific Partnership (TPP) has been signed in February 2016 (TPP,

---

(i) political and security issues; (ii) economic and sustainable development; (iii) social, cultural, and people-to-people exchanges (Sanya, 2016).

2015). Since the first LMC Mechanism was signed on 12 November 2015, China should consider playing a more active role in the MRC, expanding its involvement to sharing and managing the water resources.

References

ADB (ed.) (2004). *Greater Mekong Subregion: Atlas of the Environment.* Manila: Asian Development Bank.

ADB (ed.) (2013). *Energy Outlook for Asia and the Pacific.* Manila: Asian Development Bank.

ADB (ed.) (2015). *Renewable Energy Developments and Potential in the Greater Mekong Subregion.* Manila: Asian Development Bank.

AEC (2015). A blueprint for growth ASEAN Economic Community 2015: Progress and key achievements Jakarta: ASEAN secretariat. Retrieved from http://www.asean.org/storage/images/2015/November/aec-page/AEC-2015-Progress-and-Key-Achievements.pdf [November 2015].

ASEAN (ed.) (2010). *ASEAN Regional Guidelines on Competition Policy.* Jakarta: ASEAN Secretariat.

Barrett, S (1994). *Conflict and Cooperation in Managing International Water Resources. Policy Research Working Paper* WPS 1303. Washington: World Bank.

Bearden, BL (2010). The legal regime of the Mekong River: A look back and some proposals for the way ahead. *Water Policy*, 12(6), 798–821.

Biba, S (2012). China's continuous dam-building on the Mekong River. *Journal of Contemporary Asia*, 42(4), 603–628.

Campbell, I (2009). *The Mekong: Biophysical Environment of an International River Basin.* Amsterdam: Elsevier.

CCTV (2015). http://www.cctv-america.com/2015/11/12/asia-leaders-to-cooperate-on-use-of-lancang-mekong-river. Accessed 20 April 2016.

CIA (5 June 2013). Central Intelligence Agency, CIA World Factbook [Accessed on 26 June 2013].

Cronin, R and T Hamlin (2012). *Mekong Turning Point: Shared River for a Shared Future.* Henry L (ed.). Washington: Stimson Center.

De Stefano, L, P Edwards, L de Silva, and AT Wolf (2010). Tracking cooperation and conflict in international basins: Historic and recent trends. *Water Policy*, 12(6), 871–884.

Dinar, A, S Dinar, S McCaffrey, and D McKinney (eds.) (2013). *Bridges over Water: Understanding Transboundary Water Conflicts, Negotiation and Cooperation Second Edition.* Singapore: World Scientific Publishing.

ECA (2010). The potential of regional power sector integration: Greater Mekong Subregion (GMS) Transmission & Trading Case Study. Economic Consulting Associates, London, UK. Retrieved from http://www.esmap.org/sites/esmap.org/files/BN004-10_REISP-CD_Greater%20Mekong%20Subregion-Transmission%20&%20Trading.pdf [17 November 2014].

Eyler, B (6 March 2014). The uncertain future of the Mekong River, pp. 14–16. Retrieved from https://www.chinadialogue.net/reports/6811-The-uncertain-future-of-the-Mekong-River/en.

Goh, E (2004). *China in the Mekong River Basin: The Regional Security Implications of Resource Development on the Lancang Jiang.* RSIS Working papers; 069/04 Nanyang Technological University.

Grumbine, R, J Dore, and K Xu (2012). Mekong hydropower: Drivers of change and governance challenges. *Frontiers in Ecology and the Environment,* 10(2), 91–98.

Guangsheng, L (February 2016). *China Seeks to Improve Mekong Sub-Regional Cooperation: Causes and Policies.* Policy Report PR160225. Singapore: Nanyang Technological University.

Hensengerth, O (2009). Transboundary river cooperation and the region public good: The case of the Mekong river. *Contemporary Southeast Asia,* 31(2), 326–349.

Houba, H, KH Pham Do, and X Zhu (2013). Saving a River: A Joint Management Approach to the Mekong River Basin. *Environmental and Development Economics,* 18(1): 93–109.

Johnston, R and M Kummu (2012). Water resource models in the Mekong basin: A review. *Water Resource Management,* 26, 429–455.

King, P, J Biird, and L Haas (March 2007). Joint Initiative on Environmental Criteria for Hydropower Development in the Mekong Region. ADB Technical Report.

Kliot, N, D Shmueli, and U Shamir (2001). Development of institutional frameworks for the management of transboundary water resources. *International Journal of Global Environmental Issues,* 1(3–4), 306–328.

Kubiszewski I, R Costanza, P Paquet, and S Halimi (2012). Hydropower development in the lower Mekong basin: Alternative approaches to deal with uncertainty. *Regional Environmental Change.* Doi:10.1007/s10113-012-0303-8.

Kummu, M, M Keskinen, and O Varis (eds.) (2008). *Modern Myths of the Mekong.* Finland: Water and Development Publications. Helsinki University of Technology.

Li X (2012). Hydropower in the Mekong River Basin. *Environmental Claims Journal,* 24(1), 51–69.

Matthews, N and K Geheb (eds.) (2015). *Hydropower Development in the Mekong Region: Political, Socio-Ecology.* New York: Taylor and Francis.

Mehtonen, K, M Keskinen, and O Varis (2008). The Mekong: IWRM and Institutions. In *Management of Transboundary Rivers and Lake*, by O Varis, C Tortajada, and AK Biswas (eds). Berlin: Springer, pp. 207–26.

MRC (ed.) (2005). *Overview of the Hydrology of the Mekong Basin, Executive Summary.* Phnom Penh, Cambodia: Mekong River Commission.

MRC (ed.) (2010). *Strategic Plan 2011–2015, Mekong River Commission for Sustainable Development.* Vientiane, Lao PDR. Mekong River Commission.

Naohiro, K (2012). China's external economic cooperation: Ties to the Mekong Region. In *Rising China's Diplomatic Strategy.* Retrieved from http://www.nippon.com/en/in-depth/a00803/ [19 June 2012].

Osborne, M (2004). River at risk: The Mekong, the environment and the water politics of China and Southeast Asia. In *Lowy Institute Paper* 02. Double Bay, NSW, Australia: Lowy Institute for International Policy.

Osborne, M (2010). The Mekong River under threat. *Asia-Pacific Journal,* 8(2).

Petri P, M Plummer, and F Zhai (2012). ASEAN economic community: A general equilibrium analysis. *Asian Economic Journal,* 26(2), 93–118.

Pham Do, KH and A Dinar (2014). The role of issue linkage in managing noncooperating basins: The case of the Mekong. *Natural Resource Modelling,* 27(4), 492–518.

Pham Do, KH, A Dinar, and D McKinney (2012). Transboundary water management: Can issue linkage help mitigate conflicts and enhance cooperation. *International Game Theory Review,* 13(1), 39–59.

Phillips, D, M Daoudy, J Öjendal, A Turton, and S McCaffrey (eds.) (2006). *Trans-boundary Water Cooperation as a Tool for Conflict Prevention and for Broader Benefit-Sharing.* Stockholm, Sweden: Ministry for Foreign Affairs.

Poncet, S (2006). Economic integration of Yunnan with the greater Mekong subregion. *Asian Economic Journal,* 20(3), 303–317.

Sanya (2016). Sanya declaration. Retrieved from http://www.fmprc.gov.cn/mfa_eng/zxxx_662805/t1350039.shtml [22 April 2016].

Srivastava P and U Kumar (2012). *Trade and Trade Facilitation in the Greater Mekong Subregion.* Manila: Asian Development Bank.

Stein, A (ed.) (1990). *Why Nations Cooperate: Circumstance and Choice in International Relations.* Ithaca: Cornel University Press.

Stone, S and A Strutt (2010). Transport infrastructure and trade facilitation in the Greater Mekong Subregion. In *Trade Facilitation and Regional*

Cooperation in Asia, by DH Brooks and SF Stone (eds.). pp. 156–191. Cheltenham, UK and Northampton, MA, USA: Edward Elgar.

Suhardiman, D, M Giordano, and F Molle (2012). Scalar disconnect: The logic of transboundary water governance in the Mekong. *Society and Natural Resources*, 25(6), 572–586.

TPP (2015). The Trans-Pacific Partnership (TPP). Available at http://www.tpp.mfat.govt.nz.Accessed 20 April, 2016.

UNEP (2008). The Mekong River — survival for millions. http://www.grida.no/publications/vg/water2/page/3263.aspx. Accessed 25 April, 2015.

UNEP (ed.) (2012). *Promoting Upstream-Downstream Linkages through Integrated Ecosystem Management in the GMS*. UNEP Policy brief 8-2012, United Nations Environment Programme, Kenya.

Wang, L (2011). Is China a trade competitor of ASEAN? *Journal of Contemporary Eastern Asia*, 10(2), 1–3.

Weatherbee, D (1997). Cooperation and conflict in the Mekong River Basin. *Studies in Conflict and Terrorism*, 20, 167–184.

WLE (2015). Dams in the Mekong Basin. Vientiane, CGIAR Research Program on Water, Land and Ecosystems — Greater Mekong, Vientiane, Laos. Available at https://wle-mekong.cgiar.org/wp-content/uploads/A4_Mekong_Dams_2015.pdf. Accessed on 20 April 2016.

WLE-CGIAR (2015). Mapping the dams of the Mekong, The CGIAR Consortium Research Program on Water, Land and Ecosystems. Vientiane, Laos. https://wle-mekong.cgiar.org/maps/

WWAP (2015). The United Nations World Water Development Report 2015: Water for a Sustainable World. UN World Water Assessment Program, Paris, UNESCO.

Yongqi, H and G Anfei (2013). China strengthens ties with neighbors. China Daily Asia. http://www.chinadailyasia.com/business/2013-06/21/content_15076392.html [21 June 2013].

Yu, X (2003). Regional cooperation and energy development in the Greater Mekong Sub-region. *Energy Policy*, 31, 1221–1234.

Yu, X (2015). Water resources collaboration: Potential flagship in Lancang-Mekong cooperation mechanism, WLE Greater Mekong: MK22 project. https://wle-mekong.cgiar.org/water-resources-collaboration-potential-flagship-in-lancang-mekong-cooperation-mechanism

Ziv, G, E Baran, S Nam, I Rodríguez-Iturbe, and S Levin (2012). Trading-off fish biodiversity, food security, and hydropower in the Mekong River Basin. *Proceedings of the National Academy of Sciences of United States of America*. 109(15), 5609–5614.

Part II

WATER TREATY MODELS

CHAPTER 5

PROPOSED INTERNATIONAL LEGAL AND INSTITUTIONAL FRAMEWORK FOR CONJUNCTIVE MANAGEMENT OF SURFACE AND GROUNDWATER ALONG THE US–MEXICO BORDER REGION

MARÍA E. MILANÉS MURCIA

University of the Pacific, McGeorge School of Law
New Mexico Water Resources Research Institute

The 1906 Convention and the 1944 Treaty establish the distribution of surface water of the Rio Grande (RG), Colorado, and Tijuana Rivers between the United States and Mexico. Neither of these treaties addresses groundwater management. Only Minute 242 to the 1944 Treaty, regulates salinity for groundwater. Specifically, Minute 242.5 establishes that there is a lack of "conclusion by the Governments of the United States and Mexico for a comprehensive agreement on groundwater in the border areas." The lack of regulation has contributed to overdraft and degradation of the water quality in several aquifers along the US–Mexico border. Recommendations for an institutional and legal framework under an umbrella agreement, addressing water bank as allocation tool, attempt to fill the legal vacuum of international and interstate groundwater management in the US–Mexico border region.

J.S.D. International Water Resources Law from University of the Pacific, McGeorge School of Law. This research is part of her J.S.D.'s Dissertation developed under the supervision of Professor Stephen McCaffrey. A copy of this Dissertation is on field at McGeorge School of Law's library. The author would like to acknowledge and thank Professor Stephen McCaffrey and Professor Ariel Dinar for their orientation. The Annex for this chapter is available online at: www.worldscientific.com/worldscibooks/10.1142/9896.

In addition, these recommendations can be adapted to other transboundary basins around the world.

Keywords: Allocate; Aquifers; Border; Confined; Conjunctive use; Convention; Cooperation; Equitable; Fossil; Framework; Groundwater; Institutional; International; Management; Policy; Reasonable; Recharge; Regulation; Surface water; Transboundary; Treaty; United Nations; Water banking; Watercourses.

5.1. Introduction

This chapter proposes a new legal and institutional framework able to allocate in conjunctive use surface water and groundwater, including specific regulation management for fossil aquifers. The legal and institutional framework developed in this chapter can also be adapted to different transboundary basins around the world. This chapter has asimilarscope as the Bellagio Draft Treaty (Hayton and Utton, 1989), providing a solution to groundwater management along the US–Mexico border region.

There is no international regulation to manage groundwater along the US–Mexico border region. The lack of international regulation for groundwater has contributed to overdraft and degradation of the water quality in several aquifers along the US–Mexico border. This situation leads to the "tragedy of the commons," making it difficult to allocate groundwater for equitable and reasonable use as well as to establish cooperation between both countries. Therefore, a new international regulation is needed for the US–Mexico border region to allocate and protect groundwater (International Boundary and Water Commission [IBWC], 1973). This chapter presents a potential answer to the need of regulation to allocate in conjunctive use groundwater and surface water, as well as water from potential fossil aquifers.

The Convention Providing for the Equitable Distribution of the Waters of the Rio Grande (RG) for Irrigation Purposes, 21 May 1906 [The 1906 Treaty] ("Convention," 1906), and the Treaty relating to Utilization of Water of the Colorado and Tijuana Rivers and the RG, 3 February 1944 [The 1944 Treaty] ("Treaty," 1944) establish the distribution of surface water of the RG, Colorado, and Tijuana

Rivers between the United States and Mexico. However, neither of these treaties addresses groundwater management in their provisions. Only Minute 242 (IBWC, 1973; IBWC, 1975) regulates salinity for groundwater. Minute 242.5 establishes that there is a lack of a "conclusion by the Governments of the United States and Mexico for a comprehensive agreement on groundwater in the border areas" (IBWC, 1973).

The international regulation proposed in this chapter is addressed as an umbrella agreement based on the 1997 United Nations Watercourses Convention [The 1997 UN Convention] (UN Convention, 1997), which codifies international principles and sets guidelines to manage groundwater in conjunctive use with surface water. In addition, the proposed international regulation follows the resolution on Confined Transboundary Groundwater 1994 (International Law Commission [ILC], 1994), which recognizes "the need for continuing efforts to elaborate rules pertaining to confined transboundary groundwater" (ILC, 1994) and considers the application of the principles set forth in the 1997 UN Convention to transboundary confined aquifers.

The delimitation of the US–Mexico border region proposed in this agreement goes beyond the political border, and it is established according to the 1997 UN Convention in Article 2 defining "watercourse [as] a system of surface waters and groundwater constituting by virtue of their physical relationship a unitary whole and normally flowing into a common terminus" (UN Convention, 1997). The agreement is developed to cover the whole border region through the basin approach and for each subregion a policy will be developed.

The United States Geological Survey [USGS], (2013) defines subregion as "· the area drained by a river system, a reach of a river and its tributaries in that reach, a closed basin(s), or a group of streams forming a coastal drainage area." According to this definition, the regulation developed in this chapter provides the essential elements and principles to regulate each transboundary basin and to establish specific policies at the sub regional level according to the social, physical, and environmental conditions in each region. These policies will promote conservation and environmental protection.

In addition, the agreement includes an institutional framework where the key institution is the water bank, which provides cooperation as well as reasonable and equitable utilization, and avoids harm between the United States and Mexico. "[W]ater banking is attractive as it can allow for water to be set aside to ensure ecological flows as part of the trading process" (Le Quesne, Pegram, and Von Der Heyden, 2007) (Howe & Goodman, 1995). In this research, the water bank is a binational intergovernmental institution at the basin and subregional level able to establish the allocation among different users while protecting the environment guaranteeing ecological flow, and regulating social and environmental impacts. In addition, the proposed legal framework provides the integration of water resources management to maximize benefits along the border region at the basin level. In order to reach that goal the agreement includes a new *water use right* as a mechanism to achieve a unique system of water allocation based on uses, and treating groundwater and surface water as one source in the water bank allocation system.

5.2.   Current Issues along the US–Mexico Border

This section provides an overview of problems in the management of groundwater along the US–Mexico border. Table 5.1 summarizes the most relevant issues, which are divided into four categories: (i) Institutions, (ii) Data, (iii) Strategic planning, and (iv) other issues. For each category, a list of issues is presented, and for each issue the Good Neighbor Environmental Board (GNEB) has presented a potential solution (United States Environmental Protection Agency [US EPA], 2005).

At the institutional level, the main requirement is to identify responsibilities held by officials of the US–Mexican border region for managing its water resources. To ensure effective institutions, it is necessary to "identify jurisdictional gaps and overlaps, interpret missions to reflect changing circumstances, and leverage opportunities for stronger cross-institutional collaboration" (US EPA, 2005).

The GNEB Eighth Report provides useful and important recommendations in order to achieve more effectively managed water resources throughout the US–Mexico border region. These

Table 5.1: Issues in the US–Mexico border (US EPA, 2005).

Category	Issue	Action
Institution	Lack of management framework for groundwater	Promote binational sharing of information about transboundary aquifers
	Binational funding challenges	Restore the annual Border Environment Infrastructure Fund appropriation at $100 million
		Encourage NADB to develop additional lending vehicles
	Different legal and institutional framework	Fully exploit current institutional missions and the current legal framework
		Increase institutional flexibility and collaborative efforts
Data	Data gaps on water quantity and quality, especially groundwater	Devote more resources to data collection, especially groundwater data
	Different methods, inability to compare	Develop binational data protocols and apply them
	Inaccessibility of data	Build capacity, trust
	Limited, ad hoc data exchange systems	Establish an annual US–Mexico Water Quality Data Exchange
Strategic Planning	Limited number of programs promoting water efficiency, conservation	Identify opportunities to build conservation and efficiency into existing vehicles
	Lack of information on best practices, or prioritization systems, to resolve conflicting values and demands	Promote successful water conservation practices
		Promote dialogue, innovation, and market incentives
	Piecemeal implementation of watershed projects	Enhance binational watershed planning
		Improve data exchange and transparency for large watersheds covering multiple states and jurisdictions
		Increase institutional support for local planning efforts in smaller watersheds

(*Continued*)

Table 5.1: (*Continued*)

Category	Issue	Action
Other issues	The biggest impediment for tribal participation in the US–Mexico Border Program is a question of resources	Need to emphasis more resources for border tribes' water management
	Large number of tribes in the border	More participation of tribal groups
	Climate change and population growth	Flexibility in the agreements to adapt to new changes

recommendations focus especially on two specific issues: the lack of data and the need for strategic planning (US EPA, 2005).

The lack of water resources data must encourage those responsible for the border region to develop and sign formal water resources data agreements. These agreements must support the collection, analysis, and sharing of compatible data across a wide range of uses in order to establish cooperation among both countries (US EPA, 2005).

Currently, Minute N. 320 represents a step forward in the development of agreements able to provide cooperative efforts at the basin level. The commissioners considered that, to address cooperative measures related to transboundary issues in the Tijuana River Basin, the Commission shall undertake activities such as: "[. . .] [C]arrying out studies, investigations, inventories, maps, and/or models in order to understand or evaluate, in a coordinated manner, matters of common interest that are jointly identified" (International Boundary and Water Commission, 2015). In addition, this minute intends "to establish a program that includes binational monitoring to address the priority issues of solid waste, sediment, and water quality" (IBWC, 2015).

An important recommendation is to "ensure success of the Transboundary Aquifer Assessment Program (TAAP) to scientifically characterize aquifers that underlie the international boundary and encourage other efforts to improve data gathering and accessibility for border water resources, such as harmonization of standards" (US EPA, 2010). The U.S.-Mexico Transboundary Aquifer Assessment Act (Public Law 109-448), which authorizes TAAP, was signed into law by the President of the United States on December 22, 2006. This Act authorizes the Secretary of the Interior, through the U.S. Geological Survey (USGS), to collaborate with the States of Arizona, New Mexico, and Texas through their Water Resources Research Institutes (WRRIs) and with the International Boundary and Water Commission (IBWC), stakeholders, and Mexican counterparts to develop mapping, modeling of priority transboundary aquifers and hydrogeologic characterization. The Act addressed the multi-disciplinary, binational, scientific approaches needed to achieve all these complex, interrelated transboundary issues. Cooperation and binational teams of experts are established to identify data collection gaps and provide solutions (US EPA, 2012).

Strategic planning is another important tool for more effective management of water resources. A planning process is one of the solutions to address immediate concerns in critical areas while pursuing collaborative longer term strategies (US EPA, 2005). In this regard, monitoring efforts are being implemented along the RG Canalization Project. For example, "[i]nstallation of 53 shallow groundwater monitoring wells at 20 restoration sites will provide valuable data that will assist with planning tree planting depths and irrigation needs" (US EPA, 2014).

The fact that several wastewater treatment plants along the RG in Mexico have been completed or are under construction is a step forward toward avoiding pollution and promoting the filtration of treated water to groundwater (US EPA, 2010). Agriculture return flows represent a cause of elevated salinity levels affecting both US and Mexico water users. The New River, which originates in Mexico and empties into the Salton Sea National Wildlife Refuge, has selenium and salinity problems as well as the RG and Colorado rivers, which require monitoring by farmers to ensure that the water is suitable for crop production (US EPA, 2010).

The recent recession has impacted funding allocations along the border. Funding to improve wastewater management along the border has decreased. For example, the FY 2010 EPA budget for border water and wastewater funding was $17 million, down from a previous level of $100 million in 2001. The reduced budget leaves many border communities with fewer water and wastewater services than the rest of the country.

Another issue is that the levees need to be improved along the RG in order to avoid major flooding, especially in the Lower RG Valley (LRGV) in the event of a hurricane. The US Congress included $220 million in the American Recovery and Reinvestment Act of 2009 for crucial levee improvements along the RG (US EPA, 2010). Flood can directly damage the quality of groundwater. When surface water and groundwater are interconnected, the types of acts, plans, and management of surface water will affect the groundwater. The conjunctive use and management of both sources are essential to mitigate damage on groundwater resources.

In addition, issues with indigenous tribal groups must be addressed, including provision of access to water conveyance systems for tribes within a reasonable framework of compensation and management (US EPA, 2010). Among the main issues, tribes have suffered a loss of water rights, pumping of water from aquifers shared with other tribes, loss of wetlands and of valued species. Due to this situation, indigenous tribes have had to change their habits. For example, Mexican indigenous communities that depended on the Colorado River Delta cannot continue fishing and hunting due to the dramatic decreases in flows reaching the Gulf of California (US EPA, 2010). Executive Order 13175 (President Obama, 2009; President Clinton, 2000) requires collaboration and consultation with tribal officials. At the state and local levels, tribal communities must be included in every plan for regional water management, as has been reflected in the California Water Plans (President Obama, 2009; President Clinton, 2000).

Conservation is another important aspect along the border. The border is quite dry with the highest precipitation in the Brownsville–Matamoros area at 28 inches per year, while the Imperial Valley receives less than three inches of rain per year (US EPA, 2010). Border communities and agriculture depend on groundwater as an important source of water. Conservation is key in this region. Cities like Las Cruces, San Diego, and El Paso have notable conservation programs (US EPA, 2010). For example, Las Cruces reduced daily per capita consumption by approximately 10% between 2005 and 2008, from 143 to 128 gallons. In this context, this chapter intends to provide a potential solution to current situation along the US–Mexico border region. The development of a new international legal and institutional framework, where a water bank is the main water allocation institution can continue and ensure conservation, protect the environment and the sustainable development of the region.

5.3. A New Proposed International Legal and Institutional Framework

The new legal framework proposed in this chapter intends to provide solution to all issues along the border region. In order to do so this new legal framework or umbrella agreement is addressed as a New Minute to the 1944 Treaty, and an amendment (agreement) to the 1906 Convention, or can be considered a new agreement in consonance with the 1944 Treaty and the 1906 Convention. The intention of this chapter is to leave the door open to the legislators at the time to decide the best instrument applicable.

Minutes are amendments to the 1944 Treaty. Under treaty law an "amendment" is a new treaty, and requires ratification. However, the 1944 Treaty has a specific provision Article 25, which establishes Minutes as amendments to the Treaty 1944.

> "Decisions of the Commission shall be recorded in the form of Minutes done in duplicate in the English and Spanish languages, signed by each Commissioner and attested by the Secretaries, and copies thereof forwarded to each Government [for approval]" (Article 25, Treaty, 1944).

The 1906 Convention does not establish specific provision for amendments such as the 1944 Treaty. Therefore, an amendment to the 1906 Convention is a new treaty. Under the US Constitution Art. VI, cl. 2 a Minute or a treaty is the Supreme Law of the Land and States shall implement treaties in their states regulation framework.

Similarly, under the Mexican Constitution Article 133 treaties are the supreme law above the state and federal laws and below the Constitution.

The new legal and institutional framework (Minute, Treaty) respects the surface water distribution scheme established in the 1906 Convention and the 1944 Treaty. The purpose is to provide regulation for groundwater in conjunctive use with surface water for each basin along the border region. Fossil waters are regulated in a separate Minute, which reflects the 1994 Resolution (ILC, 1994) and provisions of the 2008 Draft Articles (ILC, 2008). The 1994 ILC Resolution uses the term "confined" to mean fossil aquifers. This chapter uses the term fossil water, which in hydrological terms means water without any connection with surface water or any other body of water. Fossil aquifers have been trapped in an underground reservoir since a previous geological age. This type of water has been accumulated in underground strata over millions of years and is therefore not a renewable resource (Science Dictionary, 2012). Currently, there is not information about the existence of fossil aquifers along the United States–Mexico border. The legislators could also incorporate the new legal and institutional framework proposed in this chapter using another instrument, such as a new treaty to manage potential fossil aquifers in a future. The main goal of the chapter is to propose a new legal and institutional framework able to protect groundwater and fossil aquifers, as well as the allocation in conjunctive use of groundwater with surface water, rather than to specify how that goal should be accomplished.

The IBWC was created in 1889, this Commission applies the boundary and water treaties between the United States and Mexico and solves differences that may arise while implementing the treaties. "The IBWC is an international body composed of the United States Section and the Mexican Section [CILA, Comisión International de Límites y Aguas], each headed by an Engineer-Commissioner appointed by his/her respective president" (IBWC, 2016). The International Boundary and Water Commission (IBWC) manages surface water along the entire border (IBWC, 2012). Minute No. 242.5 establishes that there is a lack of a "conclusion by the Governments of the United States and Mexico of a comprehensive agreement on groundwater in the border areas" (IBWC, 1973) with the only limitation for each country being the pumping of groundwater within five miles of the Arizona-Sonora border near San Luis to 197,358,000 cubic meters annually (IBWC, 1973).

According to the new regulation proposed in this chapter, the IBWC will have authority to allocate in conjunctive use groundwater and surface water along the border region. A new international regulation focusing on joint management institutions for each basin can provide the solution for managing groundwater along the US–Mexico border region.

Today, the main limitations to developing this new legal framework are political barriers and technical difficulties created by a convergence of laws from different states and countries. Another limitation is the uncertainty in evaluating and monitoring the quantity and quality of groundwater, which has been especially problematic due to unknown groundwater connectivity between aquifers that appear to be independent from each other (US EPA, 2005).

Another challenge to develop a new international legal framework for the US–Mexico border is the potential conflict between the domestic law of both countries and the new international regulation. Although a treaty prevails over common law and state law in the United States and Mexico, it is important to reconcile the two at the moment of creating a new international regulation (Aust, 2007; Perezcano Díaz, 2007).

> "The constitution of the United States declares that constitution, and the laws of the United States which shall be made in pursuance thereof, and all treaties made, or which shall be made, under the authority of the United States, shall be the supreme law of the land. It follows that a law of Congress regulating commerce with foreign nations, or among the several States, is the supreme law; and if the law of a State is in conflict with it, the law of Congress must prevail, and the State law cease to operate so far as it is repugnant to the law of the United States." *Thurlow v. Com. of Mass.* 46 US 504, 1847 WL 5992 US at 574.

International Treaties in Mexico are above the Federal and Local laws. The constitution is the only norm above International Treaties in Mexico (Perezcano Díaz, 2007; Treja García and Alvarez, 2006).

*"International treaties. They are an integral part of the supreme
law of the Union and they are hierarchically located above general
federal and local laws. Interpretation of Article 133 of the Constitution."*[1] Suprema Corte de Justicia de la Nación, Tesis: P. IX/2007,
Seminario Judicial de la Federación y su Gaceta XXV, Abril de
2007, p. 6 Registro No. 172650.

The treaty proposed in this chapter will be the supreme law
in the United States and Mexico. The Annex shows the whole
test and language of this new legal and institutional framework.
This agreement provides security for both countries and ensures the
application of its provisions at the local level. In addition, the fact
of having an international regulation among both countries brings
stability to citizens along the whole border because they will know
the amount of water (surface water and groundwater) they will
receive. Moreover, conflicts or disputes between different users and
sectors will be avoided because the regulation establishes mechanisms
to solve any issue in each of the basins along the US–Mexico border
region.

5.3.1. *Water Bank*

The water bank, as a management institution, has the goal to
develop a unique system able to combine water rights from different
states and countries into one set of water rights. It provides
the reconciliation of all different types of water rights along the
border. This institution, the water bank, will also allow addressing
a regulation from the international level to the local level where
a policy for each subregion (subbasin) will be developed according to the umbrella agreement establish in the New Minute
or international regulation. In fact, each subregion has "unique

---

[1]Original Text: *"Tratados internacionales. Son parte integrante de la ley suprema
de la unión y se ubican jerárquicamente por encima de las leyes generales,
federales y locales. Interpretación del artículo 133 constitucional."* Suprema Corte
de Justicia de la Nación, Tesis: P. IX/2007, Seminario Judicial de la Federación
y su Gaceta XXV, Abril de 2007, p. 6 Registro No. 172650.

geographic, hydrogeological, climatic and environmental idiosyncrasies of the local aquifer, responsive to local community concerns, and reflective of the values of stakeholders on both sides of the border locally-specific-tailored" (Eckstein, 2013). Because of these individuals and local characteristics, including the connectivity with surface water and groundwater, as well as between different aquifers, specific policies for each subregion will regulate and address water allocation.

The water bank is the primary institution as the vehicle used to guarantee equitable and reasonable water usage, and to ensure an ecological flow level that protects the environment and allocates water efficiently under a new water right based on uses. Water banking is a mechanism that encourages water allocation in conjunctive use through the development of a new type of water right. The water bank will provide a transition from a queuing allocation system to a trading system. This scenario provides cooperation and incentive to lower transaction costs and encourages market activity. Moreover, a water bank can regulate social and environmental impact at the local and international levels. Water banking is attractive as it can allow water to be set aside to ensure ecological flows as part of the trading process.

In addition, water use may decrease with this reform, which allows trading and transition from average to marginal cost pricing (Zilberman and Schoengold, 2005). For example, the implementation of water trading among cotton growers in the Central Valley of California reduced field level water by more than 25% while maintaining the same level of aggregate profits (Zilberman and Schoengold, 2005).

Furthermore, water banks will be used as incentives for pollution control where water quality standards will establish the type of use. Therefore, good water quality would provide water supply for all uses. Moreover, water banks can encourage flexibility, bringing about better recognition of water's value, and promoting incentives for efficient water usage (Dinar and Letey, 1991).

One of the main problems with a water bank is its impact on third parties. For example, when there are transfers of water from agriculture to urban use, there may be a reduction in return flows, which may affect the environment and other users (Dinar and Letey, 1991). The disadvantage of the transition from a queuing system (prior appropriation), or others such as a riparian or a civil system, to water trading is that the cost can be higher if the original water rights (OWRs) are not clearly defined. In addition, the cost increases when the potential framework lacks mechanisms to facilitate and monitor trades (Zilberman and Schoengold, 2005). The establishment of an international water bank along the US–Mexico border will protect each individual and third party establishing homogeneous water rights in conjunctive use for surface water and groundwater based on uses (Milanés-Murcia, 2013). The water bank will take into account the water right in the trading system, where they are developed according to the specific environmental, social, and economic circumstances for each subregion, transboundary basin, and fossil aquifer.

The laws of both countries, the United States and Mexico, allow water banking as a mechanism to allocate water and protect third parties (Secretaria de Medio Ambiente, 2011; "Banking," 1992). This proves their preference for a successful implementation of an international water bank as the instrument to allocate water along the US–Mexico border region.

Moreover, international water banks by basin will regulate the correct distribution in conjunctive use of groundwater with surface water thus allowing farmers to obtain the maximum profit from their right to use water. This is especially important during times of drought when individuals can be financially compensated by transferring their right to use water to the bank. An example at the local level of this successful instrument is the 1991 California Water Bank where the State of California was the predominant broker for water trades. One of the main goals of this water bank was the protection of fish and wildlife and their habitat. DWR and the Department of Fish and Game worked to reduce the impact of drought in the wildlife. These efforts resulted in modifications to California State Water Project operation and water bank transfers. (California Department of Water Resources [DWR],

1991) Another example of water bank is the groundwater banking and the conjunctive management of groundwater and surface water in the upper Snake River of Idaho, which revealed that "ground-water banking has the potential to reduce conflict and improve allocation of scarce water resources" (Contor, 2009).

Furthermore, water planning through a water bank can be a powerful instrument to promote changes in water usage, especially because of the yearly allocation decisions based on prior water usage. Water in conjunctive use should be allocated according to the needs and availability for each year, thus allowing the implementation of reasonable and equitable use of water yearly. A plan may determine which pool is filled first with the available water. In general, the first pool to fill is river operation, which may include environmental water; without this pool, the entire system might not be operable (NWI, 2004). Therefore, once the environmental protection is guaranteed the other needs of the basin will be covered.

In Australia, for example, the Basin states and the Commonwealth agreed to the Water Amendment Act 2008 as an addition to the Water Act (Australia Water Act, 2007) (Australia Water Amendment Act, 2008). The states agreed to give away constitutional powers, especially those needed to carry out water resource planning for the Murray-Darling Basin, to the Commonwealth via the Authority. The main purpose of this Amendment was to use planning and markets to meet environmental and economic goals. The Water Act calls for the establishment of "environmentally sustainable limits" on water withdrawal called sustainable diversion limits, which implement a broad rebalancing of water between consumptive and environmental uses (Pilz, 2010).

5.3.2. *"Basin" in the Sense of "Watercourse"*

The delimitation of the US–Mexico border region does not follow the delimitation of the border region according to Article 4 of the La Paz agreement. La Paz agreement establishes the jurisdiction of the treaty, defining the border region as the area situated 100 km on either side of the inland and maritime boundaries between the parties (La Paz, 1983). The approach in this chapter is based on the basin.where the delimitation of the US–Mexico border region is established according to Article 2 of the 1997 UN Watercourses Convention, defining "watercourse [as] a system of surface waters and groundwater constituting by virtue of their physical relationship a unitary whole and normally flowing into a common terminus" (UN Convention, 1997).[2] The application of this provision implies that the management is by basin. This means that when a basin is shared by two or more countries, the whole basin is considered the border region because the management of the basin in one country can directly affect the whole basin and therefore all riparian countries. This approach intent to provide cooperation, reasonable, and equitable use, avoiding any harm among the different countries sharing the basin. The basin includes surface water and groundwater interconnected. The hydrological delimitation of each transboundary basin establishes the jurisdiction of the joint management institutions, which addresses each individual basin as a whole where specific policies at the basin and subregional level are developed based on the new legal and institutional regulation. This approach could avoid future conflicts and guarantee the sustainable use of aquifers connected with surface water resources, as well as potential fossil aquifers, located in the border region.

---

[2]The UN Watercourses Convention 1997 is used as a model in this research. Although nor Mexico neither United States are parties to this Convention, both countries are binding by the international principles codified in the Convention (Statute of the International Law Commission, Art. 1(1) UN Doc. A/CN.4/4/Rev.2, 1982). The Convention has significant bearing upon controversies between states. Moreover, the fact that the 1997 Convention entered into force makes it applicable worldwide as the International Court of Justice has done in several occasions such as in *The Gabčíkovo-Nagymaros Project case*. In addition, the Convention "was negotiated in a forum in which virtually any interested state could participate, and therefore reflects the views of the international community on the subject. The Convention was adopted by a weighty majority of countries, with only three negative votes, indicating broad agreement in the international community on the general principles governing the non-navigational uses of international watercourses" (McCaffrey, 2007).

The new legal framework does not consider surface or ground-water but simply water of the basin as a "unitary whole" (UN Convention, 1997). In addition, the rights are not established according to the origin of the source, surface water or groundwater, but are delimited based on uses. Users will have the possibility to obtain their water from the closest source independently of whether this is surface water or groundwater, because interconnection between surface water and groundwater allows to use the concept of water of the whole basin, without distinguishing between surface water and groundwater. When water is interconnected, it moves from surface to ground and from ground to surface (Restatement of Torts, 1939) and therefore the sense of possession or property is difficult to apply. However, the concept of use is more applicable based on the availability of water each hydrological year. In this scenario, a farmer can use a specific amount of water, which will be surface water interconnected with groundwater, when the type of use and the availability of the resource for that year are clear and determined. The hydrological analysis of the entire basin and its interconnectivity determines the possibilities for using more or less water during that year without the classification of surface water or groundwater, but simply water of the basin.

The terminology "surface water right" or "groundwater right" does not apply to this legal framework, where the classification of the source is not established by surface or ground but by the interconnectivity between both sources. This element of interconnectivity is the key to determine the type of basin, which can be fossil or subject to conjunctive management. Therefore, the type of water use for each user will be based on their needs and the availability of water in the basin as a whole, surface water and groundwater, in one unique packet, or just a fossil aquifer in another. In the case of fossil aquifers, the term "basin" refers to the specific hydrological delimitation of the aquifer. Therefore, specific regulations and institutions for each type of basin are developed in this new legal framework that is presented as follows. (See the Annex).

The principles of international water law and an international institution such as the IBWC are essential for implementing this new legal and institutional framework along the US–Mexico border. The general principles of international water law are (i) equitable and reasonable utilization and participation; (ii) factors relevant to equitable and reasonable utilization that are essential to develop an allocation system based on uses; (iii) the obligation not to cause significant harm, which is directly connected to the principle of equitable and reasonable utilization, a principle that minimizes the possibilities of causing harm and demonstrates the interrelationship of the two principles in water management; (iv) general obligation to cooperate; and (v) regular exchange of data and information, which flows from the obligation to cooperate (UN Convention, 1997).

5.3.3. *Proposed Institutional Framework*

A new legal international regulation focusing on joint management institutions for each basin can provide the solution for managing groundwater along the US–Mexico border. This solution could avoid future conflicts and guarantee the sustainable use of aquifers connected with surface water, as well as fossil aquifers, located on the border. An important main limitation is the uncertainty in evaluating and monitoring the quantity and quality of groundwater, which is made especially problematic due to unknown underground water transport communicating aquifers that appear to be independent from each other (US EPA, 2005). Under this proposed legal and institutional framework, special joint management institutions for each basin would be able to obtain accurate data from both countries. The data obtained would provide the necessary information about water quality and quantity to determine the uses and the environmental needs in the basin.

Joint management institutions are flexible instruments able to implement an agreement. When regulations are strict and rigid, implementation is inefficient. In this regard, article 24 of the 1997 UN Convention envisions joint management mechanisms to provide the implementation of any plans adopted, as well as to promote the rational and optimal utilization, protection, and control of the watercourse, or basin. Article 7 of the ILC's 2008 Draft Articles also emphasizes the significance of joint mechanisms to achieve goals such as "sustainable development, mutual benefit, [...] equitable and reasonable utilization and appropriate protection of their transboundary aquifers or aquifer systems." (ILC, 2008).

In order to achieve those goals, this section presents the proposal of a model institutional framework, which suggests a potential solution to managing water resources in the US–Mexico border region. The joint management institution establishes the most appropriate mechanism for allocating water as well as determining the type of water transfers, either interbasin or intrabasin. This body will look at each riparian state and would determine the allocation of water according to the needs and development of the regions. The joint management body will have the authority to control, effectively implement, and prevent any activity against the health of the basin. It will be assisted by other institutions such as a "compliance mechanism." (ILC, 2008) This will be a state-to-state process. On a more practical level, the regulation (Minute) establishing the institution could require each state in Mexico and the United States to enforce compliance by users by having the regulation (Minute) be in accordance with their own national laws. This will allow monitoring control, ensuring the correct allocation of groundwater as well as maintaining good water quality.

In a transboundary basin legal framework, the federal governments will be seen as insurance that will provide security to the local parties in case of a conflict unable to be resolved by the parties or the joint body. Article 33 of the UN 1997 Convention provides a very useful framework for the settlement of disputes.

In addition, technical support institutions will provide scientific data about the basin. The water bank is considered the key institution and mechanism to provide allocation at the basin and subregional levels through uses.

5.3.3.1. *Institutional structure*

A joint management body will be established to manage each basin reporting to the IBWC. The Main Basin Institution will be the basin authority managing and controlling the entire basin and determining the needs of each riparian state along the basin under the supervision of the IBWC. This joint management body and specially the Main Basin Institution will study all issues and tries to provide solutions for conjunctive use of surface water and groundwater with representatives of each riparian state and the public. Their participation will be in public meetings and hearings. Following is the institutional framework at the different levels of government: International, Basin, Subregional or Subbasin, and Watershed levels, where cooperation and exchange of data and information among all institutions along the basin are essential in this institutional framework. In this regard the IBWC plays an important role having authority over other institutions and can request information at any time (Milanés-Murcia, 2013).

5.3.3.2. *International*

5.3.3.2.1. IBWC

The main institution governing water along the US–Mexico border is the IBWC, which under this new legal institutional framework will have authority to ensure the correct allocation for each basin as well as to maintain good water quality. The IBWC will be able to declare groundwater and surface water as "critical areas when water quantity is threatened by uncontrolled withdrawals or water quality is jeopardized." (Hayton and Utton, 1989) The IBWC is the main institution with competence to reallocate water uses according to recommendations from the water bank. This institution will approve the Charter, which is the regulation policy of each water bank. In addition, the IBWC will play an essential role in ensuring the conjunctive use of surface and groundwater considered as one unique source. Moreover, the IBWC will determine the potential number of fossil transboundary aquifers located in the border area. However, direct regulation of fossil aquifers is to be carried out by a technical institution under the IBWC.

5.3.3.2.2. Fact-Finding Commission

The Fact-Finding Commission is the technical institution under the IBWC. It provides solutions to hydrological issues and establishes the method to assess each basin in order to determine the connectivity of surface and groundwater. It also determines the water balance for each basin and provides annual information related to the water availability for each year.

5.3.3.3. *Basin*

5.3.3.3.1. Main Basin Institution

An individual institution by basin, known as the Main Basin Institution, controls and addresses the different issues and will be able to provide solutions at the basin-wide level and cooperate with other subbasins institutions and lower watersheds institutions. This Main Basin Institution will have to report to the IBWC, thus ensuring adequate allocation and protection of water quality. A Main Basin Institution will be established for each basin and fossil aquifer.

The Main Basin Institution will determine water availability in the basin each hydrological year, taking into account interconnected surface water and groundwater. Fact-Finding Commission and the Main Basin Institution will cooperate on this aspect. Where the connectivity of surface water and groundwater will determine the level of water availability in the basin. In those cases where groundwater does not fully follow a particular river basin, it is to be identified and assigned to the nearest or most appropriate river basin by recharge of the aquifer. This information can be used to determine the uses and at the same time maintain the minimum ecological stream flow in the basin each year.

5.3.3.3.2. Water Quality Commission and Water Quantity Commission to Inform the Main Basin Institution

Two committees of the Main Basin Institution, one for water quality and the other for water quantity, will address the needs for each basin. They will work in cooperation with the Fact-Finding Commission. These Committees will inform the Main Basin Institution, which will have the authority to establish priorities of use during drought time as well as to regulate each use. In addition, these committees will have delegated committees at the subregional level in direct cooperation with the wWater bBank in order to inform about the quality and quantity.

(i) Water Quantity Commission at the Basin level

The Water Quantity Committee will have as its main priority to ensure minimum stream flow and provide sustainable development in the use of water according to the availability for each hydrological year and to the water quality standards criteria, which may establish a specific quantity of water to ensure good water quality. This institution controls water availability by basin and works directly with the fact-finding commission and the IBWC. Its main goal is promoting the development of a common vision for each basin where surface and groundwater are treated as a single source. At this level, the basin is considered as a "unitary system of surface water and groundwater" (UN Convention, 1997). It provides a better understanding of the water-related resources, and collaborates with subregional and watershed level institutions in order to provide information, and cooperation.

(ii) Water Quality Commission at the Basin level

The Water Quality Committee would establish the most appropriate water quality standards for each basin. The Water Quality Commission at the basin level will strengthen the capacity of each subregional water quality commission. It will apply the water quality standards and criteria for water quality. The Commission will establish the ecological criteria to protect habitats along the basin based on information from each subregion water quality commission. These actions will protect surface water and underground water environment in each basin having a broader environmental perspective. In addition, it will establish the development of outreach and cooperation from the basin level to the local watershed level.

5.3.3.3.3. Water Allocation Institution (Water Bank)

Water bank means a governmental institution at the basin and subregional level that allocate water to different sectors along the basin. At the basin level, the water bank is a binational governmental institution. Subregional Water Banks collaborate with the Main Water Bank Institution. The water bank at this level "Main Water Bank Basin Institution" is composed of a Watermaster and one representative of each Subregion water bank in the basin, as well as an expert scientific team.

The water bank will be the institution directly transferring the water rights according to the use of water always following the recommendations established by both committees and by the Main Basin Institution under the direct supervision of the IBWC, in order to avoid any damage. The water bank will guarantee potable water and sanitation as well as environmental uses, and will protect current uses. The water bank as institution established at different levels of government will promote cooperation and mediation among them. The water bank will allocate water rights based on use according to the amount of available water in each hydrological year. In addition, the water bank: (i) will lease water from water rights that have been deposited in the bank, (ii) will provide safe deposit accounts, (iii) will buy water rights to be leased by the water bank, and (iv) will promote conservation programs. Users can only obtain additional water through the water bank. It is not possible to transfer water rights directly among users, only it is possible to transfer water rights through the water bank.

5.3.3.4. *Subregional or subbasin level*

Each basin will be divided into hydrologic units known as sub-regions. The subregions will be also divided into watersheds. For purposes of this institutional analysis, the RG Basin is used as an example. See Figs. 5.1 and 5.2, which illustrate how a basin will be divided institutionally according to hydrologic units. These hydrologic units will establish the jurisdiction of each institution. At the regional level, each subregion will have an institution regulating surface water and groundwater in conjunctive use. This provides a regional management mechanism that applies the subsidiary principle with the role of developing policies for each subregion according to the local needs implementing the new regulation, where

Figure 5.1: Subregions in the RG Basin.
Source: Sandoval Solis (2011).

they will follow the directives from the Main Basin Institution in order to avoid damage to the basin. In addition, each subregion encompasses a conservation area that will follow a comprehensive management plan.

Figure 5.2: Watersheds in the RG Basin.
Source: Sandoval Solis (2011).

(i) Water Quantity Commission Subregional level.

Each Water Quantity Commission at the Subregional level will work in direct cooperation with the Water Quality and Quantity Commission at the Basin level and inform them of the uses and amounts of water deposits into the bank each year and working directly with the Water Bank Allocation Institution at the Subregional level.

(ii) Water Quality Commission Subregional level.

Each water quality commission at the subregional level will work in direct cooperation with the water quality and quantity commission at the basin level. A Water Quality Commission at the Subregional level will build local capacity by ensuring, through monitoring, a good quality of water for each specific use.

(iii) Water Bank Subregional level.

Subregional water bank is an institution dependent on the Main Water Bank Institution. Its function is to control the appropriate use of each *water use right*, which is presented as follows, and to allocate these rights according to the water availability in the basin. This institution at the subregional level shall provide the legal and institutional framework for local communities, where specific policies will be developed. The Water Bank at the Subregional level will collaborate with other institutions in order to exchange data and information. At the Subregional level, each Water Bank will have a Charter, which will be developed according to information from other basin and subregional institutions along the basin. The Charter will be approved by the Main Water Bank Basin Institution and by the IBWC.

5.3.3.5.   *Watershed*

At a third stage, (Fig. 5.2) watershed institutions will ensure the correct use of water including conjunctive use of surface water and groundwater use ensuring the implementation of the legislation at the local level. The watershed institutions will inform users of their closest point of water diversion and the availability for their use each hydrological year. Local institutions as compliance mechanisms are responsible for the implementation of this legal framework.

The institution at the watershed level will ensure the implementation of the water bank through state and county mechanisms and guarantee the protection of water quality through periodical assessment. In addition, the Watershed Institution will establish the conditions for the resolution of specific watershed-related issues. These agencies can provide education about this new legal and

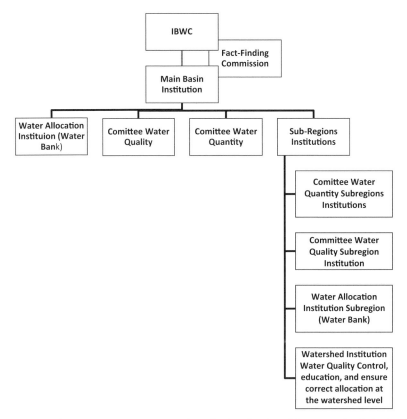

Figure 5.3: An organogram representing the institutional framework of the basin institutions.

Source Author's elaboration.

institutional framework and especially about the water bank mechanism. Figure 5.3 presents an organogram representing this institutional framework. The institutional framework for fossil aquifers would have the same structure for each fossil basin.

The key element of this institutional framework is the water bank, which is a binational intergovernmental institution at the basin and subregional (subbasin) levels. The priorities of allocations established by the water bank in this framework are (i) environmental use, (ii) human consumption, (iii) domestic and municipal uses, and (iv) conservation, agriculture and grazing. The environment has the highest priority because when the environment is protected water for human beings will be in good quality. Environmental use specifically refers to ecological flow levels, ecological services, habitats, and water quality standards able to protect water quality along the basin. The terms established in Article 3 of the 1944 Treaty are respected in the allocation process. Following priorities to the above-mentioned allocations include electric power, other industrial uses, navigation, recreation, fishing and hunting, and any other beneficial uses, which may be determined by both countries through the institutional framework.

5.4. Water Rights Arrangements to Manage Water along the US–Mexico Border

"A water right is a collectively recognized access to water resources under specific conditions defined in the right" (Colby and Bush, 1987). Examples of such conditions include location and purpose of use, quantity of withdrawals, and point of diversion.

5.4.1. *Reasons for a New Water Right in Water Transfer on the US–Mexico Border*

One of the main reasons to develop a new type of water right is that water scarcity is not an issue in the public's mind in the United States (Pilz, 2010). Currently, there is a variety of barriers in current US water policy, including a strong constitutional protection against government interference with private property rights. Among these barriers, the different state and federal water agencies have conflicting and overlapping authorities that increase the difficulties for cooperation. Exec. Order No. 12,630,53 FR 8859, 3 CFR, 1988 Comp., p. 554 sets that

> "The Fifth Amendment of the United States Constitution provides that private property shall not be taken for public use without just compensation. Government historically has used the formal exercise of the power of eminent domain, which provides orderly processes for paying just compensation, to acquire private property for public use."

A complex water law and regulation system governs water uses, including several doctrines such as the prior appropriation in the western United States (Gerlak and Heikkila, 2007; US EPA, 2005). This doctrine has been considered to "lock[s] too much water into inefficient agricultural uses and does not make enough water available for growing cities and ecosystem restoration" (Tarlock, 2001). The concept of a property right in water is especially established in the western United States. In a water market, the value of a water right has been generally considered relative to the benefits associated with owning the right and the level of protection from impairment by others (Colby and Bush, 1987). If water is not considered a property and is approached as a public good, where the right is established by use, it is more likely to face an efficient allocation according to each local circumstance. At the same time, the level of protection on use will be guaranteed if a water bank can reasonably and equitably allocate waters of the basin among different users each hydrological year while protecting third parties.

It is clear that a reform that develops a new type of public water right would be very difficult to implement in the United States. However, the development of a new US–Mexico water right for the border region could provide a unique system of water allocation based on uses, treating groundwater and surface water as one source in a water bank allocation system. This will provide security in the context of climate change, where the water bank as main institution will ensure the sustainability of water resources.

It is very difficult to efficiently allocate water because it is a very mobile resource, which flows, evapotranspires, and seeps. According to Restatement of Torts, Chap. 41, topic 3, Analysis, at 350 (1979):

> "Water, like air and light, is a fugitive, wandering thing, flowing over and through land, but seldom remaining for any length of time in one place or within the confines of any one person's possession. One's dominion over it while it is upon his land is temporary, and since it ordinarily flows onto the lands of other persons, it is limited in quantity, and a substantial use of it by one may prevent others from having it. The rights and privileges of individual users are subject to greater limitation out of regard for the common interests of all."

This natural feature makes this resource difficult to define and measure property rights in water. Water quantity as well as water quality can vary from one year to another. In addition, the diversity of uses to which water can be put in connection with its mobility generates interdependencies among water users. For example, irrigation is an offstream use that generates return flows used by downstream users. This aspect must be taken into account when water transfers are established in the area. Transfers of water can modify return flows and affect water availability for downstream users. Instream values that must be guaranteed include ecological services, habitats, water quality, wildlife protection, and aesthetics. When water is diverted there may be conflict between instream values and offstream water values (Colby and Bush, 1987). A solution for this potential conflict would be to establish priorities in case of drought and always ensure a minimum stream flow capable of protecting and guaranteeing the highest instream values. In this regard, the water bank has the authority to modify uses in case of drought and to store any excess of water in aquifers designed for this purpose promoting conservation practices.

A situation that can create an inefficient water transfer occurs when one stakeholder such as a city obtains the instream use for hydropower but does not take into account other prior instream uses such as recreation, which does not obtain compensation for this water transfer. This lack of compensation creates an instability that can damage other users. The water bank would be the ideal institution to reconcile all type of uses and users, while protecting third parties and guaranteeing the most appropriate compensation for the transfer.

A new *water use right* will be based on uses, where the right to water is ranked by users according to its use and value. This promotes conservation because otherwise, whenever a user has more water available than is needed, the water will be put to a lower value use, even though others would have a higher value or priority. This phenomenon is called diminishing marginal utility (Colby and Bush, 1987). For example, in domestic water use, water for drinking and cooking have the highest value and priority, while water for lawn-sprinkling or washing cars are at a lower usage value. In general, urban use has a higher value for the first units of water used than agricultural usage does for the same initial quantity of water. However, in the agricultural case, farmers will apply the water first to crops with the highest value. Using this theory, a water right based on use and value will promote conservation practices.

5.4.2. *Structure of a New Water Right Based on Uses*

This section proposes a potential solution to manage different water uses. It provides the analysis of the development of a new water right for the US–Mexico border region that will provide a unique system of water allocation based on uses. It treats groundwater and surface water as one source thorough one Allocation Institution (water bank), which allocates *water use rights* according to the water availability each hydrological year (Milanés-Murcia, 2013).

Each of the different types of water rights along the US–Mexico border region are transformed into *water use units* (WUU), which will be included in the *water use rights* where there is no difference among surface water and groundwater. This provides a homogenous system that will bring security when establishing water transfers because the individual will always have access to water, which can be surface water, groundwater or both depending on the availability along the basin.

5.4.3. *Bankable Water Rights*

Water rights are addressed in two different stages: the first stage addresses different types of water rights from the perspective of each jurisdiction deposited in the Allocation Institution (water bank). The second stage, establishes a transition from the OWR in each region to WUU, which will be transformed into *water use rights*. The WUU of a basin have the same water quantity, the variable factor is the quality, which will be established according to the use. The use of each *water use right* will establish the value for each WUU and which one has the highest value. For example, some domestic uses require higher water quality than others. Cooking requires higher water quality than other domestic uses such as washing a car or watering the garden.

Each use will have a specific amount of WUU depending on the water availability in the basin, taking into consideration the instream flow levels and environmental needs. The WUU can be composed of surface water and/or groundwater in conjunctive use, as water of the specific watershed, subregion and basin including the geographical origin. In addition, WUU will indicate the origin according to the water distribution under the 1994 Treaty, the 1906 Convention, and the new legal framework (minute, agreement). Only fossil aquifers will have a special type of *fossil* WUU to be included in specific water right defined as a *fossil water use right*. This system will be used for all transboundary basins throughout each country and state.

When the OWR is deposited in the water bank, the OWR is transformed into several WUU.

The units are classified for uses depending on the quality, availability, and environmental conditions in the basin.

Examples from the same basin:

- *Water use right for domestic human use in one year*
- *Water use right for irrigation of alfalfa one year*

WUU a	WUU a	WUU a
WUU b	*WUU b*	*WUU b*	*WUU b*

The first example is *water use right for domestic human use in one year*, which is water for human consumption, for a specific period of time. This *water use right* is composed of three WUU, where (a) is the specific type of water quality for that specific use (domestic use) with a specific category human use. Similarly, the second example, *water use right for irrigation of alfalfa one year* shows the use of water for irrigation of alfalfa and for one year and is composed of four WUU, where (b) is the type of water quality for this specific type of irrigation use with the specific crop category — alfalfa.

There will be no difference among riparian rights, prior appropriation or other types of water rights. The priority is based on uses, and once the institutional legal framework is implemented, all OWRs will be treated equally under the same conditions, obligations, and protections. This may cause irregularities if the OWR gave more benefits than the new *water use right*, but in this situation, monetary compensation can provide an effective solution to avoid uncertainty. Under this new concept, a water right such as a riparian right loses its characteristics and is transformed into the new WUU, which are determined according to water availability for each hydrological year and the water quality. Senior water right holders will obtain higher benefits than they would by keeping the OWR. Once the OWR is transformed into WUU, there is no possibility to revert to the OWR. However, by having had an original senior water right, the original owner would have the privilege of priority to obtain additional *water use rights* at a lower price for domestic and irrigation uses plus the compensation of depositing the senior water right into the water bank.

The main challenge is to combine surface water rights and groundwater rights located in different jurisdictions and develop a water trading system. The water trading system must take into account the different users and sectors and must provide legal and hydrological security as well as flexibility. The holder of the water right needs security and certainty of water availability or compensation in the case of changing of use in the water trading system. The type of source can create risk and insecurity; for example, intermittent streams are more uncertain than other sources such as aquifers. The development of a unique *water use right* as part of the basin without taking into account the source, groundwater or surface water, can guarantee the use of water with independency of the source, and always provide security and flexibility allowing changing the location, timing, and purpose of use. This can ensure water for different uses through the control of the water bank.

The Allocating Institution (water bank) is the institution assigning WUU to each *water use right*. The water bank follows the recommendations of the Water Quality Committee, Water Quantity

Committee, and Main Water Basin in order to determine the number of WUU, and therefore the number of *water use rights* for each year according to the water availability, the use and the water quality in the basin. The water bank is the only institution with the availability to transfer WUU and allocate *water use rights*. In addition, the water bank will be able to transfer WUU to another water bank located in a different basin when there is surplus in the basin of origin. There is not possibility to transfer WUU nor *water use rights* among users.

In order to obtain *water use rights* from the water bank, the bank will establish the price. The price of water must be established according to the use and value in each basin. In addition, the private sector cannot strategically affect the price. The price won't be affected in drought conditions. The price will be constant and won't change. The reallocation will be more restrictive, thus allowing modification of uses to primary uses, that is, domestic uses and environmental uses, which shall be guaranteed at all times. In addition, special privileges according to the economic needs of each individual will be evaluated by the Water Bank, which would reduce the price or set a free *water use right* in order to guarantee the human right to water and uses already established in the basin. Profits from the Water Bank will be used to improve infrastructure, especially on irrigation areas. Moreover, economic agents must have full access to all information about the legal and hydrologic characteristics of each basin.

The quantity of water in each hydrological year and the water quality of the basin will establish the uses of the basin. According to this, the Water Bank will establish the amount and type of *water use rights* each year. All individuals must know the privileges and restrictions associated with a *water use right* and the penalties for violation. The basic privilege is the right to use a specific amount of water during a specific time for a specific type of use. The main restriction is to use water inadequately or inappropriately to the use established in the *water use right*, so that the use could causes harm to others. Therefore, when water is used for a purpose different than the one designated in the *water use right*, there will be a violation.

A period of transition will be established to allow people get information about this new system before implementing the new regulation "*Vacatio legisis.*" The deposit of OWR will be initially voluntary. The transfer of OWRs to WUU into the Water Bank would be voluntary for a period of 15 years. This time would allow the population to understand the new system and get used to it. After this time, it will be enforced and mandatory. All OWRs must be transformed into WUU in the Water Bank, which will allocate water taking into account water availability by basin, and based on the uses and needs of users.

5.5.   Lower RG Valley

The LRGV is the subregion below Falcon International Reservoir to the Gulf of Mexico; it is of significant importance because the largest water users from the United States and Mexico are located in this region (Chowdhury and Mace, 2007). In addition, the environment depends on water management in this area. The RG discharges its water into the Gulf of Mexico; it provides nutrients required to preserve the estuarine ecosystem at the mouth of the river (Chowdhury and Mace, 2007). Water resources in the LRGV are primarily limited to the RG, which are scarce during severe droughts. This area has been selected as a case study because of the availability of surface water and groundwater data in both countries (Chowdhury and Mace, 2007; Moro, 2006).

A hydrologic analysis along the LRGV demonstrates the connectivity of surface water and groundwater in the region and therefore the applicability of the new legal and institutional framework, in establishing a water bank able to allocate surface water and groundwater as a unique source (Milanés-Murcia, 2013).

This new legal approach at the subregional level shows that there can be an improvement in water allocation from reservoirs and aquifers while guaranteeing sustainable environmental flows in the LRGV. Results from the water planning model for the RG demonstrate that the water bank policy is capable of improving water supply for agriculture, municipal water users, water conservation, and environmental protection. In addition, the economic benefits of the water bank scenario increase for both countries. In conclusion, a water bank approach involving conjunctive use of surface and groundwater will make possible to improve water use for the agricultural sector, while at the same time delivering water for the environmental requirements and securing water for municipal use.

5.6. Conclusion

This new proposed international legal and institutional framework presents a solution to manage groundwater along the US–Mexico border region. In addition, specific policies based on the international framework would provide flexibility for each subregion as well as security for stakeholders and protection for the environment. This new regulation was simulated with a specific policy in a subregion, the LRGV, where the results are very positive. Even if this new approach is different at first; the reality is that the current management of groundwater along the US–Mexico border is not working. Therefore, a new regulation adapted to the current circumstances of climate change and population growth must be applied.

The development of a binational water bank is the best potential solution to allocate water along the US–Mexico border. Water banks have been demonstrated to be an effective and efficient mechanism to encourge transfers and promote conservation. The success of this tool is due to the establishment of a capable and flexible legal framework where an institution has authority to regulate based on social, physical, and economic circumtances as well as setting a fixed price that avoids uncertainty and risk. In addition, banks are more politically accepted than private markets. Both the United States and Mexico have developed water banks to allocate their water resources. This shows the potential willingness to agree to a binational water bank at some point in the future.

In addition, this legal and institutional framework was presented to the IBWC, which considered it a good solution to allocate groundwater and solve potential conflicts along the border region. The fact that this institutional framework gives authority to the

IBWC to control the groundwater allocation was considered by them to be an important step forward to achieve a sustainable development along the border.

At the international level, the water bank approach is considered a very good solution to protect the environment and especially to implement the human right to water to local communities in the irrigation sector, where there are not clear and defined water rights. The new concept of *water use right* is considered a mechanism to provide homogenuos water right and security among stakeholders.

References

Aust, A (2007). *Modern Treaty Law and Practice.* 2nd ed. Cambridge: Cambridge University Press.

Australia Water Act (2007). Act No. 137. Retrieved from https://www. comlaw. gov.au/Series/C2007A00137 [8 May, 2010].

Australia Water Amendment Act (2008). Act No. 139 of 2008. Retrieved from https://www.comlaw.gov.au/Details/C2008A00139 [15 May 2010].

California Department of Water Resources [DWR] (1991). The 1991 drought water bank. Retrieved from http://www.waterboards.ca.gov/waterrights/water_issues/programs/hearings/usbr_dwr/docs/exhibits/cwin1e.pdf [13 June 2010].

Chowdhury, AH and RE Mace (June 2007). *Groundwater Resource Evaluation and Availability Model of the Gulf Coast Aquifer in the Lower Rio Grande Valley of Texas.* Texas Water Development Board Report 368.

Colby, SB and DB Bush (1987). *Water Markets in Theory and Practice Market Transfers, Water Values, and Public Policy.* Studies in Water Policy and Management, No. 12. Boulder and London: Westview Press.

Contor, BA (August 2009). *Groundwater Banking and the Conjunctive Management of Groundwater and Surface Water in the Upper Snake River Basin of Idaho.* Idaho: Idaho Water Resources Research Institute. Retrieved from https://www.uidaho.edu/~/media/UIdaho-Responsive/Files/research/IWRRI/publications/IWRRI_200906_GW_Banking_20090817.ashx [26 April 2016].

Convention providing for the Equitable Distribution of the Waters of the Rio Grande for Irrigation Purposes, U.S.-Mexico [Convention] (1906). 34 Stat. 2953; TS 455; 9 Bevans 924. Retrieved from http://www.ibwc.state.gov/ [27 March 2014].

Dinar, A and J Letey (1991). Agricultural water marketing, allocative efficiency, and drainage reduction. *Journal of Environmental Economics and Management*, 20, 210–223.

Eckstein, GE (2013). Rethinking transboundary ground water resources management: A local approach along the Mexico-U.S. border. *Georgetown International Environmental Law Review*, 25, 95–123.

Gerlak, AK and T Heikkila (2007). Collaboration and Institutional Endurance in US Water Policy, PSOnline www.apsanet.org. Retrieved from http://water.columbia.edu/files/2011/11/Heikkila2007Collaboration. pdf [11 March 2011].

Hayton, RD and A Utton (1989). Transboundary groundwaters: The Bellagio draft treaty. *Summer Natural Resources Journal*, 29, 663–680.

Howe, CW and DJ Goodman (1995). Resolving water transfer conflicts through changes in water market process. In: A Dinar and ET Loehman (eds.) *Water Quantity/Quality Management and Conflict Resolution, Institutions, Processes, and Economic Analyses*, Westport Preager, pp. 119–129.

Intergovernmental Agreement on a National Water Initiative Between the Commonwealth of Australia and the Government of New South Wales, Victoria, Queensland, South Australia, the Australian Capital Territory and the Northern Territory [NWI], (June 2004). Retrieved from www.nwc.gov.au/resources/documents/Intergovernmetal-Agreement-on-a-national-water-initiative.pdf [7 May 2010].

International Boundary and Water Commission [IBWC] (30 August 1973). Minute N. 242 of the: Permanent and Definite Solution to the International Problem of the Salinity of the Colorado River, U.S.-Mexico. para. 6, 24 U.S.T. p. 1968, T.I.A.S. No. 7708, 12 ILM 1105 (1973). Retrieved from the IBWC website, http://www.ibwc.state.gov [4 May 2014].

International Boundary and Water Commission (1975). Minute No. 242: Permanent and definitive solution to the international problem of the salinity of the Colorado River.*Natural Resources Journal*, 15(2), 2–9.

International Boundary and Water Commission (2012). Mission and operations specifically addresses diversion dams and related structures in El Paso area to Fort Quitman. Retrieved from http://www.ibwc.gov/Mission_Operations/Diversion_Dams.html [12 May 2012].

International Boundary and Water Commission (5 October 2015). Minute N. 320: General framework for binational cooperation on transboundary issues in the Tijuana River basin. Tijuana, Baja California. Retrieved from http://www.ibwc.state.gov/Files/Minutes/Minute_320. pdf [12 December 2015].

International Boundary and Water Commission (2016). The international boundary and water commission — Its mission, organization and procedures for solution of boundary and water problems. Retrieved from http://www.ibwc.state.gov/About_Us/About_Us.html [10 March 2016].

International Law Commission of the United Nations [ILC] (1994). Report on the Work of its Forty-sixth Session, Resolution on Confined Transboundary Groundwater Y.B. International Law Commission, vol. 2, pt. 2, p. 135. UN Doc. A/49/10.

International Law Commission of the United Nations (2008). Report on the Work of its Sixtieth Session, UN GAOR, 63d Sess., Supp. No. 10, at 19, UN Doc. A/63/10 (2008).Retrieved from http://www.un.org/law/ilc/ [8 May 2012].

La Paz (1983). La Paz Agreement between the United States of America and the United Mexican States on Cooperation for the Protection and Improvement of the Environment in the Border Area [La Paz]. August 14, 1983 T.I.A.S. No. 10827, 35 U.S.T. 2916, 1983 WL 472049. U.S. Retrieved from IBWC, http://www.ibwc.state.gov/Files/US-Mx_Boundary_Map.pdf [14 November 2013].

Le Quesne, T, G Pegram, and C Von Der Heyden (2007). *Allocating Scarce Water a Primer on Water Allocation, Water Rights and Water Market.* WWF Water Security Series 1, at 32 April 2007.

McCaffrey, SC (2007) (2nd edition). *The Law of International Watercourses 496.* The Oxford International Law Library.

Milanés-Murcia, M (14 May 2013). A new international legal and institutional framework to manage fossil aquifers and groundwater in conjunctive use with surface water along the U.S.–Mexico border: A water banking perspective. Unpublished J.S.D. dissertation, University of the Pacific, McGeorge School of Law.

Moro Ingeniería, SC (2006). Estudio de Actualización de Mediciones Piezométricas para la Disponibilidad del Agua Subterránea en el Acuífero Bajo Rio Bravo Tamps.

Perezcano Díaz, H (2007). Los Tratados Internacionales en el Orden Jurídico Mexicano, Anuario Mexicano de Derecho Internacional, vol. VII, 249–279. Retrieved from http://biblio.juridicas.unam.mx/ estrev/ pdf/derint/cont/7/art/art7.pdf [27 May 2011].

Pilz, RD (2010). Lessons in water policy innovation from the world's driest inhabited continent: Using water allocation plans and water markets to manage water scarcity. 14 *University of Denver Water Law Review*, 97.

President Barack Obama (5 November 2009). Memorandum for the Heads of Executive Departments and Agencies. Tribal Consultation,

White House. Retrieved from http://www.justice.gov/otj/pdf/obama-executive-memo110509.pdf [4 May 2011].

President William J. Clinton (6 November 2000). Executive Order 13175 — Consultation and Coordination with Indian Tribal Governments. Retrieved from http://ceq.hss.doe.gov/nepa/regs/eos/eo13175.html [4 May 2011].

Restatement of the Law of Torts, Volume IV, Division 10, Chapter 41, As Adopted by the American Law Institute. St. Paul: American Law Institute, Publishers (1939).

Sandoval-Solis, S (2011). Water planning and management for large scale river basins. Case of study: Rio Grande/Rio Bravo transboundary basin. PhD. Dissertation, The University of Texas at Austin, Austin.

Science Dictionary (2012). Definition fossil. Retrieved from http://www.science-dictionary.com/definition/fossil-water.htm [4 January 2015].

Secretatia de Medio Ambiente y Recursos Naturales (2011). Acuerdo por el que se establecen los Bancos del Agua de la Comision Nacional del Agua.Retrieved from http://www.conagua.gob.mx/CONAGUA07/Noticias/Acuerdo%20Bancos %20de%20Agua.pdf [15 May 2012].

Tarlock, D (2001). The future of prior appropriation in the New West. *Natural Resources Journal*, 41, 769–793.

Treja García, AR and R Alvarez (2006). *Los Tratados Internacionales como Fuente del Derecho Nacional*. Servicios de Investigación y Análisis, Subdirección de Política Exterior. Congreso Gobierno Mexicano.

Treaty Utilization of water of the Colorado and Tijuana Rivers and of the Rio Grande, U.S.–Mexico, [Treaty] (1944). 3 February 1944, 59 Stat. 1219; TS 994; 9 Bevans 1166; 3 UNTS 313. Available at http://www.ibwc.state.gov [September 2011].

United Nations Convention on the Law of the Non-Navigational Uses of International Watercourses [UN Convention] (1997). Entered into force on 17 August 2014. General assembly resolution 51/229, annex, *Official Records of the General Assembly, Fifty-first Session, Supplement No. 49* (A/51/49). U.N. Doc. A/RES/51/869, 21 May 1997, 36 ILM 700.

United States Environmental Protection Agency, Good Neighbor Environmental Board [US EPA] (December 2014). *Ecological Restoration in the U.S.–Mexico Border Region*. Sixteenth Report of the Good Neighbor Environmental Board to the President and Congress of the United States. Retrieved from http://www.epa.gov/sites/production/files/2014-12/documents/16th_gneb_report_english_final_web.pdf [12 March 2015].

United States Environmental Protection Agency, Good Neighbor Environmental Board (December 2012). The *Environmental, Economic and*

Health Status of Water Resources in the U.S.–Mexico Border Region. Fifteenth Report to the President and Congress of the United States.

United States Environmental Protection Agency, Good Neighbor Environmental Board (June 2010). *A Blueprint for Action on the U.S.–Mexico Border.* Thirteenth Report to the President and the Congress of the United States. Retrieved from http://www.epa.gov/ocem/gneb/ gneb13threport/eng_gneb_13th_report_final.pdf [7 May 2011].

United States Environmental Protection Agency, Good Neighbor Environmental Board (February 2005). *Water Resources Management on the U.S.–Mexico Border.* Eight Report to the President and the Congress of the United States. Retrieved from http://www.epa.gov/ocem/gneb/ gneb8threport/gneb8threport.pdf [May 5, 2011].

United States Geological Survey [USGS] (2013). Water resources of the U.S. Retrieved from http://water.usgs.gov/GIS/huc.html [2 January 2013].

Zilberman, D and K Schoengold (2005). The use of pricing and markets for water allocation. *Canadian Water Resources Journal*, 30(1), 1–10.

CHAPTER 6

A NEW PARADIGM FOR TRANSBOUNDARY WATER AGREEMENTS: THE OPPORTUNITY FOR ISRAEL AND PALESTINE

DAVID B. BROOKS* and JULIE TROTTIER[†]

*Associate, International Institute for Sustainable Development, Ottawa, Ontario, Canada

[†]Directrice de la Recherche, Centre National de la Recherche Scientifique (CNRS), ART-Dev, Montpellier

This chapter is a highly abridged version of the EcoPeace Proposal for a water agreement between Israel and Palestine. It presents the design for an agreement between Israelis and Palestinians to share water in a physically realistic, ecologically sustainable, and socially equitable manner. Existing arrangements are, at best, inadequate and, in some cases, counterproductive. The proposal relies upon ongoing monitoring and mediation to achieve equitable and sustainable use at the most local level possible. The proposal also argues that an agreement on water can be reached now, before resolving the full range of issues required in a Final Status Agreement between Israel and Palestine.

Keywords: Avoidance of significant harm; Coastal aquifer; Conflict resolution; Cross-border streams; Dead Sea; Depoliticization of water; Desalination; Desecuritization of water; EcoPeace; Final Status Agreement; Fixed allocations; Gaza Strip; Israeli Water Authority; International Water Agreements; Joint Water Committee; Jordan River; Mediation; Monitoring; Mountain Aquifer; Oslo Agreements; Palestinian Water Authority; Reasonable and equitable use; Sustainable water management; Transboundary wastewater treatment; Transboundary water; Water needs; Water rights; West Bank; Water demand management.

Although resolution of issues related to fresh water shared by Israel and Palestine will not alone bring about peace between the two peoples, in the absence of a just resolution of water issues, no peace can be complete. Further, in the absence of *sustainable* use of water by both peoples, overall social and economic development will be threatened, and so too will stability and peace for the region. Though obviously essential to any final status agreement between Israel and Palestine, remarkably little attention has been devoted to the design of the water component of the agreement, and even less to how it might be implemented.

> Treaties and institutional arrangements cannot remain static. Factors like water requirements, use patterns and efficiency of management change with time, as do water management paradigms, practices and processes. . . . It may not be an easy task to formulate dynamic treaties, but one that must be considered very seriously in the coming years (Varis *et al.*, 2008, p. xi).

6.1. Introduction

The bodies of water that are essential to both Israel and Palestine are so interconnected that any simple division of them into *our water* and *your water* is impossible. Some agreement for joint management of the shared water is essential. Further, equity and sustainability require an approach to sharing that steps away from seeing water mainly from technical and economic perspectives — what Linton (2010) calls "modern water" — and begins to look at water from social and political perspectives. Water policy must, of course, recognize hydrological and other physical limitations, but those limitations are insufficient to indicate how water is, and could be, used to satisfy changing human needs and desires, both of which influence water policy (Feitelson, 2012). This document responds to that shortcoming with its proposal for a water sharing agreement for Israel and Palestine that not only provides for equity and sustainability, but that also recognizes the context of 65 years of conflict and of Israeli water hegemony in the region.

If our work can lead to an agreement on water between Israel and Palestine, it will join a long list of other transboundary water agreements around the world. Contrary to a common impression, history demonstrates that riparian states around the world prefer to cooperate over transboundary water bodies rather than fight over them (Gleick, 2000; Jägerskog, 2003; Katz, 2011a; Kliot *et al.*, 2001; Wolf, 1998, 2007; Wouters, 2013). Indeed, as Weinthal *et al.* note (Weinthal *et al.*, 2011, p. 149), joint water resource management has "a singularly important role to play both in facilitating the rebuilding of trust following conflict and in preventing a return to conflict."

However, in contrast to the works just cited, the goal of this chapter is not just to add to the literature on the global and regional benefits from sharing rather than fighting over transboundary water resources. The analytical goal of this chapter is to demonstrate how treating water as a flow instead of a stock allows sharing in a specific region, indeed a region that is characterized as much by conflict as by cooperation. Its ultimate goal is to design a draft model water agreement for Israel and Palestine.

The second section of this chapter provides a brief discussion of water quantity and quality issues in Israel and Palestine; it also identifies which bodies of water in that region are shared and, therefore, require some form of joint management. The third and fourth sections review, respectively, the failures of existing water arrangements as they emerged from the two Oslo agreements, and the shortcomings of existing approaches to shared water management. The fifth section identifies key considerations for shared water management in Israel and Palestine, and goes on to describe organizations that can implement an approach based on those considerations. The sixth section presents the main criticisms that have been made about the EcoPeace Proposal as well as our responses to those criticisms. The final section focuses on moving water from last to first in the peace process.

6.2. Water Sources and Water Uses — Now and in the Future

Fresh water supplies are limited throughout the Middle East and North Africa (MENA), and in almost every country they are being depleted and degraded. Water withdrawals in Israel/Palestine are

Table 6.1: Water withdrawals in Israel and Palestine (MCM*/year) in about 2005.

Water Source	Israel	Palestine	Total Withdrawn	Average Annual Recharge**
Jordan River Basin	700	0	700	565
Mountain aquifer	485	115	600	550–620
Western basin	340	62	402	320–360 [12%]***
Northern basin	105	30	135	131–144 (10%)
Eastern basin	40 (insettle-ments)	23	63	95–110 (28%)
Coastal aquifer	430	125	555	330
Israel	420	5	425	250–270
Gaza Strip	10	120	130	60
Desalination	300		300	Not applicable
Reused waste water	220	0	220	220
Total	2135	240	2375	2300

Source: Modified from Lautze and Kirshen (2009), which used various sources; and EcoPeace.
*MCM: Million cubic metres.
**In contrast to other columns, the figures in this column are based on recent estimates of average yearly recharge or "sustainable yield."
***Square brackets show the proportion of saline water in each basin.

roughly 15% higher than the average annual rate of recharge (see Table 6.1). Indeed, the overdraft is likely larger than 15%, because estimates of renewable supply typically ignore the large volumes of water that should be left *in situ* to support ecosystems, provide for fisheries, flush away wastes, and so on (Gafny *et al.*, 2010; Katz, 2011b; Safriel, 2011). To make the situation worse, it is likely that climate change will lead to lower rainfall, longer droughts, and heavier storms in the whole belt of land south and east of the Mediterranean Sea. Two recent scenario analyses (Chenoweth, 2011; Feitelson *et al.*, 2011) find that, outside the Gaza Strip and provided that population growth is restrained, water resources in Israel and Palestine would be adequate to permit social and economic development. However, neither analysis is optimistic about reducing withdrawals sufficiently to provide ecosystem services.

6.2.1. *What Water is Shared and What Is Not*

Any agreement for joint management of water must be clear about exactly which bodies of water are shared. Those that are shared will be subject to any Israeli–Palestinian water agreement for joint management; those that are not shared will be managed independently by one of the two governments.

The main water bodies west of the Jordan River are shown in Fig. 6.1. All of the dozen cross-border streams that flow to the Mediterranean are shared water, as are the three that flow to the Dead Sea or the Jordan River. The western and northern basins of the Mountain Aquifer are also shared water, but the eastern basin is deemed Palestinian, even though a few of its springs emerge in Israel. The coastal aquifer is not shared; according to most hydrological analyses, it is made up of a series of lenses of permeable sandstone with only limited lateral movement of water between them. In summary, roughly two-thirds of fresh water resources can be considered as "shared water."

Special rules are needed for sharing the Jordan River because the Israel–Jordan Peace Treaty ignores Palestinian water rights. There is little interest in reopening that Treaty, but fortunately it does "work" in a physical sense because the depth of the rift valley provides a barrier against hydrological connections between Jordan on the east and Israel and Palestine on the west. Recognizing that Jordan is one of the most water-stressed states on earth (Alkhaddar *et al.*, 2005; Scott *et al.*, 2003); its allocation cannot be reduced. Therefore, the Treaty's allocation to Israel alone should be addressed as if it were apportioned jointly to Israel and Palestine. In the absence for any rationale to divide that portion, we accepted that it would be shared equally.

6.2.2. *Water Quantity: Exceeding Sustainable Limits*

Until recently, Israel was pushing to, and often beyond, the limits of the sustainable water resources available to it.[1] Although

---

[1]Final:2050 *Final Report, National Investigation Committee on the Crises in Water Management in Israel* (March, 2010), http://elyon1.court.gov.il/heb/mayim/doc/sofi.pdf. See also *Israel Water Sector Master Plan to 2050*, http://www.water.gov.il/Hebrew/ProfessionalInfoAndData/2012/05-Israel-Water-Sector-Master-Plan-2050.pdf (especially page 21).

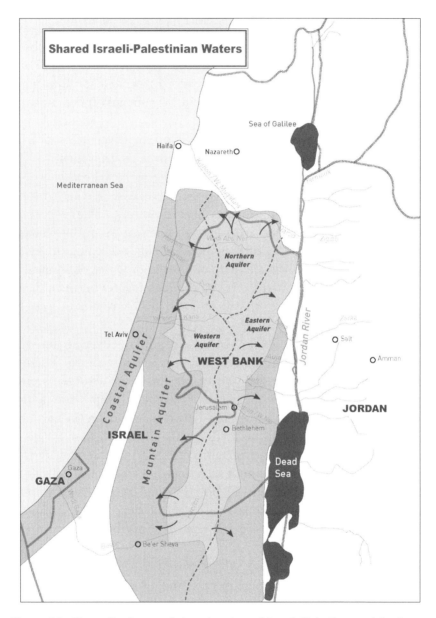

Figure 6.1: Generalized map of shared waters of Israel, Palestine, and Jordan.
Source: Adapted by the authors from EcoPeace materials.
Note: Small arrows indicate the direction of water flow within the aquifer.

desalination has provided considerable relief from concerns for drinking water supplies, it comes with a high dollar and energy cost, as well as new environmental problems and relaxation of public incentives to conserve water (Katz 2016). Ironically, desalinated water is too pure for irrigation, which remains, by far, the largest use of water throughout MENA, even in Israel where agriculture is a minor component of the economy. Palestinians, too, push against and exceed the limits of sustainable water resources, particularly in the Gaza Strip (Klawitter, 2007; Nasser, 2003). However, in contrast to Israel, agriculture remains an important part of the Palestinian economy and social fabric.

Though the largest deficits in supply involve agriculture, some Palestinians, particularly in the Gaza Strip, but also in some areas of the West Bank (such as Jenin and Hebron), do not have access to adequate quantities or qualities of fresh water (Hadi, 2003; Tagar and J-D, 2008), generally set as about 100 L per person-day. In contrast, all Israelis, with the exception of some Bedouin villages, are adequately supplied with fresh water for household use.

6.2.3. *Water Quality: Declining Everywhere and Rapidly*

Declining water quality is a major problem throughout the region. Much of Palestinian household and industrial waste water, as well as some from Israeli sources, is released without treatment into the environment. Farm run off containing fertilizers and pesticides is common from fields across the region. Less than one-third of the West Bank's Palestinian population has sewage systems connected to wastewater treatment plants; the remainder of the population relies on septic tanks and cesspits, which are commonly poorly maintained (Al-Sa'ed, 2010).

Israeli settlements in the West Bank produce nearly 18 million cubic meters (MCM) of waste water per year, of which one-third is untreated or inadequately treated. Jerusalem has a modern wastewater treatment plant for the western part of the city, but more than 11 MCM of waste water from the eastern portion and from Palestinian villages surrounding the city center flow untreated into the West Bank. Waste water treatment plants are now functioning in Al Bireh (south of Ramallah), Nablus, and Jenin. To now, the treated wastewater is released into the environment without being used for irrigation. In 2015, the Society for the Protection of Nature in Israel brought a law suit against the Civil Administration (CA)[2] of the West Bank, arguing that the quality of the water released by the Al Bireh plant damages the environment because it only carries out secondary treatment; the case is ongoing. In addition, the West Bank is dotted with hundreds of illegal solid waste dump sites producing leachate that further contaminates ground water. As a result, nearly all the streams that rise in the West Bank and flow into Israel are badly polluted (Asaf et al., 2007).

Though generally maintaining good water quality, all three subbasins of the mountain aquifer (see dashed lines and small arrows in Fig. 6.1) are increasingly threatened by seepage from solid waste dumps and from sewage channels (Tagar and J-D, 2008; Tagar et al., 2005; Tagar and Qumsieh, 2006). Water quality in the lower Jordan River was once good, but nearly all the good quality springs have now been diverted for local uses, and the river is seriously degraded by sewage, saline springs, and runoff from agricultural fields.

For many years, the quality of water in the relatively shallow coastal aquifer has been polluted by runoff of agricultural chemicals, seepage from fish ponds, and seawater infiltration. About 15% of the water pumped from the coastal aquifer does not meet drinking water standards for chloride and nitrate concentrations. Because of an even greater rate of pumping, the situation is even worse for those portions of the coastal aquifer that underlie the Gaza Strip (Bruins et al., 1991; Shomar, 2006).

---

[2]The Civil Administration is the Israeli governing body that operates in the West Bank. It was established by the government of Israel in 1981 in order to carry out bureaucratic functions within the territories occupied in 1967. Under the Oslo agreements, the West Bank was divided into three administrative divisions until a final status agreement is signed. The areas are not contiguous, but rather determined depending on the distribution of Israeli settlements and Palestinian population centers as well as on Israel's military requirements. Although some powers have been devolved to the Palestinian Authority in Areas A and B, the CA remains the ultimate authority throughout the West Bank.

6.3. Failures of the Existing Oslo Arrangements

The Israeli–Palestinian Interim Agreement on the West Bank and the Gaza Strip, known as Oslo II, was the first to be explicit about the existence of "Palestinian water rights in the West Bank" (1995, Annex III, Appendix I), but did not define them. Oslo II did establish a framework for the management of shared water resources via Article 40. Key provisions of Article 40 pertain to the establishment of a Joint Water Committee (JWC) and a Palestinian Water Authority (PWA); allocation of water between Israel and Palestine, with focus on the Mountain Aquifer; and mutual obligations to treat or reuse waste water.

Though they represent an advance compared with earlier conditions, the Oslo agreements on water fall short of those put forward in the 1997 United Nations Watercourses Convention (www.unwatercoursesconvention.org), which has now come into force, and which gives priority to reasonable and equitable use, the obligation to cooperate, and avoidance of significant harm as the three basic elements to any form of transboundary agreement (Leb, 2015).

To compound the problem, Oslo II was intended to be an *interim* agreement governing relations between Israel and Palestine during a transitional period of not more than five years beginning in May 1994. Though the termination date is long past, both Israel and the Palestine continue to operate as if the water portions of the agreement were in force.

6.3.1. *Disputes about the Extent of Failures from Continuing to Follow Article 40*

With the passage of time, the limitations of Article 40 have become increasingly clear. Three major areas of dispute are indications of systemic failure:

• Do Palestinians in the West Bank have adequate water? Many Israeli analysts claim that Israel has fulfilled its obligations under Article 40 and that the Palestinians have sufficient access to water (Gvirtzman, 2012). They point to Palestinian under-exploitation of the eastern basin of the Mountain Aquifer, and add that the Palestinians could increase their water supplies by treating sewage for reuse, as Israel does. Palestinian analysts retort that Israel obstructs development of Palestinian water infrastructure. The World Bank puts responsibility on both sides. It notes that little more than half of what Oslo II documents designated as "immediate needs" for the West Bank has been satisfied, and goes on to point out constraints "stemming from Israeli occupation, weakness in Palestinian planning and technical services, and lack of donor support or poorly articulated donor coordination" (2009, pp. 35–38).

- Do the Palestinians do enough sewage treatment on the West Bank to prevent polluted water from flowing into Israel? Israel claims that the JWC approves treatment projects, but that the Palestinians do not follow through. The World Bank did identify gaps in Palestinian institutions as one cause of delay, but also blamed the long bureaucratic approval process for water and sanitation projects, which can take up to three years (World Bank, 2009, pp. 54–58). Donors have donated heavily to Palestinian water sector (Le More, 2008). However, the functioning infrastructure is very disappointing in comparison with the funds that were committed. For example, the Northern Gaza Emergency Sewage Treatment project incorporates state-of-the-art technology, but cannot function as designed because it does not receive an adequate supply of electricity from the grid (fully 100% of the electricity consumed in the Palestinian territories comes from Israel).

- Is there overextraction from shared water? One of the main aims of the 1995 water agreement was to use "the water resources in a manner which will ensure sustainable use in the future, in quantity and quality" (Art. 40(3)c). Article 40 aimed to accomplish this by estimating the shared Mountain Aquifer's potential and then setting an annual baseline withdrawal rate as 483 MCM for Israel and 182 MCM for Palestine. Instead, the period since 1995 has been marked by regular Israeli overextraction in the western basin of the Mountain Aquifer, in violation of Oslo II (World Bank, 2009, p. 12). Israel has evaded its quota by drilling into that aquifer from inside the Green Line, where the JWC has no mandate.

6.3.2. *Bureaucratic Obstacles to Progress*

The structure of the JWC lies at the heart of the foregoing problems. At the outset, Article 40 established the JWC "to deal with all water and sewage related issues in the West Bank" (Annex III, Art. 40 ¶12). This wording excludes the Palestinians from shared management of those parts of the Mountain Aquifer that extend into Israel (Selby, 2013; Trottier, 1999). It also excludes Palestinian agencies from any role with respect to the Jordan River. Further, Oslo II mandates the JWC to serve as a vehicle for cooperation through data sharing, joint fact finding, and the resolution of water-related disputes, but does not indicate procedures for achieving these aims. Clearly, the process envisioned by Oslo II has failed to build trust between Israel and Palestine.

To complicate the situation on the West Bank, the JWC is not the only organization with jurisdiction over infrastructure and resource development. The Israeli CA (see endnote ii) also plays a role, and reinforces the asymmetry of power in decisions about water infrastructure. According to the World Bank (2009, p. 54), the CA "is seen by donors as a major constraint. One donor commented: 'First thing we request is a letter from PWA approving the project. Then we go to the JWC. But then we have to go to the CA — and there delays of two or three years are normal.'" Indeed, as shown in Fig. 6.2, whether so intended or not, the process for getting a water proposal to approval and then to implementation is bound to be slow and frustrating. For individual Palestinians, the costs in time and money of seeking CA approval for water infrastructure projects *after* they have already received approval from the JWC are highly frustrating. Consequently, they drill small, unlicensed wells, dig cisterns, and lay pipes, many of which are subsequently demolished by the CA.

6.4. Deficiencies of Conventional Approaches to Transboundary Water Management

Most transboundary agreements treat water as if it were a pie to be divided among riparian states. This traditional quantitative allocation approach is currently reflected in proposals put forward by

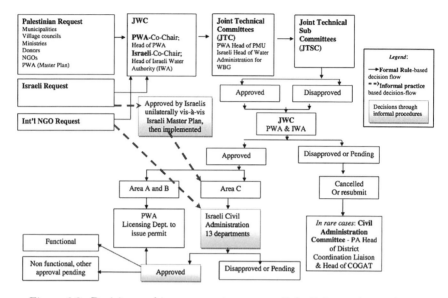

Figure 6.2: Decision-making process to approve Palestinian water projects.

Source: An agreement to share water between Israelis and Palestinians: The FoEME Proposal, revised version, p. 65.

both the Israeli and the Palestinian negotiating teams (Lautze and Kirshen, 2009; Lautze *et al.*, 2005). However, though quantitative approaches to sharing water can resolve some short-term issues, they have three long-term defects — securitization, rigidity, and ecological fiction.

- An issue becomes "securitized" when it is portrayed as an essential component of national security. It then leaves the realm of what is negotiable and can lead to compromise (Trottier, 1999, 2008; Zeitoun, 2007). Once quantitative allocations have been fixed or asserted, changing them is perceived as a threat to national security.

- Quantification also leads to rigidity. As a result of climate change, renewable water resources are likely to decrease in the Middle East, with particularly severe effects on agriculture (FAO, 2008; Freimuth *et al.*, 2007; Sowers and Weinthal, 2010). Quantitative allocations that are possible today may be impossible in a few years simply because of climate change. Further, demographic change and economic development will affect demand for water in unforeseeable ways.

- Fixed allocations also incorporate the ecological fiction that water can be treated as unchanging in space and time. In fact, water is used over and over again between the time it falls as precipitation and the time it evaporates back into the atmosphere or "disappears" into the sea or a deep aquifer. With each use, it comes under the management of a different institutional structure, which can range from an informal group of a few Palestinian farmers to the centralized organization of Mekorot, the Israeli national water company. All these structures need to be involved in implementing any agreement on sharing water. Otherwise, the agreement will fail to regulate effectively human interaction with the mobile resource, that is, water.

6.5. Designing a New Water Future for Israelis and Palestinians

Joint management of water is never easy, but it is particularly difficult for Israelis and Palestinians because such a high proportion of their water resources are hydrogeologically interconnected and because they have experienced so many years of conflict. They have also experienced different rates and patterns of economic development. Particularly since 1967, Israel's gross domestic product (GDP) per capita has greatly exceeded that of the West Bank and Gaza Strip. As one result, per capita water use in Israel is now significantly higher than in Palestine.

At the same time, Palestinians continue to depend much more on agriculture than do Israelis, both in terms of local livelihood and as a share of GDP. Hence, the value of additional water is significantly greater to Palestinian farms than to Israeli farms (Lonergan and Brooks, 1995). As farming technology improves and the economy diversifies, the total amount of water used for agriculture in Palestine can be expected to decline. Such a decline should be seen as an indication of progress. Only a few MENA nations now derive even one-fifth of their GDP from agriculture; those that do are among the poorest in the region (Beaumont, 2002).

Israel has had a highly centralized, command-and-control water management system at least since 1959, when it passed its Law on Water, which effectively nationalized all its water. The Oslo agreements and the ensuing Palestinian Water Law created the PWA as a regulatory body entrusted with implementing the provisions of the agreement concerning water (Trottier, 1999, 2007). Meanwhile, over 70% of the water actually used by Palestinians is still managed by local community- or farmer-based institutions, as it is in many other places in the world (Boelens, 2009). In effect, and with the support of some Palestinian officials, the Oslo agreements attempted to project Israeli-like water institutions onto the Palestinians (World Bank, 2009). Few Palestinians even knew about this component of the agreements, and even today most continue to abide by the existing grassroots institutions, which they perceive as effective and fair (Trottier, 1999, 2013).

Further, joint management of water shared by Israelis and Palestinians must accommodate the biophysical characteristics of lives and activities in a semiarid region of the globe. Sharp seasonal and spatial variations in rainfall are common in MENA. However, what really bedevils water planning and management in semiarid areas is year-to-year variation (Rogers and Lydon, 1994). Israel and Palestine are subject to frequent droughts, periodic "good" years of above-average rainfall, and occasional intense storms and flooding. The result is that planning and management must focus on extremes and risk minimization, not on averages and maximum utilization.

6.6.   A New Approach to Sharing Water

The essence of the EcoPeace Proposal is the use of continuous monitoring and ongoing mediation as the main management tools to achieve equity, efficiency, and sustainability. These tools provide the basis for decisions to adjust withdrawals from each well or reservoir, or to modify use of water from a spring; they also encourage interaction between state and nonstate actors. For example, ongoing mediation means that rulings or regulations can be appealed by any actor involved, whether scientist, officer of a nongovernmental organization, or member of an institution that manages water. Social and economic developments over time can be accommodated and can be integrated with geologic, hydraulic, and engineering constraints.

Israel and Palestine will necessarily always be mutually inter-dependent riparian states. They must have the right to access and use water from shared supplies. They must also accept the parallel responsibility to maintain the quality and quantity of flow in all shared water sources, within the limits set (and perhaps changed) by natural conditions. Equality in all rights and responsibilities does not mean that each party can expect to receive an equal volume of water. It does mean that each party will have equal standing within each of the organizations for joint management of shared water bodies.

Finally, in order to stay within sustainable limits of their water resources, the main focus of water management for both Israelis and Palestinians must shift from supply management to demand management (Brooks, 2006; Tal, 2006),[3] something that is rare throughout MENA (Brooks *et al.*, 2007). Water managers must spend at least as much effort finding ways to reduce demand for water as they now spend finding new sources of supply.

6.6.1. *New Organizations for Israel and Palestine: The Heart of the EcoPeace Proposal*

Figure 6.3 shows the key elements of the organizational structure for implementation of the EcoPeace Proposal; Figure 6.4 shows the flows of activities and information among them.

Two senior bodies guide the decision-making process: a Bilateral Water Commission (BWC) and a Water Mediation Board (WMB). Each of these is composed of an equal number of Israeli and Palestinian representatives plus one member from outside the region,

---

[3]See also the *Final Report of the National Investigation Committee on the Crises in Water Management in Israel* (March, 2010), http://elyon1.court.gov.il/heb/mayim/doc/sofi.pdf and the Green NGO Alternative Master Plan (2011), http://www.teva.org.il/?CategoryID=869&ArticleID=5084.

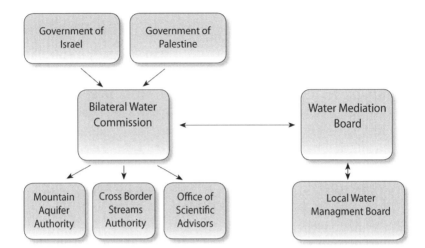

Figure 6.3: Organogram of the joint management bodies in the EcoPeace Proposal.

Source: The authors.

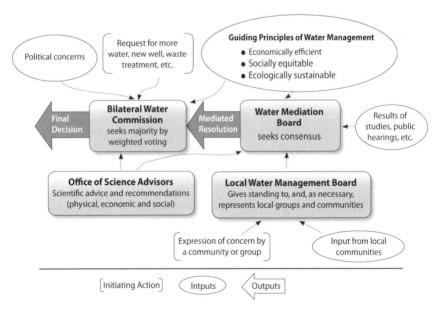

Figure 6.4: Key organizations and the flows of activities and information in the EcoPeace Proposal.

Source: The authors.

agreed to by both sides. If voting is necessary, the rules require majority (but not unanimous) support from each side, so that neither side can dominate the other.

The BWC replaces today's JWC and eliminates the need for any further approvals by the CA. It will have responsibility for all shared water (not just Palestinian water, as with today's JWC). The BWC makes key decisions on rates of extraction and delivery of water and on the removal and treatment of waste water. Its decisions are based on advice from a subsidiary body, the Office of Science Advisors, made up of staff appointed or seconded by the two governments. Should the BWC find itself unable to accept a recommendation of the Science Advisors, or should any group or community wish to oppose a decision, the WMB can take action. The WMB has a wide range of tools for resolving issues, ranging from scientific investigations to public forums. The WMB also receives advice from another subsidiary body, the Local Water Management Board, which represents local bodies in actions before the WMB. This back-and-forth process continues until the BWC receives a recommendation that it can accept. An in-depth discussion of the manner by which the WMB will promote better integration of science and democracy appears elsewhere (Trottier and Brooks, 2013). It is conceived more broadly than, but does resemble, the fact finding commission suggested in the 1997 UN Watercourses Convention.

6.7. Criticisms and Responses

To no one's surprise, the EcoPeace Proposal has received numerous criticisms about this or that provision. This section does not deal with those sorts of remarks. Rather, it looks at criticisms of the proposal as a whole.

Perhaps the most common criticism of the EcoPeace Proposal is that it is not fully formed. Although we agree that further work is needed to convert the concepts and the organizations outlined earlier into real processes and real agencies, most of them have been tried elsewhere. Only the WMB introduces more than a modest amount of innovation. From a more practical perspective, the criticism can be partly answered by suggesting a staged approach to implementation of the EcoPeace Proposal. An Israeli–Palestinian team has carried out considerable study of a joint management scheme for the Mountain Aquifer (Feitelson and Haddad, 1998, 2000), and it might be appropriate to build that agency before moving to implement the full binational structure. Al-Sa'ed (2010) argues for a similar step-by-step proposal for wastewater treatment.

Another criticism claims that the proposal requires reductions in Israeli withdrawals of water that would be "quite unprecedented" (Lautze and Kirshen, 2009, p. 201). It is true that nations have seldom voluntarily reduced their withdrawals after establishing "prior use" of that water. However, much of the Israeli increase in water use since 1967 comes from Palestinian sources under conditions of occupation. This statement does not apply to desalinated water or to most wastewater treatment plants built in Israel before 1967. However, for two reasons it does apply to many of those built since that time: first, they accept wastewater from the West Bank; and, second, in many cases, the plants located in Israel are funded with import tariffs collected by Israeli customs on behalf of the Palestinian authority on merchandise imported into Palestinian territories (Fischhendler *et al.*, 2011). Separate agreements for sharing the reclaimed water are required for such plants. If the Israelis do have to give up some quantity of water, they can expect in return to have a much better quality of water flowing to them than was formerly the case. Further, the burden of any cutbacks in water use would almost surely fall mainly on the agricultural sector (Jagerskog, 2003; Lautze and Kirshen, 2009; Lithwick, 2000; Lonergan and Brooks, 1995), which, as noted earlier, is a diminishing part of the Israeli economy. Israel is a sophisticated society that can accommodate the ensuing trade-offs and, if necessary, provide temporary subsidies to adversely affected farmers.

The late professor Shuval (2011) argued that the EcoPeace Proposal takes reallocation of the shared resources out of the hands of the two national governments and, in effect, deprives both Israel and Palestine of elements of sovereignty. Although Professor

Shuval's arguments may be literally true, they imply that Israel and Palestine can each "eat its cake and have it too." States cannot have sovereignty, at least not as that term is generally understood, over a resource that moves from one state to another, from underground to surface, and from atmosphere to surface and back again. Even though the hydrological cycle is widely understood, its implications for water management are not. And from that gap arise many of the disagreements about the proposal, as indicated in this section. We agree that allocation of water is a sensitive political and legal issue, but the very concept of joint management becomes meaningless if it starts from a premise that all existing laws must remain in place.

Of course, even if a peace agreement between Israel and Palestine is reached, water will continue to be seen as a national security issue by both sides. Deadlock could then arise on the BWC with all decisions pushed over to the WMB, which is supposed to be an instrument for mediation, not arbitration. Both sides have suffered deep wounds from the conflict, and we understand that distrust will continue. This is why we propose that decisions be made not at the state-to-state level, but at lower levels where the issues that typically arise (such as priority to domestic water) are much less polemical among either Palestinians or Israelis. This principle of subsidiarity was the cornerstone of the construction of the European Union after the Second World War. Certainly, reviews at the WMB will be able to call upon scientific expertise to dispel the prevalent idea that water problems are systematically caused by "the other side."

6.8. Moving Water from Last to First in the Peace Process

Since the start of the Oslo process in 1993, solving the water issue has been held hostage to lack of progress on the other core issues of the peace process. The stalemate is remarkable, given that almost all analysts agree that water issues are solvable and will result in the Palestinians receiving a larger proportion of shared Israeli–Palestinian water (Hadi, 2003; Shuval, 2007; Shuval and Dweik,

2007). If, as the citations indicate, resolution was possible more than a decade ago, it is all the more so today when large-scale desalination has shown itself capable of providing drinking water for a large share of household uses, which today represent more than half of total water use in Israel, at reasonable prices (Feitelson and Jones, 2014; Feitelson and Rosenthal, 2012). Indeed, so great has been the transformation of Israel's water balance because of desalination, drip irrigation, extensive recycling of water, and other technologies, along with public responses to conservation of water, that one recent book was subtitled *Israel's Solution for a Water-Starved World* (Siegel, 2015).

Certainly, resolving water issues at this time should be less contentious than doing so as part of a final status agreement that must also deal with final borders, refugees, Jewish settlements, and the status of Jerusalem. At the local level, EcoPeace's 15 years of experience with water cooperation between Jordan Valley communities on opposite sides of a border has yielded notable examples of confidence building. Its Good Water Neighbors Project demonstrates that the more frequent and intensive the cooperation, the greater the mutual understanding — and the greater the understanding, the more acceptable the results (Sagive *et al.*, 2012).

Wolf (1999, 2010) reports that most international negotiations over water during the past century have proceeded on the basis of each side recognizing the "needs" of the other side(s), rather than on *a priori* principles or rights. Equally important, transboundary water agreements typically exhibit some concept of fairness taking precedence over economic efficiency (Blomquist and Ingram, 2003; Syme *et al.*, 1999; Wolf, 2000).

But, even if EcoPeace has developed an attractive proposal, why should the Israeli government want to consider it when Israel holds almost all the trump cards? Fortunately, there are good ecological, economic, and political reasons for the Israeli government to listen now.

Regardless of where the border is eventually drawn, ecosystems in both Israel and Palestine are suffering from inadequate attention to water quality in both surface and ground water. Study after study has shown that the costs of avoiding ecological losses are small compared with those of restoring them afterward. Even the Jordan River, which today carries little more than untreated and inadequately treated sewage, might be restored to ecological health by returning some fresh water to its course, with follow-on benefits from religious visits and tourism (Baltutis, 2011; Gafny *et al.*, 2010; Hylton *et al.*, 2012; Safier *et al.*, 2011).

Much published work has claimed that Palestinian agriculture has been constrained since the 1967 war by limited access to fresh water (Baltutis, 2011; Hadi, 2003; Lonergan and Brooks, 1995). However, irrigated Palestinian agriculture relies mainly on water from farmer-managed wells and springs, and the vast majority of the irrigated plots of land are linked to one source only. As urban development occurs over previously irrigated land and as much irrigated land now lies on the other side of the separation wall, many wells now pump much less than their quota because they are linked to plots of land that are no longer irrigated. Consequently, new pioneer agricultural plots develop on previously uncultivated land, or on land where rain-fed agriculture had been carried out (Trottier, 2015). Farmers try to connect those plots to existing wells that are already functioning at full capacity. The shortages that ensue are easily solvable through the mechanisms laid out in the EcoPeace proposal. Of course, this does not mean the path of the separation wall should remain where it is, especially where it prevents previously irrigated land from being cultivated by its owners. Solving these shortages will allow farmers to pursue irrigated agriculture even before a comprehensive peace agreement includes borders approved by both sides.

Shared political gains are evident from the many places where cooperation with water has helped to resolve conflicts between nations. Jordan's former Minister of Water and Irrigation, Munther Haddadin, has written about the mutual benefits resulting from the Israel–Jordan Peace Treaty's water accord (2011, pp. 184–85).

> The main lesson learned during and after the conflict is that water can promote cooperation between adversaries as well as between allies. ··· [Israel and Jordan] realize that conflict would not bring

about more water for them but would create a zero-sum game. Conversely, cooperation can yield a positive result from which all parties can benefit.

6.9. Conclusion

EcoPeace has long maintained that water issues *need not* wait. We now assert that they *cannot* wait and that they *should not* wait. They cannot wait because under the existing situation neither side is making the best use of its fresh water, with adverse results that range from economically costly to ecologically destructive. They should not wait because an agreement to share water peacefully will be a model to show that agreements on other issues can be reached between Israelis and Palestinians. Though looking toward a Final Status Agreement, the EcoPeace Proposal is designed in a way that allows it to be adopted prior to that agreement. Only minor adjustments would be required when final borders are established. However, gains that were achieved prior to 2013 during the mission by US Secretary of State John Kerry had dribbled away by April 2014, and the easier issues, such as water, were no longer even under discussion by 2015.

The systematic focus of both parties on water quantities long maintained the bottleneck in water negotiations. Each party sought to secure a stock of water. This structured their approach to negotiations and dictated the categories they deployed to describe reality. Both parties avoided facing the fact that the quantities they discuss reflect a material reality, water that flows through several users' hands, both Israeli and Palestinian. With its massive desalination capacity, Israel now considers it enjoys water excess. This is an ideal situation from which to reconsider its interaction both with water and with its Palestinian neighbor. This proposal innovates by treating it as a flow instead of as a stock. Palestinians are located upstream on the aquifers. Israelis are located upstream for desalination capacity. Reformulating their negotiations from a struggle over quantities to a one over their interactions with a flow is now possible. Both will benefit from management that will allow the neighbor to use the same flow of water they both interact with.

When Israel passed its 1959 Law on Water, many people maintained that it had created the world's first modern water law (Burkart, 2012; Tal, 2002; Trottier, 1999).[4] If Israeli and Palestinian negotiators adopt the EcoPeace Proposal for joint management of shared water, we believe they will have created the world's first postmodern water agreement, or, as we prefer to term it, a new paradigm for managing transboundary water. Though specifically applied to water shared by Israelis and Palestinians, the general goals, the emphasis on ongoing monitoring and mediation, and the type of organizational structure are relevant to any place in the world where transboundary water divides rather than unites two or more peoples.

Acknowledgments

The authors are grateful to the staffs of EcoPeace in Tel Aviv and in Bethlehem for help in preparation of this article, and to Laura Doliner for her help in editing and formatting. This document is an abridgment of a much longer one (Brooks and Trottier, 2012) that was prepared for EcoPeace Middle East (at the time Friends of the Earth Middle East, or FoEME) and that, in its longer form, is called the EcoPeace Proposal. The first version of the EcoPeace Proposal (Brooks and Trottier, 2010) was launched in November 2010 at a workshop attended by 250 people in East Jerusalem. The revised version (Brooks and Trottier, 2012) responds to comments received at the workshop, and incorporates additional research to define the failings of existing water arrangements and to indicate how the EcoPeace Proposal would avoid or correct those failings. The full report was subsequently abridged to article length for publication in *Water International* (Brooks *et al.*, 2013), and that article received Honorable Mention for best paper of the year.

---

[4]The meaning of the word "modern," as applied to water, has changed significantly since 1959. Once complimentary because it appeared to provide an operational way to design water policy, it has since about 1990 come to be pejorative because of its focus on just a few quantitative aspects of water in society (Feitelson, 2012; Linton, 2010).

References

Alkhaddar, RM, WJS Sheehy, and N Al-Ansari (2005). Jordan's water resources: Supply and future demand. *Water International*, 30(2), 294–303.

Al-Sa'ed, R (2010). A policy framework for trans-boundary wastewater issues along the Green Line, the Israeli-Palestinian border. *International Journal of Environmental Studies*, 67(6), 937–954.

Asaf, L, N Negaoker, A Tal, J Laronne, and N Al Khateeb (2007). Trans-boundary stream restoration in Israel and the Palestinian Authority. In C Lipchin, E Pallant, D Saranga, & A Amster (eds.), *Integrated Water Resources Management and Security in the Middle East*, pp. 285–296. Dordrecht, the Netherlands: Springer.

Baltutis, J (2011). *Economic Benefits of Access to a Healthy Lower Jordan River for the Palestinian Economy*. Amman, Bethlehem, and Tel Aviv: Friends of the Earth Middle East.

Beaumont, P (2002). Water policies for the Middle East in the 21st century: The new economic realities. *International Journal of Water Resources Development*, 18(2), 315–334.

Blomquist, W and HM Ingram (2003). Boundaries seen and unseen: Resolving trans-boundary groundwater problems. *Water International*, 28(2), 162–169.

Boelens, R (2009). The politics of disciplining water rights. *Development and Change*, 40(2), 307–331.

Brooks, DB (2006). An operational definition of water demand management. *International Journal of Water Resources Development*, 22(4), 521–528.

Brooks, DB, L Thompson, and L El Fattal (2007). Water demand management in the Middle East and North Africa: Observations from the IDRC forums and lessons for the future. *Water International*, 32(2), 193–204.

Brooks, DB and J Trottier (2010). *A Modern Agreement to Share Water between Israelis and Palestinians: The FoEME Proposal*. Amman, Bethlehem, and Tel Aviv: Friends of the Earth Middle East.

Brooks, DB and J Trottier (2012). *An Agreement to Share Water between Israelis and Palestinians: The FoEME Proposal — Revised Version*. Amman, Bethlehem, and Tel Aviv: Friends of the Earth Middle East.

Brooks, DB, J Trottier, and L Doliner (2013). Changing the nature of transboundary water agreements: The Israeli-Palestinian case. *Water International*, 38(6), 671–686.

Bruins, HJ, A Tuinhof, and R Keller (1991). *Water in the Gaza Strip: Identification of Water Resources and Water Use*. Report to the

Directorate General for International Cooperation, Ministry of Foreign Affairs, Government of the Netherlands.

Burkart, L (2012). *The Politicization of the Oslo Water Agreement.* Submitted in fulfilment of the requirement for the Master in International History and Politics, Geneva, Switzerland: Graduate Institute of International and Development Studies.

Chenoweth, J (2011). Will the water resources of Israel, Palestine and Jordan remain sufficient to permit economic and social development for the foreseeable future? *Water Policy*, 13(3), 397–410.

Feitelson, E (2012). What is water: A normative perspective. *Water Policy*, 14, 52–64.

Feitelson, E and M Haddad (1998). *Identification of Joint Management Structures for Shared Aquifers: A Cooperative Palestinian-Israeli effort.* World Bank Technical Paper No. 415. Washington: World Bank.

Feitelson, E and M Haddad (eds.) (2000). *Management of Shared Groundwater Resources: The Israeli-Palestinian Case with an International Perspective.* Ottawa: International Development Research Centre; and Amsterdam: Kluwer Academic.

Feitelson, E and A Jones (2014). Global diffusion of XL-capacity seawater desalination. *Water Policy*, 16(6), 1031–1053.

Feitelson, E and G Rosenthal (2012). Desalination space and power: The ramifications of Israel's changing water geography. *Geoforum*, 43(2), 272–284.

Feitelson, E, AR Tamimi, A Bein, R Laster, E Marei, G Rosenthal, and S Salhout (2011). *Defining Water Needs for Fully Exploited Resources: A Necessary Step for Israeli-Palestinian Reconciliation.* Jerusalem: Jerusalem Institute for Israel Studies.

Fischhendler, I, S Dinar, and D Katz (2011). The politics of unilateral environmentalism: Cooperation and conflict over water management along the Israeli-Palestinian border. *Global Environmental Politics*, 11(1), 36–61.

Food and Agriculture Organization (FAO) (2008). *Climate Change: Implications for Agriculture in the Near East.* Report for 29th FAO Regional Conference for the Near East (NERC/08/INF/5). Rome: Food and Agriculture Organization of the Middle East.

Freimuth, L, G Bromberg, M Meyher, and N Al-Khatib (2007). *Climate Change: A New Threat to Middle East Security.* Amman, Bethlehem, and Tel Aviv: Friends of the Earth Middle East.

Gafny, S, S Talozi, B Al Sheikh, and E Ya'ari (2010). *Towards a Living Jordan River: An Environmental Flows Report on the Rehabilitation of the Lower Jordan River.* Amman, Bethlehem, and Tel Aviv: Friends of the Earth Middle East.

Gleick, PH (2000). How much water is there and whose is it? The world's stocks and flows of water and international river basins. In *The World's Water 2000-2001: The Biennial Report on Freshwater Resources*, PH Gleick (ed.), pp. 19–38. Washington: Island Press.

Gvirtzman, H (2012). *The Israeli-Palestinian Water Conflict: An Israeli Perspective*. Ramat Gan, Israel: Begin-Sadat Center for Strategic Studies, Mideast Security and Policy Studies No. 94.

Haddadin, MJ (2011). Water: Triggering cooperation between former enemies. *Water International*, 36(2), 178–185.

Hadi, MA (ed.) (2003). *Water in Palestine: Problems, Politics, Prospects*. Jerusalem: PASSIA Publications.

Hylton, E., *et al.* (2012). *Take Me Over the Jordan: Concept Document to Rehabilitate, Promote Prosperity, and Help Bring Peace to the Lower Jordan Valley*. Amman, Bethlehem, and Tel Aviv: Friends of the Earth Middle East.

Jägerskog, A (2003). *Why States Cooperate over Shared Water: The Water Negotiations in the Jordan River basin*. Linköping, Sweden: Department of Water and Environmental Studies, University of Linköping.

Katz, D (2011a). Hydro-political hyperbole: Incentives for over-emphasizing the risks of water wars. *Global Environmental Politics*, 11(1), 12–35.

Katz, D (2011b). Water markets and environmental flows in theory and in practice. In *Global water crisis: How can water trading be part of the solution?* J Maestu (ed.), pp. 214–232. London: Routledge; and Washington: Resources for the Future.

Klawitter, S (2007). Water as a human right: The understanding of water rights in Palestine. *International Journal of Water Resources Development*, 23(2), 303–328.

Kliot, N, D Shmueli, and U Shamir (2001). Institutions for management of transboundary water resources: Their nature, characteristics and shortcomings. *Water Policy*, 3(3), 229–255.

Lautze, J and P Kirshen (2009). Water allocation, climate change, and sustainable water use: The Palestinian position. *Water International*, 34(2), 189–203.

Lautze, J, M Reeves, R Vega, and P Kirshen (2005). Water allocation, climate change, and sustainable peace: The Israeli proposal. *Water International*, 30(2), 197–209.

Leb, C (2015). One step at a time: International law and the duty to cooperate in the management of shared water resources. *Water International*, 40(1), 21–32.

Le More, A (2008). *International Assistance to the Palestinians after Oslo: Political Guilt, Wasted Money*. London: Routledge.

Linton, J (2010). *What Is Water? The History of a Modern Abstraction.* Vancouver: University of British Columbia Press.

Lithwick, H (2000). Evaluating water balances in Israel. In *Water Balances in the Eastern Mediterranean*, DB Brooks and O Mehmet (eds.), pp. 29–58. Ottawa: IDRC Books.

Lonergan, SC and DB Brooks (1995). *Watershed: The Role of Fresh Water in the Israeli-Palestinian Conflict.* Ottawa: International Development Research Centre.

Nasser, Y (2003). Palestinian water needs and rights in the context of past and future development. In *Water in Palestine: Problems, Politics, Prospects*, F. Daibes-Murad (ed.), pp. 85–123. Jerusalem: PASSIA Publications.

Rogers, P and P Lydon (eds.) (1994). *Water in the Arab world: Perspectives and Prognoses.* Cambridge: Harvard University Press.

Safier, G, Y Arbel, G Bromberg, and E Ya'ari (2011). *Road Map for the Restoration of the Lower Jordan River.* Amman, Bethlehem, and Tel Aviv: Friends of the Earth Middle East.

Safriel, U (2011). Balancing water for people and nature. In *Water for Food in a Changing World: Contributions from the Rosenberg International Forum on Water Policy*, A Garrido and H Ingram (eds.), pp. 135–170. London: Routledge.

Sagive, M, *et al.* (2012). *Community Based Problem Solving on Water Issues: Cross-Border "Priority Initiatives" of the Good Water Neighbors Project.* Amman, Bethlehem, and Tel Aviv: Friends of the Earth Middle East.

Scott, CA, H El-Naser, RE Hagan, and A Hijazi (2003). Facing water security in Jordan: Reuse, demand reduction, energy, and trans-boundary approaches to assure future water supplies. *Water International*, 28(2), 209–216.

Selby, J (2013). Cooperation, domination and colonisation: The Israeli-Palestinian joint water committee. *Water Alternatives*, 6(1), 1–24.

Shomar, B (2006). Groundwater of the Gaza Strip: Is it drinkable? *Environmental Geology*, 50(5), 743–751.

Shuval, H (2007). Meeting vital human needs: Equitable resolution of conflicts over shared water resources of Israelis and Palestinians. In *Water Resources in the Middle East: Israeli-Palestinian Water Issues — From Conflict to Cooperation*, H Shuval and H Dweik (eds.), pp. 1–16. Berlin: Springer.

Shuval, H (2011). Comments on "Confronting water in the Israel-Palestinian peace agreement" by David Brooks and Julie Trottier. *Journal of Hydrology*, 397, 146–148.

Shuval, H and H Dweik (eds.) (2007). *Water Resources in the Middle East: Israel-Palestinian Water Issues — From Conflict to Cooperation.* Berlin: Springer.

Sowers, J and E Weinthal (2010). *Climate Change Adaptation in the Middle East and North Africa.* Dubai: Belfer Center for Science and International Affairs.

Siegel, SM (2015). *Let There Be Water: Israel's Solution for a Water-Starved World.* New York: Thomas Donne Books/St. Martin's Press.

Syme, GJ, BE Nancarrow, and JA McCreddin (1999). Defining the components of fairness in the allocation of water to environmental and human uses. *Journal of Environmental Management,* 57(1), 51–70.

Tagar, Z and E. J-D. (2008). *Lost Water in a Thirsty Land: Pollution Springs in the West Bank.* Amman, Bethlehem, and Tel Aviv: Friends of the Earth Middle East.

Tagar, Z, T Keinan, and V Qumsieh (2005). *Sewage Pollution of the Mountain Aquifer: Finding Solutions.* Amman, Bethlehem, and Tel Aviv: Friends of the Earth Middle East.

Tagar, Z and V Qumsieh (2006). *A Seeping Time Bomb: Pollution of the Mountain Aquifer by Solid Waste.* Amman, Bethlehem, and Tel Aviv: Friends of the Earth Middle East.

Tal, A (2002). *Pollution in a Promised Land: An Environmental History of Israel.* Berkeley: University of California Press.

Tal, A (2006). Seeking sustainability: Israel's evolving water management strategy. *Science,* 313(5790), 1081–1084.

Trottier, J (1999). *Hydropolitics in the West Bank and Gaza Strip.* Jerusalem: PASSIA Publications.

Trottier, J (2007). A wall, water and power: The Israeli separation fence. *Review of International Studies,* 33(1), 105–127.

Trottier, J (2008). Water crises: Political construction or physical reality? *Contemporary Politics,* 14(2), 197–214.

Trottier, J (2013). The social construction of water management at the intersection of international conflict: The case of Al Auja. *Eurorient,* (44), 161–181.

Trottier, J (2015). Le rapport à l'eau et à la terre dans la construction de territoires multisitués: Le cas palestinien. *Espace Géographique,* 44(2), 103–114.

Trottier, J and DB Brooks (2013). Academic tribes and transboundary water management: Water in the Israeli-Palestinian peace process. *Science and Diplomacy,* 2(2), 1–12.

Varis, O, AK Biswas, and C Tortajada (eds.) (2008). *Preface: Management of Transboundary Rivers and Lakes,* pp. ix–xiii. Berlin: Springer-Verla.

Weinthal, E, J Troell, and M Nakayama (2011). Water and post-conflict peacebuilding: Introduction. *Water International*, 36(2), 143–153.

Wolf, AT (1998). Conflict and cooperation along international waterways. *Water Policy*, 2(2), 251–265.

Wolf, AT (1999). Criteria for equitable allocations: The heart of international water conflict. *Natural Resources Forum*, 23(1), 3–30.

Wolf, AT (2000). From rights to needs: Water allocations in international treaties. In *Management of Shared Groundwater Resources: The Israeli-Palestinian Case with an International Perspective*, E Feitelson and M Haddad (eds.), pp. 27–59. Ottawa: International Development Research Centre; and Amsterdam: Kluwer Academic.

Wolf, AT (2007). Shared waters: Conflict and cooperation. *Annual Review of Environment and Resources*, 32(1), 241–269.

World Bank (2009). *Assessment of Restrictions on Palestinian Water Sector Development, Sector Note for West Bank and Gaza*. Washington: World Bank.

Wouters, P (2013). *International Law — Facilitating Transboundary Water Cooperation*. Stockholm: Global Water Partnership, TEC Background Papers No. 17.

Zeitoun, M (2007). The conflict vs. cooperation paradox: Fighting over or sharing of Palestinian-Israeli groundwater. *Water International*, 36(2), 105–120.

Part III

MANAGING AND VALUING WATER

CHAPTER 7

DISPUTES OVER INTERNATIONAL WATERCOURSES: CAN RIVER BASIN ORGANIZATIONS MAKE A DIFFERENCE?

SABINE BLUMSTEIN* and SUSANNE SCHMEIER[†]

*adelphi, Germany
[†]Deutsche Gesellschaft für Internationale
Zusammenarbeit (GIZ), Germany

Disagreements or full-fledged disputes continue to exist in international river basins even after the establishment of river basin organizations (RBOs) — originally often established to solve, mitigate, or prevent such disputes. However, research on transboundary river basin management as well as empirical evidence from basins around the world suggests that RBOs do make a difference by providing mechanisms for dispute resolution. This chapter asks whether and how RBOs engage in the solution of disputes that arise over water resources in transboundary basins. The chapter provides an overview of the global distribution of different RBO conflict-resolution mechanisms and analyzes in greater detail two conflict cases: the Mekong and the Nile rivers. While the findings reveal that the existence of specific conflict-resolution mechanisms does not necessarily influence the effectiveness of dispute resolution, RBOs as a whole do matter in addressing water-related conflicts through a range of mechanisms beyond pure dispute-resolution mechanisms, including the provision of forums for negotiation and exchange, data and information, or notification procedures.

Keywords: transboundary rivers; water conflicts; conflict resolution; River Basin Organizations.

7.1. Introduction

The past two decades have seen a considerable increase in the number and the responsibilities of international RBOs. This is — among many other reasons — driven by riparian states' recognition that institutionalized cooperation can help avoid or at least reduce conflicts over shared water resources and generate benefits for all riparians, especially in times of scarcity and competition. However, conflicts over shared waters have not disappeared. Instead, a number of shared basins have recently experienced significant disputes over the use and/or the protection of their water resources. And even in basins were cooperation is well established and relations among riparian states are strong, such as the Danube or the Rhine River Basin, disagreements emerge due to differences in riparian countries' interests. Most often, disagreements concern the plans of one riparian country to develop an infrastructure project on a river that might affect the river itself and the benefits other riparians gain from it (as, for instance, in the case of the Amu Darya River, where Tajikistan's construction of a hydropower dam raises fears on the Uzbek side that the project will severely reduce its own benefits from the river). Likewise, the intentional or unintentional intrusion of pollutants by one riparian country can affect the opportunities of other riparians to benefit from the watercourse (e.g., in the case of the Rhine River where upstream riparians, including Germany and France, for a long time, caused significant water pollution) and therewith cause severe disagreements among the riparian states.

The hydropolitics literature has dedicated much attention to the fact that riparians to international river and lake basins tend to cooperate over their shared water resources (Bernauer, 1997; Elhance, 1999; Swain, 2004; Wolf *et al.*, 2003) and many scholars have analyzed the multiple conditions for the establishment of joint water institutions (Dinar, 2004; Espey and Towfique, 2004; Song and Whittington, 2004; Tir and Ackermann, 2009). The fact that disputes[1] between riparians can still arise in spite of joint institutions

---

[1]Disputes have been defined in numerous ways in international law and relations scholarship — ranging from relatively broadly referring to situations in which two or more state actors pursue two irreconcilable goals or desire the same

has attracted much less attention. Existing research on the issue has focused on the presence or absence of conflict resolution mechanisms in international water treaties (rather than in more institutionalized forms of cooperation) and outlined the distribution of different types of mechanisms available (de Bruyne and Fischhendler, 2013; Giordano and Wolf, 2003; Hamner and Wolf, 1998; Sohnle, 2005; Zawahri, 2008). While there is a widespread expectation in research that conflict resolution mechanisms of RBOs lead to peaceful conflict management (e.g., McLaughlin Mitchell and Zawahri, 2015), this assumption has never really been tested (Giordano *et al.*, 2014, p. 59).

This chapter therefore focuses, first, on the question whether RBOs matter for solving disputes and, second, on whether the type of dispute-resolution mechanism they employ matters. In order to answer these two questions, we first investigate whether RBOs actually provide dispute-resolution mechanisms (and which ones) in a global overview and then focus on two specific cases — the Mekong and the Nile River Basins.

7.2.　Approaches to Dispute-Resolution over Shared Watercourses — Global and Basin-Level Insights

The ways disputes are addressed between riparian states to a shared basin differ considerably across regions and basins. This section provides an overview of how international environmental and water law requires states to address disputes over their shared resources and how dispute-settlement is operationalized across different regions, basins, and RBOs.

---

scarce resource/commodity (Galtung, 1998) to "a situation in which the two sides held clearly opposite views concerning the question of the performance or non-performance of certain treaty obligations" as the ICJ defined it in the Interpretation of the Peace Treaties with Bulgaria, Hungary, and Romania, Advisory Opinion in 1950 (1950 ICJ Rep. 65, at 74). For the purpose of this chapter, we understand by "dispute" a situation in which riparian states to a shared watercourse disagree over the use, the management and/or the protection of the watercourse and its resources to an extent that negatively influences the sustainable development of the respective watercourse and/or the overall relations between these states, independently of whether their relations are based on treaty obligations or not.

7.2.1.   The Global Level — International Water Law as a Basis for Avoiding Disputes

In order to manage cooperation between sovereign states over shared watercourses, basic principles and rules have been codified in international agreements and conventions which, together with other sources such as judicial decisions, form the basis of what is commonly referred to as international water law (e.g., Boisson de Chazournes, 2013; Caponera, 1980; Eckstein, 2002). The two major principles of today's international water law are the rule of "equitable and reasonable utilization" and the "obligation not to cause significant harm," both embedded into the overall obligation to cooperate among riparian states. Both have been codified in the United Nations Convention on the Law of the Non-Navigational Uses of International Watercourses (UN Watercourse Convention, 1997, Art. 5 and 7) as well as in the United Nations Economic Commission for Europe (UNECE) Water Convention (Art. 2) (Eckstein, 2002; Tanzi and Arcari, 2001). In order to implement these substantive provisions, international water law provides guidance on the basis of various procedural provisions, namely the requirement to notify co-riparian states of planned projects with potential transboundary impact (UN Watercourse Convention, 1997, Art. 11–19, International Court of Justice (ICJ) decision on the Pulp Mills case (Pulp Mills on the River Uruguay (Argentina v. Uruguay), ICJ, 2010).

In spite of the relatively broad acceptance of these principles within the international community, disagreements over the use, and the protection of shared water resources arise quite often across the world's river and lake basins — often concerning exactly the question of equitable and reasonable use and the avoidance of significant harm. If not solved appropriately, such disputes can harm overall country relations and hence also affect other fields of cooperation and/or negatively affect the sustainable management of the respective watercourse or even the overall peaceful development of the entire region.

In order to address such conflicts on the basis of the general duty to cooperate (UN Watercourse Convention, 1997, Art. 7), international water law makes further provisions with regard to solving water-related disputes between sovereign states (1997 UN Watercourse Convention, 1997, Art. 33), including mechanisms for negotiation, mediation, conciliation, arbitration, or impartial fact-finding. While negotiation usually provides the first step for dispute resolution, it might not always succeed. If parties cannot reach an agreement through negotiation, they may therefore also rely on an external party in form of a mediator that assists in finding a solution for the conflicting parties or engage in a conciliation process (Art. 33, 2; see also Salman, 2013). Alternatively, states can seek to solve a dispute by referring the case to an arbitration tribunal or the ICJ (Art. 33, 2) whose finding are then legally binding to the conflicting parties, or other forms of adjudication or arbitration. This approach to solving conflicts has indeed been relatively common as cases such as the 1997 Gabčíkovo–Nagymaros Project (Hungary/Slovakia) case and the 2010 Pulp Mills on the River Uruguay (Argentina v. Uruguay) case — both submitted to the ICJ — as well as other cases treated by international arbitration mechanisms (e.g., the 2013 Indus Waters Kishenganga Arbitration (Pakistan v. India)) suggest. If such measures are unable to resolve the issue, as a final resort, "the dispute shall be submitted, at the request of any of the parties to the dispute, to impartial fact-finding" (Art. 33, 3). As such, a commission including the conflicting parties as well an external member would be set in place to collect and examine all available facts on the dispute and make a recommendation for an "equitable solution of the dispute, which the parties concerned shall consider in good faith" (Art. 33, 8).

International (water) law is hence very clear on how to address disputes potentially emerging among riparian states over their shared water resources. These provisions, however, need to be implemented at the basin level and put into the respective basin practice.

7.2.2. *The Basin Level*

The implementation of international norms for the governance and the management of shared water resources are done on the basis of basin-specific treaties and through RBOs. Worldwide there are more than 400 international water treaties (Giordano *et al.*, 2003), many of them containing mechanisms governing the respective watercourse in general and — in some cases — for dispute resolution in particular. Moreover, there are more than 100 RBOs,[2] established to implement the different provisions of basin-specific treaties in a more long-term institutionalized manner and to provide an overall forum for cooperation among riparian states.

Looking specifically at those basins that are endowed with RBOs, one finds that 63 out of 121 RBOs possess clearly defined dispute-resolution mechanisms.[3] The remaining 58 RBOs have no specifically defined mechanism for addressing disputes in case they arise in the respective basin (Schmeier, 2013, p. 106; Schmeier, 2014, p. 62).

The geographical distribution of RBOs with and without clearly defined dispute-resolution mechanisms reveals some interesting observations (see Fig. 7.1): First, and somewhat surprisingly, a significant number of RBOs in Europe and North America — that is, in regions where cooperation over shared water relies on a long history of intensive cooperation — do not have any dispute-resolution mechanisms defined in the respective underlying treaty (in Europe, for instance, 13 out of the 32 RBOs studied do not define dispute-resolution mechanisms in their underlying legal documents). This might be due to the fact that in these regions, cooperation — generally and beyond water resources — has been well established for a long time. Consequently, a number of other formal and informal means for dispute resolutions were in place already or have developed

---

[2]In this chapter, we base our analysis on a set of institutions governing international watercourses that are generally considered to be RBOs. Some of them do not meet the strict definition of an RBO put forward in Schmeier *et al.*, 2016. However, these institutions might be of relevance for addressing disputes in shared basins and will therefore be considered as well.

[3]Data on dispute-resolution mechanisms across RBOs (both with regard to their availability and their geographical distribution as well as to their actual design) is based on the Transboundary Freshwater Dispute Database (TFDD)'s RBO Database, http://www.transboundarywaters.orst.edu/research/RBO/.

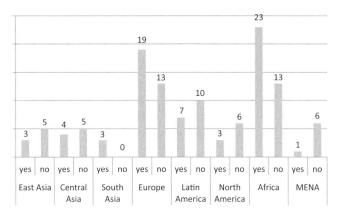

Figure 7.1: Regional distribution of dispute-resolution mechanisms in RBOs.

in parallel to water-related and more general environmental cooperation in the region (including the 1992 UNECE Water Convention or the 1991 Convention on Environmental Impact Assessment in a Transboundary Context). RBOs hence did simply not require any specific dispute-resolution mechanisms to be included in their legal frameworks as riparian states would — in the unlikely situation of a conflict occurring — resort to other means.

On the other hand, a considerably high share of African RBOs has dispute-resolution mechanisms defined in their treaties (23 out of 36). This can be explained by a number of reasons. First of all, many African basins had experienced conflicts over water resources in the past, highlighting the need to dispute-resolution mechanisms from the very beginning of the institutionalization process. Consequently, riparian states had an interest in including the required provisions when negotiating cooperation agreements. For example, the 2011 Water Charter in the Niger River Basin, a basin that has been facing severe conflicts over scarce water over the past decades, developed as an additional legal commitment to cooperation, emphasizes the importance of dispute-resolution mechanisms by having an entire chapter of the charter addressing this matter in significant detail (Niger Water Charter, Chap. 10). Many of the agreements underlying institutionalized water cooperation in Africa (including subsequent legal arrangements such as water charters or protocols) have also been influenced significantly by the international community, which considers clearly defined dispute-resolution mechanisms as a prerequisite for successful cooperation over international watercourses (Wolf, 1997) (e.g., the Agreement on the Zambezi Watercourse Commission [ZAMCOM] or the Convention for the Establishment of the Lake Victoria Fisheries Organization [LVFO], both containing very specific provisions on how disputes that arise in the context of their institutionalized cooperation should be settled).

Across RBOs that have defined dispute-resolution mechanisms in their constituting agreements, a number of different mechanisms can be identified. Generally, dispute-resolution mechanisms can be distinguished along three categories — bilateral negotiations, RBO-internal mechanisms, and external actors' involvement. Often, states have opted to establish more than one step in the respective dispute-resolution mechanism, structuring the processes into two instances with different mechanisms to be applied.

As a first step of dispute resolution, most cooperation arrangement over shared waters with defined dispute-resolution mechanisms (which is the case for 62 RBOs; see Fig. 7.2) refer to negotiations among the conflicting partners as the primary means of dispute-resolution (see Fig. 7.3). This is for instance the case in the Niger Basin Authority (NBA) where any dispute that may arise between the parties "shall be amicably settled through direct negotiations" (NBA, 1980). In some instances, RBOs provide internal mechanisms,

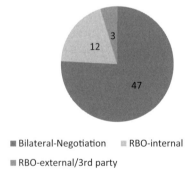

Figure 7.2: Distribution of dispute-resolution types for the first (or single) instance.

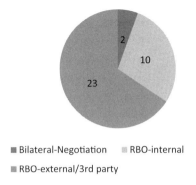

Figure 7.3: Type of dispute-resolution mechanisums for second instance.

such as voting or an internal arbitration. For example, the International Joint Commission (IJC) between Canada and the United States refers a dispute to the Commission, its highest decision-making organ, to decide upon by majority vote. In even fewer instances (three cases) RBOs rely on external actors such as the ICJ for conflict resolution. The Zambezi River Authority (ZRA) for example may refer any dispute to an Arbitrator or Board of Arbitrators appointed by the parties (Agreement 1987, Art. 32).

For the second instance (if defined — not all agreements foresee a second step in the dispute-resolution process), the picture is quite different. Instead of relying on negotiations between the parties, most cooperation mechanisms foresee the involvement of external actors and third parties for solving the conflict (see Fig. 7.3). The Organisation pour la Mise en Valeur du Fleuve Sénégal (OMVS), for example, foresees the consultation of the Commission of Mediation, Conciliation, and Arbitration of the African Union (AU) once direct negotiations among member states has failed.

7.3. Disputes and Their Resolution in Two Basins — Insights from Case Studies

In order to better understand how specific disagreements or disputes are actually approached by basin states, the remaining part of this chapter will therefore look at two different case studies: the Mekong River Basin and the Xayaburi Hydropower Project (XHP) and the Nile River Basin with the Grand Ethiopian Renaissance Dam (GERD). These cases represent two of the four well-known conflicts on international rivers in recent years, all related to hydropower development[4] — in addition to the aforementioned Rogun Dam dispute between Tajikistan and Uzbekistan and the Kishenganga Dam dispute between India and Pakistan. Both cases represent basins where RBOs — at a different level of institutionalization and development — are present. They can hence provide insights into whether and how RBOs matter for solving disputes on international watercourses.

Each case study first provides an overview of the overall legal and policy provisions for water resources governance in the respective basin with a particular focus on formally defined dispute-resolution mechanisms (or the lack thereof). It then presents a specific dispute or contested issue and describes the evolution of the conflict and its eventual resolution in order to then draw lessons on which factors determined the resolution (or the lack thereof) of the conflict, with a particular focus on the role RBOs play in addressing such disputes and reconciling member states' interests. Both case study analyses are based on a range of different sources, including official agreements, news reports as well as technical studies. The analysis takes into consideration events up to February 2016.

7.3.1.   *Case Study I: The Mekong River Basin and the XHP*

7.3.1.1.   *The cooperation framework in the lower Mekong basin*

Cooperation in the lower Mekong Basin (LMB) is based on the 1995 Agreement on the Cooperation for the Sustainable Development of the Mekong River Basin (Mekong Agreement). The agreement commits all parties "to cooperation in a constructive and mutually beneficial manner for sustainable development, utilization, conservation, and management of the Mekong River Basin water

---

[4]Hydropower development has proven to be the single most important source of conflict over international watercourses (de Stefano *et al.*, 2012).

and related resources" (Preamble). It includes a number of international water law provisions, including the principle of equitable and reasonable utilization (Art. 5) and the obligation not to cause significant harm (Art. 7) as well as the principle of notification (Art. 5 and 7).

In order to ensure such long-term cooperation "in all fields of sustainable development, utilization, management and conservation of the water and related resources [···] in a manner to optimize the multiple-use and mutual benefits of all riparians" (Art. 1), the agreement establishes the Mekong River Commission (MRC). The MRC consists of a high-level governing body (Council), a technical implementation body (Joint Committee [JC] and a Secretariat, charged with rendering "technical and administrative services" (Art. 28) for cooperation. Over the years, the Secretariat has grown significantly and today represents a comprehensive institution that does not only provide numerous technical, administrative, and financial services to Mekong cooperation but also plays an important role in setting the agenda for and determining the development of the Mekong River's resources. In the past years, the MRC has initiated an organizational reform process — aiming at rendering the institution more effective by decreasing the number of regionally implemented functions (and related costs) by transferring implementation responsibility to the member states — that is, considerably affecting the work of the organization (MRC, 2014b; Schmeier, 2010; The Diplomat, 2015).

Under the auspices of the MRC, a number of procedures have been established that further operationalize the provisions of the 1995 Mekong Agreement[5] and aim at ensuring the implementation of the underlying water law principles. These Procedures, together with Guidelines for Implementation for some of the Procedures, provide further guidance on the interpretation of the 1995 Mekong Agreement and its implementation in day-to-day Mekong management.

---

[5]2001 Procedures for Data and Information Exchange and Sharing (PDIES), 2003 Procedures for Notification, PNPCA, 2003 Procedures for Water Use Monitoring (PWUM), 2006 Procedures for Maintenance of Flows of the Mainstream (PMFM), 2006 Procedures for Water Quality (PWQ).

As will be shown in the course of this chapter, the Procedures for Notification, Prior Consultation and Agreement (PNPCA) can be regarded as particularly important for the sustainable management of the river's resources but also as particularly contested in disputes between member states concerning the use and the development of these water resources.

With regard to dispute resolution, the 1995 Mekong Agreement emphasizes MRC's role to "address and resolve issues that may arise from the use and the development of the Mekong River Basin water and related resources in an amicable, timely and good neighborly manner" (Preamble). This is reconfirmed in Art. 34 of the Agreement, instructing the MRC to "make every effort to resolve the issue." The responsibility for this lies with MRC's highest governing body, the Council, which is mandated to "entertain, address and resolve issues, differences and disputes" (Art. 18). In case issues remain unresolved by the Council, the 1995 Mekong Agreement foresees a referral of the issue back to member states' governments for bilateral resolution or — if all parties to the dispute agree — to a third party (Art. 35). There is no further specification of how dispute-resolution is to be undertaken beyond diplomatic means or which third parties to involve and how. In comparison to other agreements for cooperation of shared water resources, the provisions for dispute resolution are relatively weak. It has been argued that MRC's "direct intervention role in conflict management remains unclear" (Hirsch and Jensen, 2006, p. 120).

Over the past decades, a number of disagreements have arisen between member states of the MRC, most often related to the use of the Mekong's water resources and the development of infrastructure schemes. These include the conflict between Cambodia and Vietnam on the management of the Sesan River and in particular the Yali Dam which had caused repeated flooding for downstream Cambodia, the disagreements between MRC member countries and China over the potential holding back of water behind Chinese Mekong dams, causing droughts in the LMB in 2010, or the more organizational disagreements concerning the location of the MRC Secretariat (2007–2009) and the selection of a new chief executive officer (CEO) in 2010/2011 and repeatedly in 2014/2015 (Schmeier, 2013, pp. 158/159, 164/165). The most prominent conflict, providing ample of insights into how the MRC can and cannot address disputes, was the conflict over the Xayaburi Dam, which will be studied in the next section in more detail.

7.3.1.2. *The dispute around the XHP*

The XHP is one of 11 planned dams on the Mekong mainstream in the LMB — nine of them being planned in Laos as part of the country's overall ambitious hydropower development strategy. Constructed downstream of the city of Luang Prabang, it will consist of an 830-m long and 49-m high dam which will create a reservoir of an estimated 60–90 km length. Equipped with 10 turbines, its main purpose is to generate electricity at an estimated capacity of 1260 MW. Ninety-five percent of the electricity will be sold to Thailand on the basis of a power purchase agreement (PPA) with the Electricity Generating Authority of Thailand (EGAT), the remaining 5% will be fed into the Lao national grid.

The project is being developed by Ch. Karnchang, a Thai construction company. Based on a memorandum of understanding (MoU) signed in 2007 with the Lao government Ch. Karnchang has the right to develop and operate the project for a period of 30 years as a build–operate–transfer project (BOT). Subsequent to the signature of the MoU, Ch. Karnchang engaged in the necessary preparatory measures, including a feasibility study and an Environmental Impact Assessment (EIA), undertaken in 2007/2008. On this basis, a Concession Agreement with Ch. Karnchang was signed to implement this US$3.5 billion project, mainly financed by Thai commercial banks, backed by Thai government guarantees.

Although enthusiastically referred to as a "run-off-river"-project by the developers and the Lao government, the project will influence the Mekong River and its ecosystem as well as its people. In addition to the immediate local environmental and social consequences of every hydropower project, the XHP is expected to have some significant long-term impacts that affect large parts of the LMB — especially with regard to fish migration and fisheries (a significant source of livelihoods for riparian populations) as well as sediment transport and hence agriculture, a particularly important sector in the basin.[6]

Based on the requirements of the PNPCA, the Lao government notified the MRC (i.e., the MRC Secretariat which subsequently passed on the notification to the JC) of its intention to build the project in September 2010.[7] This opened a notification and prior consultation process according to the MRC's PNPCA[8] (for an overview of the process, refer to Annex I): A JC Working Group, consisting of representatives of the member countries, was established to steer the consultation process. In addition, a Task Group was established within the MRC Secretariat to provide the technical insights and interpretation of the data and information submitted by Laos on the basis of the technical expertise present within the MRC Secretariat and its various technical programs as well as the support from external consultants and experts on specific topics (namely

---

[6]For example, the Mekong's water is crucial for agriculture in the LMB which employs up to 85% of the population in Cambodia, Laos, and Vietnam, and produces more than 15% of the global rice production. Furthermore, fisheries is an important source of livelihoods as well as economic development, with two-thirds of the population in the LMB being involved in fisheries activities at least part time and fisheries representing a major source of the subsistence as well as export economy and the fisheries industry being worth total value between $5.6 billion and $9.4 billion (Schmeier, 2013, pp. 121/122; Economist, 2016).

[7]Whether the time of notification is in line with the 1995 Mekong Agreements provisions for "timely notification" and the PNPCA Guideline's request for "at least 6 months prior to commencement of project implementation, preferably greater" remains unclear. It is extremely difficult to identify the exact point of commencement of the XHP — especially since the Lao government — all the way through to 2013 — continued to claim it was pursuing preparatory works only that had nothing to do with the XHP itself. This does, however, also reveal a fundamental weakness of the 1995 Mekong Agreement and its subsequent Procedures (Rieu-Clarke, 2015, p. 14 ff.) that will not be discussed here.

[8]It should be noted here that originally, the Lao government's intention was to submit the project for notification only, aiming at avoiding a potentially lengthy consultation process (with the argument that the project's impacts would be minor according to Art 5). However, in informal discussions the MRC Secretariat's then CEO convinced the Lao government to submit the project for consultation, making it the first ever project undergoing such process.

fisheries and sediments). Over the next six months, these groups were working on the technical assessment of the material submitted and the draft of a review report. In parallel, public consultations on the project were held in Cambodia, Thailand, and Vietnam (though not in Laos).

After a number of internal drafting and review rounds, the finalized report of the Working Group was submitted to the MRC Secretariat in March 2011 (MRC, 2011a). In addition to a general overview of the project (design), it contained a comprehensive analysis of various aspects of the project's potential impacts. It found that there were a number of gaps and areas of uncertainty remained (MRC, 2011a, p. i). In spite of these knowledge gaps, it could already point to some problematic issues, namely the fact that the project design was neither consistent with the MRC's Preliminary Design Guidance[9] nor with best international practice (MRC, 2011a). This concerned, in particular, the highly critical areas of fish migration and sediment transport.

In addition to the report itself, countries could file replies to the report and explain their interpretation of the results and their conclusions on how to continue in this matter. This was done by all MRC member states except for Laos, all of them raising their concerns about the project and emphasizing the need for further investigation. In its reply to the PNPCA report, Vietnam for instance clearly stated that it "strongly suggests that the decision on the XHP as well as all other planned hydropower projects on the Mekong mainstream be deferred for at least 10 years" (MRC, 2011d, p. 3). And even Thailand, a beneficiary of the project and itself supporting the project indirectly through government guarantees, raised its concerns, stating that "the sustainability of the project is still questionable" (MRC, 2011b, p. 2).

---

[9]The 2009 Preliminary Design Guidance for Proposed Mainstream Dams in the Lower Mekong Basin defines a number of technical criteria that hydropower projects on the mainstream have to comply with (MRC, 2009). They have been agreed to by all MRC member states at the Council level.

In April 2011 and in line with the provisions of the PNPCA, the JC came together to discuss its results of the PNPCA Review Report. Due to opposing interests between Laos and the two downstream countries,[10] JC members were not able to find a solution to the issue — neither with regard to whether the project was to move ahead nor with regard to the more formal question whether the consultation process was now over. The Lao government insisted that the six months consultation period was over and that it could hence move ahead with the project. Since then, it has held on to this interpretation, regarding all additional communication with and all information provided to the MRC as a gesture of good will rather than an activity it would have been obliged by the 1995 Mekong Agreement and related documents.

As a minimal consensus, and in line with the provisions of the 1995 Mekong Agreement (Art. 18), the matter was referred to the MRC Council, scheduled for late 2011. In the meantime, throughout the year 2011, developments moved increasingly fast and along a number of parallel and partially overlapping routes. Disagreements between the MRC's member states — most openly between Laos and Vietnam — became increasingly loud.

Meanwhile, downstream riparians increasingly raised their voice against the project: In May 2011, the Vietnamese government officially requested Government of Laos (GoL) to stop the XHP and demanded a 10-year deferral of all mainstream dams (MRC, 2011d, p. 3). In November 2011, the government of Cambodia followed this example and also officially requested Laos to stop the project. The

---

[10]Disagreements concerned, in particular, remaining gaps of knowledge and a lack of a full understanding of the project's impacts on both the basin's environment and its people and the consequences that would need to be drawn from such lack of a full understanding of the project's consequences. While the Lao side argued that more analyses could be undertaken in the course of the project's construction (including the development of mitigation measures for some of the potential impacts, especially in the field of fish migration and sediment transport), Cambodia and Vietnam insisted on knowledge gaps being closed first and mitigation measures being tested for effectiveness first before the construction of the project.

MRC itself had already called for a 10-year deferral of all mainstream dams in 2010, stating that existing knowledge on their potential impacts was too limited (MRC, 2010a, p. 24).[11]

On the other hand, the Lao government was pushing the XHP ahead, both at the political and legal level and by actually pursuing construction on site. Already in April 2011, more or less in parallel to the JC's negotiations over the Project Review Report, significant construction works were reported (Bangkok Post, 2011). The Lao government, however, claimed these to be merely preparatory in nature. In order to underline its claim to move ahead, the Lao government hired Pöyry, an international consultancy firm, to assess its compliance with the MRC's PNPCA requirements. The final report as it was released in August 2011 concluded — on the basis of both a technical and a legal analysis of previous developments — that "in the case of the Xayaburi HPP, the decision whether or not to proceed with the project rests solely with the Government of Laos" (Pöyry, 2011a, p. 45). Moreover, it made a number of ambitious claims concerning the project's impacts, including "current flow regime of the Mekong River should not have major impact from Xayaburi" (Pöyry, 2011b, p. 13) and that other effects, namely on sediments and fish migration, could be successfully mitigated through state-of-the-art technology. In this context, some additional mitigation measures for potential environmental effects were indeed included at that stage, for example, additional fish migration devices and a more elaborate sediment flushing system. Ultimately, these statements (together with the changes on the project) aimed at underlining the rightfulness of Laos moving ahead with the construction of the project.

---

[11]In a consultant report — initiated by the MRC — remaining uncertainties with regard to the economic, social, environmental, and regional cooperation impacts let to the conclusion that "Decisions on mainstream dams should be deferred for a period of ten years with reviews every three years to ensure that essential deferment-period activities are being conducted effectively" (MRC, 2010a, p. 24). While the report had originally been agreed to by all MRC members, Laos withdrew its agreement later, claiming that it was a mere consultants' study, not representing the MRC's position on mainstream dams.

Based on a draft version of the Pöyry Report, the Lao Government had already in June 2011 informed the developer, Ch. Karnchang that the consultation period was now officially over and that construction could hence officially start. A similar informa- tion was officially forwarded to the Thai government in October 2011, together with the formal information that the construction of the project would start soon.

The MRC Council met in December 2011. This meeting can be considered as an important attempt to bring the Xayaburi dispute into MRC's realm again, avoiding an escalation of the conflict outside of an institutionalized cooperation mechanism. However, the Council could not come to a decision. The GoL continued to emphasize its rights to move ahead with the project and claimed that the albeit limited impacts of the projects could be mitigated by measures integrated during the construction process. Downstream countries, on the other hand, opposed the project. Likewise, the question of whether the notification process was officially over resurfaced again. While GoL argued that it had complied with all PNPCA requirement by notifying the project and engaging in a six months consultation process (independently of its results or the lack thereof), downstream Cambodia and Vietnam regarded the process as not finished yet. Consequently, their interpretation was that the project could not be continued by GoL. This question can be regarded as one of the main contested issues within the disagreement over the XHP and within the Mekong legal framework overall.

In spite of the remaining disagreements, government representa- tives could agree that there was a general need to further study the overall sustainable development of hydropower in the LMB, including the impacts of mainstream hydropower projects (MRC, 2011e). This was the beginning of the so-called Council Study, a comprehensive study of the impacts of hydropower developments (later watered down to infrastructure projects more generally) on the Mekong mainstream (though not specifically focusing on the XHP). The MRC Secretariat commenced work on the study immediately and a first concept note was provided to member countries in November 2012

(MRC, 2012a).[12] Results have, however, not been produced until the time of writing of this chapter.

The conflict dragged on and at some stages escalated throughout 2012: In April 2012, both a representative of the Cambodian National Mekong Committee (CNMC) and the Minister for Water Resources issued statements that the project should be halted and that Cambodia was considering taking the case to an international court (RFA, 2012). Although such international arbitration of adjudication never actually happened, the mere fact that one of the disputing parties was considering this option shows how critical the XHP was perceived to be for riparian states' development. At the same time, the project moved ahead. The official groundbreaking ceremony was held in November 2012. This finally made it clear to everyone that the Lao government was not to stop the project because of concerns of neighboring countries, being entirely convinced that all potential negative impacts (that it widely neglected) could be mitigated by state-of-the art technology.

Although Thailand is the main beneficiary of the electricity generated by the XHP and the Thai government has been backing the project politically and economically, there has been increasing resistance from the Thai civil society against the project. Local fishermen and civil society groups engaging for their rights fear the negative impacts of the project on the ecosystem and the development opportunities for Thailand's northeastern region. In September 2012, Thai civil society groups have therefore taken the XHP issue to the Thai Court, claiming that in providing guarantees for Thai banks financing the project, the Thai government had neglected both international and, in particular, Thai national requirements

---

[12]Implementation of the work, however, dragged on for much longer. First, member countries and, in particular, the Lao government delayed the required provision of comments to the concept note for a long time. Consequently, the first draft inception report for the Council Study (MRC, 2014a) was not finalized until mid-2014. Until now, no significant analytical work for this study has been undertaken.

for large infrastructure projects (such as some requirements concerning EIAs) and has thus acted against the interest of the Thai people.

Until and then during the 2012 Council Meeting (held in January 2013 (MRC, 2013a), disagreements were still not solved. The Lao government continued to justify the project and its rights to move ahead. The Lao representative argued that especially with the design changes (a new sediment flushing system and improved fish migration devices) there would now be no significant impacts on the river and neighboring countries. Downstream Cambodia and Vietnam continued to oppose the project.[13] And beyond the XHP itself, Vietnam insisted that "each riparian country should show their responsibility by assuring that any future development and management of water resources proposed in the basin should be considered with due care and full precaution based on best scientific understanding of the potential impacts" (MRC, 2013a). Consequently, downstream riparians repeatedly called for a halt of XHP and all mainstream projects until the potential impacts and the effectiveness of potential mitigation measures were better understood. The disagreement hence remained unresolved until present while construction of the dam is progressing fast.

At the same time, it became visible that discussions about the XHP increasingly took place outside of the MRC's realm — at least with regard to the official negotiations. MRC had somewhat lost the driver's seat position in this process and remained stuck in a situation in which there was neither a solution on the basis of its legal and policy provisions insight nor an alternative dispute-resolution mechanism available. This would prove to be one of the main impediments to MRC's effectiveness in the matter of infrastructure developments in the basin for the upcoming years as well.

---

[13]MRC 2013 Minutes of the MRC Council, 16 and 17 January 2013 in Luang Prabang, Lao PDR (which have not yet been released as the content remains contested between Laos and the downstream countries) (MRC, 2013a and MRC, 2013b).

7.3.1.3. *The role of the MRC*

The example of the XHP illustrates clearly the role of the MRC as an RBO in the process of addressing disputes among member countries with regard to the use of their shared resources. On the one hand, the MRC has not been able to directly solve the disagreement between Laos and the other riparian states over question whether or not to build the project. It can hence be argued that the MRC failed in solving the dispute. On the other hand, the MRC has been successful in, first, navigating the disagreement into orderly processes from the beginning on, and in, second, improving the design of the project and hence contributing to more sustainable water resources management in the basin.

With regard to the dispute itself and the way it was addressed by MRC member states in the context of the PNPCA, it must be stated that the dispute has not been solved so far. This is mainly due to three issues — all relating to the provisions of the PNPCA itself.

First, it was contested when the PNPCA process would actually be over. Laos claimed that after the six months period stipulated in the PNPCA (Art. 5.5.1), it had complied with all requirements and was allowed to construct the project. Cambodia and Vietnam (and to some extent even Thailand), on the other hand, claimed that the process was not finished yet in April 2011. Cambodia, for instance, stated in its reply to the Prior Consultation Report (MRC, 2011c), that "the six months period for PC is not enough to cover many efforts" (MRC, 2011c, p. 2). Thailand and Vietnam also called for an extension of the consultation period.

Second, an in relation to the first challenge, the period of prior notification as stipulated in the PNPCA was contested. While the PNPCA stipulates that consultation should last six months from the date of receiving the documents (Art. 5.5.1) and that an extension should be permitted by a decision of the JC (Art. 5.5.2), it remains unclear under which conditions such extension should be granted. Since any decision taken by the JC — according to Art. 27 1995 Mekong Agreement — has to be taken by consensus, the question of a formal extension of the process could never be clarified.

Consequently, Laos moved ahead with the project while downstream countries claimed this to be a breach of the 1995 Mekong Agreement.

And third, disputed issues relating to the actual meaning of the PNPCA process and its influence on national and regional decision making could not be solved. Since Chapter II of the 1995 Mekong Agreement stipulates that "prior consultation is neither a right to veto a use nor a unilateral right to use water by any riparian without taking into account other riparians' rights" (1995 Mekong Agreement), the PNPCA does neither provide a go-ahead for the notifying party nor a veto power for the potentially affected party. Instead, states always have to strike a balance between their interests. This was, however, extremely difficult to achieve under given circumstances.

Overall, the ambiguity of the 1995 Mekong Agreement and, in particular, the PNPCA and its legal provisions has hindered effective dispute-resolution around the XHP. Consequently, some authors have argued that the XHP process failed because of "the ambiguity within the text of the 1995 Mekong Agreement and related procedures" (Rieu-Clarke, 2015, p. 3). Although a number of actors, including MRC's Development Partners in their statement during the January 2013 Council Meeting,[14] have called for a revision of the PNPCA, it seems unlikely that there will be agreement to alterations of the 1995 Mekong Agreement of the PNPCA in the near future given the current political situation in the LMB.

Beyond the PNPCA process, however, the MRC has had an important influence on the issues relating to the XHP project. The MRC has made a difference with regard to three dimensions — first, the cooperation process itself — ensuring that cooperation and communication means remained open among disputing parties — second, the provision of data and information that can guide more sustainable water resources management, and third, more technical aspects of the project itself.

---

[14]Development Partners emphasized that, "all ambiguities regarding the application of the PNPCA be resolved before any future mainstream project proceeds" (MRC, 2013c).

First, the MRC has provides member states with a negotiation forum through which they could address specific issues — such as the XHP — in the context of cooperative and integrated river basin management. Regular meetings of the MRC Council and the JC have allowed for maintaining communication channels even in times of dispute and have, moreover, required all member states to share information with each other. Moreover, the MRC Secretariat as well as various working and expert groups on specific topics relating to hydropower development in the basin have ensured the constant flow of information on the project, its impacts and the possibilities to mitigate those impacts between the countries.

In this context, the second key contribution of the MRC so sustainable water resources management even under conflicting interests is its role as a basin knowledge hub, gathering, analyzing, and disseminating data on the state of the basin, the different pressures it faces and the impacts of specific projects as well as the potential for mitigating them (e.g., the MRC's State of the Basin Report, MRC, 2010b). In this context, the MRC Preliminary Design Guidance has played a particularly important role. Developed in 2009, the Preliminary Design Guidance (MRC, 2009) is a document adopted by all MRC member states that provides very detailed guidance on how hydropower projects on the Mekong mainstream have to be designed. This concerns technical design issues (e.g., the length and width of navigation locks), but also the mitigation of negative environmental effects (e.g., by requiring that "fish passage facilities for both upstream and downstream passage must be incorporated into all dams on the mainstream," with the even more specific requirement to ensure "safe passage for 95% of the target species under all flow conditions," MRC, 2009, p. 12). The Preliminary Design Guidance has, indeed, significantly influenced the discussion on the XHP. A number of actors, including the Lao government, the developer, and a consulting firm advising the Lao government on project-related matters have referred to it, emphasizing that the project would be in line with the requirements of the MRC as defined in the Preliminary Design Guidance (GoL, 2012 and Pöyry, 2012).

Based on the MRC's technical guidance and its overall role as a basin knowledge hub, changes of the project have indeed been initiated. For instance, the original spillway outline design has been adapted by introducing additional large capacity low level outlets equipped with radial gates and additional fish migration facilities have been included into the design (Pöyry, 2012). While it is unlikely that these mitigation efforts will be sufficient to counter the expected negative environmental (and related socioeconomic) effects of the XHP, the MRC has nevertheless played an important role in triggering changes that would otherwise not have been undertaken at all.

Overall, it can hence be confirmed that the MRC does play a crucial role in ensuring sustainable management of shared water resources in the basin and guiding individual national development projects toward more sustainability. While a lot remains to be done and sustainability is by far not ensured yet in the Mekong River Basin, the counterfactual situation — unilateral dam development without the MRC as a body coordinating and guiding water resources development in the basin — would be much worse. The MRC as an RBO does thus play a crucial role in managing disputes that arise between riparian states over the use and protection of their shared resources. However, it does so in a much broader way that was to be expected from the mere analysis of specific dispute-resolution mechanisms.

7.3.2. *Case Study II: The Nile River Basin and the GERD*

7.3.2.1. *The cooperation framework in Nile basin*

The Nile River Basin and its water resources have been a source of conflict and cooperation between the 11 riparians for many decades. While a number of multilateral RBOs have been established within the White Nile Basin (e.g., the LVFO or the Lake Victoria Basin Commission [LVBC]), there is only one RBO that incorporates downstream riparians along the Blue Nile Basin (Ethiopia, Sudan, and Egypt) — the so-called Nile Basin Initiative (NBI). NBI's main role so far has been to provide a platform for exchanging and collecting research data on the Nile Basin as well as to identify investment opportunities for joint development projects. The NBI was established at a regional meeting of the Nile Basin countries in 1999 with the objective "to achieve sustainable socioeconomic development through equitable utilization of, and benefit from, the common Nile Basin water resources" (NBI Act, 2002). As the RBO has always been meant to be an interim institution it lacks any binding regional treaty or agreement. However, the NBI Act from 2002 outlines the RBO's main institutional structure, including a high-decision-making body in form of the Council of Ministers of Water Affairs (Nile-COM), a Technical Advisory Committee (Nile-TAC), and a permanent Secretariat (Nile-SEC) based in Entebbe, Uganda. The Secretariat as the permanent structure of the NBI is not only responsible for administrative and financial management of the RBO but also for the implementation of basin programs. The NBI Act makes not further reference to principles of international water law or even more specific dispute-resolution mechanisms or procedures.

The more recent process over the Cooperative Framework Agreement (CFA), which aims to establish a permanent Nile River Basin Commission (NBC) once the agreement has come into force, has been unilaterally pursued by the lower Nile Basin riparians (White Nile) together with Ethiopia. In contrast to the NBI the founding agreement of the CFA acknowledges the possibility of arising disputes and makes provisions for the resolution of such (thereby heavily relying on the UN Watercourse Convention). In Article 33, the agreement outlines that dispute arising between riparians should first be tried to solve through the NBC or another third party, an arbitration procedure or may be submitted to the ICJ. In case such dispute-resolution fails, the dispute can be submitted to a fact-finding commission to make recommendations for the solution of the dispute (Annex Fact Finding Commission) which is, however, not binding to the members.

The CFA has not yet entered into force but is likely to do so in the near future (once six riparians have ratified the document).

Once into force, the new NBC will replace the NBI. However, as Egypt and Sudan are not signatories to the CFA the agreement will have no legal effect on them.

In the past, the lower Nile Basin riparians have encountered a number of disputes (e.g., Salman, 2013; Swain, 1997). In particular, there has been a long-standing disagreement regarding the binding nature of several colonial water agreements (including among others the 1929 Nile Waters Agreement and the 1959 Nile Water Agreement) which divide the Nile water resources between Sudan and Egypt without considering water allocation to upper riparians. None of the other Nile states has, therefore, ever considered itself bound to any of these agreements.

Another closely related field of dispute has emerged along the negotiations around a permanent Nile agreement (CFA) which started not long after the establishment of the NBI. While Sudan and Egypt insist on including their claims on acquired historical rights as well as a veto power on any project along the Nile (as given to them in the aforementioned treaties) into the agreement, all other riparians reject these claims. Attempts to overcome the dispute had been unsuccessful, leading to the de facto split of the NBI in 2010/11. Six of the upstream equatorial countries as well as Ethiopia (the so-called Entebbe Group) have since signed the CFA and three (Ethiopia, Ruanda, and Tanzania) have already ratified the agreement.[15] The dispute over the CFA culminated in the temporal withdrawal of Sudan and Egypt from the NBI in 2010. While Sudan resumed participation in 2014, Egypt still remains absent form NBI processes.

7.3.2.2. *The dispute around the GERD*

Although the upstream riparians, and in particular Ethiopia, have repeatedly claimed rights to the Blue Nile water resources, there had been no serious challenge to the position of Egypt and Sudan

---

[15]Compare NBI website: http://www.nilebasin.org/index.php/spotlight/99-cfa-overview and http://www.nilebasin.org/index.php/about-us/the-nb-cooperative-framework.

until Ethiopia announced its plans to construct GERD in April 2011 (Ethiopian News, 2011).[16] The dam is being built along the mainstream of the Blue Nile in the northwestern region of Ethiopia close to the border of Sudan. The main purpose of GERD is the generation of hydropower (up to 6000 MW) to be used locally as well as an export commodity to neighboring countries such as Sudan and Kenya. With a storage capacity of 74 billion m^3 the dam will hold more water than the average annual flow of the Blue Nile.[17] Up on completion in 2017, GERD will be the largest such project on the African continent. Because downstream riparian Egypt opposes any upstream construction of any structures that could potentially change the current state of water flow, the Government of Ethiopia was not able to raise money from international actors and hence entirely relies on national funds to raise the four billion USD for GERD's construction. The government has therefore issued several bonds and raises further money through donations as well as taxes (Ighobor and Bafana, 2014).[18]

For Ethiopia, GERD is a project of national pride and one among a range of projects currently in progress to boost the countries industrial development and regional economic integration (compare Ministry of Finance and Economic Development [MOFED], 2010). Government officials have repeatedly emphasized the national as well as regional benefits that can be derived from GERD (e.g., Daily Ethiopia, 2012). Most prominently, the hydropower generated from GERD will provide important electricity needed to boost Ethiopian's economy and also generate income through electricity sales to neighboring countries. Ethiopia furthermore argues that the control of the water flow will also facilitate flood management, reduce evaporative

---

[16]Increasing political stability, economic growth, and changing regional power relations have put Ethiopia in a position to realize a project as GERD (compare Cascao, 2009; Abebe, 2014, pp. 41–43).

[17]The project is realized by the Italian construction company Salini Impregilo which is also involved in other hydropower projects in the country, including Gibe III.

[18]Additionally, a loan from China provides funding for the construction of transmission lines.

losses, and decrease sediment inflows into downstream reservoirs such as Rosaries, Merowe, and the Aswan High dam, and therefore provide benefits to downstream riparians. However, a number of uncertainties and possible negative impacts on downstream states remain (IPoE, 2013; Non-partisan Eastern Nile Working Group, 2014). First of all, the exact social and environmental impacts on downstream riparians are to date unknown as only a preliminary assessment of transboundary impacts in downstream areas had been conducted prior to the start of construction. It was only in April 2015 after several rounds of negotiations that Ethiopia together with Sudan and Egypt in a joint effort appointed two European consultancy firms with assessing the dam's social and environmental impacts on downstream countries.[19] Considering that reduction in downstream stream-flow will at least take place during the filling process of GERD's reservoir (compare Zhang *et al.*, 2015), some environmental and social impacts are likely to be expected during this period.

Ethiopia has furthermore not yet signed any agreements on the sale of the generated electricity to neighboring countries (which is a precondition for acquiring investments and constructing necessary transmission lines).[20] This in turn could affect the quantity of water that can be released from the dam to downstream states (the fewer electricity will be produced, the less water will be released through the dam's turbines). There are also uncertainties with regard to the safety of a saddle dam which is meant to prevent the spilling of water from GERD whose foundations (weathered rock) are likely to exhibit weak zones that could allow significant seepage or, in worst case, even cause the rupture of the dam, if not monitored carefully. Finally, concerns have been raised regarding the capacities of GERD's release

---

[19]Originally, the French company BRL Ingénierie was selected to conduct the two impact and the Dutch company Deltares, favored by Egypt, was chosen as a subcontractor. However, Deltares withdrew from the project and was replaced by another French company (see page 24).

[20]Recently, Ethiopia and Sudan, however, signed an agreement on investigating how to connect both countries' power grids (Sudan Tribune, 2015a).

outlets and whether they can provide the required quantity of water releases.[21]

The dam project is generally perceived as a major challenge to the current status quo and the 1929 and 1959 agreements which Egypt still considers binding.[22] Egypt therefore is the main opponent of the project as the country fears that water flow within its part of the basin will be significantly diminished once GERD has been finalized. The downstream country is furthermore concerned that GERD could not only be used to produce hydropower but also to divert water from the Blue Nile and to open the doors for further upstream developments. Considering that the Nile waters are the main water sources of the country and are a significant factor for the irrigation-based agricultural sector that employs over 30% of the population, the Nile water is of high political relevance.[23] The loss of control over the Nile water resources is therefore perceived as a serious national security threat and has also been communicated as such within Egypt for several decades.[24]

Although earlier documents made notifications of a hydropower plant (e.g., MOFED, 2010), the construction of GERD was only officially announced by the Ethiopian Government in April 2011 without prior notification to any other riparians via the media (for an overview of the process, refer to Annex II).[25] Though Egyptian

---

[21] These last two uncertainties stem from a lack of technical information provided by Ethiopia and could hence turn out to be insignificant once the required information is made public.

[22] The treaties from 1929 and 1959 grant 55.5 billion m^3 of the estimated total 84 m^3 of Nile water to Egypt and 18.5 billion m^3 to Sudan. According to the 1929 agreement, Egypt furthermore has a veto right on any planned measures along the Nile that could affect its interests.

[23] The Nile River provides 96% of Egypt's renewable freshwater resources.

[24] For decades, Egyptian politicians have supported a discourse which closely connects the countries' security to the flow of the Nile waters. The former Egyptian president Anwar Sadat several times even emphasized that Egypt would be willing to fight a war over the Nile waters.

[25] Already in February 2011, Ethiopia's Prime Minister Meles Zenawi presented the plans for the construction of a hydropower dam, then called Project X, along the Blue Nile to the Ethiopian Parliament (Ministry of Foreign Affairs, 2014; Whittington *et al.*, 2014, p. 5).

officials expressed their disapproval, there was only limited opposition at this particular time as Ethiopia's announcement fell in the time of the Arab Spring and the protests against Egyptian President Hosni Mubarak. Despite Egypt's objection, Ethiopia started construction in April 2011 and will most likely complete construction in 2017.

The relations between Ethiopia and Egypt experienced a critical point in mid-2013 after Ethiopia temporarily diverted the water flow to build the dam walls. This provoked a series of verbal exchanges and culminated in June 2013 when during a Government Meeting President Morsi promised to "defend each drop of the Nile water with our blood" and high Egyptian government officials proposed the forceful destruction of GERD and the support of antigovernment rebels, being unaware of the live broadcast of their discussion on national TV (Kingsley, 2013; Raus, 2013).

While Sudan initially also opposed the construction of GERD, it soon changed sides, realizing the different benefits it could derive from cooperation with Ethiopia (Daily Ethiopia, 2012; Tesfa-Alem Tekle, 2013). Sudan is particularly interested in purchasing electricity and could also benefit from decreasing siltation accumulating in its own dams and from a more regulated flow to increase agricultural production.

In parallel to mutual allegations between Ethiopia and Egypt and the launch of GERD construction, negotiations between the opposing parties took place from the very beginning of the conflict. These negotiations were particularly facilitated through the Government of Sudan, although external actors like the World Bank also tried to play a facilitating role. In May 2012 Ethiopia, Egypt, and Sudan agreed to establish — as outlined in the procedures of the UN Watercourse Convention (1997, Art. 33) — an IPoE composed of two representatives from each country as well as four international experts. The panel members subsequently reviewed the GERD design documents that were made available by Ethiopia at this time in order to estimate the impacts on the downstream areas and furthermore inspected the construction site in Ethiopia. The panel's final report was submitted to the parties in May 2013. However, Egypt and Ethiopia disagreed on the panel's main findings and the interpretation of the report. While Ethiopia argued that the panel's report shows that GERD offers "significant benefits which would accrue to all the three basin countries as the project would not result in any significant adverse impact on the two downstream countries" (Ministry of Foreign Affairs, 2013), Egypt maintained the "environmental and socioeconomic report fails to address the impacts on the downstream countries" (Ministry of Water and Energy, 2014).

The report has only been made accessible to the public in 2014 by International Rivers (International Rivers, 2014).[26] Looking at the report itself, one finds that it is largely general in nature and that no section in the report provides a straightforward interpretation of the technical design documents. It, however, underlines the lack of available data and information on a number of important issues, such as impacts of changes in sediments, and that many key studies are out-of-date and do not take major changes in the dam design into consideration (the design of the dam has experienced major changes over the years). Finally, the IPoE report recommends the conduction of a detailed transboundary environmental and social impact assessment that should quantify expected impacts (IpoE, 2013, pp. 42–43).

To follow-up on the implementation of the IPoE's recommendations and prepare the conduction of impact studies, the three parties launched a series of tripartite ministerial meetings between November 2013 and September 2014. At the last ministerial meeting in September 2014 the three countries decided to establish a Tripartite Technical Committee (TTC) comprising of four representatives from each country (Sudan Tribune, 2015a). The TTC convened several times to discuss the preparation and implementation of the proposed impact studies. Among others it provided a platform to share some further technical studies that hadn't previously been made available and guided the selection process on the consultancy firms to conduct

---

[26]International Rivers is an international NGO that critically observes the construction of dams and campaigns for the rights of dam affected people. It has been criticized by Ethiopia to take side in favor of Egypt.

the environmental and social impact studies as well as a study on hydrological modeling (Masriya, 2014). After selecting the two consulting companies BRL Ingénierie and Deltares in early 2015, the three countries, however, disagreed on the exact study details until one of the consulting companies (Deltares) finally withdrew from the contract. The company declared that under the given conditions imposed by the TTC and BRL Ingéniere, it could not guarantee the production of a high-quality independent study.[27] The withdrawal of Deltares further prolonged the initiation of the impact studies. It was only in December 2015, after negotiations moved to the ministerial level again, that the Foreign and Water Resources Ministers of the three countries agreed to replace Deltares by the French ARTELIA Group (Sudan Tribune, 2015b).

These trilateral negotiations happened outside NBI structures and culminated in the signing of a presidential agreement in March 2015 — the Agreement on Declaration of Principles between Egypt, Ethiopia, and Sudan. This agreement was praised as an important breakthrough in the negotiation process. The declaration is based on principles of international water law as, among others, reflected in the UN Watercourse Convention (1997). In the agreement, Egypt for the first time officially acknowledges Ethiopia's rights to develop the Nile water resources falling within its territory (principle of equitable and reasonable use, see Art. 2) while Ethiopia at, the same time, commits itself to avoid to significantly affect the potentials of water use in Egypt (principle of no significant harm, see Art. 3). The declaration furthermore specifies the objective of the project as to which "the purpose of GERD is for power generation" (Art. 2). This clearly addresses Egypt's concerns of potential upstream consumptive uses, such as for irrigation purposes, which would reduce water availability downstream. The agreement also reemphasized the need for the three parties to conduct the impacts studies as recommended by the IPoE (see previous paragraph). The

---

[27]Compare Deltares website: https://www.deltares.nl/en/news/deltares-with draws-from-gerd-studies/ [accessed 20 September 2015].

parties furthermore express their commitment to develop guidelines and rules on the process of dam filling as well as to coordinate the annual operation of their major dams along the Nile River. This point addresses the diverging interests between Egypt and Sudan on the future operation of GERD.

The original time frame foreseen in the agreement for the implementation of these activities was 15 months after signing the agreement. However almost a year after concluding the agreement, the three parties are still engaged in preparatory discussions on the technical design details and will hence not be able to implement the activities outlined in the agreement in the given time frame.

Despite the difficulties that followed regarding the implementation of the agreement (neither the impact studies have yet been conducted nor operational guidelines for dam filling and operation have been negotiated), the signing of the document can be seen as an important first step toward defusing the conflict around GERD. Both, Egypt as well as Ethiopia, made important concessions and for the first time acknowledge main principles of international water law. While Egypt is now in a position where it officially acknowledges the rights of upstream countries to develop the Nile River resources and hence does not question the mere existence of the GERD anymore, Ethiopia has committed itself toward coordinating the filling and the operation of the dam with its downstream neighbors — addressing one major issue of controversy. Politicians from both countries have emphasized that relations between them have improved over recent months (Reem, 2015) and also media reports in both countries have markedly toned down conflict rhetoric (e.g., El-Bey, 2015; Sewilam, 2015). With regard to the latter it can be observed that media coverage on GERD issues in Ethiopia as well as Egypt have started to increasingly cover views from the respective other side, for example, through interviews with technical experts. Newspaper articles have furthermore generally shifted from defending their own national views (mostly in very emotional ways) toward covering more technical issues around the dam.

7.3.2.3. *The role of the NBI*

The earlier outlined process shows that important steps toward conflict resolution around GERD have been taken since the beginning of construction and that the dispute between the riparians, although far from being solved, has lost much in intensity. While the NBI did not contribute to diplomatic negotiations between the three parties, it nonetheless contributed to dissolving the conflict in more indirect ways. The case shows that although an RBO might not matter in a narrow conflict resolution role (and hence the presence or absence of a specific conflict resolution mechanism) it can still make a difference through more indirect means of conflict mitigation.

With regard to the dispute around GERD and the lack of direct involvement by the NBI, two points need to be emphasized that can explain this noninvolvement. First, Egypt as well as Sudan suspended their NBI membership just prior the announcement of Ethiopia's plans to construct GERD. Therefore, the conflict took place at a time when the two major conflict parties did not fully participate in the RBO's activities. Although Egypt and Sudan did not entirely terminate their membership and still engaged in different NBI activities (Egypt for instance still appointed NBI's Executive Manager between 2010 and 2012 and both countries participated in different technical work groups) the NBI lacked any official mandate to facilitate negotiations between the parties at the diplomatic level.

Second, even if Sudan and Ethiopia would have been fully participating in NBI activities at the time the conflict broke out, it would have been difficult if not impossible for the RBO to function as a "neutral" platform for the conflict parties to negotiate a potential solution at the political level. Because of the underlying dispute around the overall allocation of Nile water resources which have not been addressed by the RBO and which have divided the NBI in two opposing groups (downstream Sudan and Egypt on the one side and upstream Ethiopia as well as the Equatorial States on the other) addressing the key issues of concern around the GERD conflict would have very likely been unfruitful.

Despite the lack of direct influence on the conflict resolution process, the NBI has made a difference through its broader activities around data and information sharing and increasingly distributing this knowledge to the broader public. The RBO's increasing media outreach activities have contributed toward a growing focus on the benefits that can be derived from cooperation and by doing so also to defusing the conflict around construction of GERD. In recent years, the NBI has developed a strong and proactive involvement with media houses, individual newspapers, and journalists as well as social media in order to improve the reporting on different Nile issues, such as the potentials for benefit sharing, informing about various national and joint activities, and distributing the results of different technical studies. It has furthermore been engaged in a range of capacity building activities (e.g., training of journalists). With these activities the NBI aims at informing the public and improving the knowledge about various Nile Basin issues. Considering the lack of neutral reporting in many Nile countries on contested issues, including the construction of GERD, these activities are an important step toward creating public understanding of diverging interests and perceptions and to build confidence.

Similarly to the Mekong, the Nile case study furthermore illustrates the general importance of data and information sharing. The case around GERD illustrates that potential negative as well as positive impacts of hydropower projects are not always straightforward and can be interpreted in different ways. It is therefore particularly important to have reliable data and information which is available to all riparians. As previous research has already emphasized, uncertainties and misunderstandings around the dam's hydrological impacts on downstream riparians have contributed to the intensification of the dispute between Ethiopia and Egypt (Whittington *et al.*, 2014). The two consulting companies which have now been awarded with the mandate to evaluate the environmental and hydrological impacts of the dam will hence play a major role in the process of dispute resolution in the future. The technical studies on impacts of GERD could help to further facilitate negotiations around a possible solution of the dispute. However, if they include major uncertainties or allow for different interpretations, they could also contribute to a stalemate of negotiation process.

Summarizing, one can say that although the NBI did not directly contribute to conflict resolution between the parties it nonetheless supported the process by influencing national discourses on contested Nile issues through its various media outreach activities. Considering that any final solution on the conflict will require substantial domestic support this role of the RBO is an important contribution toward long-term dispute resolution.

7.4. Conclusion

As experiences from around the world indicate, disagreements over the use of shared water resources can emerge anytime — especially in times of rapid socioeconomic, political, or environmental change. Sometimes, simple disagreements grow to veritable conflicts that threaten not only the sustainable management of water resources but also the overall development of entire regions. This chapter therefore addressed the role of international RBOs in solving disputes over the use of shared water resources and their respective dispute-resolution mechanisms. The analysis shows that RBOs do matter for addressing water-related disputes in international basins — but not necessarily on the basis of their dispute-resolution mechanisms in a narrow sense. Instead, RBOs have proven to be important for addressing conflicts through a number of their typical tasks: First of all, RBOs provide a forum for negotiation. As shown in the Mekong case, the presence of the MRC provided a platform for the member states to exchange their views on the XHP and to start a negotiation process, which helped avoid a further escalation of the conflict. This holds particularly true if compared with other hydropower projects in the world — such as the Rogun project between Tajikistan and Uzbekistan, for instance — where conflicts have escalated in a much faster and a much more intensive way because no exchange and negotiation was possible in a structured and institutionalized manner.

Second, RBOs ensure the gathering, analysis, and sharing of data and information. In the case of the Mekong, Laos shared important data and information on the XHP design with other members through the MRC Secretariat. This allowed other parties to assess the potential impacts of the dam on their parts of the basin and request Laos to make changes on the dam design — changes that have indeed been implemented to some extent. Moreover, the exchange between Laos and the MRC has prompted the Lao government to ask the developer to gather more data than originally intended for the XHP (especially on fish migration). This data will not only help to mitigate some of the impacts of the project, but also provides an important knowledge base for the entire basin — if shared in a sufficiently transparent manner. Through this data and information sharing role RBOs can also help reframe conflicts into more technical challenges rather than security-driven national political consideration as exemplified by the NBI. The RBO's activities regarding knowledge distribution through national media is an important contribution to desecuritize national discourses around the construction of GERD and hence a precondition for any final resolution of the dispute.

Finally, RBOs help address potentially conflictive issues relatively early on through notification mechanisms. In the case of the Nile and the dispute around GERD, the lack of any prior notification mechanisms and guidelines on the sharing of data and information on planned infrastructure measures has allowed the dispute to emerge in the first place. The failure of Ethiopia to notify downstream neighbors about the construction of the dam and to provide necessary technical data on the design of GERD as well as expected downstream impacts from it has raised great concern in downstream countries, in particular Egypt, which heavily relies on the water resources of the Nile. The lack of communication and uncertainty about the design of the dam and its downstream impacts has caused fear in Egypt that it would be deprived of its "fair share" of water resources — even if actual impacts might be fewer than expected. In the case of the MRC, on the other hand, the existence of a predefined mechanism for notification (the PNPCA) has allowed to bring the dam developing state and the potentially affected state together relatively early on. Even if the PNPCA has proven less well-designed and effective than originally hoped for, it has helped to channel disagreements and avoided an escalation such as in the Nile River Basin.

Overall, the chapter has shown that RBOs make a difference with regard to water resource conflicts, although not necessarily through their specific dispute-resolution mechanism. Future research on conflict-resolution within international river basins should therefore increasingly focus on broader RBO governance mechanisms (beyond narrow dispute-resolution mechanisms — if defined at all) and their role in not only solving disputes that arise over water resources in transboundary basins, but also proactively avoiding them in the first place. Only such a wider focus on RBO governance instruments will help to improve our understanding of how RBOs can contribute to solving water resources conflicts most effectively (and how their capacities in doing so could be improved).

References

Abebe, D (2014). *Egypt, Ethiopia, and the Nile: The Economics of International Water Law* (Public Law and Legal Theory Working Paper No. 484).

Agreement on the Cooperation for the Sustainable Development of the Mekong River Basin signed on April 5, 1995. Chiang Rai: Thailand.

Bangkok Post (17 April 2011). *Xayaburi Dam Starts on Sly.* http://www.vietnamica.net/xayaburi-dam-starts-on-sly/. [Accessed 21 December 2014].

Bernauer, T (1997). Managing international rivers. In *Global Governance: Drawing Insights from the Environmental Experience*, O Young (ed.), pp. 155–195. Cambridge: MIT Press.

Boisson de Chazournes, L (2013). *Fresh Water in International Law* (New edition). Oxford: Oxford University Press.

Caponera, DA (1980). The Law of International Water Resources: Some General Conventions, Declarations, and Resolutions adopted by Governments, International Legal Institutions, and International Organizations, on the Management of International Water Resources. In *Food and Agriculture Organization. Legislative study*, Vol. 23. Rome: Food and Agriculture Organization.

Cascao, AE (2009). *Institutional Analysis of the Nile Basin Initiative: What worked, what did not work and what are the emerging options?*

Nile basin Focal Project Report. Retrieved from http://hdl.handle.net/
10568/21547 *Convention on Environmental Impact Assessment in a
Transboundary Context* (Espoo, 1991).

Convention Creating the Niger Basin Authority signed on 21 November 1980, Farnah.

Daily Ethiopia (14 April 2012). *Sudan's Support for the Grand Ethiopian
Renaissance Dam Project.* Retrieved from http://news.sudanvision
daily.com/details.html?rsnpid=209069. [Accessed 28 July 2016].

de Bruyne, C and I Fischhendler (2013). Negotiating conflict resolution
mechanisms for transboundary water treaties: A transaction cost
approach. *Global Environmental Change*, 23(6), 1841–1851.

deStefano, L, L de Silva, P Edwards, and A Wolf (2012). *Updating the
International Water Events Database.* UN World Water Assessment
Programme, Side Publication Series. Paris: UNESCO.

Dinar, A (2004). Treaty principles and patters: Negotiations over International Rivers, Baltimore. PhD Thesis, Johns Hopkins Institute.

Eckstein, GE (2002). Development of international water law and the UN
Watercourse Convention. In *Hydropolitics in the Developing World.
A Southern African Perspective*, A Turton and R. Henwood (eds.),
pp. 81–96. Pretoria: African Water Issues Research Unit (AWIRU) and
International Water Management Institute (IWMI).

Economist (2016). Requiem for a river. Can one of the great waterways
survive its development? *Economist.* Retrieved from http://www.eco
nomist.com/news/essays/21689225-can-one-world-s-great-waterways-
survive-its-development. [10 November 2015] El-Bey, D (31 December
2015). Questions in Khartoum. *Al-Ahram Weekly.* Retrieved from
http://weekly.ahram.org.eg/News/15114/17/Questions-in-Khartoum.
aspx. [Accessed on 05 January 2016].

Elhance, A (1999). *Hydropolitics in the 3rd World: Conflict and Cooperation
in International River Basins.* Washington: United States Institute for
Peace Press.

Espey, M and B Towfique (2004). International bilateral water treaty
formation. *Water Resources Research*, 40(4), W05–S05.

Ethiopian News (2 April 2011). *Ethiopia Launched Grand Millennium
Dam Project, the Biggest in Africa.* http://www.ethiopian-news.
com/ethiopia-launched-grand-millennium-dam-project-the-biggest-in-
africa/ [Accessed on 2 February 2015].

Galtung, J. (1998). *Frieden mit friedlichen Mitteln: Friede und Konflikt,
Entwicklung und Kultur.* Friedens- und Konfliktforschung: Vol. 4.
Opladen: Leske + Budrich.

Giordano, MA and AT Wolf (2003). Transboundary freshwater treaties. In
Water Resources Management and Policy Series, M. Nakayama (ed.),

pp. 71–100. International Waters in Southern Africa. Tokyo: United Nations University Press.

Giordano, M, A Drieschova, JA Duncan, Y Sayama, L de Stefano, and AT Wolf (2014). A review of the evolution and state of transboundary freshwater treaties. *International Environmental Agreements*, 14(3), 245–264.

Government of Laos (GoL) (30 March 2012). *Xayaburi Hydroelectric Power Project. Peer Review of the Compliance Report Made by Pöyry.* Retrieved from http://www.poweringprogress.org/download/Reports/2012/April/Final-report-V1.pdf.

Hamner, JH and AT Wolf (1998). Patterns in international water resource treaties: The Transboundary Freshwater Dispute Database. *Colorado Journal of International Environmental Law and Policy* 1997 Yearbook.

Hirsch, Philip and Jensen, Kurt Morck (2006): *National interests and transboundary water governance in the Mekong*, Australian Mekong Resource Center/Danish International Development Assistance, 5/2006.

Ighobor, K and B Bafana (December 2014). Financing Africa's massive projects. *Africa Renewal*, p. 6. Retrieved from http://www.un.org/africarenewal/magazine/december-2014/financing-africa%E2%80%99s-massive-projects [14 February 2014].

International Court of Justice (ICJ) (2010). Pulp Mills on the River Uruguay (Argentina v. Uruguay). http://www.icj-cij.org/docket/index.php?p1=3&p2=3&case=135&p3=4 [4 November 2015].

International Panel of Experts (IPoE) (2013). *Grand Ethiopian Renaissance Dam Project: Final Report.* Addis Ababa, Ethiopia. Retrieved from http://www.internationalrivers.org/files/attached-files/international_panel_of_experts_for_ethiopian_renaissance_dam-_final_report_1.pdf. [2 March 2015].

International Rivers (2014). GERD Panel of Experts Report: Big Questions Remain. 31 May 2013, Addis Ababa, Ethiopia [Last modified 2 March 2015]. http://www.internationalrivers.org/gerd-panel-of-experts-report-big-questions-remain

Kingsley, P (11 June 2013). Ethiopia rejects Egyptian protests over Nile Dam. *The Guardian*. Retrieved from http://www.theguardian.com/world/2013/jun/11/ethiopia-rejects-egyptian-protests-nile-dam [28 July 2016].

Masriya, A (23 September 2014). Ethiopia hands Egypt safety studies of main dam: Ministry of Water Resources. *Ahram Online*. Retrieved from http://english.ahram.org.eg/News/111470.aspx.

McLaughlin Mitchell, S and NA Zawahri (2015). The effectiveness of treaty design in addressing water disputes. *Journal of Peace Research*, 52(2), 187–200.

Ministry of Finance and Economic Development (MOFED) (2010). *Growth and Transformation Plan. 2010/11–2014/15*. Addis Ababa. http://www.mofed.gov.et/English/Resources/Documents/GTP%20English2.pdf [28 January 2016].

Ministry of Foreign Affairs (2013b). The International Panel of Expert's report on the Grand Renaissance Dam submits its report to respective leadership. *News Release*. June 14. http://www.mfa.gov.et/weekHornAfrica/morewha.php?wi=1026#1026 [3 March 2015].

Ministry of Water and Energy (16 January 2014). Setting the record straight: What really transpired during the third tripartite ministerial meeting of Egypt, Ethiopia and Sudan. *News Release*. http://www.mowr.gov.et/index.php?pagenum=0.1&ContentID=108 [2 January 2015].

MRC (31 August 2009). *Preliminary Design Guidance for Proposed Mainstream Dams in the Lower Mekong Basin*. Vientiane, Lao PDR. http://www.mrcmekong.org/assets/Publications/Consultations/SEA-Hydropower/Preliminary-DG-of-LMB-Mainstream-dams-FinalVersion-Sept09.pdf. [10 November 2015]

MRC (October 2010a). *Strategic Environmental Assessment of Hydropower on the Mekong Mainstream*. ICEM/MRC.

MRC (2010b). *State of the Basin Report 2010*. Vientiane: MRC.

MRC (24 March 2011a). *Prior Consultation Project Review Report. Procedures for Notification, Prior Consultation and Agreement (PNPCA). Proposed Xayaburi Dam Project—Mekong River*. Vientiane, Lao PDR.

MRC (April 2011b). *Reply to Prior Consultation*. Submitted by the Thai National Mekong Committee. Bangkok, Thailand.

MRC (13 April 2011c). *Reply to Prior Consultation*. Submitted by the Cambodia National Mekong Committee. Phnom Penh, Cambodia.

MRC (15 April 2011d). *Reply to Prior Consultation*. Submitted by the Vietnam National Mekong Committee. Hanoi, Vietnam.

MRC (8 December 2011e). *Minutes of the 18th Meeting of the MRC Council*, Siem Reap, Cambodia. http://www.mrcmekong.org/assets/Publications/governance/Minutes-of-the-18th-Council.pdf. [10 November 2015]

MRC (28 November 2012a). *Concept Note on the Follow-Up of the MRC Council Meeting Decision of 8 December 2011 to Conduct a Study on Sustainable Management and Development of the Mekong River Including Impacts by Mainstream Hydropower Projects*. MRC Secretariat. Vientiane, Lao PDR.

MRC (17 January 2013a). *Minutes of the Meeting of the MRC Council.* Luang Prabang, Laos (not published).

MRC (17 January 2013b). *Statement by H.E. Dr. Nguyen Thai Lai, 19th Meeting of the MRC Council.* Luang Prabang, Lao PDR. http://www. mrcmekong.org/news-and-events/speeches/statement-by-h-e-dr-nguyen-thai-lai-19th-meeting-of-the-mrc-council/. [10 November 2015]

MRC (17 January 2013c). *Joint Development Partner Statement. 19th MRC Council Meeting.* Luang Prabang, Lao PDR, http://www. mrcmekong.org/news-and-events/speeches/joint-development-partner-statement-19th-mrc-council-meeting-17-january-2013/. [10 November 2015].

MRC (7 July 2014a). *The Study on the Sustainable Management and Development of the Mekong River, Including Impacts of Mainstream Hydropower Projects. Inception Report.* Final Draft, MRC Secretariat. Vientiane, Lao PDR.

MRC (26 June 2014b). *MRC Council Reaches Conclusions on Pressing Issues.* http://www.mrcmekong.org/news-and-events/news/mrc-council-reaches-conclusions-on-pressing-issues/.[10 November 2015]

Non-partisan Eastern Nile Working Group (13–14 November 2014). *The Grand Ethiopian Renaissance Dam: An Opportunity for Collaboration and Shared Benefits in the Eastern Nile Basin.* Working Group Convened at the Massachusetts Institute of Technology. http://web.mit. edu/jwafs/pubdocs/GERD/MIT_NILE_GERD_BRIEF_FINAL.pdf [Accessed on 31 May 2015].

Pöyry (2011a). *Xayaburi Hydroelectric Power Project. Run-of-River Plant. Compliance Report.* Zurich, Switzerland/Vientiane, Lao PDR.

Pöyry (2011b). *Xayaburi Hydropower Plant, Lao PDR. Background Material on Pöyry's Assignment.* 9 November 2012. Zurich, Switzerland/ Vientiane, Lao PDR.

Pöyry (16 July 2012). *Xayaburi Run-of-River HPP. Presentation to Government of Lao PDR and Other Interested Stakeholders.* Luang Prabang, Laos. Retrieved from https://www.tem.fi/files/42855/Appen dix_1_Presentation_of_Poyry_at_meeting_of_16072012.PDF. [10 November 2015]

Reem, L (9 April 2015). Step ahead on the dam. *Al-Ahram Weekly.* Retrieved from http://weekly.ahram.org.eg/News/10947/17/Step-ahead-on-the-dam.aspx. [12 February 2016]

RFA (19 April 2012). *Cambodia Warns Laos over Mekong Dam. Phnom Penh threatens to take Laos to court if it moves ahead unilaterally with the Xayaburi dam project.* http://www.rfa.org/english/news/ cambodia/dam-04192012143244.html. [29 March 2014]

Rieu-Clarke, A (April 2015). Notification and consultation procedures under the Mekong Agreement: Insights from the Xayaburi Controversy. *Asian Journal of International Law, 5(1), 143–175.*

Salman, SM (2013). The Nile Basin Cooperative Framework Agreement: A peacefully unfolding African Spring? *Water International,* 38(1), 17–29.

Schmeier, S (10 June 2010). *The Organizational Structure of River Basin Organizations Lessons Learned and Recommendations for the Mekong River Commission (MRC).* Paper Prepared for the Mekong River Commission (MRC). http://www.mrcmekong.org/assets/Publica tions/governance/MRC-Technical-Paper-Org-Structure-of-RBOs.pdf [10 November 2015].

Schmeier, S (2013). *Governing International Watercourses. River Basin Organizations and the Sustainable Governance of Internationally Shared Rivers and Lakes.* London: Routledge.

Schmeier, S (2014). The institutional design of river basin organizations — empirical findings from around the world. *International Journal of River Basin Management,* 13(1), 51–72.

Schmeier, S, AK Gerlak, and S Blumstein (2016). Clearing the muddy waters of shared watercourses governance: Conceptualizing international River Basin Organizations. *International Environmental Agreements: Politics, Law and Economics,* 16(4), 597–619.

Sewilam, M (26 March 2015). A win-win situation. *Al-Ahram Weekly.* Retrieved from http://weekly.ahram.org.eg/News/10775/17/A-win-win-situation.aspx [12 March 2015]

Sohnle, J (2005). Nouvelles tendances en matière de règlement pacifique des différends relatifs aux ressources en eau douce internationales. In *Les resources en eau et le drout international,* L Boisson de Chazournes and S Salman (eds.), pp. 389–426. Leiden: Martinus Nijhoff Publishers.

Song, J and D Whittington (2004). Why have some countries on international rivers been successful negotiating treaties? A global perspective. *Water Resources Research,* 40(5), 1–18.

Sudan Tribune (22 July 2015a). *Sudan Seeks to Purchase Electricity from Ethiopia.* http://www.sudantribune.com/spip.php?article55797.

Sudan Tribune (29 December 2015b). *Sudan, Egypt and Ethiopia Reach Agreement on Renaissance Dam.* http://www.sudantribune.com/spip. php?iframe&page=imprimable&id_article=57526 [2 February 2016].

Swain, A (1997). Ethiopia, the Sudan, and Egypt: The Nile River dispute. *Journal of Modern African Studies,* 35(4), 675–694.

Swain, A (2004). *Managing Water Conflict: Asia, Africa and the Middle East.* London: Routledge.

Tanzi, A and M. Arcari (2001). *The United Nations Convention on the Law of International Watercourses: A Framework for Sharing.* International and national water law and policy series. London: Kluwer Law International.

Tesfa-Alem Tekle (14 December 2013). "No political motive" behind Sudan's support for Ethiopia's Nile dam: Ambassador. *Ethiopian News.* http://www.ethiopian-news.com/political-motive-behind-sudans-support-ethiopias-nile-dam-ambassador/ [11 February 2016].

The Diplomat (2015). Why the Mekong River Commission May Be in Peril. The future of the body hangs in the balance amid financial and performance concerns. *The Diplomat.* [10 October 2015].

The Nile Basin Initiative Act (NBI) (2002). An Act to confer legal status in Uganda on the Nile Basin Initiative, and otherwise give the force of law in Uganda to the signed Agreed Minute No. 7 of the 9th Annual Meeting of the Nile Basin States held in Cairo, Egypt, on 14th February 2002; and to provide for other connected or incidental matters.

Tir, J and J Ackermann (2009). Politics of formalized river cooperation. *Journal of Peace Research*, 46(5), 623–640.

UN Watercourse Convention (1997). United Nations Convention on the Law of the Non-Navigational Uses of International Watercourses.

United Nations Convention on the Protection and Use of Transboundary Watercourses and International Lakes, United Nations Economic Commission for Europe (UNECE) adopted on March 17, 1997, Helsinki, Finland.

Whittington, D, J Waterbury, and M Jeuland (2014). The Grand Renaissance Dam and prospects for cooperation on the Eastern Nile. *Water Policy*, 16(4), 595–608.

Wolf, AT (1997). International water conflict resolution: Lessons from comparative analysis. *International Journal of Water Resources Development*, 13(3), 333–366.

Wolf, A, S Yogge, and M Giordano (2003). International waters: Identifying basins at risk. *Water Policy*, 5(1), 29–60.

Zawahri, N (2008). Designing river commissions to implement treaties and manage water disputes: The story of the Joint Water Committee and the Permanent Indus Commission. *Water International*, 33(4), 464–474.

Zhang, Y, P Block, M Hammond, and A King (2015). Ethiopia's Grand Renaissance Dam: Implications for downstream riparian countries. *Journal of Water Resources Planning and Management*, 141(9), 05015002.

Annexes

Annex I: Overview of XHP Events

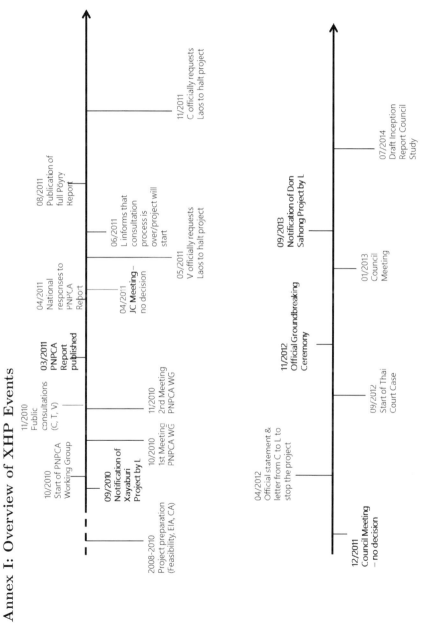

Annex II: Overview of GERD Events

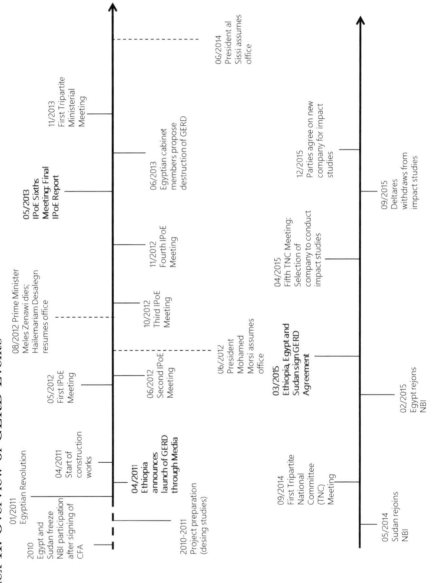

2010
Egypt and
Sudan freeze
NBI participation
after signing of
CFA

01/2011
Egyptian Revolution

04/2011
Start of
construction
works

**04/2011
Ethiopia
announces
launch of GERD
through Media**

2010–2011
Project preparation
(desing studies)

05/2012
First IPoE
Meeting

06/2012
Second IPoE
Meeting

06/2012
President
Mohamed
Morsi assumes
office

08/2012 Prime Minister
Meles Zenawi dies;
Hailemariam Desalegn
resumes office

10/2012
Third IPoE
Meeting

11/2012
Fourth IPoE
Meeting

**05/2013
IPoE Sixths
Meeting: Final
IPoE Report**

06/2013
Egyptian cabinet
members propose
destruction of GERD

11/2013
First Tripartite
Ministerial
Meeting

06/2014
President al
Sissi assumes
office

05/2014
Sudan rejoins
NBI

09/2014
First Tripartite
National
Committee
(TNC)
Meeting

02/2015
Egypt rejoins
NBI

**03/2015
Ethiopia, Egypt and
Sudan sign GERD
Agreement**

04/2015
Fifth TNC Meeting:
Selection of
company to conduct
impact studies

09/2015
Deltares
withdraws from
impact studies

12/2015
Parties agree on new
company for impact
studies

CHAPTER 8

TRANSBOUNDARY WATER MANAGEMENT ALONG THE TAGUS RIVER BASIN IN THE IBERIAN PENINSULA: SUSTAINABLE WATER ALLOCATION OF THE AQUEDUCT TAGUS-SEGURA

MARÍA E. MILANÉS MURCIA

Sindicato Central de Regantes del Acueducto Tajo-Segura
University of the Pacific, McGeorge School of Law
New Mexico Water Resources Research Institute

Spain and Portugal have established cooperation mechanisms to manage their shared water resources in order to avoid any potential conflict. Cooperation is clearly reflected in the 1998 Albufeira Convention, which provides a legal framework to regulate all transboundary basins between both countries to protect surface water and groundwater, as well as the aquatic and terrestrial ecosystems that depend on them for the sustainable use of water resources. The 1998 Albufeira Convention establishes as one of the uses of the Tagus Basin Gthe transfer of water interbasin such as the Aqueduct Tagus-Segura (ATS). According to this Convention, the management of water uses and the right to use water shall be addressed to guarantee the sustainable use of water that is already established. The ATS is a use guaranteed and protected under international water law. The analysis of the ATS in the context of the international legislation to mitigate water scarcity, and droughts provides the strategies to promote resilience to climate change and the impacts of drought conditions in the society in a sustainable manner while ensuring the fundamental rights.

Keywords: Agriculture; Allocation; Aqueduct; Convention; Cooperation; Desertification; Directive; Drought; European Union; Human rights; Interbasin transfers; International legal framework; Management plans;

Portugal; Segura; Solidarity; Spain; Spanish law; Sustainable; Tagus; Transboundary; Treaty; United Nations; Watercourses; Water right.

8.1. Introduction

The Tagus River is the longest watercourse of the Iberian Peninsula. It is a transboundary river shared by Spain (called Río Tajo), and Portugal (called Rio Tejo). The Tagus River rises in the Sierra de Albarracín of eastern Spain, and flows westward across Spain and Portugal for nearly 1000 km to empty into the Atlantic Ocean near Lisbon (Encyclopedia Britannica, 2015). The total drainage basin is approximately 81,447 km^2, of which 25,666 km^2 are in Portugal and 55,781 km^2 in Spain. The River Tagus provides water to the Aqueduct Tagus-Segura (ATS), which transfers water from the headwater of the Tagus River to the Segura River, and guarantees the sustainable development of one of the driest regions in Europe, avoiding the desertification of southeast Spain (Sindicato Central de Regantes del Acueducto Tajo-Segura [SCRATS], 2015). The Tagus River is an essential source of water for the population, the environment, the agriculture sector, and the economy of both countries (Encyclopedia Britannica, 2015).

Spain and Portugal have established cooperative mechanisms to manage their shared water resources in order to avoid any potential conflict (Spanish Government, "The International Duero," 2015). Both countries have developed institutional cooperation to allocate water resources along the border since the 19th century (Spanish Government, "The International Duero," 2015). Cooperation must also be reflected at the national level between regions in Spain. Cooperation is clearly established in the 1998 Albufeira Convention (Convention on Cooperation for the Protection and Sustainable Use of Waters in Portuguese–Spanish River Basins [Albufeira Convention], 1998), which provides a legal framework to regulate all transboundary basins

The author would like to acknowledge and thank Professor Ariel Dinar, Professor Stephen McCaffrey, and Professor Alexander Fernald for their orientations, and NM EPSCoR grant no. #IIA-1301346. The author specially acknowledge in memory of Mr. José Manuel Claver, the President of the Sindicato Central de Regantes del Acueducto Tajo-Segura.

including Miño, Limia, Duero, Guadiana, and Tagus. However, in Spain, there is a lack of cooperation among autonomous communities to manage water transfers from the Tagus Basin.

The ATS is not a source of conflict between Spain and Portugal. Moreover, Portugal has never complained about the use of the water transfers from the Aqueduct specially because the 1998 Albufeira Convention has always been complied by both countries. However, water transfers from this Aqueduct represent a source of dispute between Spanish riparian autonomous communities along the Tagus Basin and the autonomous communities in southeastern Spain, which receives the water transfers. Castilla-La Mancha, one of the Tagus Basin riparian autonomous communities, demands the immediate cessation of the flow of water to the southeast Spanish as political tensions grow with increasing water scarcity and drought. The southeast regions that need water for drinking and irrigation ensure that the water transfers comply with the law (Sevillano and Vazquez, 2015). This situation has brought serious uncertainty to over 2.5 million people, which depend on the Aqueduct water transfers to continue living in southeastern Spain.

International treaties are incorporated as national law once they are officially published in the Spanish Official Gazette (Boletín Oficial del Estado [BOE]), and thus, they are Spanish law and must be applied in Spain. In this regard, according to the 1998 Albufeira Convention, the Aqueduct Tagus Basin is a use already established and its stable and continuous use must be protected and guaranteed through cooperation between all affected parties the riparian autonomous communities and the southeast of Spain.

The analysis of international legal instruments addressing water scarcity, droughts, and fundamental rights provide the strategies to mitigate the effects of climate change and the impacts of drought conditions in the society in a sustainable manner. Among these strategies, the ATS is the tool that guarantees water consumption to natural parks, millions of trees and ensures the sustainable development in southeast Spain while ensuring the ecological flow in the Tagus Basin.

The main goal of this chapter is to demonstrate that under international water law, the ATS is a protected use of the Tagus Basin. Therefore, stable and continuous water transfers must be respected by law between different autonomous communities in Spain for present and future generations. Moreover, the study of the ATS as a regional allocation mechanism that allocates water from the Tagus reflects the implementation of the principles established in the 1998 Albufeira Convention, the Water Framework Directive 2000 (WFD) (Directive 2000/60/EC), the 1997 United Nations Convention on the Law of the Non-navigational Uses of International Watercourses, the 1994 United Nations Convention to Combat Desertification (UNCCD) in Those Countries Experiencing Serious Drought, and the 1992 Convention on the Protection and Use of Transboundary Watercourses and International Lakes. In addition, the analysis of legal instruments such as the principle of solidarity, customary law, the concept of sustainable development, and European policies provide strategies to promote resilience to climate change and the impacts of drought conditions.

8.2.   Geographical Location and Characteristics

The scope of the 1998 Albufeira Convention is to protect surface water and groundwater as well as the aquatic and terrestrial ecosystems that depend on them, and provide for the sustainable use of water resources in all transboundary basins between Spain and Portugal including Miño, Limia, Duero, Guadiana, and Tagus (Albufeira Convention, 1998). Fig. 8.1 shows all transboundary basins in the Iberian Peninsula.

The Tagus River is a transboundary river shared by Spain and Portugal. This river provides water to the ATS, which is the essential source of water for southeast Spain including the regions of Almería, Alicante, and Murcia. The planning project of the Aqueduct occurred in 1933 and was included in the national hydrological plan aimed to solve the shortage of water resources in southeast Spain. The ATS came into operation in 1979, to support the irrigation and domestic water supply of the population living in the Júcar and Segura basins (SCRATS, 2015; Spanish Government Tagus Basin Management Agency [SGTBMA], 2015). Fig. 8.2 presents the ATS location and scheme.

Figure 8.1: Transboundary basins between Spain and Portugal regulated by the 1998 Albufeira Convention.

Source: Gobierno de España, Ministerio de Agricultura, Alimentación y Medio Ambiente. http://www.magrama.gob.es/es/desarrollo-rural/temas/politica-fores tal/desertificacion-restauracion-forestal/lucha-contra-la-desertificacion/z_antigua_ acuerdos.aspx.

The reservoirs of Entrepeñas and Buendia regulate the Upper Tagus Basin and the use of the ATS. The water transfers are established according to the water level in both reservoirs, which have a total capacity of $2443 \, \text{hm}^3$ ($1 \, \text{hm}^3 = 1$ million m^3). These reservoirs belong to the state and are managed by the *Confederación Hidrológica del Tajo*, which is the management institution by basin in Spain. The start of the ATS is located in the Bolarque Reservoir. The Bolarque Reservoir, with a total capacity of $35.64 \, \text{hm}^3$, has two main functions: first, the production of hydroelectric energy and second, to be the nexus between the Tagus and Segura basins. The Aqueduct links the Bolarque Reservoir on the Tagus River with the Talave Reservoir on the Segura and is $292 \, \text{km}$ in length. The water is conveyed through a channel that has a capacity of $33 \, \text{m}^3/\text{s}$,

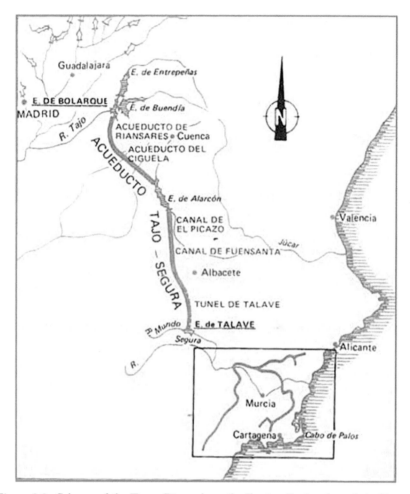

Figure 8.2: Scheme of the Tagus River along the Iberian Peninsula and the Tagus-Segura Aqueduct.

Source: Gobierno de España, Ministerio de Agricultura Alimentación y Medio Ambiente, Confederación Hidrográfica del Segura. https://www.chsegura.es/chs/cuenca/infraestructuras/postrasvaseTajoSegura/infraestructura01.html.

with stretches through sections of tunnels and aqueducts. This Aqueduct can warrant a transfer of 600 hm^3 (155 hm^3 to domestic water supply and 445 hm^3 for irrigation), while it was expected to transfer 1000 hm^3, the average annual volume transferred is 350 hm^3 (SGTBMA, 2015).

In addition to its original purpose, the ATS is used today to supply water to the National Park Tablas de Daimiel in the Guadiana Basin, and to to transport water from the Alarcón reservoir to Albacete, which is located in the Castilla La Mancha Autonomous Community, for irrigation and drinking uses (SGTBMA, 2015). The basic rule of the Aqueduct has always been to prioritize the demands of the Tagus Basin, including environmental needs. Spanish law always preserves the preferences of the donor basin and respects the determinations of its water planning (Spanish Act 21/2013, BOE n. 296).

The post-transfer system is a complex structure of canals beginning at the Talave Reservoir on the Segura River. This infrastructure enables the management, transport, and final distribution of water to the various recipient zones in southeastern Spain. The Ojos Dam distributes the water through different channels: the right bank channel, the Almería channel, the main left bank channel, the Crevillente channel, the La Pedrera reservoir, and the Campo de Cartagena channel. This infrastructure allows efficient water distribution and the best available technology is applied to ensure low water use (Soto Garcia *et al.*, 2014).

The average yearly water volume transferred into the Segura Basin from 1979 to 2014 was 328,000,000 m^3 per year (55% of the allowed maximum). Volumes transferred for public use have not varied greatly over time, unlike irrigation transfers, whose average yearly sum was 204,000,000 m^3, almost half of the allocated quantity (Soto Garcia *et al.*, 2014).

8.3. Interaction between International and National Law

International law directly interacts with national law. "States see the interaction between international and national law in two different ways monism and dualism traditions" (Peace and Justice Initiative, 2016). States with a monism system incorporate immediately international law with the act of ratifying an international treaty. However, states with dualism tradition must first translate international law into national legislation through a specific reception act before it can be applied by their national courts (Peace and Justice Initiative, 2016).

Neither the Spanish Constitution nor other laws provide any specific provision regarding customary international law. However, a large number of customary international norms have been expressly incorporated into the Spanish law without any specific reception act. This incorporation has been done directly in the Constitution and in State laws. Spanish courts have applied customary international norms, which have not expressly been incorporated by any reception act. Thus, the application of customary international law can be considered monism in Spain (Pastor Ridruejo, 2015).

However, the Spanish system regarding the internal application of treaties can be qualified as dualism because it requires a reception act. In this case, the reception act is the publication of the treaty in the Official Gazette of the Spanish State. Under Article 96.1 of the Spanish Constitution, international treaties are incorporated as national law once they are officially published in Spain and only after publication will they be applied in the Spanish territory. Similarly, the Spanish Civil Code in Article 1.5, modified by Decree 31 of May 1974, establishes that the publication of a treaty in the Official Gazette of the Spanish State is the specific requirement to be incorporated into the Spanish law. Once a treaty is published, it forms part of the law of Spain and must be ascertained and administered by the Spanish courts of justice.

In addition, the Constitution in Article 96.1 also establishes that the termination, modification, or cessation of a treaty cannot be done by a Spanish law. International treaties are above national law and below the Constitution in Spain. A treaty prevails over national law. Thus, as a matter of Spanish law, the Constitution would prevail over all other sources of law in the event of a conflict, while international agreement will prevail over state law. This is also reflected in Article 28 of the 2014 Spanish Treaty Law, which also establishes that termination and modification of a treaty can only be done by the general norms of international law (Pastor Ridruejo, 2015).

In this regard, for example, the 1998 Albufeira Convention was incorporated as Spanish law published in the Official Gazette, BOE

n. 37, 12 February 2000. After this, the Convention is law in Spain and therefore its provisions govern the management of the Tagus River at the national and international levels.

The reception of European Union Law such as the WFD (Directive 2000/60/EC) has a different approach than for treaties in Spain. "The European Community is the most highly developed, and most legally complex, international regional organization" (McCaffrey *et al.*, 2010). Member States have to transpose European directives into national law and communicate the measures adapted to the Commission. Article 93 of the Spanish Constitution establishes that "[by] means of an organic law, authorization may be granted for concluding treaties by which the exercise of powers derived from the Constitution shall be vested in an international organization or institution." This Article 93 has only been applied to European integration issues, giving powers to the European Community to legislate in certain materials such as environment (Leal-Arcas, 2005). The transposition of the WFD (Directive 2000/60/EC) into Spanish law was made by Article 129 of the Act 62/2003 regarding fiscal, administrative, and social measures (Spanish Act 62/2003, BOE n. 313) which amended the consolidated text of the Water Act, approved by Royal Legislative Decree 1/2001. However, "Spain should ensure the timely adoption of the River Basin Management Plans and further work is needed to ensure WFD is fully transposed in all intra-community River Basin Districts" (European Commission, 2015).

8.4. The International Legal Framework of the Transboundary Tagus River Basin

The legal framework of the transboundary Tagus River Basin management includes several agreements developed to promote cooperation (General Secretariat, Council of the European Union, 2008). This chapter focuses on the 1998 Albuferia Convention, which establishes the flow regime for the basin (Spanish Government "The International Duero," 2015) and the WFD. The 1998 Albufeira Convention reflects the principles of the WFD (Directive 2000/60/EC, 2000; General Secretariat, Council of the European Union, 2008).

Both instruments were discussed during the same period and include the same aims (General Secretariat, Council of the European Union, 2008). The WFD has a number of objectives, such as promoting sustainable water usage, environmental protection, and mitigating the effects of droughts (Directive 2000/60/EC). The European Commission emphasizes the need for a combination of adaptation measures in water policies to address water scarcity and drought (European Commission, 2012). In this line, the analysis of the implementation of the 1998 Albufeira Convention, as well as the WFD and the policies developed to manage each river basin can shed light on how to effectively achieve the goals proposed by the Directive.

In addition, this chapter analyzes several treaties to which Spain and Portugal are parties of, such as the 1997 UN Watercourses Convention, and the 1994 UNCCD. Furthermore, it examines the 1992 Convention on the Protection and Use of Transboundary Watercourses and International Lakes (UNECE Water Convention), which promote cooperation among regions and establish in their provisions the reasonable use of water and the nonsignificant harm principles. Moreover, the treaty on the functioning of the European Union (EU) established the solidarity principle, which provides harmonization in the EU Customary law at the local level is also analyzed as an instrument to maintain uses already established and recognized among the parties. The analysis of all these treaties and legal instruments demonstrates that the ATS is a current use and an established use, which is protected and guaranteed for future generations by these treaties, which are incorporated as Spanish law and therefore they prevail over state law and must be implemented at the national level in Spain (Pastor Ridruejo, 2015).

8.4.1. *Background and the 1998 Albufeira Convention*

The Treaty of Limits (1864) stipulated that shared boundary resources should be used for mutual benefits and with no harm to another party. The result of the cooperation between Spain and Portugal is the evolution of several agreements addressing specific issues such as the production of hydroelectric power (Spanish

Government "The International Duero," 2015). It was in 1994 with the Oporto Declaration between Spain and Portugal when the bilateral cooperation in the field of transboundary river basin management took its first steps. The 1998 Albufeira Convention aims to integrate surface water, groundwater, and ecosystems related to them for each basin. The cooperation is established through an exchange of information, specific institutions to provide consultancy, the adoption of measures to achieve the implementation in both countries, and the flow regimen. The 1998 Albufeira Convention in Article 20 establishes two main institutions: "the Conference of the Parties" and "the Commission." Representatives of each country and a Ministry or delegate person from each country who presides over the Cconference, and meet when a party requires compose the Conference of the Parties. The Commission is composed by a delegation from each party and has the competences of interpretation and application of the Convention.

In addition, the Convention in Article 31 addresses the possibility of amendment when there is agreement between the parties. In fact, the parties agreed on a new flow regimen in the Protocol reviewing the Albufeira Convention in 2008 ("Revision Protocol," 2008). The Convention in Article 16 establishes the flow regime for each basin based on the ground of the sustainable use to cover the needs of present and future generations. Article 5 of the Protocol set the flow regime for the Tagus River, where two gauges control the minimum integration flow Salto de Cedillo and Ponte de Muge. The integral flow level is controlled weekly, every three months, and annually. The annual integral flow level is $2700 \, \mathrm{hm}^3$ below Salto de Cedillo and $1300 \, \mathrm{hm}^3$ in Ponte de Muge. Both countries shall manage water of the Tagus Basin maintaining these flow levels as agreed in the 2008 protocol ("Revision Protocol," 2008).

The 1998 Albufeira Convention in Annex I establishes as use the transfer of water interbasin already established, such as the ATS. Moreover, the Convention in Article 15 set the management of water uses and the right to use water according to the sustainable use of water uses already established. Following Article 15, the ATS is a "use already established" and therefore this use contains the right to use. According to Article 15, the flow level transferred of the ATS is a use, which was established and must be guaranteed at the national level with stable water transfers and water availability in order to protect the population, national parks, millions of trees, and farmland depending on it. Article 16 addresses the flow level management and specifically set the need to guarantee current uses. The ATS is a current use, which started operations even before the Convention was signed according to the Spanish Act 21/1971, 19th June, which is analyzed in Section 8.5 of this chapter.

Under the 1998 Albufeira Convention, which is Spanish law as it was explained earlier, the ATS is a "use" already established and therefore must be respected by law between different autonomous communities in Spain for present and future generations. In the hypothetical case that a Spanish law aims to terminate the Tagus-Segura water transfers, the 1998 Albufeira Convention prevails over the national law maintaining the water transfers as a use already established according to the 1988 Albufeira Convention.

In addition, Article 4 of the 1998 Albufeira Convention set the objectives and mechanisms for cooperation. The parties must act in order to mitigate the effects of droughts and water scarcity, this implies the cooperation to provide water surplus to drought regions such as southeastern Spain. Moreover, the 1998 Albufeira Convention expressly establishes the use of water in a sustainable manner, which is also the object of the Convention. The ATS represents a model of sustainability use of water as is analyzed through this chapter in Section 8.6.

8.4.2.   *The Water Framework Directive*

The Albufeira Convention is in line with the Directive 2000/60/EC of the European Parliament and of the Council of 23 October 2000 (Directive 2000/30/EC), which establishes a framework for community action in the field of water policy. Through the WFD, the EU has established a community framework for water protection and management (Directive 2000/30/EC). "Member States must identify and analyze European waters, on the basis of individual river basin and district. They shall then adopt management plans and programs of measures adapted to each body of water" (Directive 2000/30/EC). This Directive has a number of objectives, such as preventing and reducing pollution, promoting sustainable water usage, environmental protection, improving aquatic ecosystems, and mitigating the effects of floods and droughts. Its ultimate objective is to achieve "good ecological and chemical status" (Directive 2000/30/EC) for all community waters by 2015. The analysis of the implementation of the Directive and the policies developed to manage each river basin can shed light on how to effectively achieve the goals proposed by the Directive. In addition, the study of regional allocation mechanisms such as aqueducts and other instruments would provide strategies to promote resilience to climate change and the impacts of drought conditions. "Climate change is expected to increase the existing stresses on water as changes in precipitation, combined with rising temperatures" (European Commission, 2012). The current climate change situation is expected to increase the existing stresses on water through issues such as changes in precipitation, and rising temperatures (European Commission, 2012). Although, the WFD has provided guidelines to manage water scarcity and droughts, the present and forecasted effects of climate change demand additional measures at the legislative level to provide resilience and ensure water availability to dry areas such as southeastern Spain.

The purpose of the WFD is "to establish a framework for the protection of inland surface waters, transitional waters, coastal waters, and groundwater which: [···] (e) Contribute to mitigating the effects of floods and droughts" (Directive 2000/60/EC). The WFD specifically emphasizes the need to mitigate the effects of droughts and establishes as a mechanism to do so a framework for the protection of water. The WFD does not specifically address how to mitigate the effects of droughts in dry regions which are dependent on a water basin. It provides a nonexclusive list of supplementary measures which Member States within each river basin district may choose to adopt as part of the program of measures required under Article 11(4). Supplementary measures may be designed and implemented in addition, to the basic measures, in order to achieve the environmental objectives of Article 4. The supplementary measures list includes demand management measures, *inter alia,* promotion of adapted agricultural production such as low water requiring crops in areas affected by drought (Directive 2000/60/EC). An example of the implementation of this demand management measure is the ATS in Spain, where the best available technology is applied to ensure low water use (Isilestudio, 2008).

According to the WFD, the irrigation of dry land by the ATS promotes adapted agricultural production through mechanisms such as drip irrigation technology and low water requiring crops. However, the way the WFD addresses drought is only to meet the environmental objectives. The social and economic impacts of drought on society are not addressed in the WFD.

The WFD approaches drought as an unforeseen or exceptional circumstance, which must be solved to achieve good water status. In case of drought, all practicable steps must be taken "to mitigate the adverse impact on the status of the body of water" (Directive 2000/60/EC). Moreover, the WFD establishes that if droughts are the result of "circumstances of natural cause of force majeure, which are exceptional and could not reasonably have been foreseen, in particular prolonged droughts, the Member State may determine that additional measures are not practicable, subject to Article 4(6)" (Directive 2000/60/EC). The WFD addresses drought as a negative effect on the good water quality of the basin but does not address the negative impact on the society depending on a specific basin. There is no protection for arid or semiarid regions such as the southeast of Spain, which suffers a structural deficit of water resources for use by the population and for irrigation.

Under the EU Water Framework Directive "member States shall collect and maintain information on the type and magnitude of the significant anthropogenic pressures to which the surface water bodies in each river basin district are liable to be subject to, in particular estimation and identification of the impact of significant water flow regulation, including water transfer and diversion, on overall flow characteristics and water balances" (European Commission, 2012). At the regional level, this assessment is essential to guarantee the correct allocation of water among users according to their uses, especially in drought regions such as southeast of Spain where the ATS provides water to one of the most arid regions in the EU. In fact, "south-eastern Spain [the Murcia and Valencia regions and eastern Andalucía] is experiencing an exceptional drought over the last 25 years" (European Commission, 2014). These current "extremely dry" conditions have occurred on other occasions since 1990, with the result of desertification because the soil water content was drastically depleted (European Commission, 2014).

The European legislation lacks a specific regulation for establishing a framework that is able to mitigate the impact of drought on society and the economy. This is especially relevant in the agricultural sector, which is the largest water user in Europe. The WFD does not establish any protection for agriculture and the dignity of farmers to continue with their activity in case of drought. Under the *Universal Declaration of Human Rights*, "everyone, as a member of society, has the right to social security and is entitled to realization, through national effort and international co-operation and in accordance with the organization and resources of each State, of the economic, social and cultural rights indispensable for his dignity and the free development of his personality" (U.N., 1948). Farmers, as members of society, have the entitlement to cultural rights indispensable for their dignity. When water from the ATSaqueduct Tajo-Segura is not sufficient, additional sources of water must be guaranteed in order to protect agricultural activity and therefore farmers' dignity. The WFD lacks a regulation ensuring the supply of water for agricultural activities in case of drought. There is therefore no protection of the use of water for agricultural purposes, which means farmers' dignity as a fundamental human right is not protected.

The European Commission emphasizes the need for a combination of adaptation measures in water policies to address water scarcity and drought (European Commission, 2012). The EU has developed a desertification and drought-related policy according to which it established implicit requirement of the WFD to manage properly water quantity in the EU. "The Environmental Council of 30th October 2007 supported the Commission's 2007 Communication and invited the Commission specifically to review and further develop the water scarcity and drought policy by 2012" (European Commission, 2007). The Report on the Review of the European Water Scarcity and Droughts Policy, 2012 specifically establishes that "the use of European Investment Bank (EIB) funds for Member States actions to address [water scarcity and drought] WS&D is still low" (European Commission, 2012). Moreover, there are still limitations in the integration of Drought Management Plans with river basin management plans (European Commission, 2012). In addition, "[l]imited progress has been made with the use of EU Solidarity Funds in the area of droughts" (European Commission, 2012). There are several gaps in the current Water Scarcity and Droughts Policy, such as conceptual gaps, information gaps, as well as policy, governance, and implementation gaps (European Commission, 2012). While the assessment and management of flood risk is regulated under the Directive 2007/60/EC, there is not any specific directive related to water scarcity and droughts.[1] The lack of a legal instrument and inadequate policies to address water scarcity and droughts contributes to economic and social disequilibrium between regions in the EU.

Although the WFD incorporates the transfer and diversion of water as mechanisms to manage water flow, there is no specific provision addressing transfer of water in order to mitigate the effects of drought in society and more specifically in the agricultural sector. This situation is affecting southeastern Spain, which requires additional measures to protect society, the sustainable development of the region, and current agricultural practices and uses. Therefore, there is a clear need to regulate the assessment and management of

---

[1]The main limitation to developing new legislation addressing water quantity is established in Art. 192(2)(b) of Treaty of the Functioning of the European Union (OJ C83/47, 30 March 2010), which requires unanimous voting in the Council in order to legislate in respect of "quantitative management of water resources or affecting, directly or indirectly, the availability of those resources" (OJ C83/47, 30 March 2010). The current situation clearly demonstrates that the WFD and related policies are not sufficient to mitigate the effect of WS&D in the EU. In this regard additional options must be proposed for a legal and institutional framework capable of addressing this challenge.

water scarcity and droughts where aqueducts must be recognized as a tool to promote integrity between drought management plans with river basin management plans. In addition, EU Solidarity Funds must be used to provide solutions to avoid social and economic impacts in specific dry regions such as southeast Spain. A potential solution in case of drought and lack of surplus flow from the Tagus Basin would be the development of new aqueducts infrastructure from other surplus basins such as the Ebro and Duero as well as the use of desalination in combination with water from the Tagus Basin. The EU Solidarity Funds would be used to build such infrastructure promoting solidarity among different regions and improving the economy and social life of millions of people in Spain. This would be the solution to the current hydrologic disequilibrium between the north and south in Spain.

For example, while regions along the Ebro Basin suffer regular floods, causing serious damages to the society and the environment, the southeast of Spain lacks of water, which is the result of serious water scarcity and droughts. In fact, only the region of Aragón has lost €25 million due to floods in 2015. Moreover, agricultures from the three regions Navarra, Aragón, and Rioja estimated a loss of over €50 million due to flood damage the same year ("El Gobierno de Aragón," 2015). In addition, floods have very negative environmental impacts such as damage in water quality due to too much sediment and nutrient entering a waterway. "Other negative effects include loss of habitat, dispersal of weed species, the release of pollutants, lower fish production, loss of wetlands function, and loss of recreational areas" (Office of the Queensland Chief Scientist [OQCS], 2015). Coastal marine environments are also affected by floods, which cause serious damage due to the introduction of excess sediment and nutrients, and pollutants. This situation affects "aquatic habitats, lower water quality, reduce coastal production, and contaminate coastal food resources" (OQCS, 2015). Therefore, the solution to mitigate the effects of floods and droughts is the development of an interbasin infrastructure composed of dams and canals, which would be able to store and transfer the excess of water to the ATS system.

8.4.3. *Convention on the Law of the Non-navigational Uses of International Watercourses 1997*

The 1997 Convention on the Law of the Non-Navigational Uses of International Watercourses codifies the international principles of nonsignificant harm, cooperation, and reasonable use of water. The Convention entered into force on 17th August 2014 (Watercourses Convention, 1997). Portugal signed this Convention in 1997 and Spain adhered to it in 2009 (United Nations Convention on the Law of the Non-Navigational Uses of International Watercourses, [Watercourses Convention], 1997) and was published in the Spanish Official Gazette July 2014 (BOE, n. 161, 3rd July, 2014).

The Convention in Article 5 establishes the principle of reasonable utilization and participation and Article 6 set the factors relevant to determine the principle of equitable and reasonable utilization. These factors are geographic, hydrographic, hydrological, climatic, ecological, and subject to other factors related to social and economic activities. Moreover, Article 6 includes the analysis of the population dependent on the watercourse, the effects of the use or uses, existing and potential uses, conservation, protection, development, and economy of use, and the availability of alternatives, of comparable value, to a particular planned or existing use. The application of all these factors establish the reasonable use, which as we can see is determined according to the needs and uses established for each region.

If we apply the factors reflected in Article 6 to our specific case, the ATS, it is proved the reasonable use of interbasin water transfers to southeast Spain. Regarding the analysis of the population factor, the number of people affected by the lack of drinking water in case of interruption or termination of these transfers will be over 2.5 million. About the geographic, hydrographic, and hydrological factors, southeast Spain is a very dry area affected by water scarcity and drought. Moreover, the area lacks its own water resources able to cover all the needs and uses. Regarding the availability of alternatives of comparable value, desalination would be a potential solution. However, desalination cannot be an alternative to the ATS due to the large number of issues involved; these issues are presented in Section 8.6.4 of this chapter.

The analysis of the factor related to social and economic activities illustrates that the activities related to the water transfers from the Aqueduct contribute a total of €2.36 billion to the Spanish gross domestic product (GDP) (PricewaterhouseCoopers [PWC], 2013), an analysis of this factor is especially addressed in Section 8.6.2 of this chapter. Other factors are ecological and conservation, where water transfers from the Aqueduct provide conservation to several national parks and over 40 million trees. In addition, according to Spanish law ecological flow along the Tagus River are guaranteed. In this regard, Section 8.6.3 of this chapter provides a detail analysis of ecological flows and environmental conservation.

In addition, Article 6 set one relevant factor the "existing and potential uses of the watercourse" (Watercourses Convention, 1997). The ATS is an existing use of the Tagus as has been established in Section 8.4.1 of this chapter during the analysis of the 1998 Albufeira Convention. In this regard, the Aqueduct as a use of the Tagus Basin is protected and ensure at the international level as a reasonable use according to the 1997 UN Watercourses Convention.

Furthermore, Article 10 set that "[i]n the event of a conflict between uses of an international watercourse, it shall be resolved with references to articles 5 to 7, with special regard being given to the requirements of vital human needs" (Watercourses Convention, 1997). The ATS provides water for the southeastern Spain's requirements of vital human needs, specially drinking water. Thus, in case of any potential conflict of uses in the Tagus Basin, article 10 of the 1997 UN Watercourses Convention guarantees the use of the aqueduct.

8.4.4. *United Nations Convention to Combat Desertification in Those Countries Experiencing Serious Drought and/or Desertification, Particularly in Africa 1994*

Spain and Portugal signed the UNCCD in 1994 (UNCCD, 1994). The Convention was published in the Spanish Official Gazette February 1997 (BOE n. 36, 11 February 1997). The Convention in Article 10 set the obligation to develop a National Action Program, which "shall specify the respective roles of government, local communities and land users and the resources available and needed" (UNCCD, 1994). Spain has complied with this obligation developing a National Action Program for Desertification (Orden ARM/2444/2008) (Spanish Government, 2008). However, drought mitigation and solutions to ensure and to provide water to a specific dryland region of southern Spain is not addressed.

Article 3 of the UNCCD established that "the Parties should, in a spirit of international solidarity and partnership, improve cooperation and coordination at sub-regional, regional and international levels, and better focus financial, human, organizational and technical resources where they are needed" (UNCCD, 1994). This Article incorporates the principle of solidarity to achieve the objectives of the UNCCD. Solidarity shall be established at the subregional, regional, and international levels. This means cooperation to prevent drought impacts between countries and within a country. The allocation and distribution of water in a reasonable use according to the uses already established in each subregion and each region mitigates the effects of droughts and ensures the sustainability of the region. A way to achieve this goal is as Article 3 establishes through "better financial, human, organizational and technical resources where they are needed" (UNCCD, 1994) such as the development and maintenance of infrastructure to transfer water from surplus basins to drylands regions.

The UNCCD also includes a specific Annex addressing the regional implementation for the Northern Mediterranean. Annex IV establishes the cooperation at the regional level between country parties, in order to mitigate the effect of droughts (UNCCD, 1994). To this end, different regions (autonomous communities) in Spain should cooperate to mitigate the effect of droughts guaranteeing uses through solidarity at the international, regional, and subregional levels. Based on this cooperation at different levels of government, the protection of the ATS as an instrument to mitigate the effects of droughts in southern Spain shall be ensured and implemented as well as additional measures to achieve this goal at the international and national levels.

8.4.5. *Convention on the Protection and Use of Transboundary Watercourses and International Lakes 1992*

Spain ratified this Convention in February 2000 and Portugal in December 1994 (United Nations Economic Commission for Europe Convention on the Protection and Use of Transboundary Watercourses and International Lakes [UNECE Water Convention], 1992). The Convention was published in the Spanish Official Gazette April 2000 (BOE n. 81, 4 April 2000). This Convention focuses on cooperation between member countries concerning the protection and use of transboundary water resources. The Convention promotes international cooperation for the prevention, control, and reduction of transboundary water pollution and sustainable use of transboundary waters (UNECE Water Convention, 1992). Under the 1998 Albufeira Convention, Spain and Portugal commit to achieve the sustainable development of the Tagus River, where the ATS promotes the sustainable use of the Tagus River as in the 1992 UNECE Water Convention. At the national level, in Spain, pollution along the Tagus River is an issue, especially the bad water quality due to sewage coming from Madrid and the industries located around Madrid and Guadalajara. This is mainly a problem of water purifying, which has not been solved yet. It is not admissible to use more water from the Entrepeñas and Buendia dams upstream to dilute the pollution. This is against Spanish law, the WFD, the 1998 Albufeira Convention, and the 1992 UNECE Water Convention. Moreover, this situation confuses the ecological flows with flow dilution of discharges, which is a legal fraud that could also have very negative effects on the ATS water transfers (El Soto, 2008; Iagua, 2015). Section 8.6.3 of this chapter provides an analysis of ecological flows along the Tagus Basin.

8.4.6. *Solidarity Principle*

The solidarity principle is reflected in the EU legislation (Treaty of Lisbon, 2007) (consolidated versions of the Treaty on European Union and the Treaty on the Functioning of the European Union, [TEU] 2012). The EU addresses solidarity as normally associated with national welfare, including social policies with political and human rights dimensions. The concept of solidarity has also a substantial role at the supranational level. In fact, EU Treaties, the Charter of Fundamental Rights, EU law and Court of Justice's judgments contain numerous references to solidarity, albeit in different contexts (Center of European Law, 2013). Solidarity is considered as a fundamental value of the EU (Articles 2 and 3(3) TEU); solidarity between EU peoples while respecting their history, their culture, and their traditions; solidarity between generations; financial solidarity among EU citizens; solidarity among Member States (TEU, 2012). The solidarity at the national and supranational levels must be in the same line in order to avoid conflict affecting the welfare development and human rights of a region. For example, solidarity among member states recognized in Article 3 TEU must be also included among different regions in the same state. This would promote cooperation among different levels of government and equal welfare in different regions of the EU.

Article 222 of the Treaty on the Functioning of the European Union set the solidarity clause, under which "[t]he Union and its Member States shall act jointly in a spirit of solidarity if a Member State is [···] the victim of a natural or man-made disaster. The Union shall mobilize all the instruments at its disposal, by the member States, to: [···] (b) assist a Member State in its territory, at the request of its political authorities, in the event of a natural or man-made disaster" (TEU, 2012).

The European Commission defines drought and desertification as a natural disaster. "Drought and desertification, two closely related natural events, can have significant impacts on the environment, society and the economy" (Joint Research Center [JRC], 2015). As it was reflected in the analysis of the WFD, "[c]limate change is expected to increase frequency, duration and severity of droughts in many parts of the world" (JRC, 2015; Rosenthal, 2008). Drought is a natural disaster, which under article 222 of the Treaty on the Functioning of the European Union, the Union and Member States shall act jointly in a spirit of solidarity providing solutions to mitigate the effects of droughts in southern Spain. These solutions must be as it has been addressed earlier through the development of new infrastructure able to transfer water from surplus basins to the ATS and southeastern Spain. Although the Union and Member States intend to follow the principle of solidarity, the fact is that this principle has not been applied to the economy and society of southern Spain, which is suffering due to the droughts in the region without a clear plan to solve that situation. Moreover, the lack of solidarity from other regions (autonomous communities) in Spain specifically central and northern regions toward the south, is causing significant impacts on the environment, society, and the economy of southern Spain. In fact, Aragón, at the regional level, has passed a law concerning its own waters and rivers in order to avoid any transfer of water from the River Ebro to southeastern Spain (Aragón Act, 2014; Valencia, 2015). According to Article 149 of the Spanish Constitution, this law is against the Spanish Constitution based on the lack of authority of Aragón to legislate when "water flows among more than one autonomous community" (Spanish Constitution, 1978) such as the River Ebro.

Uncertainty about the future of available water resources is affecting the society and can cause serious harm in the economy of the region, which is mainly focused on agricultural activities. The population needs the guarantee of the human right to water, where enough amount of water is ensured in order to continue their social and economic uses and activities while safeguarding the sustainable development of the region. The lack of solidarity between regions in Spain needs to be addressed at the EU level in order to ensure water to semiarid regions such as southern Spain.

8.4.7.   *Regional Customary International Law*

Article 38(1)(b) of the International Court of Justice (ICJ)'s Status refers to "international custom, as evidence of a general practice accepted as law." In addition to this rule which is applicable to all states, "it is also possible that a practice be regional or even local, and give rise to a corresponding rule binding only on the states that have engaged in the practice" (McCaffrey, 2006). The ICJ in *the Rights of Passage Case*, 1960 ICJ 6, 39, "sees no reason why long continued practice between two States accepted by them as regulating their relations should not form the basis of mutual rights and obligations between the two States." In this regard, the continuous use of water of the River Tagus as interbasin water transferred has already been accepted as a practice. Thus, the continuous practice of the ATS transferring water shall be categorized as a regional customary law and thus autonomous communities should respect this practice in Spain.

8.5.   National Regulation Management of the Aqueduct Tagus Segura

The ATS started operations according to the Spanish Act 21/1971, 19th June, which in Article 1 set the maximum annually amount of $600 \, \text{hm}^3$ water surplus transferred from the Tagus Basin to the Segura Basin. Moreover, once the construction was complete, the law allowed the transfer of the maximum annual amount of $1.000 \, \text{hm}^3$. The effective transfers of water from the Tagus Basin to the Segura Basin started in 1979, and were established in 1971 before the 1998 Albufeira Convention entered into force.

The water surplus transferred has been modified. The Central Commission for Exploitation of the Tagus-Segura adheres to the rules of operation set in the Spanish Act 21/2015 of 20 July 2015 and in the Royal Decree 773/2014, of 12 September 2014. The law set fourth different levels according to the amount of water in the Entrepeñas and Buendía Dams.

The Spanish Act 21/2013[2] and Spanish Act 21/2015 approve regulation management for the ATS. The Act 21/2015 includes a number of provisions relating to the Tagus-Segura, to comply

---

[2]Spanish Act 21/2013, 9th December. BOE N. 296. The Constitutional Court declared null some articles of this law due to a default form when the Aragon's report was not included. Therefore, the Constitutional Court establishes that the null of this law "should be deferred for a period of one year" which shall run from the date of publication of the decision in the Official Gazette (BOE) (5 February 2015). This gives time to incorporate the Aragon's report and therefore remediate the default form of the law.

with the judgment of the Constitutional Court of February 5. This judgment was declared unconstitutional because several provisions relating to the ATS, which were introduced through amendments during the parliamentary process of the Act 21/2013, of December 9, environmental assessment, by the formality has been omitted audience to the Autonomous Community of Aragón, provided for in Article 72.3 of the Statute of Autonomy. After this, the current management of water transfers is established according to Royal Decree 773/2014 and Act 21/2015, which provide a transfer system on a monthly basis, depending on the total water supply available in the reservoirs Entrepeñas and Buendia dams in the Upper Tagus River at the beginning of every month. Where the maximum annual amount transferred is 650 hm^3 (600 hm^3 for the Segura and 50 hm^3 for the Guadiana).

The Royal Decree 773/2014 establishes regulation for water transfer based on these four levels (Table 8.1).

Level 3 establishes the minimum water transfers of 20 hm^3 according to monthly values established in the following Table 8.2.

Level 3 is considered an irregular hydrological situation; the relevant agency shall authorize at its own discretion a transfer of up to 20 hm^3 per month.

The Act 21/2015 defines the rules of exploitation at four different levels (Table 8.3).

Table 8.1: Regulation for water transfer under the Royal Decree 773/2014.

Royal Decree 773/2014	Water Level in Entrepeñas and Buendía Dams	Water Level in Both Dams during the Last 12 Months	The Relevant Agency Shall Authorize per Month a Transfer of:
Level 1	≥1300 hm^3	≥1200 hm^3	60 hm^3
Level 2	<1300 hm^3 without reaching level 1	<1200 hm^3	38 hm^3
Level 3	Water level per month established according to Table 8.2		20 hm^3
Level 4	<400 hm^3		No transfer allowed

Table 8.2: Monthly values established at level 3 under the Royal Decree 773/2014.

	Oct	Nov	Dec	Jan	Feb	Mar	Apr	May	Jun	Jul	Aug	Sep
$m^3 \times 10^6$	613	609	605	602	597	591	586	645	673	688	661	631

Source: Retrieved from https://www.boe.es/diario_boe/txt.php?id=BOE-A-2014-9336. (B.O.E., no. 223, 13 September 2014, pp. 71634–71639).

Table 8.3: Rules of exploitation under the Spanish Act 21/2015.

Act 21/2015	Water Level in Entrepeñas and Buendía Dams	Water Level in Both Dams during the Last 12 Months	The Relevant Agency Shall Authorize per Month a Transfer of:
Level 1	$\geq 1500\,\text{hm}^3$	$\geq 1000\,\text{hm}^3$	$68\,\text{hm}^3$
Level 2	$<1500\,\text{hm}^3$ without reaching level 3	$<1000\,\text{hm}^3$	$38\,\text{hm}^3$
Level 3	Exceptional hydrological situations, which will take place when the water level between Entrepeñas y Buendía do not exceed, at the beginning of each month, the values to be determined by the Tagus Hydrological Plan in force. The Government by Royal Decree may set for level 3 the maximum monthly transfer that the competent authority may authorize based on motivate and discretion reasons.		
Level 4	$<400\,\text{hm}^3$		No transfer allowed

The Royal Decree 1/2016 of 8 January, on the review of approved hydrological plans Cantabrian river basin districts West, Guadalquivir, Ceuta, Melilla, Segura, and Júcar, and the Spanish part of river basin districts of the Eastern Cantabria, Minho-Sil, Duero, Tagus, Guadiana, and Ebro, establishes for the Tagus River Basin indicators and operating thresholds (Spanish Government, 2016). The headwater system of the Tagus River Basin as defined in Article 2 of the hydrological plan is applicable to the special plan action in situations of alert and temporary drought and will be consistent with those rules set in the Act 21/2015 of 20 July 2015 and the Royal Decree 773/2014 of 12 September 2014.

The current severe drought situation in the basin suggests according to Orden AAA/2787/2015, of 18 December 2015 that the level of water transfer is 3 and the amount of water authorized to be transferred applying the rules set in Act 21/2015 and the Royal Decree 773/2014 it was only $6\,hm^3$ from Entrepeñas and Buendía dams for December 2015. This uncertainty, and dramatic situation where the government discretionally can establish the level of water transfers during severe drought and water scarcity in the southeast shows the need to legislate according to the treaties and principles already analyzed, which ensure the use of stable water transfers and water availability to southeast Spain.

8.6. Sustainable Water Allocation of the Aqueduct Tagus-Segura

The ATS presents a solution to the current dry conditions in southeast Spain. This Aqueduct has been providing drinking water to over 2,500,000 people, where during summer the population increases to over three million people. In addition, the Aqueduct provides water to protect natural parks, and 140,000 hectares of farmland since 1979 (SCRATS, 2015).

The concept of sustainable development was adopted by the European Commission in the 2009 Review of EU sustainable development strategies (SDS) in July 2009 (European Commission, 2009). The European Council also confirmed that "[s]ustainable development remains a fundamental objective of the European Union under the Lisbon Treaty" in December 2009 (Council of European Union, 2009).

The concept of sustainable development "stands for meeting the needs of present generations without jeopardizing the ability of future generations to meet their own needs – in other words, a better quality of life for everyone, now and for generations to come" (European Commission, Environment, 2015). The concept includes the integration of different sectors of society from local to global, as well as social, economic, and environmental aspects, which are all interconnected in regional and global human progress. An analysis of some of these aspects, such as appropriate use of water in irrigation, economic impact of the ATS, ecological flow, and food security show how this Aqueduct guarantees the concept of sustainable development. In addition, each of these aspects reflects the factors establish in Article 6 of the 1997 UN Watercourses Convention.

8.6.1. *Appropriate Use of Water in Irrigation*

The ATS applies the supplementary measures established in the WFD. The land irrigated by the ATS promotes adapted agricultural production through mechanisms such as drip irrigation technology and the use of low water requiring crops (Soto Garcia *et al.*, 2014). Among this technology, *localized irrigation systems* apply water directly where the plant is growing, thus minimizing water loss through evaporation from the soil. This ensures the most effective use of water. However, the problem of water scarcity and drought in southeastern Spain needs additional solutions to mitigate the effects of climate change in the context of the EU to ensure the sustainable development of the region.

The reuse of water is also applied in irrigation practices. In fact, the WFD addresses the reuse of water as an additional measure to mitigate water scarcity (Directive 2000/60/EC). Reuse of water has a high value for agriculture because it ensures the continuity of water use. The Spanish Royal Decree 1620/2007 (BOE, n. 294) establishes specific national regulation of the reuse of water. In the Murcia region alone, the average annual volume of reused water was $103\,\text{hm}^3$ during the period 2002–2011 (Soto Garcia *et al.*, 2014).

8.6.2. *Economic Impact of the Aqueduct*
Tagus-Segura

Agriculture is essential for the Spanish economy and the progress of the country. Water transfers from the ATS related to the agrofood industry contributes a total of €2.36 billion to the GDP (PricewaterhouseCoopers, 2013). In addition, agriculture promotes the development of industries connected to the sector such as transport, engineering, and sanitation. Agricultural activities related to the ATS generate more than 100,000 jobs. Moreover, water from the Aqueduct creates over 320,000 indirect jobs, contributing to the development of the country. This is especially important in the current economic crisis in Spain. Water profitability per m^3 is very high between €0.60/m^3 and €1.00/m^3. Moreover, profitability can be as high as €3/m^3 in greenhouses (Soto Garcia *et al.*, 2014). There is a high level of exports from the southeast. In 2013, 69% of national vegetable exported were from southeast Spain; this represents a total of €1 billion (FEPEX, 2013).

The ATS is also a source of income for other autonomous communities in Spain through payments to donor regions. The total amount paid to the autonomous communities located in the Tagus Basin is €405.33 million. This implies an additional benefit from the Aqueduct to other regions (SCRATS, 2015).

8.6.3. *Environmental Conservation and Ecological Flow*

The ATS provides ecological value to society by protecting national parks and improving the environment (PricewaterhouseCoopers, 2013). An example of this environmental protection is the Spanish Act 13/1987, 17 July 1987, enacted to provide water for environmental purposes through the ATS to the Tablas de Daimiel National Park (Spanish Act 13/1987, BOE n. 171). This National Park receives water from the ATS, thus maintaining its ecological value. Moreover, the Aqueduct irrigates 44,000,000 trees (SCRATS, 2015), which contribute to mitigate desertification and improve air quality by sequestering CO_2 from the atmosphere according to the measures established under the UNCCD in those countries experiencing serious drought 1994.

According to the WFD and the international legislation analyzed in this chapter, the ATS ensures the protection of the Tagus Basin. Under the Tagus Basin Hydrological Plan the ecological flow is guaranteed. In fact, the Tagus Basin hydrological plan establishes a minimum flow of $6\,m^3/s$ in Aranjuez and $10\,m^3/s$ in Toledo and Talavera. These flow levels meet the requirements of both the biological and physical habitats of the species in those river sections (Spanish Government, 2009). The total water resources in the Tagus Basin are about 10,000 hm^3/year, and the maximum volume transferred is 600 hm^3, which is barely 5.5% (SCRATS, 2015).

The ATS does not cause environmental harm to the Tagus Basin. In 2008, an environmental study developed by the Universidad Politécnica de Madrid addressed the minimum stream flows in the stretch of the river between Bolarque and Aranjuez. This study was developed according to the term "good ecological status" established under the WFD and transposed into the Spanish Water Law (Royal Decree 1/2001, BOE n. 176). "Good surface water status" means the status achieved by a surface water body when both its ecological status and its chemical status are at least "good" (Directive 2000/60/EC). The results of this study show that the environmental demand established under the Law 52/1980 in 6 m^3/s was respected (Spanish Act 52/1980, BOE, 256). This study concluded that the ATS is not causing harm to the ecological flow and therefore, the good water status in the Tagus River is guaranteed (Universidad Politécnica de Madrid, 2008).

In 2013, the Company Ingeniería y Ciencia Ambiental, SL developed an additional study addressing ecological flow in the Tagus River through physical habitat modeling in the stretch between Bolarque Dam and Jarama River. This study was established according to the Order ARM/2656/2008, which approves the hydrological Plan. The results of the study established that the minimum stream flow 6 m^3/s under the law in the Bolarque-Aranjuez section is compatible with the methods set in the hydrological plan to calculate ecological flow through physical habitat modeling because the habitat result obtained is between 30% and 80% according to the hydrological plan (Ingeniería y Ciencia Ambiental, S.L., 2013). The conclusions of these two studies prove that the ATS is not causing harm to the environment or negative impact on the ecological flow in the Tagus River. The main environmental impact is sewage coming from Madrid and Guadalajara, which use more water from the dams upstream to dilute pollution as it was showed above in Section 8.4.5.

8.6.4. *Desalination*

Desalination has been considered as a potential solution to obtain more water for agricultural proposes. However, desalination cannot be an alternative to the ATS due to the large number of issues involved. Among these issues, the higher level of energy consumption is particularly important. While the consumption of energy for the Aqueduct is $0.87\,\text{kWh/m}^3$, the consumption for desalination is between 3.5 and $4\,\text{kWh/m}^3$. The substitution of the ATS with desalination would therefore require four times the current energy consumption (Soto Garcia *et al.*, 2014). Moreover, this increase would be unacceptable to the EU, which is committed to reducing the level of energy consumption by 20% by 2020. Another negative effect of desalination would be the increase of greenhouse gases, where the use of desalination would increase the emission of CO_2 by 400% (Soto Garcia *et al.*, 2014).

An additional issue with desalination is the quality of the water, which is not appropriate for irrigation because of the high level of boron it contains. This would harm crops such as lemon trees, orange trees, peach trees, apricot trees, and fig trees. Moreover, desalinized water is very low in nutrients and minerals. This leads to the need to add fertilizers, with the associated additional cost of production and energy consumption in manufacture. Finally, the cost of desalinizing water would be €1 m^3, while the current cost of water from the ATS is €0.10/m^3 (Soto Garcia *et al.*, 2014).

8.6.5. *Food Security*

The Food and Agriculture Organization of the United Nation has estimated that the demand for food is likely to grow by 70% by 2050 (European Commission, Joint Research Center, 2015). The Joint Research Centre (JRC) is the European Commission's in-house science service and carries out research in order to provide independent scientific advice and support to EU policy. Among one of the challenges addressed by the JRC is to establish international trade from productive agricultural areas to deficit areas, through greater integration of regional agricultural polices (European Commission, Joint Research Center, 2015).

It is therefore highly relevant that regions with a combination of water, sun, soil, and excellent climate conditions such as southeastern Spain can produce large amounts of food, which can be exported to other regions ensuring food security in EU. For example, exports from southeast Spain, which is irrigated with water transfers from the ATS, included 3,199,626 tons of vegetables and 2,025,855 tons of fruits in 2013. An interesting aspect of this is that the EU is by far the largest consumer of these exports at 90% (FEPEX, 2013).

The Spanish Government and the European Union should protect semiarid regions with privileged soil and climate conditions, which are able to produce large amount of food. The JRC has also established that these regions in the EU can "contribute to global food security, being important suppliers of agricultural and food products in a growing world market" (JRC, 2014). In the context of climate change, it is essential to protect those productive regions, which ensure the production of food for present and future generations. In order to protect this source of food, the first step is to ensure the availability of water for the irrigation of semiarid regions.

As we have seen, according to the European legislation, treaties, and the principles of international water law, the ATS fulfills the concept of sustainable development as it protects the environment for present and future generations while promoting the development of the region.

8.7. Conclusions

The Tagus River represents an important source of water for both countries and shall be managed in order to mitigate serious droughts and the effect of climate change. The 1998 Albufeira Convention establishes in its provision the interbasin water transfers as a use of the Tagus Basin. Moreover, the 1998 Albufeira Convention set that uses already established must be guaranteed and protected and this is the case of water transfer from the ATS. The ATS is a vital source of water for the society and economy in Southern Spain. The 1997 UN Watercourses Convention protects vital uses of water needed in a society to maintain their current uses. In this regard, the ATS is the only source of water for over 2.5 million people in southern Spain. Moreover, the social and economic development of the region depends directly on this source. The dramatic droughts demand more sources of water to satisfy the needs of this region. The application of the solidarity principle, where other regions consent the transfer of surplus flow to the thirsty south, is a solution that would ensure the life and stability of millions of people in the region. Moreover, it is essential to develop a Water Scarcity and Drought Directive in order to protect semiarid regions in the European Union, such as southeastern Spain, which are able to ensure food security for Europe and other countries.

The population from southeastern Spain has the fundamental right to the dignity to continue with their activity and living in this specific region. In this regard, the national law does not provide a stable framework where water transfers are guaranteed in order to protect their dignity. The level of water transfer is confusing and the government has the aleatory authority to decide the amount of water transfers. This create uncertainty and does not apply the principles reflected in the 1998 Albufeira Convention, the European legislation, the 1997 UN Watercourses Convention, the 1994 UNCCD, and the 1992 Water Convention.

Thus, a law is needed to ensure stable water transfer from surplus basins to southeastern Spain. Moreover, there is the need of a national hydrological plan where the major surplus basins are interconnected and with reservoirs able to transfer water using the infrastructure already placed in the ATS. If all basins were interconnected and the surplus was stored in underground reservoirs, conservation will be guaranteed and the high level of evaporation will be reduced. In addition, the development of an infrastructure connected with the ATS will provide stable and continuous water transfers.

References

Aragon Act 10/2014, de 27 de noviembre, de Aguas y Ríos de Aragón. Boletín Oficial de Aragón (BOE) número 241.

Center of European Law, Jean Monnet Centre of Excellence (2013). European Union: Solidarity in Question, King's College London, University of London, Legal Workshop 21 June 2013.

Communication from the Commission to the European Parliament, the Council, the European Economic and Social Committee and the Committee of the Regions—Mainstreaming sustainable development into EU policies: 2009 Review of the European Union Strategy for Sustainable Development (2009). Retrieved from http://eur-lex.europa.eu/legal-content/EN/TXT/?uri=CELEX:52009DC0400 [7 March 2015].

Convention on Cooperation for the Protection and Sustainable Use of Waters in Portuguese-Spanish River Basins [Albufeira Convention] (1998). Spain and Portugal, 30 November 1998 Albufeira. BOE n. 37, 12 February 2000.

Council of European Union (2009). Review of the EU Sustainable Development Strategy—President Report—16818/09, Brussels 1 December 2009. Retrieved from http://register.consilium.europa.eu/doc/srv?l=EN&f=ST%2016818%202009%20INIT [15 March 2015].

Directive 2000/60/EC of the European Parliament and of the Council of 23 October 2000 Establishing a Framework for Community Action in the Field of Water Policy (2000). *Official Journal of the European Union* (L 327)1. Retrieved from http://europa.eu/legislation_summaries/agriculture/environment/l28002b_en.htm [7 March 2015].

El Gobierno de Aragón cifra en 25 millones de euros las pérdidas ocasionadas por la crecida del Ebro (3 June 2015). *El Mundo*. Retrieved from http://www.elmundo.es/espana/2015/03/05/54f85858ca474179108b45 72.html [4 June 2015].

El Soto (2008). *Las aguas fecales de los ríos Manzanares y Jarama están siendo utilizadas para regar los cultivos de la Región*. Retrieved from http://www.elsoto.org/noticia-riego-aguas-fecales-agosto-2008. htm [7 March 2014].

Encyclopedia Britannica (2015). Tagus River. Retrieved from http://goblal. britannica.com [5 February 2015].

European Commission (2009). Communication from the Commission to the European Parliament, the Council, the European Economic and Social Committee and the Committee of the Regions—Mainstreaming sustainable development into EU policies: 2009 Review of the European Union Strategy for Sustainable Development. Retrieved from http://eur-lex.europa.eu/legal-content/EN/TXT/?uri=CELEX:52009DC0400 [May 2014].

European Commission (2012). Communication from the Commission to the European Parliament, the Council, the European Economic and Social Committee and the Committee of the Regions. Report on the Review of the European Water Scarcity and Droughts Policy. COM (2012) 672 final, Brussels, 14 November 2012.

European Commission (2014). Exceptional drought in south-eastern. *Joint Research Center News*. Spain, 12 August 2014. Retrieved from https://ec.europa.eu/jrc/en/news/exceptional-drought-in-south-eastern-spain [5 April 2015].

European Commission, Environment (2007). Water scarcity and droughts in the European Union. Retrieved from http://ec.europa.eu/environ ment/water/quantity/eu_action.htm#2007_com [7 February 2015].

European Commission, Environment (2015). Sustainable development. Retrieved from http://ec.europa.eu/environment/eussd/ [7 March 2015]. The Commission provides a detail analysis of the concept of Sustainable Development.

European Commission, Joint Research Center (2015). Global Food Security. Retrieved from https://ec.europa.eu/jrc/en/research-topic/global-food-security [5 March 2015]

European Commission (2015). Commission Staff Working Document. Report on the implementation of the Water Framework Directive River Basin Management Plans Member State: Spain Accompanying the document Communication from the European Commission to the European Parliament and the Council. The Water Framework Directive and the Floods Directive: Actions towards the 'good status' of EU water and to reduce flood risks/*SWD/2015/0056 final*/

Federación Española de Asociaciones de Productores Exportadores de Frutas, Hortalizas, Flores y Plantas [FEPEX] (2013). Exportaciones Españolas de Frutas y Hortalizas, 2013. Retrieved from http://www. fepex.es/datos-del-sector/exportacion-importacion-espa%C3%B1ola-frutas-hortalizas [May 2013].

General Secretariat, Council of the European Union (2008). The Albufeira Convention–an example of bilateral cooperation in the management of shared river basins with the benefit of compliance with the WFD. ENV 136, 7167/08 Annex, Brussels, 29 February 2008.

Iagua, (2015). Ecologistas alertan de los problemas de gestión de riego y con-taminación del Jarama, May 2015. Retrieved from http://www.iagua. es/noticias/espana/13/06/25/nueva-temporada-de-riego-en-el-jarama-viejos-conflictos-32187 [7 March 2014].

Ingeniería y Ciencia Ambiental, S.L. (2013). Estudio del Régimen de Caudales Ecológicos en el Rio Tajo Mediante Modelación del Hábitat Físico. Tramo Embalse de Bolarque-Río Jarama. Sindicato Central de Regantes del Acueducto Tajo-Segura, 2013.

Isilestudio (2008). Informe Técnico Sobre Necesidades Hídricas de los Cultivos de la Zona del Post-Trasvase. Estudio Preliminar Sobre el Ahorro Previsible de Agua en Cítricos Mediante la Aplicación de Estrategias de RDC en al Zona del Post-Trasvase [on file with SCRATS's Library] April 2008.

Joint Research Center (2014). European Commission, exceptional drought in southeastern Spain. Joint Research Center News, 12 August 2014.

Joint Research Center [JRC] (2015). Desertification and Drought. European Commission. Retrieved from https://ec.europa.eu/jrc/en/research-topic/desertification-and-drought [4 April 2015].

McCaffrey, S, D Shelton, and J Cerone (2010). Public International Law: Cases, problems, and texts. LexisNexis.

McCaffrey, S (2006). Understanding International Law, 47 LexisNexis.

Leal-Arcas, R (2005). The Reception on European Community Law in Spain, Hanse Law Review, Vol. 1 No. 1. p. 18.

Office of the Queensland Chief Scientist [OQCS] (2015). What are the Consequences of Floods. Retrieved from http://www.chiefscientist.qld.gov.au/publications/understanding-floods/flood-consequences [22 March 2015].

Orden AAA/2787/2015, December 18 (2015). Establishing a transfer of 6 million cubic meters, which is authorized from the reservoirs of Entrepeñas-Buendía, through the Tajo-Segura, for the month of December 2015. BOE N. 306 of 23 December 2015, pp. 121479–121479. BOE-A-2015-14025.

Orden ARM/2444/2008, August 12 (2008). Approving the National Action Programme to Combat Desertification in compliance with the UN Convention to Combat Desertification. BOE n. 200, August 19 2008, pp. 34836–34837. BOE-A-2008-14048.

Ordern ARM/2656/2008, September 10 (2008). Approving the Hydrological Plan. BOE n. 229, September 22 2008, pp. 38472–38582. BOE-A-2008-15340.

Pastor Ridruejo, J (2015). *Curso de Derecho Internacional Público y Organizaciones Internacionales*, 19th Ed. Madrid, Spain: Tecnos (Grupo Anaya, S.A.).

Peace and Justice Initiative (2016). How does international law apply in a domestic legal system? Retrieved from http://www.peaceandjusticeinitiative.org/implementation-resources/dualist-and-monist [15 January 2016].

PricewaterhouseCoopers Asesores de Negocios. [PWC] (2013). Economic Impact of the Aqueduct Tagus-Segura, (Consulting Report). PricewaterhouseCoopers Asesores de Negocios, S.L. Madrid, Spain.

Ratification of UN Convention to Combat Desertification (UNCCD) (1997). BOE n. 36, February 11 1997, pp. 4353–4375. BOE-A-1997-2888.

Revision Protocol of the Convention on Cooperation for the Protection and Sustainable Water Use of the Luso-Spanish Hydrographic Basins, between Spain and Portugal (2008). Albufeira, Portugal, 30 November 1998, Madrid and Lisbon 4 April 2008. BOE n. 14, Sec. I, p. 3425, 16 January 2010.

Royal Decree 1/2016, January 8. Approving the revision of the Water Plans for river basin districts of West Cantabrian Guadalquivir, Ceuta, Melilla, Segura, Júcar, and the Spanish part of the river basin districts of the Eastern Cantabria, Minho-Sil, Duero, Tajo, Guadiana and Ebro. BOE N. 16 of 19 January 2016, pp. 2972–4301. BOE-A-2016-439

Royal Decree 1620/2007, 7 December, por el que se establece el régimen jurídico de la reutilización de las aguas depuradas, BOE, n. 294.

Royal Decree 1/2001, 20 July por el que se aprueba el texto redundido de la Ley de Aguas. BOE, n. 176 -A-2001-14276.

Royal Decree 773/2014, 12 September. Approving rules governing the transfer of the Tagus-Segura. BOE N. 223, of 13 September 2014, pp. 71634–71639. BOE-A-2014-9336

Royal Decree 8/1995, 4 August. Urgent measures to improve the utilization of the Tajo-Segura are adopted. BOE N. 188 of August 8 1995, pp. 24433–24434. BOE-A-1995-18965.

Rosenthal, E (3 June 2008). In Spain water is a new battleground. *The New York Times.* Retrieved from http://www.nytimes.com/2008/06/03/world/europe/03dry.html?scp=1_sq=Spain+water_st=nyt&_r=0 [3 March 2008].

Sevillano, E and C Vazquez (14 August 2015). El Trasvase Tajo-Segura abre un foco de conflicto entre comunidades. El País. Retrieved from http://politica.elpais.com/politica/2015/08/14/actualidad/1439579972_676774.html [7 March 2016].

Sindicato Central de Regantes del Acueducto Tajo-Segura [SCRATS] (2015). Un Poco de Historia. Retrieved from http://www.scrats.com/ [5 March 2015].

Soto Garcia, M, V Martínez Álvarez, and B Martín Górriz (2014). El Regadío en la Región de Murcia. Caracterización y análisis mediante indicadores de gestión. Sindicato Central de Regantes del Acueducto Tajo Segura, 2014.

Spanish Act 21/2015, 20 July. Amending Law 43/2003 of 21 November, Forestry. BOE N. 173, of 21 July 2015, pp. 60234–60272. BOE-A-2015-814.

Spanish Act 21/2013, 9 December. Environmental Assessment. BOE N. 296 of 11 December 2013, pp. 98151–98227. BOE-A-2013-12913.

Spanish Act 62/2003, 30 December. Fiscal, Administrative, and Social Measures. BOE N. 313 of 31 December 2003.

Spanish Act 13/1987, 17 July. Derivation of volumes of water in the Upper Basin of the Tagus, through the Aqueduct Tagus-Segura, on an experimental basis, towards the Tablas de Daimiel National Park. BOE N. 171, of 18 July 1987, pp. 22079–22079. BOE-A-1987-16792.

Spanish Act 52/1980, 16 October. de regulación del régimen económico de la explotación del acueducto Tajo-Segura. BOE n. 256.

Spanish Act 21/1971, 19 June. Joint use of the Tagus-Segura. BOE N. 148 of 22 June 1972, pp. 10115–10116. BOE-A-1971-778.

Spanish Constitution (1978). BOE N. 311 of 29 December 1978, pp. 29313–29424. BOE-A-1978-31229.

Spanish Government. Ministry of Agriculture, Nutrition, and Environment (2016). The Tagus Hydrological Plan 2015–2021. Memoria Anejo 3. Retrieved from http://www.chtajo.es/Informacion%20Ciudadano// PlanificacionHidrologica/Planif_2015-2021/Documents/PlanTajo/PHT 2015-An03.pdf [17 January].

Spanish Government. Ministry of Agriculture, Nutrition, and Environment (2015). The International Duero. Retrieved from http://www.chtajo.es [5 March].

Spanish Government. Ministry of Agriculture, Nutrition, and Environment, Tagus Basin Management Agency, (Confederación Hidrológica del Tajo) [SGTBMA] (2015). Aqueduct Tajo-Segura. Retrieved from http://www.chtajo.es/Confederacion/Infraestructuras/Paginas/Acued uctoTajoSegura.aspx [10 March 2015].

Spanish Government, Ministry of Environment Rural and Marine Environment (2008). National Program to avoid Desertification. Agosto 2008. Retrieved from http://www.magrama.gob.es/es/biodiversidad/publica ciones/pand_agosto_2008_tcm7-19664.pdf [4 May 2015].

Spanish Government (2009). Ministerio de Agricultura, Alimentación y Medio Ambiente, Confederación Hidrológica del Tajo, Plan Hidrológico 2009–2015. Retrieved from http://www.chtajo.es/Informacion%20 Ciudadano/PlanificacionHidrologica/Planif_2009-2015/Paginas/Proy PHC_2009-2015.aspx.

Treaty on European Union and the Treaty on the Functioning of the European Union, Consolidated version [TEU] (2012). *Official Journal of the European Union* C326 Vol. 55, 26 October 2012.

Treaty of Lisbon amending the Treaty on European Union and the Treaty establishing the European Community, signed at Lisbon, 13 December 2007, *Official Journal of the European Union* 2007/C 306/01.

Treaty on boundaries between Spain and Portugal from the mouth of the Minho River to the junction of the river Cay and with the Guadiana (1864). [Treaty of Limits, 1864]. Spain and Portugal, Signed at Lisbon on 29 September 1864. United Nations Treaty Series n. 906.

United Nations Convention to Combat Desertification in those Countries Experiencing Serious Drought and/or Desertification Particularly in Africa [UNCCD] (1994). U.N. *Treaty Series*, Vol. 1954, pp. 3, Paris, 14 October 1994.

United Nations Convention on the Law of the Non-Navigational Uses of International Watercourses [Watercourses Convention] (1997). United Nations *Treaty Collection*, Chapter XXVII, 12, A/RES/51/229 Status. UN Doc. A/RES/51/869, 21 May 1997, 36 ILM 700 (1997). BOE N. 161, 3 July 2014, pp. 50889–50905. BOE-A-2014-6964.

United Nations Economic Commission for Europe. Convention on the protection and use of transboundary watercourses and international lakes [UNECE Water Convention] (1992). United Nations Treaty Collection, Chapter XXVII, *Treaty Series*, Vol. 1936, p. 269. Helsinki, 17 March 1992. BOE N. 81, 4 April 2000, pp. 13849–13857. BOE-A-2000-6440.

United Nations Universal Declaration of Human Rights [U.N.] (1948). General Assembly Resolution 217 A(III), Paris (December 1948). Retrieved from http://www.ohchr.org/EN/UDHR/Pages/Introducti on.aspx [June 2014].

Universidad Politécnica de Madrid (2008). Determinación del Régimen de Caudales Mínimos en el Tramo Bolarque-Aranjuez del Río Tajo. Sindicato Central de Regantes Acueducto Tajo-Segura.

Valencia recurrirá ante el Constitucional la Ley de Aguas y Ríos de Aragón por "blindar el Ebro" (8 January 2015). *elEconomista.es*. Retrieved from http://ecodiario.eleconomista.es/valenciana/noticias/6376431/ 01/15/Consell-presentara-recurso-de-inconstitucionalidad-a-la-Ley-de-Aguas-de-Aragon-por-ser-argucia-para-blindar-el-Ebro.html [10 March 2015].

CHAPTER 9

INSTITUTIONAL SETTINGS IN TRANSBOUNDARY WATER MANAGEMENT: LESSONS FROM THE FERGANA VALLEY AND THE LOWER JORDAN BASIN

CHRISTINE BISMUTH* and BERND HANSJÜRGENS[†]

*Helmholtz Center Potsdam — GFZ German Research Centre for Geosciences
[†]Helmholtz Center for Environmental Research — UFZ Leipzig

Both the Fergana Valley in Central Asia and the Lower Jordan River Basin are international hotspots in water management. The irrigation and land use systems in both basins have seen important changes during the last century and the economic, social, and political stability in those regions depends largely on the availability and fair distribution of the basins' water resources. How these water resources are managed depends in many ways on the different institutional settings and their adaptation capacities. In both regions, path dependencies, resulting from the construction of major water engineering projects (MWEPs) and existing institutional settings, constrain the introduction of integrated water resources management (IWRM) within a transboundary context. Those constraints can only be lifted by the introduction of adaptive and participative instruments.

Keywords: Major water engineering projects; transboundary water management; path dependencies; Red Sea — Dead Sea Conveyance Project; Fergana Valley; IWRM; International Water Law.

9.1. Introduction

Transboundary water management should provide for the effective and fair allocation of water, but implementing strategies which guarantee the design of adequate institutions between upstream and downstream users faces often major obstacles. The absence of adequate institutions frequently leads to conflicts between riparian states. The question of conflict and cooperation among water users has been dealt with extensively in the literature (see, e.g., Dombrowsky, 2008). However, how these effective and fair institutions are to be developed is still a challenge that remains largely to be explored.

Our research on institutions in the Fergana Valley and the Lower Jordan Valley was part of the Interdisciplinary Research Group *Society–Water–Technology* (IRG SWT) of the Berlin Brandenburg Academy of Sciences and Humanities. Over the project period of three and a half years, the IRG SWT analyzed how MWEPs shape the ecological, social, and economic development of a region in terms of path dependencies (Hüttl *et al.*, 2016). This analysis was centered on two case studies: the Lower Jordan River Basin with its planned Red Sea–Dead Sea (RSDS) Conveyance Project and the Fergana Valley with the Great Fergana Channel conveyance systems. Both case studies are situated in transboundary surroundings that are considered to be political hotspots with respect to the management of transboundary river basins (and nonwater protracted conflicts).

Our analytical method was inspired by the diagnostic approach of Ostrom and Cox (2010) and Ostrom (2009). The evaluation framework (see Table 9.1) is divided into different system classes and their arrays. The choice of these system classes corresponds widely to the selected thematic foci of the IRG, namely water (resource system class), society (governance and social system class), and technology (technological system class) (Hoechstetter *et al.*, 2016).

In this chapter, we focus on the institutions and processes within the governance systems in transboundary water man. By analyzing and comparing the governance systems in the two case studies — the Fergana Valley and the Lower Jordan Basin Valley — we draw some general lessons for the institutional settings of transboundary water management conditions. We include the rules and regulations as set by the International Water Law in our analysis.

More specifically we focus on the following questions:

- What influence does the International Water Law have on the management of transboundary river basins?

Table 9.1: Evaluation framework for the Fergana Valley and the Lower Jordan Basin.

	Systems and Processes		
Natural Conditions and Resource Systems	*Governance Systems*	*Social Systems and Stakeholder Concerns*	*Technological Systems*
Geographical attributes and boundaries	Rules, norms, and property right regimes	Group attributes and leadership	Technological attributes and performance levels
Economic value of relevant ecosystem services	Governance mode	Capacity and social capital	Monitoring (environmental, technical, social, economic)
Productivity and effectiveness	Participatory processes	Acceptance of and familiarity with technology used	Human resources
Resource challenges (e.g., climate and demographic change)	Network structure (centrality, adaptiveness, connectivity, number of levels)	Economical and societal challenges (e.g., global economic crisis, world market prices for resources and goods, political events)	Technical challenges (e.g., material property restrictions, distances, size)

	Outcomes	
Ecological Performance (e.g., exploitation, ecosystem resilience and resistance, biodiversity, sustainability)	*Economic Performance (e.g., efficiency, cost-recovery, cost–benefit ratio, external costs)*	*Social Performance (e.g., equity, accountability, sustainability)*

Notes: Based on Ostrom and Cox (2010) and Ostrom (2009); modified from Hoechstetter *et al.* (2016).

- How responsive is the International Water Law with respect to new challenges such as climate change?
- What are the common characteristics of the institutional settings in the Fergana Valley and the Lower Jordan Basin Valley and what lessons can be derived from the analysis?

Based on the findings of our analysis, we discuss in a last step the question what would be the core elements of an adaptive and participative water basin management in International Water Law?

9.2.   The International Water Law and the Concept of IWRM

The IWRM within the limits of river basins is the most advanced water management concept (Mager, 2015). Particularly, the European Water Framework Directive (WFD) explicitly pursues such a river basin approach (European Community, 2000). The European Union member states are required to deliver a river basin management plan for each river basin, including all relevant data on the basin and its main characteristics (e.g., socioeconomic data and major uses). The states are obliged to monitor and to evaluate achievements made in attaining the overarching goal of a "good ecological status" of the river body. An economic analysis of water uses within the river basin must be carried out. Furthermore, the WFD requires that the public participate in establishing the river management plans.

One particular blueprint for the WFD has been the activities within the International Commission for the Protection of the Rhine (ICPR), one of the oldest and successful river commissions in Europe. Following the example set by the ICPR, other international river commissions such as for the Danube or the Oder have been founded. In these commissions, river management plans, international measures for flood protection, as well as activities for the rehabilitation of the rivers are coordinated in workgroups focused on specific themes and in which civil society actively participates. The reintroduction of salmon into the Rhine River is just one concrete result of the active involvement of civil society in its management.

However, apart from the WFD, International Water Law shares the same general weakness of all international laws: there is no institution with undisputed powers to enforce its rules (Mager, 2015). In fact, there are only three undisputed rules of customary International Water Law. These are:

(i) The rule of equitable and reasonable utilization;
(ii) The no-harm rule;
(iii) The duty to cooperate (Mager, 2015).

In 1997, the General Assembly of the United Nations passed the *UN Convention on Non-Navigational Uses of International Water Courses* (United Nations, 2014). The convention came into force almost 17 years later in May 2014. It requires that a state sharing an international watercourse with other states should utilize the watercourse in its territory, in a manner that is equitable and reasonable *vis-a-vis* the other states sharing it. In order to ensure that their utilization of an international watercourse is equitable and reasonable, states are to take into account all relevant factors and circumstances (Mccaffrey, 2008). Another key provision established in the convention is found under Article 7 which imposes the obligation not to cause significant harm (Mccaffrey, 2008). The states must "take all appropriate measures to prevent the causing of significant harm" to other states sharing an international watercourse. Besides the codification of customary International Water Law, the convention establishes information and notification duties as well as consultations and negotiations in the case of planned measures. The convention has been criticized as being weak on environmental issues and for not taking into consideration the human right to water.

International Water Law is criticized for being inadequate to meet the challenges posed by climate change, such as increasing climate variability, more intense and frequent flood and drought events and, for many transboundary basins, a significant reduction in the annual mean discharge (Eckstein, 2009; IPCC, 2014). Eckstein (2009, p. 434) criticizes that the "applicability and value of the principles of equitable and reasonable utilization and of no significant harm are limited in the context of climate change. Both principles focus entirely on ensuring the rights of nations rather than on responding to climatic variability." Consequently, current International Water Law, instead of creating options for improved governance of transboundary watercourses, consolidates in some cases historically grown structures and, in the worst case, inhibits adaptation (Bismuth *et al.*, n.d.).

Here, we leave the introduction to the concepts of IWRM and the example of the ICPR, a possible benchmark for water management, and now turn to the situation in the Fergana Valley and the Lower Jordan Basin.

9.3. Historical Developments and Geographical Overview of the Two Case Study Regions

9.3.1. *The Fergana Valley*

The Fergana Valley irrigation system along the ancient Silk Road in Central Asia is among the eldest of the world. Water has been directed to the fields by gravitation since the Neolithic started to water wheat and barley. Rice, wheat, and wine were grown in the oasis along the rivers, as well as alfalfa for the valley's famous breed of horses. The Fergana Valley is among the most fertile regions in Central Asia, but also among the most densely populated. Glaciers in the Kirgiz high mountainous regions and rain and snowfall during winter seasons provide the lion share of water the Fergana Valley receives. The climate during the cultivation season is hot and dry.

In the early 19th century, the Fergana Valley gradually fell under Russian influence. The Russian Empire was interested in colonizing "Turkmenistan," as this region with unclear boundaries was called, to become independent from imports of cotton dominated by Anglo-Saxons, and to build up an independent cotton production industry. Moreover, Turkmenistan is located in the way of the empire's pursuit of reaching the Indian Ocean (Fig. 9.1).

From Russian colonization until the present, the Fergana Valley has succumbed to several transformations. While life and working practices in the Fergana Valley during early colonization times remained unchanged, with increasing connection to Russian production and market centers, the production of cotton gained growing

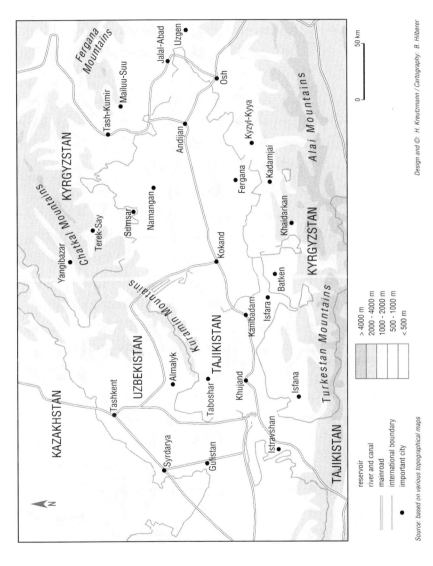

Figure 9.1: Topographic map of the Fergana Valley (Kreutzmann, 2016).

importance (Jozan, 2012). That said, major changes only occurred during the Soviet period. With increasing mechanization of the production and manufacturing process within the cotton sector, and also with improved transportation, the dream of a Central Asian cotton production center for the Soviet Union was realized (Abdullaev *et al.*, 2007; Jozan, 2012). This was done through comprehensively expanding the irrigation areas, and in doing so, reshaping the irrigation schemes. Since the late 1930s, when the Fergana Valley Channel was built, hundreds of kilometers of irrigation and drainage channels (all of which have to be maintained) have dominated the geography of the Fergana Valley.

Even though traditional farming systems were merged into the socialist kolkhoz systems, the old decision structures to direct the complex irrigation systems remained in force and were adapted to the new socialist system. As such, the mirhabs (the managers of opening and closing the water channel gates and inspector of irrigation quantities) kept their functions in the socialist production system, and the emerging new Central Asian States inherited socialist management and decision structures following the collapse of the Soviet Union. Cotton remains subject of state-controlled policies, especially in Uzbekistan, while the secondary crops sustain the local rural populations in the Fergana Valley (Abdullaev *et al.*, 2007).

The key source of irrigation in the region is the Toktugul Reservoir upstream of the Syr Darya Basin (in Kirgizstan) with an effective exploitable storage capacity of 14 billion m^3. It was built in 1976 primarily to deliver the valley with sufficient water in summer for cotton production. Its second purpose was the production of energy during winter months. During the Soviet Union era, it was in the hands of Moscow to balance the diverse interests and needs of the Central Asian Republics (i.e., water for cotton and food production for downstream users, energy needs for upstream users), but after the collapse of the Soviet Union, a political vacuum appeared while the newly established Republics were trying to consolidate their independence.

It was the extension of the irrigation areas for cotton, not only in the Fergana Valley, but also in Kazakhstan and further downstream of the Syr Darya that has led to the drying up of the Aral Sea. Furthermore, rising salinity levels in the irrigation water downstream of the Fergana has salinized the soils, which have formed toxic dusts around the Aral Basin when combined with pesticide residues, severely impacting the health of this region's inhabitants.

International initiatives and donor organizations have tried to prevent further decline in the Aral Sea and to rehabilitate the environment. They have created international programs insisting on regulations and institutions to manage the Central Asian trans-boundary waters. However, these efforts have produced limited restoration of the Aral Sea. While the international engagement started off with the safeguarding the Aral Sea as the focus of its interests, the predominant subject matters are now security, stability, and climate change. Diverging interests on quantities, primary uses, and distribution of the available water resources form the character of the relationships between Uzbekistan, Tadzhikistan, and Kirgizstan. Population growth, and social, economic, and political turmoil are further increasing the tensions between the riparian Central Asian Republics.

9.3.2.   *The Lower Jordan Basin*

The Lower Jordan River Basin is another political hotspot in the context of transboundary water. As the final recipient of the Jordan River, the Dead Sea faces declining sea levels as is the Aral Sea (Fig. 9.2). Agriculture is the main user of available water resources as is the case in the Fergana Valley. High population growth rates and the negative impacts of climate change have put further pressure on available water resources in the Lower Jordan River Basin. But while the irrigation system of the Fergana Valley suffers from rather low efficiency, at least the Israeli's part of the Lower Jordan River Basin has one of the most efficient irrigation systems in the world. Nevertheless, use and distribution of the available water resources are the most important issues in the discussions among the riparian states of the Lower Jordan River Basin (Lebanon, Syria, Israel, Palestine Territories, and Jordan).

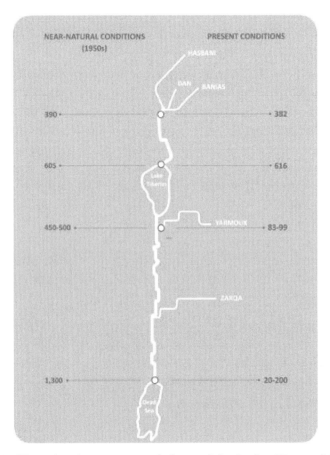

Figure 9.2: Natural and present water balance of the Jordan River and the Dead Sea (UN-ESCWA and BGR, 2013).

Source: Compiled by ESCWA-BGR based on Courcier et al. (2005); GRDC (2011); Palestine Irrigation Service, 1944–1946 and HSI, 1946–2008.

The Lower Jordan River Basin (from hereafter: Lower Jordan) has been subject to major changes since the 1950s with the construction of Israel's National Carrier diverting water from Lake Tiberias to the south of Israel. While the inlet flow into the lake has remained nearly constant, the outflow from the lake into the Lower Jordan has decreased dramatically (also it must be said, as a result of the dams built by the Kingdom of Jordan and by Syria on the Yarmouk River).

Not only has the water flow of the River Jordan declined by 95%, but also the water quality has deteriorated considerably — turning the Lower Jordan River into a sewage carrier (Bamya *et al.*, 2012).

Droughts, rising water deficits, groundwater depletion, and saltwater intrusion into the aquifers have increased environmental concerns about the state of the water resources. The need to halt the further decline of the Dead Sea is calling not only for the rehabilitation of the Lower Jordan River, but has also led to the development of new water sources by seawater desalination. The latest plans are to desalinate water from the Red Sea to use for the supply of drinking water for Amman (in Jordan) and Eilat (in Israel) and to convey the brine to the Dead Sea. Differing project alternatives and the environmental consequences of RSDS conveyance project had been studied by the World Bank on the initiative of Israel and Jordan (Allan *et al.*, 2012). However, institutional and transboundary water management matters were outside the scope of the different studies within this project (Bismuth, 2016).

9.4.   Regional Institutions, Regulations, and Tools

9.4.1.   *The Interstate Water Law in Central Asia*

Following the collapse of the Soviet Union in 1991, a political and ecological reorganization was required of the previously centralized water control and management, and cooperation had to be established between the concerned central Asian republics. The necessity to cooperate led to signing an accord between the five central Asian republics of Kazakhstan, the Kyrgyz Republic, the Republic of Uzbekistan, the Republic of Tajikistan, and Turkmenistan: *The Agreement on Cooperation in the field of Joint Water Resources Management and Conservation of Interstate Sources*, signed on 18 February 1992. In the agreement the same allocation terms set by the Soviet Union were used (Eschment, 2011). The treaty established the Intergovernmental Water Management Commission (ICWC) to ensure strict compliance with the rules on time and amount of water releases from main reservoirs and on the distribution of the agreed quantities of water. The objectives of the statutes of the ICWC are far-reaching in principle and include, *inter alia*: the common goals of economical use of water; maintaining the water quality required; ensuring a sufficient flow of water into the Aral Sea; restoring the ecosystem; and implementing a coordinated social and economic development program (Mager, 2015). In 2008, the status of the ICWC was redrafted adding functions for making suggestions to improve international agreements on shared water management and to assist the governments in their cooperation with international organizations (Mager, 2015). Other new features include training and educational activities and coordinating the needs of irrigated agriculture and hydropower generation.

In 1993, the International Fund for Saving the Aral Sea (IFAS) was established with the specific task of obtaining financial resources from foreign donors to save the Aral Sea (Mager, 2015).

As a result of noncompliance with former ICWC decisions of water allocations, Kazakhstan, Kyrgyzstan, and Uzbekistan concluded the *Agreement of the Use of Water and Energy Resources* in the Syr Darya Basin on 17 March 1998, known as the Bishkek Agreement. The parties agreed to decide annually on the use of the Naryn–Syr Darya Cascade water for the dual purposes of irrigation and hydropower production. In fact, the agreement maintains the old Soviet principle "water against energy." However, this agreement was rarely respected and can be regarded as failed. Also, several attempts to adapt the agreement failed due to diverging interests, mainly between Uzbekistan and Kirgizstan.

In fact, all the water-related treaties and accords in Central Asia can be regarded as failed (Eschment, 2011). Besides the fact that competences between regional organizations and national authorities were never clearly defined, the contracts do not include sanctions for cases of nonexecution or effective mediation mechanisms (Mager, 2015). Additionally, neither ecological matters nor the effects of climate change were considered. In principle, the water allocation system follows the rules stemming from the former Soviet times, an agreement that was already showing its limitations during the Soviet regime. A very important reason for the failure of all treaties is the lack of political will to establish common functioning institutions with adequate control and sanctioning mechanisms and the necessary competences to implement the measures (Eschment, 2011). The lack of reliable databases, monitoring systems, and the transparent exchange of information are further reasons for noneffective transboundary water management.

9.4.2. *Interstate Water Law in the Jordan River Basin*

As there are to date no water-related agreements concerning the upper Jordan River between Israel and Lebanon, or Israel and Syria, we focus in our analysis on the treaties between Israel, the Palestine Territories, and the Kingdom of Jordan. Syria is only regarded as far as the Yarmuk River is concerned.

Existing water accords between the riparian states play an important role in defining rules for the management of the common water resources. In our analysis we will not consider the *Johnston Plan* from 1953, as this plan has never been formally adopted and falls short in sustainable groundwater use, environmental needs, and the impacts of population growth and climate change on the availability of water resources (Bismuth, 2016).

The agreement on the utilization of the water of the Yarmuk River between the Syrian Arab Republic and the Kingdom of Jordan was signed in 1987 (Syrian Arab Republic and Jordan, 1987). It foresaw the establishment of a joint Syria–Jordan commission for the implementation of construction work on the Maqarin Dam. The dam was finally completed in 2011, but so far the dam's reservoir remains unfilled. Droughts and increased water withdrawal by Syria reduced the annual flow of the Yarmuk River to the reservoir. Since the agreement was signed, more than 30 dams and 300 wells have been erected in the basin (UN-ESCWA and BGR, 2013).

Israel and Jordan signed a peace treaty in 1994. This treaty implicitly refers to the three main water law principles of the above-mentioned international customary water law (i.e., rule of equitable and reasonable utilization, no-harm rule, and duty to cooperate), but adapts them to the special political situation in the region. The parties agreed on the allocation of shared water resources from the

Yarmuk and Jordan rivers. The accord settled the establishment of a Joint Water Committee (JWC). The cooperation on water issues and the exchange of relevant data on water resources are synchronized by the committee. Joint monitoring stations are to be established and the disposal of untreated wastewater into the river is forbidden.

In Annex III, Article 40 of the *Oslo II Agreement* between the Palestinian Authority and Israel (Israeli Government and PLO, 1995) the share and distribution of water resources and the establishment of a Palestinian Water Administration Authority have been settled. The exact allocation has been postponed until the Permanent Status Negotiations and Agreement is finalized. The two parties agreed to establish a JWC for the interim period. As all decisions of the JWC have to be made unanimously, this provides the Israeli side with a de facto veto right over projects under the administration of the Palestinian Authorities. Furthermore, projects outside the area of the Palestinian administration need the approval of the civil administration, which is in effect a branch of the Israeli Defense Ministry. As a consequence of the political lockdown, the protection and the development of the water resources is seriously hampered by the diverging interests of the Israeli and Palestinian sides, not only regarding water-related issues, but also with the occupation of the Palestinian areas. It can be said that the Israeli occupation is obstructing a sustainable management of the shared water resources. It might not be the only reason, but it is an important one.

During the negotiation process of the RSDS conveyance project and for the *Water Swap Memorandum of Understanding* (MoU), the Palestinians saw the opportunity to use the project as a bargaining chip in the peace treaty negotiation process, as well as an instrument to achieve national sovereignty (Fischhendler *et al.*, 2013). The MoU falls short of addressing institutional regulations for the management of a complex transboundary water project. Especially between Israel and the Palestine Authority, the MoU agreements reduce the problems between the two parties to merely quantitative aspects (Bismuth, 2016; Mager, 2015).

A common characteristic of all three accords mentioned is that they are ambiguous, vague, and voluntarily, leaving room for interpretation by each party. Rules on compliance and control, and mechanisms for mediation in case of conflict between parties are not established, nor in operation (Dombrowsky, 2003).

9.5. Comparison of the Interstate Institutions of the Selected Case Studies

A common characteristic of both case studies is that water issues and water projects are seen as a part of the nation-building effort, especially for new emerging states such as the territory of the Palestine Authority, which could get a statehood status in the near future, and the Central Asian republics, which were founded in 1993 after the collapse of the Soviet Union (see also Trottier and Brooks, 2013). The water policies in Israel can be seen in this perspective too, as within the state building process and since the foundation of Israel as a state in 1948 water and land policies have always been a major building block in Israel's consolidation policy. This approach is at odds with the features of International River Basins, and particularly contradicts any IWRM approach. The conflicts become apparent when it comes to the rules concerning water allocation. In both case studies, the water allocation system regards only quantitative aspects of the uses. They leave no option for addressing changing societal or economic developments, or changes in the natural available water resources. For example, the allocations fixed in the Oslo II agreements are already difficult to achieve at present during the recent series of long droughts in the basin, and give constant ground for water disputes between Israel and the Palestine Authority. There are similar situations in the relationship between Uzbekistan and Kirgizstan, as well in the relationship between Uzbekistan and Tadzhikistan where the distribution of water between cotton production and energy production continuously adds fuel to the ongoing conflicts. As a consequence, these regulations fail in day-to-day practice, as they neither provide answers to newly emerging economic needs, nor to social or environmental needs. In other words, a quantitative approach alone on the allocation of water resources impedes the ability to adapt to climate change, changing societies, and other emerging needs.

In both case studies, transboundary management structures are either weak or absent. This is a direct cause of the above-mentioned reason of water being part of a national building effort. As long as riparian states regard water as a national issue, the institutions set up to deal with transboundary (i.e., international) issues of water management will remain weak, and thus fail in the majority of the cases. Only when it can be proven that the economic benefits from shared management are greater than those from purely nationalistic ones, different approaches might be achievable.

For example, in Europe, it was the Sandoz catastrophe which led to the collapse of the Upper Rhine, and the concentrated efforts of all riparian states to restore the river that provided the evidence for the benefits that resulted from stringent standards and common action plans. And thus, the Rhine basin turned into a striking example of how cooperation generates welfare for the whole society and for the environment. Clear regulations, a stringent monitoring program, the sharing of data, and comprehensive action programs were the basis of this success. All those elements are missing in the Fergana Valley case study and in the Jordan Basin.

Trust is an element mostly missing in both case studies. The sharing of data and information is not transparent and leaves discretionary room for interpretation. Even though Israel is exceptionally transparent in publishing its own water use data, when it comes to the West Bank this information is not accessible, leaving room for different interpretations and disputes. The water data from the Kingdom of Jordan seems to be little more than wishful thinking than solid facts (see Bismuth, 2016; Mager, 2015) concerning the data situation in the Lower Jordan basin. With regards to Central Asia, the data situation becomes even worse. Until present, it has been extremely difficult to implement a common monitoring network for water and climate research purposes between Uzbekistan and Kirgizstan due to the lack of political will, despite of agreements on research.

Regulations and transboundary institutions in both case studies lack any mechanisms to allow for the participation of the public in water management. Even though public participation is not a core element in International Water Law, the *Aarhus Convention* has recognized its importance for environmental planning issues (UNECE, 1998). The WFD was one of the first European directives to integrate public participation in water management as one of its core elements. Also, the concept of IWRM advocates public participation in water management. But the institutional settings in the two case studies both at an international level and at the different national levels lack any approaches to integrate public participation. Access to information is only fully granted to the public in the case of Israel. Even in the democracy of Israel, the participation of the civil society in water authority bodies is weak (Kislev, 2011). The international agreements in our studies ignore that public participation in water management creates partnerships, provide legitimacy to water management plans and to social instruments, and improves capacity and ownership (Gupta *et al.*, 2013).

9.6. Core Elements of Adaptive and Participative Water Basin Management in International Water Law

The two case studies illustrate the weakness and the failures of the International Water Law, although we find in many other cases positive examples of institutional settings to be further developed within International Water Law. However there has rarely been a fundamental discussion on the question how International Water Law should be designed to address questions of climate change, changing societies, or upcoming new priorities and needs. Especially in regions under water stress and in regions which are mostly affected by climate change, answers have to be found how the water law can both be flexible enough to react to changing environments on one side, and on the other stringent enough not to leave room for competing interpretations and further disputes. An especially important question is how to address water allocation as transparent, socially equitable, and fair in transboundary water management.

9.7.   Water Allocation Linked to the Availability of Renewable Water Resources

Maximum allocation quotas are inflexible with regards to new requirements or to climate change. We would gain flexibility if we used set percentage quotas related only to the amount of the renewable water resources available annually based on continuous monitoring and measurements. During drought, the usable amount would be less, while in wetter years overflows could go into storage systems or left to the environment. The percentage rate should be set by nature. As such, we would attain both flexibility and rigidity.

9.7.1.   *Qualitative Objectives Linked to the Ecological Status of a River Course*

Qualitative objectives are not merely water quality standards but they refer also to the structure and the biological aspects of a river. For example is the existence of artificial barriers like dams determining for the ecological status of a river. Qualitative aspects in transboundary water management are often overlooked, despite their important influence on the usability of water resources. With the adoption of the principle of the objective of "a good ecological status," it is possible to unite both aspects in water management: the quantitative with the qualitative. Such an approach would require the establishment of long-lasting management plans in order to reach the objective combined with an efficient monitoring and data collection system.

9.7.2.   *Monitoring and Data Collection, and Sharing(?)*

The proposed allocation system would require continuous monitoring and data management. Innovative remote sensing geotechnologies offer new possibilities to provide decision makers with necessary information (Löw *et al.*, 2014). Monitoring, data collection, and sampling could be performed by independent international bodies or by research institutions. Information should be accessible for the public and data management would be transparent and understandable.

9.7.3. *Instruments for Mitigation and Conflict Resolution*

Any international agreement requires clear rules in cases of conflict and diverging interests. It would be beneficial to integrate appeals to international water courts (if needed) as a mechanism. Likewise, it is important to include mechanisms of sanctions in cases of disrespect/noncompliance. It seems that we have much more powerful enforcement instruments available in the case of international financing institutions than in the case of International Water Law. Possibly we can learn something from the mechanisms applied in finance.

9.7.4. *Transboundary Management Body with Clearly Designed Duties and Responsibilities*

Transboundary water management calls for the establishment of a common authority as a discourse platform on transboundary water management aspects within basins. Rules and duties should be clearly designed. It would be essential that the formulation of legal binding management and development plans be among the responsibilities in accordance with the defined overarching objectives. The specific abilities of the member organization should be taken into consideration. The organization should include the civil society and guarantee the participation of the public in the decision-making process.

9.7.5. *Economic Instruments*

The efficiency of water management can be raised by the integration of economic instruments in water law. For example, the WFD demanding the full cost recovery principle in measurement plans. Such an instrument can avoid costly and unnecessary activities, and is an incentive for developing cost saving alternatives. And it is essential for the equitable distribution of cost burdens.

9.8. Concluding Remarks

Both case studies illustrate that international coordination and cooperation needs to be strengthened. However, we have to be aware that general objectives have to be broken down into reliable, practical, and concrete corner stones. The transformation of institutions is a slow process, and even more so with regard to existing legacies. It is especially important to build inclusive institutions, which help to overcome asymmetries of powers. International organizations including financial organizations could phase more emphasis on the implementation of the principles of IWRM. Monitoring and evaluation criteria play a critical role in IWRM determining whether standards have been met or more interventions are needed (Lim, 2014). The implementation process of the WFD alone would deliver substantial material for a comprehensive analysis of the determinants for success and failures under different political, societal, and geographical conditions. Combined with an analysis of present transboundary treaties and conventions, this would be a first step toward the development of adaptive strategies for a rapidly changing world (see, e.g., Dombrowsky, 2007, 2008). If we want to face the present and upcoming challenges, we must emphasize research focusing on increasing the resilience of coupled socioecosystems.

References

Abdullaev, I, M Giordano, and A Rasulov (2007). Cotton in Uzbekistan: Water and Welfare. In *The Cotton Sector in Central Asia Economic Policy and Development Challenges*, D Kandiyoti (ed.), pp. 112–128. London: The School of Oriental and African Studies University of London.

Allan, JA, AIH Malkawi, and Y Tsur (2012). *Red Sea–Dead Sea Water Conveyance Study Program. Study of Alternatives. Preliminary Draft Report*. Washington: World Bank Publications. Retrieved from http://siteresources.worldbank.org/INTREDSEADEADSEA/Resources/Study_of_Alternatives_Report_EN.pdf [January 2015].

Bamya, S, N Becker, EJ Saaf, and D Katz (2012). *Towards a Living Jordan River: A Regional Economic Benefits Study on the Rehabilitation of the Lower Jordan River*. Amman, Bethlehem, Tel Aviv: Friends of the Earth Middle East. Retrieved from http://foeme.org/uploads/136732 71311~%5E$%5E~Economic_Benefits_Study_English.pdf [June 2014].

Bismuth, C (2016). Water resources, cooperation and power asymmetries in the water management of the Lower Jordan Valley: The situation today and the path that has led there. In *Society–Water–Technology: A Critical Appraisal of Major Water Engineering Projects*, RF Huettl, O Bens, C Bismuth, and S Hoechstetter (eds.), pp. 189–204. Dordrecht: Springer.

Bismuth, C, K Unger-Shayesteh, F Löw, T Schöne, S Hoechstetter, O Bens, and RF Hüttl (n.d.). How Earth Observation Technologies may help to dismantle path dependencies in water management: The example of the Fergana Valley. *Environmental Earth Sciences, 2* (Sustainable Resource Water Management in Central Asia).

Dombrowsky, I (2003). Water accords in the Middle East peace process. In *Security and Environment in the Mediterranean — Conceptualising Security and Environmental Conflict*, HG Brauch, PH Liotta, A Marquina, P Rogers, and ME-S Selim (eds.), Vol. 16, pp. 729–744. Berlin, Heidelberg, New York: Springer.

Dombrowsky, I (2007). *Conflict, Cooperation and Institutions in International Water Management — An Economic Analysis*. Cheltenham, UK and Northampton: Edward Elgar.

Dombrowsky, I (2008). Konflikt und Kooperation an grenzüberschreitenden Flüssen. Wasser-Zukunftressource zwischen Menschenrecht und Wirtschaftsgut, Konflikt und Kooperation. Potsdam (2008): 57–70. *Brandenburgische Landeszentrale Für Politische Bildung*, 57–70.

Eckstein, G (2009). *Water Scarcity, Conflict, and Security in a Climate Change World: Challenges and opportunities for International Law and Policy*. Retrieved from http://papers.ssrn.com/sol3/papers.cfm?abstract_id=1425796 [December 2015].

Eschment, B (2011). *Wasserverteilung in Zentralasien. Ein Unlösbares Problem? Friedrich Ebert Stiftung*. Berlin: Friedrich Ebert Stiftung. Retrieved from http://www.fes.de/international/moe [March 2013].

European Community (2000). Directive 2000/60/EC of the European Parliament and of the Council of 23 October 2000 establishing a framework for Community action in the field of water policy. *Official Journal of the European Parliament, L327* (September 1996), 1–82. doi:10.1039/ap9842100196.

Fischhendler, I, AT Wolf, and G Eckstein (2013). The role of creative language in addressing political asymmetries: The Israeli-Arab Water

Agreements. In *Shared Borders, Shared Waters*, SB Megdal, RG Varady, and S Eden (eds.), pp. 53–74. Leiden: CRC Press. Retrieved from http://www.transboundarywaters.orst.edu/publications/publications/CH04. Fischhendler-Wolf-Eckstein.pdf [November 2013].

Gupta, J, A Akhmouch, W Cosgrove, Z Hurwitz, J Maestu, and O Ünver (2013). Policymakers' reflections on water governance issues. *Ecology and Society*, 18(1). doi:10.5751/ES-05086-180135.

Hoechstetter, S, C Bismuth, and H-G Frede (2016). Major water engineering projects: definitions, framework conditions, systemic effects. In *Society–Water–Technology: A Critical Appraisal of Major Water Engineering Projects*, RF Huettl, C Bismuth, S Hoechstetter, and O Bens (eds.), pp. 33–46. Dordrecht: Springer.

Hüttl, RF., O Bens, C Bismuth, and Hoechstetter, S. (eds.). (2016). *Society–Water–Technology: A Critical Appraisal of Major Water Engineering Projects* (Water Reso.). Heidelberg: Springer Netherlands: Dordrecht. doi:10.1007/978-3-319-18971-0.

IPCC (2014). *Climate Change 2014: Synthesis Report. Contribution of Working Groups I, II and III to the Fifth Assessment Report of the Intergovernmental Panel on Climate Change.* Geneva, Switzerland: IPCC.

Israeli Government and PLO (1995). *Israeli-Palestinian Interim Agreement on the West Bank and the Gaza Strip.* Signed in Washington, DC. 28 September 1995 (Oslo II). Retrieved from http://mfa.gov.il/MFA/ForeignPolicy/Peace/Guide/Pages/THEISRAELI-PALESTINIAN IN TERIM AGREEMENT.aspx [June 2014].

Jozan, R (2012). *Les Débordements De La Mer d'Aral.* Paris: Presses Universitaires de France.

Kislev, Y (2011). *The Water Economy of Israel.* Jerusalem: Taub Center for Social Policy Studies in Israel. Retrieved from http://departments.agri.huji.ac.il/economics/teachers/kislev_yoav/water_English edition.pdf [May 2013].

Kreutzmann, H (2016). From upscaling to rescaling — The Fergana Basin's tranformation from Tsarist irrigation to water management for an independent Uzbekistan. In *Society–Water–Technology: A Critical Appraisal of Major Water Engineering Projects*, RF Huettl, O Bens, C Bismuth, and S Hoechstetter (eds.), pp. 113–127. Dordrecht: Springer. doi:10.1007/978-3-319-18971-0.

Lim, M (2014). Is water different from biodiversity? Governance criteria for the effective management of transboundary resources. *Review of European, Comparative and International Environmental Law, 23*(1), 96–110. doi:10.1111/reel.12072.

Löw, F, E Fliemann, and CM Biradar. 2014. *Quantification of the land use and land cover dynamics in the Fergana Valley. Technical Report, ICARDA.*

Mager, U (2015). International water law: Global developments and regional examples. *Miscellanea Juridica Heidelbergensia,* JF der R.-K.-U. Heidelberg, (ed.), Miscellane, Vol. 3. Heidelberg: Jedermann-Verlag Heidelberg.

Mccaffrey, BSC (2008). Convention on the Law of the Non-Navigational uses of International Watercourses. *United Nations Audivisual Library of International Law,* 1–4.

Ostrom, E. (2009). A general framework for analyzing sustainability of social-ecological systems. *Science,* 325(5939), 419–422. doi:10.1126/science.1172133.

Ostrom, E and M Cox (2010). Moving beyond panaceas: a multi-tiered diagnostic approach for social-ecological analysis. *Environmental Conservation,* 37(4), 451–463. doi:10.1017/S0376892910000834.

Syrian Arab Republic and Jordan (1987). *Agreement Concerning the Utilization of the Yarmuk Waters* (with annex). Signed at Amman on 3 September 1987. Retrieved from http://www.internationalwaterlaw.org/documents/regionaldocs/Jordan-Syria-1987.pdf [April 2014].

Trottier, J and CB Brooks (2013). Academic tribes and transboundary water management: Water in the Israeli-Palestinian peace process. Retrieved from http://www.sciencediplomacy.org/files/academic_tribes_and_transboundary_water_management_science_diplomacy.pdf [July 2014].

UN-ESCWA and BGR (2013). *Inventory of shared water resources in Western Asia: Chapter 6 Jordan River Basin.* Beirut: United Nations Economic and Social Commission for Western Asia; Federal Institute for Geosciences and Natural Resources. Retrieved from http://waterinventory.org/sites/waterinventory.org/files/chapters/chapter-06-jordan-river-basin-web.pdf [December 2013].

UNECE (1998). Convention on Access to Information, Public Participation in Decision-Making and Access to Justice in Environmental Matters (Aarhus Convention) done at Aarhus, Denmark, on 25 June 1998. Retrieved from unece.org.

United Nations (2014). *Convention on the Law of the Non-Navigational Uses of International Watercourses, New York, 21 May 1997.* United Nations.

CHAPTER 10

REGIONAL COOPERATION IN RIVER BASIN REHABILITATION: ESTIMATING ECONOMIC BENEFITS OF ALTERNATIVES FOR JORDAN RIVER RESTORATION

NIR BECKER* and DAVID KATZ[†]

*Department of Economics and Management,
Tel-Hai College, Upper Galilee, Israel

[†]Department of Geography and Environmental Studies,
University of Haifa, Haifa, Israel

The Jordan River, one of the world's most famous, has been reduced to a little more than a drainage ditch after years of neglect. However, given its rich heritage and environmental importance, rehabilitation of the Lower Jordan River (LJR) brings with it the potential for significant cultural, ecological, and economic benefits. This regional benefits study estimated the magnitude of the economic benefits Jordanians, Palestinians, and Israelis may achieve from river restoration. The study used different nonmarket valuation techniques to help identify the scale of benefits that can be derived from various rehabilitation scenarios, addressing both flow magnitude and water quality. The results identify several positive-sum outcomes from rehabilitation of the LJR, especially from a regional perspective. As such, it points to the potential for rehabilitation of the river to provide shared benefits and common interests among parties in a region more typically characterized by political conflict and stalemate.

Keywords: Jordan River; Non-Market Valuation; Cost–Benefit analysis.

10.1. Introduction

The Jordan River is one of the world's most famous rivers, immortalized in the holy books of Judaism, Christianity, and Islam. Site of numerous biblical events, including the baptism of Jesus, it remains an important cultural reference for half of the world's population. Prior to the modern period, the river flowed freely creating lush fluvial and wetland ecosystems, rich in biodiversity. The river system also serves as one of the most important migratory flyways on the planet with an estimated 500 million birds traveling its length twice annually (Turner *et al.*, 2005).

Unfortunately, the lower stretch of the Jordan River, the same stretch immortalized in the religious texts, has been reduced to little more than a drainage ditch after years of upstream water diversions, pollution, and overall neglect. Currently, both government agencies and nongovernmental organizations (NGOs) have drafted plans to rehabilitate the river. Given its rich cultural heritage and environmental importance, rehabilitation of the LJR brings with it the potential for significant cultural, ecological, and economic benefits to all nations involved. Thus, rehabilitation of the shared river, which in the past has served as a source of conflict in a troubled region, has the potential to enhance cooperation between the local populations — Israeli, Jordanian, and Palestinian — providing them with common objectives and shared benefits.

The region suffers from a shortage of natural water resources, with all three countries below the well-known Falkenmark index's criteria for chronic water scarcity (Falkenmark and Lindh, 1976). The relatively recent advent of large-scale desalination in Israel, however, has somewhat reduced the pressures on natural water supplies and has increased possibilities for both regional cooperation over water issues as well as allocations of water for environmental purposes (Aviram *et al.*, 2014; Tal and Katz, 2012). Because desalination is relatively expensive, however, it is imperative to estimate and compare the potential benefits of all competing alternative uses of water, including that used for river restoration. This study is an attempt to identify and measure the potential economic benefits that can be derived from various rehabilitation scenarios for the LJR.

In the coming sections we present a brief background on the river and plans for its rehabilitation, followed by a description of study methods which provide estimates of the potential economic benefits to the three local populations of alternative rehabilitation plans, using three different nonmarket valuation methods (travel cost, contingent valuation, and choice modeling [CM]). After presenting the results of the valuation methods, we then compare these benefits to the costs of supplying the necessary water for environmental flows. Finally, we conclude with a discussion of the findings and their implications for broader regional cooperation.

10.2.   Background on Lower Jordan River and Rehabilitation Plans

10.2.1.   *Water Quantity and Quality*

The LJR and its tributaries are shared among Israel, Jordan, Syria, and the Palestinian Authority. It is the longest permanent river in the region, stretching an aerial distance of 105 km, with an actual stream channel length of 217 km from the Sea of Galilee to the Dead Sea (Fig. 10.1). The river is gently sloped from an altitude of 212 m below sea level to an altitude of 428 m below sea level. The LJR can today be divided into three sections: from the Sea of Galilee to the confluence with the Yarmouk River in which both sides of the LJR flow through Israel; from the entrance of the Yarmouk River into the LJR to Bezeq Stream in which the LJR serves as the border between Israel and Jordan; and from Bezeq Stream (near the border with the West Bank) to the Dead Sea, in which the LJR serves as the border between the West Bank and Jordan. The LJR is currently a military zone, serving as a border between Jordan to the east and Israel and the West Bank to the west. Access to the river is therefore extremely limited for Jordanians and Israelis and almost nonexistent for Palestinians. This lack of access has limited the public awareness of the state of the river, and, as a result, involvement in river advocacy.

According to recent studies the LJR system carried an average of 1.3 billion cubic meters of fresh water from the Sea of Galilee to

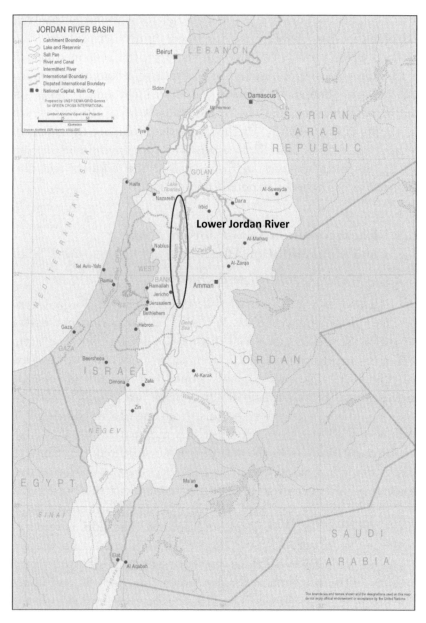

Figure 10.1: Map of the Jordan River Basin.

Source: UNEP Grid map. http://www.grid.unep.ch/index.php?option=com_content&view=article&id=73&Itemid=400&lang=en&project_id=137.

the Dead Sea every year until the 1930s (Anisfeld and Shub, 2009). Beginning in 1932 with the construction of Degania dam at the Jordan River's exit from the Sea of Galilee, the process of regulating the flow of the LJR began in earnest. Between 1946 and 1964, the river's flow regime was modified through interventions to prevent winter flooding, greatly reducing flow variability. In the mid-1960s, Israel and Jordan undertook major national water infrastructure projects to divert water of the LJR and its tributaries for domestic and agriculture use through the construction of the Israeli National Water Carrier and the King Abdullah Canal, respectively. Syria and Jordan also constructed smaller diversions along the Yarmouk River, the LJR's largest tributary, including construction of the Unity Dam in 2007. As a result of all of the diversions, capturing the majority of the Yarmouk's flow and further reducing the base flow of LJR to 20–30 million cubic meters (mcm) in 2009 (Gafny *et al.*, 2010) — less than 5% of its natural rate. Even including floodwaters, the annual flow of the Jordan is still less than 10% of its natural levels.

Water quality in the river has also deteriorated significantly over the past half century. This is not only due to reduced assimilative capacity due to reduced flows. It is also due to substantial inputs of pollutants, both intentionally and otherwise. In order to improve water quality in the Sea of Galilee, Israel constructed a pipeline in the 1960s that diverts water from saline springs that once flowed into the Sea of Galilee into the LJR instead. This caused a significant increase in the LJR's salinity because the saline water bypasses the Sea of Galilee. In addition, sewage from communities along both sides of the river has been discharged into the LJR continuously until recent years with dramatic effects on the river's health. Agricultural runoff has also contributed sediment and nutrient loads, including high amounts of organic pollution, to the river.

According to Hillel *et al.* (2015) the average electrical conductivity of the LJR is 12 mS/cm, over an order of magnitude higher than values typical for freshwater rivers. According to the same source, the mean salinity rate was over 3000 mg/L, reaching over 4000 mg/L in the dry season. The combination of reduced flow and poor water quality led to a 50% decrease in the river system's biodiversity over the past several decades (Gafny *et al.*, 2010).

The lack of flow in the LJR has also had a major impact on the state of the Dead Sea. The level of the terminal lake of the river has been dropping by over 1 m each year, continually breaking its own record as the lowest place on earth. As a result, the Dead Sea has already lost a one-third of its surface area (Glausiusz, 2010). The decreasing water levels are primarily due to water diversion from the LJR — the main water source for the Dead Sea (Lansky and Denta, 2015). The declining levels have brought about numerous ecological and environmental problems, including drying up of many freshwater springs along the coastal area and creation of thousands of sinkholes along the shore, causing significant damage to property and infrastructure.

10.2.2.   *Rehabilitation of the LJR*

The 1994 Peace Treaty signed by the governments of Israel and Jordan calls upon the signatory parties to cooperate with regard to the Jordan River in order to provide "ecological rehabilitation of the Jordan River," "environmental protection of water resources to ensure optimal water quality," "nature reserves and public areas," and "tourism and local heritage" (Environment Annex IV). The 1995 Interim Peace Agreement between Israel and the Palestinian Liberation Organization (PLO), established by the Palestinian Authority, did not specifically address the Jordan River, but did mandate that the parties work together to prevent environmental degradation (Article 12) and prevent water pollution and to promote the use of water resources in a sustainable manner (Article 40).

Over the last decade, the three parties have made some strides in reducing the discharge of waste into the LJR. The Israeli, Jordanian, and Palestinian governments are currently taking steps to significantly reduce the flow of untreated sewage into the LJR including the activation or planned several new sewage treatment plants in the Jordan Valley, Beit She'an, and Jericho regions. However, because effluent is a substantial component of the LJR flow, these efforts may not only reduce pollution loads, but also reduce river flow in an already denuded river. In this respect, the Israeli government has taken a first step in this direction by approving the allocation of 30 mcm per year of high quality water to be returned to the LJR. Relative to historical flows, such an amount is minor, however, it is expected to compensate for the reduced effluent inputs.

Governmental agencies at both the national and subnational levels, as well as NGOs, have begun to develop plans for large-scale rehabilitation of the LJR. These plans include restoration of some of the historical flow, continued efforts to reduce pollution, restoration of ecological habitat, and development of nature and cultural tourism along the river. It is hoped that such rehabilitation will bring about significant environmental, social, and economic benefits. The study presented in this chapter was undertaken within the framework of a regional rehabilitation plan for the LJR developed by the international NGO EcoPeace/Friends of the Earth — Middle East (EcoPeace, 2015). The purpose of the study was to gauge the potential economic benefits from rehabilitation of the LJR. This study was conducted by a team of Israeli, Jordanian, Palestinian, and international researchers using three different nonmarket valuation techniques.

10.3. Background on Nonmarket Valuation and Literature Review

Rehabilitation of the LJR involves numerous economic costs and benefits, including some that are more easily measured, such as the cost of infrastructure needed, and those that are more difficult, such as the value of ecosystem services. In this study, we employ multiple methods to value the benefits of rehabilitation of the LJR and compare them to the opportunity costs of the water (i.e., the value of the water as it is currently used). This section provides a general background on nonmarket economic valuation methods as well as a review of some of the past such studies conducted on aquatic ecosystems in the region.

10.3.1.   *Nonmarket Valuation Methods*

Environmental services and improvements thereof are what economists call "nonmarket goods," to indicate that these are not purchased directly, as are typical commodities. For market goods, welfare effects are tracked by changes related to changes in prices. As there are no clear markets for public goods and environmental services, estimation of the economic welfare they provide cannot be made from direct observations of transactions of the goods in question.

There are two main types of valuation methods by which these potential welfare effects can be estimated: (i) Revealed preference methods and (ii) Stated preference methods.

Revealed preference approaches involve estimation of value for environmental/recreational goods from observations of behavior in the markets for related goods (Freeman, 2003).

One of the more popular revealed preference methods, and one used in this study, is called the travel cost method (TCM). The TCM seeks to measure the economic benefits of outdoor recreation by estimating how changes in the environmental quality attributes of a site are likely to affect visitation rates.

The stated preference approach to valuation involves derivation of values for environmental goods from responses to questions about preferences for the good/service (Freeman, 2003). Typically, stated preferences are garnered via survey-based studies that ask respondents to reveal information about their preferences or willingness to pay (WTP) or accept compensation for an environmental good or service. The primary benefits of stated preference models include their ability to assess total economic value (as opposed to just recreational value or land-use value, etc.), including both use and nonuse values. Nonuse values include economic benefits by persons not directly consuming the good or services, such as satisfaction from knowing that a good exists or that it will remain available for future use and for future generations (Krutilla, 1967). While stated preference methods allow for valuation of future changes in provision of environmental goods or services, revealed preferences do not.

Two types of stated preference methods were used in this study on the LJR: the contingent valuation method (CVM) and choice modeling (CM).

The CVM involves directly asking respondents about their monetary valuation over a specific environmental change/improvement (Freeman, 1993).

CM is another stated preference valuation method that is applied to estimate the value of hypothetical recreational and environmental goods (e.g., Adamowicz *et al.*, 1994; Hanley *et al.*, 1998; Opaluch *et al.*, 1993). In the application of CM, survey respondents are presented with a series of choice sets, each containing options of goods with different attributes (e.g., different levels of quality), with each associated with a given cost. Respondents are asked to choose their preferred alternative from among those offered in the set. Attribute levels are varied from one alternative to the next in an experimental design (for a review, see Bennett and Blamey, 2001).

An advantage of CM vis-à-vis CVM is that the former does not rely on direct declarations of WTP, but rather, discerns the WTP based on the preferences of the respondents given various costs for obtaining given attribute levels. As such, relative to CVM, CM can provide a more detailed understanding of respondents' utility functions (Young, 2005). In addition, it may reduce the possibility that respondents answer strategically rather than indicating actual preferences (Young, 2005), as it is more difficult for subjects to behave strategically when they must choose among several different situations and make tradeoffs.

10.3.1.1. *Combining stated and revealed preference approaches*

A great deal of research has been done in the field of applied environmental economics which implements elements of both stated- and revealed-preference approaches in order to mutually validate responses from each method. Several empirical studies that have evaluated the veracity of stated preference models (by, for instance, comparing them with results from revealed preference models) have found them to provide reliable estimates of WTP (e.g., Carson *et al.*, 1996; Loomis, 1989; Reiling *et al.*, 1990; Teisl *et al.*, 1995), although some have found discrepancies between the approaches (e.g., Shechter *et al.*, 1998). In many cases, stated preference data can also be calibrated via revealed preference data over the same nonmarket good. In this manner, efficiency and accuracy of benefit estimation is improved in both measurements of WTP for changes in quality and quantity (e.g., Cameron and Englin, 1997; Huang *et al.*, 1997; Layman *et al.*, 1996).

Several studies have combined stated- and revealed-preference approaches in order to take advantage of the strengths and mitigate the weaknesses of each approach. Notably, Whitehead *et al.* (1998, 2000) and Whitehead (2002) proposed a combined revealed and stated behavior estimation method to measure recreation benefits for a quality improvement. In this method, sometimes dubbed contingent behavior modeling, one starts by estimating the travel and time costs of a recreation trip as the implicit cost of the trip, and then estimating a correlation between the trip costs and trips taken as a measure of quantity. Estimation of changes to quality are often determined via pooled data from recreation sites with different quality levels; correlations can then be made between quality levels and the number of trips taken (e.g., Kaoru *et al.*, 1995). The stated preference methods can be used directly to value quality changes at a single site by presenting respondents with questions of hypothetical quality changes (e.g., Boyle *et al.*, 1994; Carson and Mitchell, 1993).

A major advantage to such a combined revealed and stated approach is that it allows for benefit estimation that extends beyond the scope of historical data, for example, it allows for estimation of how travel behavior would be expected to change under various future scenarios. Such a contingent behavior approach has been proved externally valid when compared to revealed preferences. For example, Loomis (1993) found that intended and actual length of stay were not different given a constant level of lake quality.

10.3.2. *Review of Economic Studies of Aquatic Restoration in the Region*

In recent environmental assessments, there has been extensive use of a mixed method of stated- and revealed-preference approach in order to value transboundary environmental restoration projects. In each study it is evidenced that findings from nonmarket valuation methods are self-reinforcing, by incorporating cultural and ecological values that typically are nonmarket in nature. Here we review some key valuation studies that have valued nonmarket aspects of waterways in Israel, Jordan, and the Palestinian Territories, especially those with a transboundary focus. In general, benefits evaluation that provides market values in addition to cultural indicators provides substantial leverage to supporting projects for restoration and conservation of the areas. In turn, the economic findings suggest that in many of these projects, there are major potential for political gains in addition.

Becker and Katz (2006) investigated nonmarket value of conservation of the Dead Sea basin using both contingent valuation and TCM. The three local populations (i.e., Israeli, Jordanian, and Palestinian) were found to have substantial levels of WTP in order to preserve cultural and environmental heritage in the Dead Sea basin region, and the magnitude of WTP was found to be consistent between the two approaches. Such an analysis provides substantial strength to the conservation efforts in the region up to that point had relied on ethical and ecological arguments (e.g., tourism and wildlife conservation) without a comparative economic valuation.

Jabarin and Damhoureyeh (2006) examined the recreational patterns of the Dibeen National Park in Jerash, Jordan in order to determine the potential value of the park. They do a cross-comparison between CVM and TCM conducted via survey to see the value Jordanians place on maintaining and improving the park. Valuation results from the two methods are mutually supportive and in turn reinforce the goals of a biodiversity strategy that the Government of Jordan was just launching at the time of the study within the Dibeen and Ajloun regions.

Abramson *et al.* (2010) looked at the potential for reduced environmental degradation and subsequent health and security threats in areas affected by the Israeli–Palestinian conflict. Using CVM the study found that both Israelis and Palestinians value the water use in similar fashions and have comparable WTP. The authors then took these results as the basis for a cost benefit analysis of various rehabilitation policy options.

In studies of stream restoration in Israel using CM, Barak (2010) and Barak and Katz (2015) found that respondents' valuation of stream recreational amenities was roughly equally divided between those that are in-stream based (e.g., swimming, fishing, and boating), and those that are based on recreational opportunities along the streams' banks (e.g., walking trails, picnicking, etc.).

Becker and Friedler (2012) examined economic benefits of a restoration project that has taken place since the mid-1990s to restore the Alexander–Zeimar basin, which is a transboundary stream between the West Bank and Israel that has been used as a sewage outlet since the 1950s. The study supplements a scientific hydrological model with market and nonmarket valuations through travel costs to estimate conditions a *priori* and ex-post the restoration plan took effect. The cost–benefit analysis focused on a series of different restoration options versus the current restoration plans. The authors concluded that there is only a positive net benefit to both parties when a complete cleanup of the river occurs.

The studies outlined above demonstrate the use of nonmarket and market methods in order to value nonmarket public goods in the Israeli–Jordanian–Palestinian region. It also emerges that in such valuation studies, it has become common practice to combine stated and revealed preference techniques. It is clear in these studies that the management of public goods to maximize their public benefits is aligned with the public's WTP for such services.

10.4. Methodology

In order to estimate the economic value of rehabilitation of the LJR, three teams (one from each country), under the coordination of the NGO EcoPeace/FoEME, administered nearly identical surveys. The surveys explained the current status of the LJR, and each gathered information regarding respondents' relative preferences for each one of four possible rehabilitation scenarios covering two levels of flow and two levels of water quality. The four scenarios presented are as follows:

- **Scenario 1** — increased flow to 220 mcm/y, roughly seven times current flow, of moderate quality
- **Scenario 2** — increased flow to 220 mcm/y, roughly seven times current flow, of good quality
- **Scenario 3** — increased flow to 400 mcm/y, roughly 13 times current flow, of moderate quality
- **Scenario 4** — increased flow to 400 mcm/y, roughly 13 times current flow, of good quality

As the respondents were unfamiliar with flow and water quality parameters, each scenario was also described in terms of the expected attributes associated with each in terms of recreational opportunities (e.g., boating, swimming, fishing) and levels of ecological functioning. In order to facilitate understanding, the scenarios were represented by illustrations as well as written descriptions, as depicted in Fig. 10.2. Respondents were also able to ask questions for clarification if need be.

Each survey utilized three different methods to estimate WTP for the four scenarios:

(i) Contingent behavior TCM
(ii) CVM
(iii) CM

TCM: The surveys explained the current status of the LJR and gathered data on respondents' current use of the LJR in order to determine a baseline, for use in the TCM. The contingent behavior TCM approach was used in order to assess future changes in visitation frequency under the different scenarios. Travel cost was assessed by calculating average cost of travel[1] from the area in which

---

[1]Average travel cost = (average fuel cost) × (average car fuel efficiency) × (distance travelled to LJR).

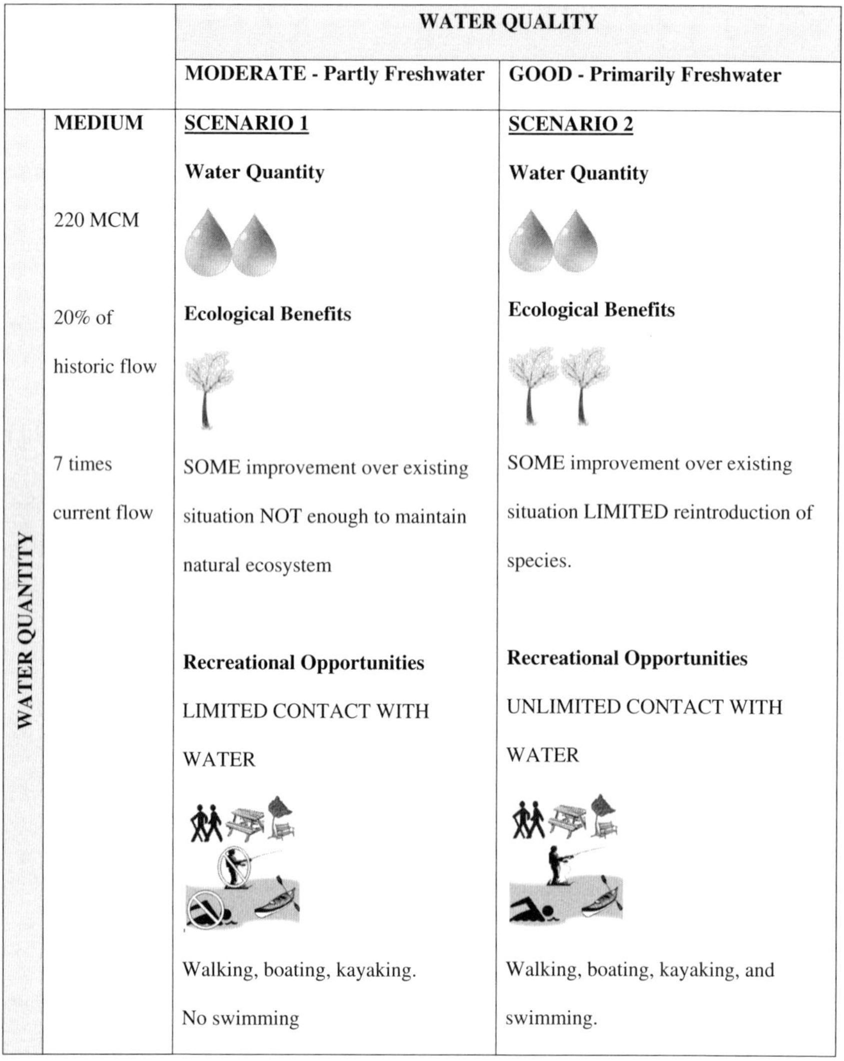

		WATER QUALITY	
		MODERATE - Partly Freshwater	GOOD - Primarily Freshwater
	MEDIUM	**SCENARIO 1**	**SCENARIO 2**
		Water Quantity	**Water Quantity**
	220 MCM		
	20% of historic flow	**Ecological Benefits**	**Ecological Benefits**
WATER QUANTITY	7 times current flow	SOME improvement over existing situation NOT enough to maintain natural ecosystem	SOME improvement over existing situation LIMITED reintroduction of species.
		Recreational Opportunities LIMITED CONTACT WITH WATER	**Recreational Opportunities** UNLIMITED CONTACT WITH WATER
		Walking, boating, kayaking. No swimming	Walking, boating, kayaking, and swimming.

Figure 10.2: Schematic illustrating four rehabilitation levels and respective attributes.

the respondents live to the LJR as well as a value for time spent at the LJR.[2]

---

[2]Time was calculated as 25% of average salary multiplied by the average time spent in travel to and from the LJR.

	SCENARIO 3	SCENARIO 4
HIGH	Water Quantity	Water Quantity

400 MCM		
	Ecological Benefits	**Ecological Benefits**
40% of		
historic flow		
	SIGNIFICANT improvement over	SIGNIFICANT improvement over
13 times	existing situation	existing situation
current flow	LIMITED reintroduction of species.	SUBSTANTIAL reintroduction of species
	Recreational Opportunities	
	LIMITED CONTACT WITH	**Recreational Opportunities**
	WATER	UNLIMITED CONTACT WITH
		WATER
	Walking, boating, and kayaking. No swimming.	Walking, boating, kayaking, and swimming.

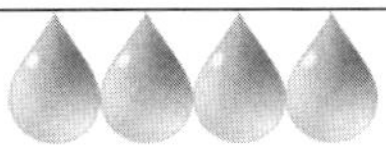

Figure 10.2: (*Continued*)

CVM: Respondents were asked to indicate their annual WTP in order to ensure the rehabilitation of the LJR at the levels indicated in the four scenarios. Respondents were reminded of their budget constraints. The CVM was in the format of a payment card, with options ranging from 0 to 150 shekels for the Israelis and Palestinians and 0 to 30 Jordanian dinars for the Jordanians,[3] with an additional, open-ended option if the indicated WTP was more than 150 shekels/30 dinar annually. A series of follow-up questions was presented after the payment card, in order to assess the extent to which responses were indicative of use and nonuse values, as well as whether the responses were internally consistent.

CM: Respondents were presented with four choice sets, each containing three possible outcomes — the current status and two of the four rehabilitation scenarios. Each of the two rehabilitation scenarios in each choice set was presented together with an associated price, while the current status was an option available at no additional cost. The respondents were asked to choose their preferred outcome, given the associated price for each of the four choice sets.

A final section of the survey obtained data on relevant socioeconomic and demographic variables. This information was used to gauge how representative the surveyed sample was relative to the population.

10.4.1. *Survey Administration*

Pilot versions of the survey were administered in order to ensure understanding of the issue involved. Initial versions were adjusted by, for instance, replacing detailed text with shorter descriptions and visuals as displayed in Fig. 10.2. The final version was tested as well, in order to ensure understanding and in order to ensure that the length was not prohibitive. Upon successful initial outcomes, the final survey version was administered broadly among the full sample.

During 2011–2012 three consultancies administered the survey in various locations throughout their respective countries, in order to capture regionally and socioeconomically representative cross sections of the population. Sites near the Lower Jordan were oversampled in order to capture the population currently visiting

---

[3]At the time of the study, in early 2013, one Israeli shekel was equal to 0.27 US dollars while one Jordanian dinar was equal to 1.41 US dollars.

Table 10.1: Survey sample distribution.

	Israelis	Jordanians	Palestinians	Total
Locals	394	178	276	**848**
Tourists	91	101	98	**290**
Total	**485**	**279**	**374**	**1138**

the location. Other locations in which the survey was administered included bus and train stations, shopping centers, and other public places. Surveys were administered face to face,[4] with those administering available for clarification questions. We checked continuously that there were no ongoing issues with filling out the questionnaires.

Surveys were reviewed by the consultancies teams. Unfinished surveys were eliminated from the sample. So too were all irrational answers; for instance, when somebody is willing to pay more for inferior scenario, this is considered irrational in nature. Surveys containing "protest zeros" were also eliminated from the sample.[5] In the end, surveys from 848 local residents and 290 international tourists were included in the sample. The breakdown by country is provided in Table 10.1.

10.5. Results

This section presents the results of the nonmarket valuation studies for the various rehabilitation scenarios examined, as well as a comparison of these benefits to the associated costs of implementation in

---

[4] An initial attempt to administer at least some of the surveys online proved unsuccessful, with low response rates. Results from the few successfully completed surveys were included in the overall analysis.

[5] "Protest zeros" are a phenomenon in which the respondent indicates that the environmental good or service is indeed important to them, but indicates no WTP for such (Freeman, 2003). A lack of WTP may stem from a number of reasons, including a feeling that another party is responsible or a lack of belief that the payment would actually result in the outcomes described. Whatever the rationale, such protest zeros are problematic in that it is not possible to translate the respondent's utility into WTP. As such, such responses were omitted from the calculations of overall WTP.

order to calculate the net benefit of an intervention. First, the results of the three methods of nonmarket valuation are presented. Only a summary of the results is presented herein. This is followed by a description of the calculation of the costs of implementation, which covers the opportunity cost of the water, as well as the infrastructure and operations and maintenance necessary to deliver the water at the specified quantity and quality. Finally, a comparison of benefits and costs is presented.

10.5.1.   *Benefits from Nonmarket Valuation*

10.5.1.1.   *Contingent behavior TCM results*

For all four rehabilitation scenarios examined, estimated visitation rates among all three populations are expected to rise. Table 10.2 presents the expected change in visits per capita as well as the expected increase in consumer surplus (a measure of economic welfare) per visit for each of the three populations and for each of the four scenarios (S1–S4). International visitors are not included in this estimate in order to highlight changes in economic welfare to the population of the countries in the region. As such, they should be seen as a lower bound estimate of actual economic benefits.

Table 10.3 presents the total annual economic benefits for each population (Israeli, Jordanian, and Palestinian) for each scenario.

Table 10.2: Change in annual visits per capita (VPC), visits (in thousands), and consumer surplus (CS) per visit (in USD).

		S1	S2	S3	S4	S5
Israelis	ΔVPC	0.21	0.41	0.68	1.53	
	ΔVisits	322.1	639.5	1.061	2387	
	ΔCS	**2.98**	**11.07**	**10.23**	**20.73**	
Jordanians	ΔVPC	0.82	1.87	1.87	4.21	
	ΔVisits	983.5	2.160	2.243	5.015	
	ΔCS	**3.65**	**3.94**	**5.23**	**8.78**	
Palestinians	ΔVPC	0.54	1.01	1.39	2.73	
	ΔVisits	248.2	464.8	638.7	1.256	
	ΔCS	**5.55**	**12.65**	**13.51**	**13.70**	

Table 10.3: Annual benefits for alternative rehabilitation scenarios using different valuation methods (in millions of USD).

		S1	**S2**	**S3**	**S4**	**S5**
TCM	Israelis		1.0	7.1	10.9	49.5
	Jordanians		3.6	8.5	11.7	44.0
	Palestinians		1.4	5.9	8.6	17.2
	Total		**5.9**	**21.5**	**31.2**	**110.7**
CVM (total)	Israelis		33	64	78	134
	Jordanians		47	84	98	170
	Palestinians		10	19	21	46
	Total		**90**	**167**	**197**	**349**
CVM (use values +	Israelis		16	31	37	63
option values only)	Jordanians		22	39	46	79
	Palestinians		5	9	10	22
	Total		**42**	**79**	**93**	**165**
CM	Israelis		8.8	17.4	9.0	17.6
	Jordanians		6.0	8.9	6.7	9.6
	Palestinians		4.0	7.2	4.7	7.9
	Total		**18.8**	**33.5**	**20.4**	**35.1**

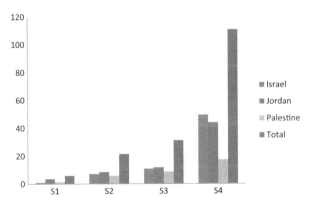

Figure 10.3: Annual benefits from increased visitation (TCM survey) (millions of USD).

On a per visit level of analysis, unsurprisingly, Scenario 1 (lower flow and lower quality) generated the least amount of benefits for each, while Scenario 4 (higher flow and higher quality) generated the most (Table 10.3). The benefits differ greatly both across scenarios and across populations, however, for all three populations there seemed to be a preference for higher water flow, even at the expense of lower quality, as indicated by the higher benefits for Scenario 3, relative to Scenario 2. The demand curve for an improved LJR is highly nonlinear for all populations, with a significant jump in benefits from Scenario 3 to Scenario 4. This indicates that the populations do value increased ecological functioning and/or better water quality that allows for full human contact with the water.

Estimated Palestinian benefits on a per visitor level are significantly higher than those estimated for either Israelis or Jordanians. While several possible explanations can be surmised for such a result, the difference is most likely due to the current restrictions on movement and access to the site. In using a contingent behavior method, the survey estimated the expected increase in visitation, assuming freedom of access. Since current access is restricted to most of the Palestinian population, it is likely that much of the value is reflective simply of having access to visit the site. Thus, in this case, while the relative differences between scenarios are instructive of economic benefits, the absolute values may not be directly comparable to those of Israelis and Jordanians, for whom access is less of an issue. At national level, the Palestinian results are not higher than those of the other two populations, given the smaller population of the Palestinians.[6]

10.5.1.2.   *CVM results*

Results of the CVM section of the survey indicate significantly higher economic benefits from the various restoration scenarios (Table 10.3). These values are presented graphically in Figure 10.4. Again, these figures include values attributed only by the domestic populations, and thus should be viewed as lower bound estimates.

As with the TCM results, respondents value both quantity and quality, but indicate a clear preference for the amount of water flowing in the river over the difference in water quality. The benefit

---

[6]The population included for calculations was that of the West Bank (including East Jerusalem) only. It did not include that of the Gaza Strip.

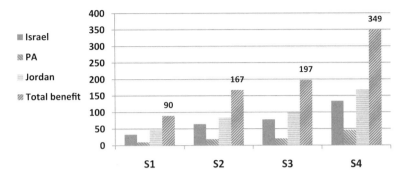

Figure 10.4: Annual benefits from CVM survey (millions of USD).

levels are substantially higher than the corresponding results from the TCM contingent behavior survey as reported in the previous section. As noted earlier, because CVM captures both use and nonuse values, it should not be surprising that the results for CVM present higher values.

Figures for Jordanian benefits are the highest. Possible explanations for differences between methods will be discussed more at length in the "Discussion" section, however, the result is likely due to the primary role the Jordan Valley plays in Jordanian recreation, relative to Israeli, which has many more popular recreational options, and relative to Palestinian, for which the majority of the population has limited experience with the Jordan Valley due to travel restrictions.

From questions included in the survey, it was possible to distinguish between use and nonuse values in the CVM results. Total WTP for each of the scenarios and each of the countries is divided roughly equally between use and nonuse values (Table 10.3). For this calculation, option values — that is, the value of maintaining the option of utilizing the river in the future, were included as use values. From analysis of the differences between use and nonuse values it seems that use values account for slightly less than half of total value.

10.5.1.3.   *CM results*

Results from the CM experiment are substantially different from those obtained using either the TCM or CVM (Table 10.3 and

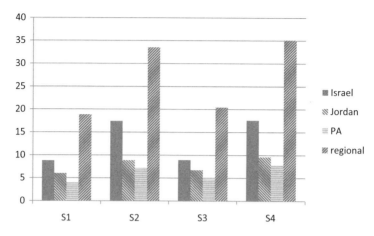

Figure 10.5: Annual benefits from CM survey (millions of USD).

Fig. 10.5). In terms of order of magnitude they are similar to those of the TCM; this, despite the fact that CM is, like CVM, a stated preference model that should capture both use and nonuse values. However, unlike either the case of TCM or CVM, results from the CM indicate a distinct preference for water quality over water quantity for all countries. The benefits for an increase in quantity from 220 mcm/y of flow to 400 mcm/y keeping with quality level fixed was marginal, while the increase in benefits from increasing quality while keeping flow rates constant was substantial.

10.5.1.4. *Ancillary benefits from downstream water availability*

The above benefit estimates, using each of the three valuation methods, capture only the value of in-stream uses of the water in the LJR. They do not capture benefits from having more water available downstream. These could include either use of the water at its lowest level prior to the junction with the Dead Sea, or the benefits from increased flow into the Dead Sea, which would slow the drop in its level, a serious environmental problem in its own right. While these ancillary benefits from rehabilitation are likely substantial, no attempt to quantify them was made in this study. Thus, the benefits estimates given should be seen as lower bound estimates.

10.5.2. *Costs of Implementation*

The basis for the costs of water supply are estimated by the consulting firm DHV (Safier, 2011), which calculated the infrastructure costs, as well as the opportunity costs of water (e.g., losses by current users) to achieve a flow level of 220 mcm/y at a salinity level of 750 mg/L — the specifications of Scenario 2 in this study (Safier, 2011). The study found that it would be difficult to meet the 750 mg/L standard with only 220 mcm/y while also maintaining the minimum monthly base flows needed for rehabilitation. It, therefore, based its calculations on supplying 238 mcm/y, the minimum amount of water needed for both 220 mcm/y and various monthly minimum flow specifications. The DHV report presented costs in net present value (NPV) terms using a 4% discount rate and a 30-year time frame. The estimate of the cost for achieving Scenario 2 was $868 million. This figure was based on numerous assumptions regarding necessary actions and the associated costs that will not be elaborated at length here. The primary assumption was that roughly 100–120 mcm/y would come from increased flows from the Sea of Galilee, which has salinity levels of roughly 250 mg/L. The remaining roughly 100 mcm/y would come from a variety of other actions. The primary costs, as estimated by DHV can be summarized as follows:

- $183 million in lost revenues for the farmers in the LJR basin
- $243 million in lost revenues for the farmers in the Upper Jordan River basin
- $325 million to substitute flow in Israel's National Water Carrier with increased desalination of Mediterranean seawater
- $93 million for treating the saline water carrier and its brine beyond what is currently planned, and transfer of the brines to the Dead Sea
- $25 million for further transfer of treated effluents from Haifa Bay to the Spring Valley Regional Council for use by farmers.

Associated input costs such as electricity, were assumed fixed, and associated environmental costs (externalities) were not taken into account. These costs notwithstanding, there are several reasons to believe that this cost estimate is upwardly biased. First, the costs were based on infrastructure costs and lost revenues to Israeli farmers, assuming that all the necessary water would be provided by Israel. However, the opportunity cost of water in Israel, as measured either by replacement cost or the return on water used in agriculture (water productivity), is several times higher in Israel than in Jordan or Palestine. Second, the estimates include lost revenue to farmers, rather than simply lost profits (producer surplus), as is common in benefit–cost analyses. This was done to reflect both the losses in terms of return on sunk costs for equipment as well as lost salaries to farmers in the region, assuming no alternative source of income. Such assumptions are highly restrictive and conservative, and likely elevate true costs. Thus, the cost estimates can be viewed as an upper bound.

It is possible to meet both the 220 mcm/y and the moderate water quality (e.g., 1000 mg/L salinity) criteria, that is, Scenario 1, without additional water. In order to calculate the cost of Scenario 1, we took the average cost of supplying 238 mcm/y of water from the DHV estimate and deducted the cost of the additional 18 mcm/y. This gives an annual cost of nearly $4 million less than Scenario 2. Providing the extra freshwater to the LJR from natural sources to meet 400 mcm/y criteria would almost guarantee water of good quality (Scenario 4). Thus, the cost of Scenarios 3 and 4 is likely identical, though additional efforts to control for runoff and other point and nonpoint source pollutants to achieve good water quality may, increase the cost of Scenario 4 slightly. The cost of desalination was used as an upper bound cost estimate of supplying additional water, under the assumption that desalination represents the replacement cost of cutting withdrawals from the basin. This cost was estimated at $0.625 per cubic meter.[7] Supplying an additional 162 mcm/y to

---

[7]This figure is based on Becker *et al.* (2010), adjusted for changes in electricity prices and exchange rates. This estimate does not include the costs of transfer of the water to the Jordan Basin. It is based on the assumption that naturally flowing water would be left instream to flow into the Lower Jordan from the Sea of Galilee, and that the corresponding losses to national water networks would be compensated for by desalinated sea water.

Table 10.4: Estimated annualized (30 years) costs of rehabilitation scenarios (in million USD/y).

Quality \ Quantity	Moderate	Good
220 MCM/Y	Scenario 1 $46m	Scenario 2 $50m
400 MCM/Y	Scenario 3 $151m	Scenario 4 $151m

Scenario 2 to meet the 400 mcm/y would cost roughly $101 million per year. Desalination is not currently directly utilized to supply Jordanian or Palestinian supplies, and much research has shown that a large quantity of water could be obtained at a lower marginal cost than desalination (e.g., FoEME, 2010), Thus, it should be viewed only as an upper bound estimate of the cost of "new" water. In reality, the costs are likely lower.

Given these assumptions, the estimates for the costs of the four scenarios chosen are summarized in Table 10.4.

10.5.3. *Comparing Costs and Benefits*

10.5.3.1. *Domestic net benefits*

Given the estimates of benefits from the nonmarket valuation methods and the estimate of costs from the DHV study with the associated adjustments as detailed in the previous section, it is possible to conduct a basic benefit–cost analysis. Benefits and costs are presented in Table 10.5, ordered by method.

When using the CVM total benefits, the highest of those measured, taking only domestic benefits into consideration, benefits outweigh costs for rehabilitation for all four scenarios, that is, when pooling the benefits of all three populations. In the case of Jordan, the benefits to Jordanians alone are higher than the total estimated costs for the 220 mcm flow scenarios (Scenarios 1 and 2), although not for the higher flow scenarios (3 and 4). If nonuse values are eliminated, total benefits outweigh costs only for Scenario 2, although the benefits for Scenario 1 are only slightly lower than the estimated costs.

When taking benefits as measured using the CM and contingent behavior TCM, the benefits, even when pooled, are outweighed by

Table 10.5: Annual benefit–cost comparisons.

		S1	S2	S3	S4
COSTS	Total Costs	46	50	151	151
TCM	Total Benefits	5.9	21.5	31.2	110.7
	Net Benefits	40.1	28.5	−119.8	−40.3
CVM (total)	Total Benefits	90	167	197	349
	Net Benefits	44	117	46	198
CVM (use values + option values only)	Total Benefits	42	79	93	165
	Net Benefits	−4	29	−58	14
CM	Total Benefits	18.8	33.5	20.4	35.1
	Net Benefits	−27.2	−16.5	−130.6	−115.9
All Three	Range	6–90	22–167	20–197	35–349
Valuation Methods	Average	38	74	83	165

the costs for all four scenarios (the higher end estimate for Scenario 4 is presented in the table — the lower end estimate is identical to that of Scenario 3).

10.5.3.2. *Incorporating international tourists*

It is important to note that the above benefit estimates included only those from domestic tourists. International tourists were not included in the above analysis as the benefits measured are those accrued by the visitors themselves, and not the state. However, it is important to note that well over 1 million international tourists visit the Jordan River each year. This number can be expected to increase with the rehabilitation of the Lower Jordan. From the surveys collected from international tourists, it is clear that they also place a strong value on the quality of the Lower Jordan and that this would affect the quality of their visits. Table 10.6 presents the calculated increase in consumer surplus per visit for international tourists in each of the scenarios as calculated form surveys collected. The values are substantial for all scenarios. For those surveyed in Israel and Palestine, the values are much higher even than those of domestic visitors (compare to Table 10.3).

Table 10.6: Additional consumer surplus
per visit — International tourists (in USD).

	S1	S2	S3	S4
Israelis	6.1	14.4	14.3	17.2
Jordanians	3.4	3.9	4.5	6.3
Palestinians	12.5	19.1	19.1	23.3
Average	7.3	12.5	12.6	15.6

Regarding water quality, in both the low flow (220 mcm/y) and high flow (400 mcm/y) scenarios net benefits were higher for the higher water quality scenarios (2 and 4). This is because the difference in costs between the low and high quality water scenarios, with a given flow level, were small or nonexistent, while the benefits differ substantially. Thus, should rehabilitation be pursued, it should be done so at higher water quality levels, regardless of the amount of water dedicated for flows.

It is not possible from the surveys issued to estimate the expected increase in international tourism as a result of river rehabilitation. For many international tourists the region is a repeat destination in which the LJR could play an important role, while for others, such a visit is a once in a lifetime experience and thus, visitation rates for them would not be expected to increase. Moreover, should the LJR become a more significant element of the international tourists' itinerary, it is unclear the extent to which the stay at the LJR would add to the overall time spent in the region, and the extent to which stay at the LJR would come at the expense of stay in other local tourist sites.

It is possible, given the existing data, to calculate the number of international tourists that would need to visit in order for benefits to exceed the costs of rehabilitation. This can be calculated by dividing the net cost (cost minus total domestic benefits) by the average consumer surplus per visit by international tourists as presented in Table 10.6. The results of such calculations, using total benefits from the TCM and the CVM (use values only) methods are presented in Table 10.7. As can be seen, the values range from 1 to 9.6 million

Table 10.7: Additional international tourist visits necessary for positive net benefits (million days for all three populations combined).

	S1	S2	S3	S4
TCM	4.7	2.3	9.6	2.6–3.3
CVM (use + option values only)	nb > 0	nb > 0	8.6	nb > 0

Note: nb > 0 indicates the net benefits were positive when evaluating domestic tourism, and thus no additional international tourists would be necessary to justify the given scenario on economic grounds.

additional tourist days, depending on the scenario and method in question. According to World Bank statistics, the region receives roughly 7.5 million entries per year (World Bank, 2016). As such, achieving the necessary additional number of tourist days to generate positive benefits is feasible. In addition, it is important to note, that this analysis does not take into consideration potential benefits for the host countries in terms of money spent by international tourists in the region. Profits from such sales could be considered as additional benefits for the three economies.

10.6. Discussion and Conclusions

The results presented in this chapter vary considerably by the valuation method used. However, it is clear that the benefits from rehabilitation of the LJR are substantial. Furthermore, it is also very clear that all three populations value highly the restoration of the river, providing a shared interest that could serve as a basis for regional cooperation. In all cases, the estimated costs are within the range of estimated domestic benefits (Table 10.5). A comparison of average benefits (the average of the three methods) to the estimated costs shows that the benefits are roughly equal to the costs for Scenarios 1 and 4 and greatly exceed the costs for Scenario 2, while falling short of the costs for Scenario 3 when looking at the direct benefits to the local population only. Adding the economic benefits associated with international tourists to those of the domestic populations could tip the balance strongly in favor of at least 3 of the 4 scenarios.

Several issues are worth noting in terms of interpretation of the results. First, the only method according to which net benefits for all scenarios were positive was the CVM. In this method, nonuse values accounted for a large share of the benefits and were essential in terms of the scenarios passing a benefit–cost type analysis. Furthermore, when looking at total benefits, the benefits to Jordan alone outweigh the costs. If, however, one restricts the estimates to just use value benefits, then only when benefits are pooled do they surpass the estimated costs. It means that regional cooperation, or at least coordination, would be necessary for an economically beneficial rehabilitation project. Such a situation is not surprising given the public good nature of the shared resources involved.

With two of the three methods (TCM and CVM) there was a strong preference for quantity of water over quality; that is, relative to Scenario 1, an increase in water quantity was valued more than an increase in water quality. This was not the case with the CM method. Given inconsistency of the CM results with those of the other two, together with questions raised by some of those surveyed, these results are likely the least reliable of the employed three methods. However, given supply of a certain quantity of water, be it 220 or 400 mcm/y, the additional costs to improve to good quality are economically justified. That is, the additional benefits from improvement of water quality outweigh the additional costs (indeed, in the case of annual flow of 400 mcm, there may, in fact, be little additional costs). Thus, should a policy of rehabilitation be pursued, regardless of the flow level chosen, attaining good water quality standards is economically efficient.

It is also important when interpreting the results to remember the self-imposed constraints, limitations, and biases built in to the valuation and cost estimations. In terms of the benefits, only in-stream values of the LJR were estimated. Ancillary benefits from the additional water provided downstream, whether it be reused offstream or whether it flow into the Dead Sea, are likely substantial, but are not included in the assessment. Thus, true benefits are likely higher. In contrast, cost estimates take the cost of desalination as the marginal cost of water, despite the fact that lower cost options are almost certainly available and include lost revenues of farmers, rather than lost producer surplus. Thus, the true costs are likely lower. Given these built in biases, the above estimates are conservatively biased against rehabilitation. Therefore, cases in which benefits outweigh costs can be seen as robust.

This analysis focused primarily on estimating economic benefits to the local populations surrounding the LJR. It is clear that there would be many additional benefits not included in this estimate. From a global perspective, these additional benefits include the value to the international community of rehabilitation of a historic site with a rich cultural and religious heritage. From a local and regional perspective, the project could serve as a catalyst for broader regional cooperation. Geostrategic considerations of enhancing regional ties and cooperation have been critical in galvanizing governmental support for other joint regional development projects such as the proposed Red–Dead Canal between the Red Sea and the Dead Sea. As a shared public good, rehabilitation of the LJR could provide similar such benefits. In addition, it would provide a meeting place in which populations from across the region could interact in a setting in which they share common experiences and objectives. This, in and of itself, is a rare occurrence in the region and could be a welcome development.

The region is still experiencing increasing population growth, and with it, continued demands for scarce water. The Jordan basin in particular is under growing pressure to supply water to the large numbers of refugees coming from Syria. It is clear from this study that the LJR is highly valued by all of the residents of the region; however, the opportunity costs of supplying the necessary amount of water are also quite high. The advent of desalination has allowed for serious consideration of additional flows for stream flow restoration purposes and is also facilitating increased regional cooperation over water resources. The cost of desalination, which serves as a proxy for the marginal cost of water in the region, has declined dramatically over the past decade. As it continues to do so, the opportunity cost of restored river flows should drop proportionately, making river rehabilitation an ever more attractive option. While fully restoring historical flows to the Jordan is unlikely, even partial rehabilitation can bring about substantial environmental, social, and economic benefits to the region and reverse the trajectory of the river from a polluted drainage canal back to a thriving ecosystem worthy of its great legacy.

Acknowledgments

This chapter presents work conducted by the authors together with Saeb Bamya, of CORE Associates, Palestine, and Ele Jan Saaf, of SaafConsult BV, Jordan, and with the assistance of Jennifer Helgeson of the London School of Economics. The study was done with the financial support of EcoPeace/Friends of the Earth–Middle East (FoEME) within the framework of the organization's development of a regional master plan for rehabilitation of the Jordan Valley basin.

References

Abramson, A., A Tal, N Becker, N El-Khateeb, L Asaf, A Assi, E Adar (2010). Stream restoration as a basis for Israeli–Palestinian cooperation: a comparative analysis of two transboundary streams." *International Journal of River Basin Management*, 8(1), 39–53.

Adamowicz, WL, JJ Fletcher, and T Graham-Tomasi (1994). Functional form and the statistical properties of welfare measures — Reply. *American Journal of Agricultural Economics*, 76(4), 958–959.

Anisfeld, S, and J Shub. 2009. Historical flows in the Lower Jordan River. New Haven, CT: Yale School of Forestry and Environmental Studies.

Arrow, K, R Solow, PR Portney, EE Leamer, R Radner, and H Schuman (1993). Report of the NOAA panel on contingent valuation. *Federal Register* 58 (10), 4601–4614, Aviram, R, D Katz, and D Shmueli (2014). Desalination as a game-changer in transboundary hydro-politics. *Water Policy*, 16(4), 609–624.

Barak, B (March 2010). How much are we willing to pay for a clean stream? Report published by Zalul (In Hebrew).

Barak, B and D Katz (2015). Valuing instream and riparian aspects of stream restoration — A willingness to tax approach.*Land Use Policy*, 45, 204–212.

Becker, N and E Friedler (2012). Integrated hydro-economic assessment of restoration of the Alexander-Zeimar River (Israel-Palestinian Authority). *Regional Environmental Change*, 12(4), 1–12.

Becker, N and D Katz (2006). Economic valuation of resuscitating the Dead Sea. *Water Policy*, 8(4), 351–370.

Bennett, J and R Blamey (2001). *The Choice Modelling Approach to Environmental Valuation* p. 269. Northampton: Edward Elgar Publishing.

Boyle, KJ, WH Desvousges, F Reed Johnson, RW Dunford, and SP Hudson (1994). An investigation of part-whole biases in contingent valuation studies. *Journal of Environmental Economics and Management*, 27, 64–83.

Cameron, TA and J Englin (1997). Respondent experience and contingent valuation of environmental goods. *Journal of Environmental Economics and Management*, 33, 296–313.

Carson, RT and RC Mitchell (1993). The value of clean water: the public's willingness to pay for boatable, fishable, and swimmable quality water. *Water Resources Research*, 29, 2445–2454.

Carson, R., N Flores, K Martin, and J Wright, (1996). Contingent Valuation and Revealed Preference Methodologies: Comparing the Estimates for Quasi-Public Goods. *Land Economics,* 72(1), 80–99.

EcoPeace (2015). Regional NGO master plan for sustainable development in the Jordan valley. http://foeme.org/www/?module=projects&record_id=205 [26 September 2015].

Falkenmark, M and G Lindh (1976). *Water for a Starving World.* Boulder: Westview Press.

FoEME (2010). *Towards a Living Jordan River: An Economic Analysis of Policy Options for Water Conservation in Jordan, Israel and Palestine.* Draft Report. Amman, Bethlehem, Tel Aviv: EcoPeace/Friends of the Earth Middle East.

Freeman, AM (2003). *The Measurement of Environmental and Resource Values : Theory and Methods.* Washington: Resources for the Future.

Gafny, S, S Talozi, B Al Sheikh, and E Ya'ari (2010). *Towards a Living Jordan River: An Environmental Flows Report on the Rehabilitation of the Lower Jordan River.* Amman, Bethlehem, Tel Aviv: Eco-Peace/Friends of the Earth Middle East.

Glausiusz, J. (2010). New life for the Dead Sea? *Nature*, 464, 21 April 2010. 1118–1120.

Hanley, N, RE Wright, and V Adamowicz (1998). Using choice experiments to value the environment: Design issues, current experience and future prospects. *Environmental and Resource Economics*, 11(3–4), 413–428.

Hillel, N, S Geyer, T Licha, S Khayat, JB Laronne, and C Siebert (2015). Water quality and discharge of the lower Jordan River. *Journal of Hydrology*, 527(August), 1096–1105.

Huang, JC, TC Haab, and JC Whitehead (1997). Willingness to pay for quality improvements: Should revealed and stated data be combined? *Journal of Environmental Economics and Management*, 34, 240–255.

Jabarin, AS and SA Damhoureyeh (2006). Estimating the recreational benefits of Dibeen national park in Jordan using contingent valuation and travel cost methods. *Pakistan Journal of Biological Sciences*, 9(12), 2198–2206.

Kaoru, Y, VK Smith, and JL Liu (1995). Using random utility models to estimate the recreational value of estuarine resources. *American Journal of Agricultural Economics*, 77, 141–151.

Krutilla, J (1967). Conservation reconsidered. *American Economic Review*, 57(4), 777–786.

Lansky, N and E Denta (2015). *Factors Causing the Accelerated Drop in the Dead Sea Level over the Past Decades.* Report GSI/16/2015. Jerusalem: Geological Survey of Israel (In Hebrew).

Layman, RC, JR Boyce, and K Criddle (1996). Economic valuation of the Chinook Salmon Sport Fishery of the Gulkana River, Alaska, under current and alternate management plans. *Land Economics*, 72, 113–128.

Loomis, J (1989). Test-retest reliability of the contingent valuation method: A comparison of general population and visitor responses. *American Journal of Agricultural Economics*, 71, 76–84.

Loomis, JB. (1993). An investigation into the reliability of intended visitation behavior. *Environmental and Resource Economics*, 3(2), 183–191

Opaluch, JJ, SK Swallow, T Weaver, CW Wessells, and D Wichelns (1993). Evaluating impacts from noxious facilities: Including public preferences in current siting mechanism. *Journal of Environmental Economics and Management*, 24, 41–59.

Reiling, SD, KJ Boyle, ML Phillips, and MW Anderson (1990). Temporal reliability of contingent values. *Land Economics*, 66(2), 128–134.

Safier, G (November 2011). Roadmap for the rehabilitation of the Lower Jordan River. Report by Friends of the Earth—Middle East.

Shechter, M, B Reiser, and N Zaitsev (1998). Measuring passive use value: Pledges, donations and CV responses in connection with an important natural resource. *Environmental and Resource Economics*, 12, 457–478.

Tal, A and D Katz (2012). Rehabilitating Israel's streams and rivers. *International Journal of River Basin Management*, 10(4), 317–330.

Teisl, MF, KJ Boyle, DW McCollum, and SD Reiling (1995). Test-retest reliability of contingent valuation with independent sample pretest and posttest control groups. *American Journal of Agricultural Economics*, 77(3), 613–619.

Turner, M, K Nassar, N Khatib (2005). Crossing the Jordan — Concept Document to Rehabilitate, Promote Prosperity and Help Bring Peace to the Lower Jordan River Valley. EcoPeace/Friends of the Earth Middle East. Amman, Bethlehem and Tel Aviv.

Whitehead, JC, J Huang, GC Blomquist, and RC Ready (1998). Construct validity of dichotomous and polychotomous choice contingent valuation questions. *Environmental and Resource Economics*, 11(1), 107–116.

Whitehead, JC., TC Haab, and JC Huang (2000). Measuring recreation benefits of quality improvements with revealed and stated behavior data. *Resource and Energy Economics*, 22(4), 339–354.

Whitehead, JC (2002). Incentive incompatibility and starting point bias in iterative valuation questions. *Land Economics*, 78, 285–297.

World Bank (2016). World development indicators database. http://databank.worldbank.org/data/home.aspx.

Young, RA (2005). *Determining the Economic Value of Water: Concepts and Methods*. Washington: Resources for the Future.

INDEX